Reading: Tests and Assessment Techniques

Second edition

Peter D. Pumfrey

Hodder and Stoughton
In association with the United Kingdom Reading Association

British Library Cataloguing in Publication Data

Pumfrey, Peter D.
Reading: tests and assessment techniques.—
2nd ed.—(UKRA teaching of reading monographs)
1. Reading—Great Britain—Ability testing
I. Title II. United Kingdom Reading Association
III. Series
428.4′076 LB1050.46

ISBN 0-340-35632-4

First published 1976
Second edition 1985

Printed in Great Britain for
Hodder and Stoughton Educational,
a division of Hodder and Stoughton Ltd,
Mill Road, Dunton Green, Sevenoaks, Kent,
by Bulter and Tanner Ltd, Frome.

Contents

List of figures and tables

Preface

The original edition of *Reading: Tests and Assessment Techniques* appeared in 1976 as one of the first group of United Kingdom Reading Association Teaching of Reading Monographs. The book has proved invaluable to teachers, educational psychologists and other educationists. However, after nearly ten years the field has changed considerably: far more tests are available and their purposes and the contexts in which they are used are somewhat different from those of the mid-seventies. This second edition is thus most timely. The sources of information have been updated and extended. Additional suggestions concerning the uses of different types of reading tests and techniques in the assessment of reading and the diagnosis of difficulties have been incorporated. The entries describing particular reading tests have been thoroughly checked and revised where necessary. A number of old tests have been deleted. Over a hundred and twenty new test information sheets have been included in the revision which contains descriptions of more than twice as many tests as the original. The classification system devised by the author enables teachers rapidly to identify tests suited to their professional concerns. It is anticipated that teachers will find the revision even more useful than the volume it now replaces.

Asher Cashdan
Sheffield City Polytechnic

Acknowledgments

I have been greatly helped in the preparation of the second edition of this monograph by my colleagues in the Department of Education of the University of Manchester.

In addition, the work was furthered by the willing cooperation of the many reading test constructors, publishers and distributors whose addresses are given in Appendix I of this monograph.

Special mention must be made of Claudia Casey of the International Reading Association; Dr J. Chapman of the Open University; Dr W. B. Dockrell of the Scottish Council for Research in Education; Dr K. L. Dulin of the University of Wisconsin-Madison; Martha Clark of the Centre for Applied Linguistics; Dr A. C. Croft and Dr W. B. Elley of the New Zealand Council for Educational Research; R. A. Davies formerly of the City of Manchester College of Education; Judy Eppinger of the Australian Council for Educational Research; J. M. Ewing of Dundee College of Education; Dr R. Fletcher of the City University, London; Martyn Goff of the National Book League; Dr T. Gorman of the National Foundation for Educational Research and Assessment of Performance Unit of the Department of Education and Science; Dr G. Gredler of the University of North Carolina; T. A. Kelly of Sandwell Child Psychology Service; Ms E. MacErlain of the Ontario Institute for Studies in Education; Dr J. V. Mitchell of the Buros Institute of Mental Measurements; D. V. Moseley of the University of Newcastle-on-Tyne; Anne O'Sullivan of St Patrick's College, Dublin; Dr M. Newton of the University of Aston in Birmingham; Ruth Nichols of Berkshire LEA; Dr M. C. Roe of the Inner London Education Authority; Betty Root of the Centre for the Teaching of Reading, University of Reading; Dr G. D. Spache of Spache Educational Consultants; Dr R. Summer of the National Foundation for Educational Research; Dr W. H. Teale of the University of California; G. E. F. Trickey of the London Borough of Barking and Dagenham LEA; Professor P. E. Vernon of the University of Alberta; A. Wells of the Adult Literacy and Basic Skills Unit; and Dr J. A. Wilson of the Northern Ireland Council for Educational Research. All have given freely of their time in either discussing specific tests or assessment procedures with which they are concerned, or in enabling me to obtain information on related issues.

Whilst this work has been greatly facilitated by the above, I must acknowledge the help and encouragement given to me by the General Editor of this series, Asher Cashdan, Head of the Department of Communication Studies, Sheffield City Polytechnic.

Department of Education,
University of Manchester
1985

Peter D. Pumfrey

Introduction

Since the publication of the first edition of this monograph considerable developments have taken place in the range of reading tests and assessment techniques available to and used by teachers. During this period two important and still unresolved controversies have exercised professionals interested in the relevance of reading tests to our understanding of the nature of the reading process, its development and the alleviation of avoidable reading difficulties.

The first of these centres on the 'top-down' versus 'bottom-up' issue. Namely, are the sub-skills of reading best acquired through reading? Is the practice of a complex skill (reading) the most effective way of mastering apparently less complex ones (e.g. letter sounds)? Alternatively, does the mastery of the apparently less complex skill facilitate the development of fluent reading?

Proponents of the first position are likely to consider the use of diagnostic reading tests as unnecessary. Oversimplified, their position is summarised by the statement, 'We learn to read by reading.' Had this approach been completely successful, it is doubtful whether professional interest in reading tests would have developed as it has. Opponents to the first position find that, for example, the use of reading tests in identifying a child's specific strengths and weaknesses can enable the teacher to help a child more effectively than would have been the case without such information.

One of the most significant developments in the teaching and testing of reading has derived from the theory and practice of individualised precision teaching. To engage in precision teaching requires four related activities: firstly, the statement of a behavioural objective or objectives; secondly, an assessment of the learner's current level of performance; thirdly, an instructional unit designed to facilitate the learner's mastery of the objective or objectives; and finally, an assessment of the learner's attainment of the initial objectives. This approach has contributed significantly to increases in the reading attainments of disadvantaged children in the USA and elsewhere. Whilst few would claim it as the only way to learn to read or to teach reading, its contribution cannot be ignored.

There have been many attempts at analysing the skills involved in fluent reading and of reading at all stages in its acquisition. Numerous studies of early, pre-reading predictors of later success or failure in reading have been reported. Whilst such studies have added to our understanding, they have not resolved the controversy.

It is my considered opinion that the two positions are not mutually exclusive. It is likely that the ability to conceptualise the reading process, to predict success or failure in reading, and to be able to modify the predictions for children with reading difficulties will require a synthesis of both 'top-down' and 'bottom-up' orientations.

The second ongoing controversy concerns the respective usefulness of norm-referenced and criterion-referenced reading tests. Over recent years, the former have tended to lose, and the latter gain, popularity with teachers. The pedagogic value of conventional test theory, and the edifice of normative testing that has been erected upon it, has been called into question.

Fortunately, teachers' appreciation of the respective strengths and weaknesses of both approaches to the testing of reading is growing. This awareness is but one aspect of the profession's development. The interdependence of the two orientations is increasingly recognised.

To reject as worthless the information that reading tests can provide would be as indefensible as treating such data as the only criteria for individual and institutional decision making. Reading tests and assessment techniques serve many purposes. Without them the profession would be less able to demonstrate its accountability to our pupils, their parents, society and ourselves.

Reading tests can make a contribution to the improvement of standards of literacy in our schools. By helping teachers become more aware of children's attainments in and attitudes towards reading, by increasing our understanding of the nature of the reading process and of the specific difficulties faced by many children learning to read, the incidence of reading failure can be reduced.

To use reading tests effectively it is essential that every teacher should be aware of the complexity of the reading process and of the characteristics of reading tests. She must also consider the relationships between the objectives of the reading programme, the methods and materials to be utilised and the assessment of the programme's effectiveness. Thus she needs to be aware of the various uses to which reading tests can be put and of the complementary relationship between the teaching and testing of reading.

These points are considered briefly in this monograph. It is intended primarily as a source of information concerning a selection of reading tests that will be of interest and use to the teacher of any age group of children.

To this end it is in two sections. Section I briefly outlines the justification of the use of reading tests, gives a description of some important dimensions of reading test interpretation and outlines the nature and uses of the informal reading inventory. Section II gives information about tests available for specified purposes and age ranges of children. The Appendices contain some major sources of information on the testing of reading.

A more extended consideration of important concepts related to the measurement of reading abilities, of both local and national sources of reading test information together with examples of some uses of reading tests, is given in a companion volume to this monograph (Pumfrey, 1977).* Whilst the monograph and book have a related theme, each publication can be read independently.

* PUMFREY, P. D. (1977) *Measuring Reading Abilities: concepts, sources and applications*. London: Hodder and Stoughton (obtainable from the author at the University of Manchester).

In the text which follows, references have been placed at the end of each chapter.

Section I

General Considerations

1 The Uses of Reading Tests

The nature of reading: some considerations

Most of the readers of this monograph will be concerned with teaching children to improve certain aspects of their reading skills. Yet, when asked the deceptively simple question 'What *is* reading?', opinions among teachers (and others) vary greatly. This very question was put in discussion at a recent in-service course for teachers. Results showed that opinions were partly related to the abilities and ages of the children taught, to the length of teaching experience of the teachers and also to the extent that they were aware of current investigations into this topic.

The reading process is far more than a simple, almost mechanical, 'decoding of print to sound' skill whereby the presentation of a flash-card to an infant school child elicits the appropriate oral response. It is more than being able to answer questions on the explicit content of a passage, i.e. 'What was the boy's name in the story you have just read?' In essence, reading is a constructive thinking process. The competent reader is aware of both the explicit and implicit meanings of, for example, proverbs. He can 'read between the lines'. Reading is an active means of information processing. It is both a contributor to and a determinant of cognitive abilities. To argue that modern technology will make reading 'unnecessary' is to misunderstand the nature of the reading process.

Additionally, reading is characteristically developmental. Thus the relative importance of particular skills at a given stage in the development of the abilities characteristic of the competent reader will inevitably vary. The instruction appropriate to an infant is typically different from that required (but rarely given except by 'remedial' teachers) at the secondary or tertiary stages of education. Despite such differences, it should be appreciated that even at the very earliest stage of teaching reading, it is *not* predominantly a mechanical process. One need only ponder the child's tremendous oral language base on which reading is developed to take the point. From the very start the process of reading is concerned with the extraction of meaning for the child from the printed text.

What is a reading test?

A reading test is a means of determining with some precision the extent to which a child has approached one or more goals of a school's reading instruction programme. Such an instrument may measure attainments in or attitudes towards reading.

The careful selection of the material that comprises a given test enables the user to obtain information economically in terms of her own and her pupil's time. This selection also ensures that the test is valid, reliable and well-organised. Thus reading tests are primarily efficient and valid means of obtaining information. There is no way by which the effectiveness of the teaching of reading can be assessed other than through the use of reading tests of one type or another.

There are many ways in which the teacher may assess reading progress. The familiar standardised objective reading test is only one type. There are others that are equally, if not more, important.

Objectives, methods and the assessment of reading

The main function of the teacher of reading is to bring about improvements in the pupil's level of reading competence. To be effective, this teaching must be closely related to the rest of the educational programme. Nevertheless, this monograph is deliberately and justifiably focused on the testing of reading.

The changes in performances which the teacher expects her pupils to achieve in reading constitute the goals of her reading programme. It is important that these goals be specified in advance of instruction: it is helpful for a teacher to know explicitly what she expects her pupils to achieve. In my view, the goals should be specified in terms of behaviour that is both *observable* and *measurable*. This requires considerable thought on the part of the teacher. Having specified her objectives in operational terms, however, it is then far easier to select or devise a valid reading test.

In reading, as in any other educational endeavour, objectives, teaching methods and resources and the assessment of the results of the teaching and learning that have occurred are inter-related aspects that must be considered simultaneously. This is presented diagrammatically in Figure 1.

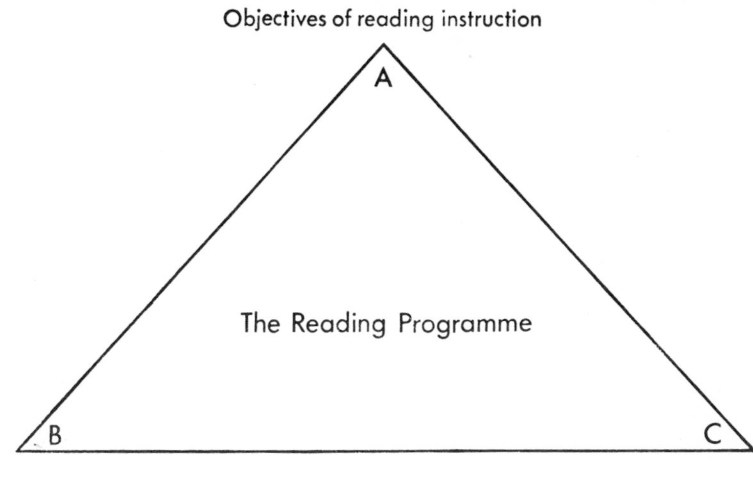

Figure 1
Essential elements of any reading programme

Why use reading tests?

The purpose in testing reading is to provide the teacher with the information that is needed in order to decide the strategy required to improve the children's reading competencies. This purpose may be achieved in the following six ways.

(i) *Finding a starting point for instruction*

If a teacher is faced with a child or a group of children about whose reading abilities she knows little, the use of a reading test can help her decide where to start with them. Knowing the characteristics of a particular age group can help, as also can one's observation and analysis of the children's general behaviour. The use of standardised tests can usefully moderate the first of these and checklists of reading behaviours can do the same for the second. An Informal Reading Inventory (hereafter IRI) can also be used in this situation as can any teacher-constructed test that has been found of value in such circumstances (see Chapter 3, p. 26). In essence the teacher is using the information obtained from reading tests and assessment techniques to match the instructional materials to the pupil's particular pattern and levels of reading attainments.

(ii) *Comparing reading standards in the class with national norms*

It is easy for a teacher to be unaware of the relative reading attainments and attitudes of her pupils compared with other groups. She might legitimately be concerned with whether the group's scores were in line with national norms or not. It is here that standardised objective tests of reading have much to offer as they will allow such comparisons to be made. Such tests also enable the teacher to judge whether reading standards are changing or not from year to year. However, there is the problem that test content can become more and more out of date each year and changes in reading test scores may reflect this factor rather than genuine differences in reading standards. Recent developments in item banking and test construction are reducing such problems.

(iii) *Comparing reading standards of pupils within a class*

It is important for the teacher of reading to be aware of the extent of inter-individual differences in the reading abilities of her pupils. Tests can provide this kind of information and help the teacher to make decisions about how best to organise groups of children for reading instruction.

(iv) *Measuring progress in reading*

Progress can be assessed in a number of ways—books read, skills mastered, or gains made *vis à vis* other pupils. The differences between test scores obtained at the start of a period of reading instruction and those obtained at the end provide one quite useful measure. Objective standardised tests can be used for this purpose. Diagnostic tests can be used to assess progress in the mastery of specific skills.

(v) *Assessing the effectiveness of various approaches to the teaching of reading*

Reading tests can be used to evaluate the effectiveness of existing practices and of innovations in the teaching of reading. The many schools concerned with the various investigations into the efficacy of the Initial Teaching Alphabet and the *Breakthrough to Literacy* scheme will be well aware of this use of reading tests. Provided that appropriate records are kept, both the short-term and long-term effects of innovations can be objectively appraised. The latter may be particularly important as short-term gains are sometimes achieved at the expense of long-term objectives.

(vi) *Diagnosing the reading difficulties of individuals*

Diagnostic reading tests enable the teacher to identify the child's particular skill deficiency as an essential first step in reducing its adverse effects on his reading. Typically, such tests provide a profile of the child's abilities and permit a comparison of relative strengths and weaknesses.

In some instances a child's reading difficulties may be directly attributable to an abnormality of some kind—a disorder or disease of sight or hearing, perhaps. If this can be identified through testing it can often be treated directly and relieve the reading difficulty. However, in the vast majority of cases of difficulties in reading, highly specific causes of this kind cannot be identified. Teachers and researchers are well aware that for almost every child that has a given pattern of strengths and weaknesses in skills purporting to underlie reading ability and who is unable to read, one can find a child with a similar profile who can read proficiently in spite of it.

This points to our incomplete understanding of and control over the development of the ability to read. It also indicates that we must be wary about the conclusions we draw from any diagnosis. To diagnose accurately does not necessarily imply the ability to treat effectively. Nonetheless, diagnostic procedures based on reading tests, though imperfect, provide a valuable point of departure from which to further our understanding of the reading process and our ability to help our pupils to overcome reading difficulties.

A perspective on the six uses of reading tests

The diagnosis of reading difficulties is not an esoteric exercise carried out solely by specialists. It is carried out at many levels. The class teacher is constantly involved in the informal diagnosis of children's reading difficulties. If this approach is not successful, the class teacher may well initiate a more systematic examination of a child's reading difficulties still within the classroom, using a recognised diagnostic reading test, e.g. the *Standard Reading Tests* battery, *Neale Analysis of Reading Ability* (see Section II, pp. 194 and 146). If the child continues to experience difficulties, referral may then be made to someone with more specialised knowledge and expertise such as an educational psychologist or a remedial teacher.

Provided that she is interested in the diagnosis and treatment of reading difficulties, the teacher who notices that a child is having some problem with reading usually asks herself a number of related questions. These might be:

1 What exactly is the child's difficulty?
2 What is causing the problem?
3 Can anything be done to help the child overcome the difficulty?
4 Specifically *what* can I do to help the child?
5 How effective is the help given?
6 How adequate was my original diagnosis?

Diagnostic reading tests can often provide answers to the first question. They can also suggest possible causes of a child's particular difficulty. The answer to the third question is largely determined by the teacher's understanding of reading as a developmental process.

Also bearing on it, the manuals of a number of diagnostic reading tests provide general guidelines on the treatment of certain reading problems. However, relatively few provide detailed advice for the teacher on the fourth question. An answer to it is usually dependent on the teacher's ingenuity plus her knowledge of a variety of materials and approaches to skill mastery and motivation. Either informal observation or the use of more systematic testing will meet the fifth question. Any answer to the sixth is usually related to the effectiveness of the teacher's intervention. If it does not enable the child to overcome his difficulty, the original diagnosis may be called into question and the whole series of questions repeated.

During such a revision, the teacher learns more about the nature of the reading process, individual differences between pupils and the effectiveness of a given intervention. She also becomes conscious of the uses and limitations of diagnostic reading tests in assisting her to teach efficiently.

At all levels the diagnosis of reading difficulties is a process of hypothesis generation followed by an intervention, the effects of which lead to a further modification of the hypothesis and thus of the intervention. For example, 'Tommy cannot synthesise simple three- and four-letter phonically regular words; why not? Perhaps it is because . . . , so I will get him to . . . and see whether it will help him cope. If it doesn't, I'll have to think again.'

The following points underlying the diagnosis of reading difficulties should be borne in mind:

(i) Diagnosis is an integral part of effective teaching;
(ii) Diagnosis is intended to facilitate the child's acquisition of specified skills or attitudes;
(iii) Diagnosis is not a once-for-all-time activity but is a continuous process in education;
(iv) Diagnosis is centred on the individual's particular reading difficulty;
(v) Diagnosis of reading difficulties requires that the teacher be aware of the importance of the other language arts of listening, speaking and writing;
(vi) Diagnosis of reading difficulties often requires more than an assessment of cognitive skills as reading difficulties may be symptomatic of a wide range of causative factors;
(vii) Diagnosis should involve the use of standardised test procedures where appropriate, but the teacher needs to be aware of the limitations of currently available instruments in this field and to be willing to use other types of tests such as criterion-referenced tests and informal reading tests;
(viii) Because our understanding of the reading process is not complete, the diagnosis of a reading difficulty should be based on a pattern of scores, ratings, reading errors or miscues;
(ix) The heart of diagnosis is the intelligent interpretation of a series of careful, reliable observations coupled with the ability to relate the interpretation to a plan for remedial teaching, and finally;
(x) Only by developing and refining diagnostic procedures can our understanding of the reading process and our ability to prevent and alleviate reading difficulties be furthered.

N.B. The use of the terms 'diagnosis' and 'treatment' are seen by some reading experts as being based on a medical model inappropriate to education. The processes involved in relation to reading difficulties are sometimes said to be better represented by the concepts of 'identification' and 'alleviation'. At present readers will find both sets of concepts in widespread use in the professional literature.

Who else may need the information reading tests provide?

Whilst the preceding six considerations are likely to be of major interest to the classroom teacher, other people have an interest in the testing of reading. Local Education Authorities (LEAs) might well consider that standardised objective tests of reading provide a useful way of monitoring the extent to which the schools are, or are not, helping to produce a literate population. The results of such testing could also be used when deploying limited resources to places where the need appears greatest. With the facilities currently available for the easy storage and very rapid analysis of such data, there are good reasons for expecting that in the near future all LEAs will have a regular programme of objective testing in the basic subjects at both the primary and secondary level. A recently completed survey (Pumfrey, 1984) showed that 81 out of 104 LEAs in England and Wales carry out authority-wide testing of reading at one or more age levels.

Parents generally want their children to become fluent and enthusiastic readers. If their children's schools are sufficiently concerned with their own effectiveness in this respect to test reading regularly, this can be interpreted by parents as explicit recognition of a mutually valued educational objective.

To the pupil of any age the informal and formal testing of reading can help to give a sense of direction. Children and adults generally learn more effectively when they are able to quantify and record their own progress. For example, individual records such as those contained in the SRA Reading Laboratories, the Ward Lock Reading Laboratories and in the Stott *Programmed Reading Kit* Record Card use the impetus provided by knowledge of reading test results to maintain children's motivation to read at a high level.

The testing of reading and related skills forms an important area of educational research. Such research is often criticised because it does not provide the unambiguous and definitive pointers to action that many teachers would like. We all have a tendency to hope for simple answers to complex questions. Reading research is trying to provide us with insights into a phenomenon as complex as anything that man has yet considered.

The teacher as tester

'I've never needed to use a reading test in all my years of teaching reading.' This was a statement made by a primary school teacher who was clearly competent at helping her pupils learn to read. She had taught in the same school for a number of years. The school was one which considered the teaching of reading an important educational objective (as do most schools). Less typically, her pupils were all making excellent, albeit varied, progress in their reading. They also showed considerable and sustained enthusiasm in reading-related activities. It was the type of class that the majority of teachers who had visited described as 'excellently taught', 'a joy to see', 'I'd like my children to attend such a class in such a school.'

Having observed this teacher at work, it was clear that with individual children she was constantly using *informal testing* of their mastery of reading skills. As a result of this information she would modify the content and sequence of learning experiences to which the child was exposed. She also kept a systematic record of the type of difficulties that had been observed, together with comments on the effectiveness of what she had arranged to alleviate the difficulty. However, she did *not* consider this to be 'testing reading'. This excellent teacher had mistakenly identified the process of testing solely with the administration of a particular type of standardised reading test.

The testing of reading is no more than the careful sampling of some important aspects of a child's behaviour related to reading. This testing can be done informally and/or formally. Both aspects of the process are important. They are not mutually exclusive. Even the exceptionally competent teacher of reading is likely to be more effective if she recognises the value of both approaches.

Further reading

(See Appendix 2, pp. 305–33)

ASSESSMENT OF PERFORMANCE UNIT of the Department of Education and Science (1982) *Language Performance in Schools: Primary Survey Report No. 2*. London: HMSO.

ASSESSMENT OF PERFORMANCE UNIT of the Department of Education and Science (1984) *Language Performance in Schools: 1982 Primary Survey Report*. London: Assessment of Performance Unit.

ASSESSMENT OF PERFORMANCE UNIT of the Department of Education and Science (1983) *Language Performance in Schools: Secondary Survey Report No. 2*. London: HMSO.

ASSESSMENT OF PERFORMANCE UNIT of the Department of Education and Science (1985) *Language Performance in Schools: 1982 Secondary Survey Report*. London: Assessment of Performance Unit.

CHAPMAN, L. J. and CZERNIEWSKA, P. (1978) *Reading: From Process to Practice*. London: Routledge and Kegan Paul in association with The Open University.

PUMFREY, P. D. (1984) 'Monitoring the reading attainments of ethnic minority children: national survey of LEA practices.' *New Community*, **XI**, 3, 268–77.

SMITH, F. (1973) *Psycholinguistics and Reading*. New York: Holt, Rinehart and Winston.

SMITH, F. (1982) *Understanding Reading* (3rd edition). New York: Holt, Rinehart and Winston.

2 How can a Reading Test be Selected?

A classification of reading tests

There is a tremendous variety of reading tests and assessment procedures available. It is helpful for the teacher who intends using some to have a conceptual framework within which to classify and think about them. This immediately presents the problem of which characteristics can best be used as a basis for a comprehensive classification. For example, is it helpful to group tests as individual or group, oral or silent, timed or untimed, multiple choice or constructed response? Should tests be grouped according to form, content, age group or method of administration? Important as such points are, to consider these before having thought about the *purpose* for which the test is required is putting the cart before the horse.

Having established the general purpose, there are three important dimensions that must be considered simultaneously if the teacher is to select a test which will provide the information she requires in the most efficient manner. These dimensions provide a useful framework within which *any* reading test whatsoever may be classified. The dimensions are as follows: firstly, which of the *goals* of the reading programme does the test claim to measure? Secondly, from what kind of *source* is the information collected? Thirdly, what is the level of interpretation to be: that is, to what *use* will the information collected be put?

Each of these dimensions can be sub-divided as follows:

(i) The *goals* of the reading programme can be formulated in terms of
 (*a*) attainments (reading skills), and
 (*b*) attitudes towards the activity.

(ii) The three major *sources of information* can be described as:
 (*a*) informal tests of reading,
 (*b*) standardised tests of reading, and
 (*c*) criterion-referenced tests of reading.

(iii) The *level of interpretation*: basically there are the following three levels of reading test interpretation, each level related to different uses:
 (*a*) descriptive,
 (*b*) diagnostic: (1) historic, (2) predictive, and
 (*c*) evaluative.

These three major aspects (i, ii and iii) of reading tests can be represented visually as in Figure 2. A further consideration of these three dimensions will help to clarify a number of points that are central to the effective use of reading tests by the teacher.

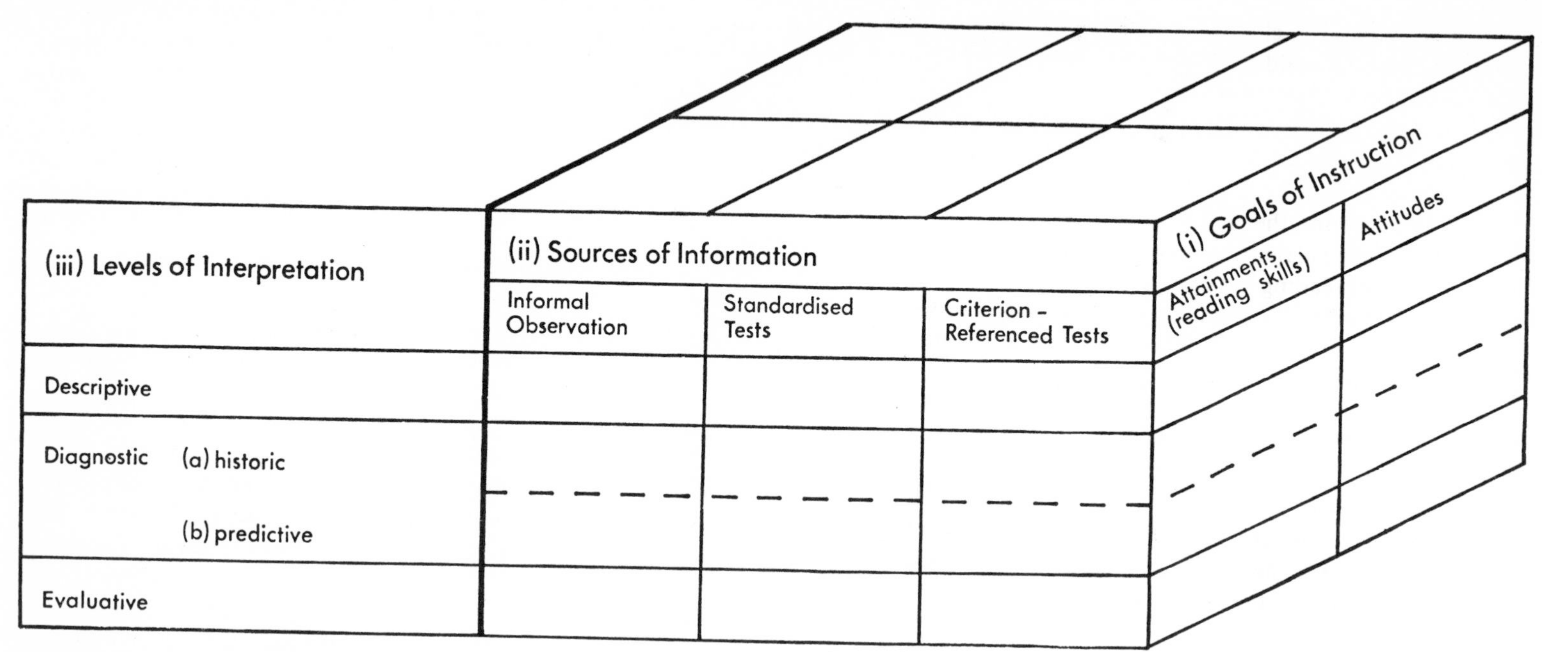

Figure 2
Model for the classification of reading tests in relation to objectives of reading instruction, sources of information and levels of interpretation

(i) *Goals*

Most teachers of reading would agree that two of their aims are 'To enable every child to become a competent reader' and 'To enable every child to obtain pleasure from reading'. The disadvantage of goals expressed in this way is that it is difficult to assess the extent to which they have been achieved. It is important that the goals of the reading programme be defined in terms of objectives that can be observed, taught and/or learned, and measured.

To define goals in this way is a far from easy task. However, there are useful guidelines to help the teacher (Vargas 1977; Smith *et al.*, 1977; Ainscow and Tweddle, 1979; Wulf and Schave, 1984).* Thus objectives can be broken down from general to specific ones. For example, the operational definition of *one part* of a general objective in the cognitive area could be 'The child can *name* flash cards correctly.' Here the type of behaviour is unambiguously defined. Once this has been done, the particular content to which it applies can be specified. Having carried out such an analysis, the selection of an appropriate test of reading is made much easier because the teacher knows exactly what her objectives are. A fuller account, together with examples, of how to write behavioural objectives in the reading field is given in a companion volume (Pumfrey, 1977, pp. 129–34).

(ii) *Sources of information*

(*a*) Informal tests of reading

The teacher of young children in the early stages of reading acquisition should hear her pupils read individually, regularly and frequently as *one part* of the reading programme. The information that the teacher can obtain in such a situation helps her to identify the children who are having difficulties and also the type of difficulties they are experiencing. However, to do so efficiently requires that the teacher use an adequate method of recording the child's responses and analysing error patterns. The error pattern will suggest ways of helping the child and, at an informal level, the teacher can then evaluate the efficacy of whatever interventions she puts in train. Such informal analyses and records mean that the teacher is more likely *consciously* to recognise important diagnostic indicators and develop constructive ways of responding to them. She becomes less dependent on an intuitive and unsystematic approach to the identification and remediation of children's reading difficulties. Her professional expertise is increased. She can communicate her activities to colleagues. The use of a simple type of error recording and analysis is described in Chapter 3. The system can be adapted by any teacher at any level to suit her particular requirements.

Most teachers readily make up attainment tests for their pupils without having studied the theory of test construction. Frequently these tests are devised almost on the spur of the moment to establish the extent to which the pupils have mastered a particular skill that has been taught. For example, a teacher might arrange for groups of children to work on material intended to help them identify the consonant blends at the start of certain words by using item 15 from Stott's *Programmed Reading Kit* (Stott, 1971). To see whether the children were able to generalise their skill to other situations, the teacher could think of a number of different yet structurally similar words and check whether the children were able to identify the initial consonant blends. It is unlikely that she would systematically consider all the possible words she might use, but would rapidly decide on a list of twenty or so that seemed to her pertinent to the skill she wished to test. The informality in the construction, administration and interpretation of such tests is readily apparent. Their major strength lies in the skill of the teacher in choosing valid items.

Currently there is a move to help teachers construct rather more adequate attainment tests in areas such as reading. The Educational Testing Service, Princeton, New Jersey, publish two small pamphlets called 'Making a Classroom Test—A Guide for Teachers' and

* Full references are given at the end of the chapter.

'Short-cut Statistics for Teacher-made Tests'. These can be obtained for a nominal sum. They tend to emphasise the considerations normally borne in mind by test constructors when making up a standardised test, but are still of value to the teacher interested in ensuring that her own informal classroom tests are good ones.

Quite useful reading comprehension tests can be readily constructed using the 'cloze' technique (Rye, 1982). All that is required here is to take an appropriate passage and block out some of the words. The child's task is to read the passage and deduce the missing words from the context. The same technique is also used in both standardised and criterion-referenced reading tests (e.g. *Cloze Reading Test*, Section II, p. 113).

The Informal Reading Inventory (IRI) is described at length in Chapter 3, because it is an important assessment procedure for the classroom teacher bringing the strengths of informal and criterion-referenced testing together. It is considered by the author as one of the most promising approaches to assessment available to the teacher of reading.

The use of reading tests by a teacher means that careful *observation* of the pupil's reading behaviours can take place. Such observations, if systematic, planned, recorded, analysed and their interpretation acted upon, can enable the teacher to assess reading competencies, to measure progress and to diagnose difficulties.

(*b*) Standardised tests of reading

The two most important characteristics of standardised tests are that they have been designed to discriminate between children and their norms are established on a specified group. Their use enables the teacher to answer questions such as 'Is Peter's reading comprehension ability using a multiple choice test superior to John's?' The distinction between the informal test, which also is able to provide an answer to this question, and the formal *standardised* test is that the latter gives an answer with a known degree of precision. Children can be compared with their immediate peers and also with the scores of the sample on whom the test has been standardised.

A refinement of this approach leads to the standardised diagnostic reading test. This type of test can give a number of scores for the individual child on different aspects of the reading process. These scores are sometimes presented in the form of a profile from which the diagnosis of areas of difficulty can be made and ideas for remedial work generated. For example, the *Neale Analysis of Reading Ability* (see Section II) gives scores for speed, accuracy and comprehension. It also provides an analysis of the specific reading errors made by the child.

The interpretation of standardised reading test profiles is a complex subject. It is discussed in the companion volume to this monograph. An understanding of the reliabilities of the subtest scores and of their intercorrelations is necessary if a profile is to be interpreted adequately (Pumfrey, 1977).

National surveys of reading are based on standardised objective tests. For example, the *Southgate Group Reading Tests* 1 and 2 (see Section II, p. 192) and various of the standardised tests produced by the NFER-Nelson have been used extensively. The Assessment of Performance Unit of the Department of Education and Science has developed a related system whereby national standards in reading attainments and other aspects of language can be monitored and changes over time identified. This type of test is extremely important, but it should not blind the teacher to the availability of other sources of information that may be more appropriate to her pupil's needs and her school's resources. It must be borne in mind also that many standardised objective reading tests are very limited in the range of skills they measure.

(*c*) Criterion-referenced tests of reading

Some tests of reading are based on the premise that *all* children need to master certain reading skills if they are to cope adequately with skills at progressively higher levels of complexity. The focus of attention is *not* on the individual differences between children, but on a comparison of the child's abilities in relation to that level which it is deemed reasonable and necessary that he achieve. For example, it might be considered that *all* children need to be able to recognise the twelve words in English that comprise about one quarter of typical written material (McNally and Murray, 1984). Immediate recognition of these twelve words can be regarded as a criterion of reading performance. The teacher is concerned that *all* children achieve this goal and is not particularly interested in the fact that, if they do, the twelve-word test no longer serves to help her to discriminate between the children in terms of relative ability. Similarly, the headmistress of an Infants' school who aims to have all children reading *at least* to a certain book in a graded series, is stressing a criterion goal.

Criterion-referenced tests are primarily concerned with the child's ability to cope with items representative of a specified criterion of reading competence. Such tests are usually made up on the basis of a detailed analysis of the content of reading instruction. Jackson's *Phonic Skills Tests* is an example (see Section II, p. 180) of this type of test. Many of the diagnostic reading tests contained in the handbook by Daniels and Diack are also criterion-referenced tests. The material was first published in book form during 1958 and reached its 14th impression in 1979. The tremendous popularity of this battery of tests suggests that many practising teachers find them helpful in diagnosing difficulties.

The criterion-referenced approach to the testing of reading is built into some graded reading series such as the series *Programmed Reading* by McGraw-Hill. In these books a test of the material covered forms an integral part of the programme. It must be coped with adequately before the child proceeds to a more advanced level of work. The same is true of the Macmillan Reading Programme. The graded reading and language development programme *Reading 360* includes evaluation packs that enable the teacher to assess pupils' mastery of specific skills as they progress through the materials. The system integrates teaching and testing.

One further homely example might help clarify the concept of criterion-referenced measurement for those to whom it is unfamiliar. At the back of many books in series of graded readers there is a list of the words used in the reader. When a child comes to the teacher saying that he has finished reading the book and asking if he can go on to the next one in the series, after checking that the child has understood the story, the teacher typically asks the child to read the 'out of context' list of words at the back of the book. If the child can read them, he is given the next book in the series. If he cannot, he is usually referred to another book of similar level to that which he claims to have completed, or certain work is prescribed on the basis of the material he obviously has not mastered. This is using the 'out of context' words as a criterion-referenced test based on a content analysis of the reader.

The criterion-referenced test of reading is related to the informal approaches that can be used by the teacher in the closeness of its link with the child's reading programme. It is a move away from the normative standardised test approach. Currently a number of criterion-referenced reading tests are being developed and there are sound reasons for teachers welcoming such instruments.

At the same time it should be remembered that any criterion-referenced reading test such as the Dolch *Basic Sight Word Test* (TRN 25, p. 209) inevitably has a normative aspect in the same way that any normative test has a criterion-referenced one. For this reason, some test constructors have tried to combine the advantages of criterion-referenced measurement of reading skills with normative scores, e.g. the *Woodcock Reading Mastery Tests* (TRN 197, p. 274).

(iii) *Level of interpretation*

It was suggested earlier that interpretation of the information obtained from any reading test or assessment procedure can be considered at three major levels:

(*a*) descriptive;
(*b*) diagnostic: (1) historic, (2) predictive; and
(*c*) evaluative.

The first level, *descriptive*, merely enables the situation as it is now to be described with some precision. It is frequently found in official reports and surveys.

The second, *diagnostic*, is of much more importance to the teacher. It has two aspects, the historic and the predictive. The former is concerned with the possible causes of a child's current pattern of reading competencies. The latter is forward looking. It is concerned with the interpretation of findings in terms of planning some kind of instructional programme to take the child on to the next stage of reading development.

Interpretation of information at the level of *evaluation* involves considering the effectiveness of the reading programme in the context of the overall values of the teacher and the school and the resources available to help achieve the various goals of the curriculum. For example, how important is it that children should read and enjoy the activity? Are there not other educational goals of equal importance? What resources, in terms of teacher, and pupil time and school capitation allowance, should be allocated to the teaching and learning of reading? What improvements might reasonably be effected?

In practice the teacher moves rapidly between these three levels of interpretation. Any reading test can be used at any level but some tests are more appropriate to one than the others.

If John obtains a reading age of six years on a reading test, that is a descriptive statement. If the teacher looks at the pattern of errors in his responses and at the boy's situation in general, she is shifting her level of interpretation to diagnosis, either historic and/or (more usefully) predictive. If the teacher then questions the efficacy of the reading programme, her goals and the resources that are brought to bear on achieving them, the information obtained from the reading test or other assessment procedure is being considered in a much wider sense. It is being used evaluatively.

It is not unknown for teachers to say of reading tests, 'It's not what I really wanted, but it is the only one available at our school.' Or even worse, 'I only know of one reading test' (usually the Schonell *Graded Word Reading Test* or the *Burt* (*Rearranged*) *Word Reading Test*, itself replaced in 1976 by the *Burt Word Reading Test 1974 revision*).

These are two examples of test selection determined by relatively unimportant considerations. If the proposed three-dimensional model is applied, the teacher is more likely to be able to select appropriately from the vast array of reading tests and assessment procedures available those which are best suited to her particular purpose.

Using the three dimensions

The value when thinking about reading tests of using the three dimensions given in Figure 2 is shown in the following two typical teaching situations.

A teacher might ask 'How do the reading standards of my class compare with national norms?' Here she is interested in the goal of *attainment* in certain reading skills. The source of information most appropriate would be a nationally *standardised test* of the reading skill or skills under consideration. The initial emphasis of interpretation would be *descriptive*.

When thinking about arranging appropriate word-attack experiences for a child, the teacher may wonder precisely where a pupil's knowledge of phonics is weak. Here also her concern is with the goal of *attainment*. The source of information could be a *criterion-referenced test* such as Jackson's *Phonic Skills Tests* (see Section II). In this instance the emphasis of interpretation is *diagnostic*.

In Tables 7a and 7b and 8a and 8b, pp. 43–4, 45–6, the reading tests described in Section II of this monograph have been categorised according to the model described. It is anticipated that this will help the teacher to locate reading tests or assessment procedures that will suit these varied purposes for children of different age groups.

Normative and criterion-referenced tests: some further points

The Secretary of State for Education and Science has recently (1984) suggested that, because educationists have concentrated their attention on normative rather than on criterion-referenced assessment of pupil performance, too many pupils are doomed inevitably to being labelled as (relative) failures. In fact the two approaches to assessment are complementary rather than mutually exclusive.

Examinations in music are based on Grades extending from Grade 1 to Grade 8. The tests at each grade level are criterion-referenced. What candidates need to know and do is explicitly stated. However, of those taking the examinations, some candidates fail, some just pass whereas others may obtain scores of 100%. If every child passed Grade 1 for a given instrument with a mark of 100%, there would quite probably be a demand that the *absolute* standard be raised. The British driving test is often cited as another example of a criterion-referenced test in which the performance criteria for success in terms of knowledge of the Highway Code and mastery of specified driving skills are explicitly stated. Even though the criteria for success are publicly notified, there is a very high initial failure rate. It is also interesting to note that 'successful' candidates still contribute to a regular national carnage on the roads that could, possibly, be reduced by having a driving test that required higher standards.

Turning to reading, to possess a sight vocabulary of, say, 200 specified words would represent a criterion that could guide (or direct) instruction. Some pupils would achieve the criterion more rapidly than others.

It is also the case that many normative reading tests contain items that appear in criterion-referenced reading tests. The child's ability to complete a sentence by selecting one word from five alternatives is an example.

The danger of any form of testing is its 'backwash' effect on the curriculum and methods used in schools. It has been said that the power to test *is* the power to determine the curriculum. Hence narrowly defined performance criteria for success can lead to a limiting and restricted education.

Deciding on the required standards for a criterion-referenced test is very difficult. Perfect, or near perfect, scores are required where the skill is important for future learning, where objective items allow guessing and where the criterion objective specifies mastery. The validity of standards is not easily determined.

Criterion-referenced reading tests are increasingly being used by schools to implement diagnostic-prescriptive reading programmes. A number of widely-used basal reading schemes incorporate criterion-referenced testing to assist the teacher in the identification and alleviation of reading difficulties. *Reading 720* published by Ginn (USA) is an example. It is an American system similar in some respects to *Reading 360* produced by Ginn (UK) and mentioned earlier in this chapter.

Teachers need to understand the respective strengths and weaknesses of normative and criterion-referenced tests. They will then be able to select instruments appropriate to particular educational purposes. In summary, if the teacher is interested in how students are performing in relation to national and/or local standards, a norm-referenced or standardised reading test should be used. If the focus of interest is on eliciting diagnostic information about a pupil's performance on a particular skill, an objectives-based or criterion-referenced reading test should be used. In making such decisions, it is always important to appreciate that every normative reading test has a criterion-referenced aspect and that every criterion-referenced reading test has a normative aspect. Though the two approaches differ significantly in certain respects, there is not as great a difference between them as recent publicity has suggested. This is not to say that no differences exist. In Table 1, p. 17, norm-referenced and criterion-referenced reading tests are contrasted in relation to important issues in educational assessment.

Diagnostic-prescriptive teaching of reading

This approach involves a six-stage, sequential/spiral hypothesis generation and testing strategy. The stages are shown in Figure 3 (p. 18). The reading behaviours of competent readers are more wide-ranging, complex and efficient than those of beginners. Whether or not reading can, to advantage, be analysed into hierarchies of skills is a complex and unresolved issue. What is clear is that reading tasks *can* be ordered in terms of their relative difficulty levels for groups and individuals. Variations in either the form or the content of such tasks can differentially affect task difficulty. On the basis of such orderings of operationally defined tasks, a pupil's individual strengths and weaknesses can be identified. This information can be linked to instructional procedures and materials designed to promote developments enabling the pupil to master previously unmastered tasks. Whilst diagnostic-prescriptive teaching of reading is most commonly associated with an objectives-based curriculum utilising criterion-referenced tests, the approach can also incorporate normative testing. Because reading instruction is both systematic and develop-

Table 1
Normative and criterion-referenced reading tests contrasted

ISSUE	Norm-referenced	Criterion-referenced
Purpose	To assess inter- and intra-individual differences in reading attainments and attitudes to reading in a specified group of pupils.	To assess the extent to which specified operationally defined reading objectives have been achieved.
Focus	1 Generalised skills and reading abilities and attitudes. 2 Latent traits inferred from pupils performances.	1 Specific and narrow reading skills and behaviours. 2 Detailed task-analysis.
Construction	1 Based on conventional test theory using item analyses with given limits to Facility and Discrimination indices of items. 2 Specification of the group to which the test is to be applied is of the essence. 3 Mathematical basis of measurement well developed and articulated.	1 Tests are based on items developed from an analysis of the objective to be mastered. 2 Explicit normative considerations are irrelevant because the successful mastery of the criterion by all pupils is the objective. 3 Mathematical basis of criterion-referenced measurement is still in the early stages of development.
Standards	Test results usually compared with children of the same age and from the same population.	Test results compared to an explicit criterion of mastery, e.g. number of items correct for a given objective.
Reporting results	Standard scores (e.g. deviation quotients, 'z' scores, T scores, stens, stanines), percentiles, and reading ages.	Percentage scores on number of items correct for a given objective.
Teaching implications	1 Items must *not* be taught as doing so would invalidate the norms that have been obtained. It would also be impossible to interpret the scores of pupils after such teaching. 2 Does not provide a clear guide to required instructional content but can suggest *method.* 3 Focuses attention on normative standards.	1 The items have been selected as both desirable and able to be mastered by pupils. The content of the test *must* be taught. 2 Provides guidance concerning instructional materials. Tests can be directly linked to such resources. 3 Narrowness of objectives can restrict curriculum adversely.

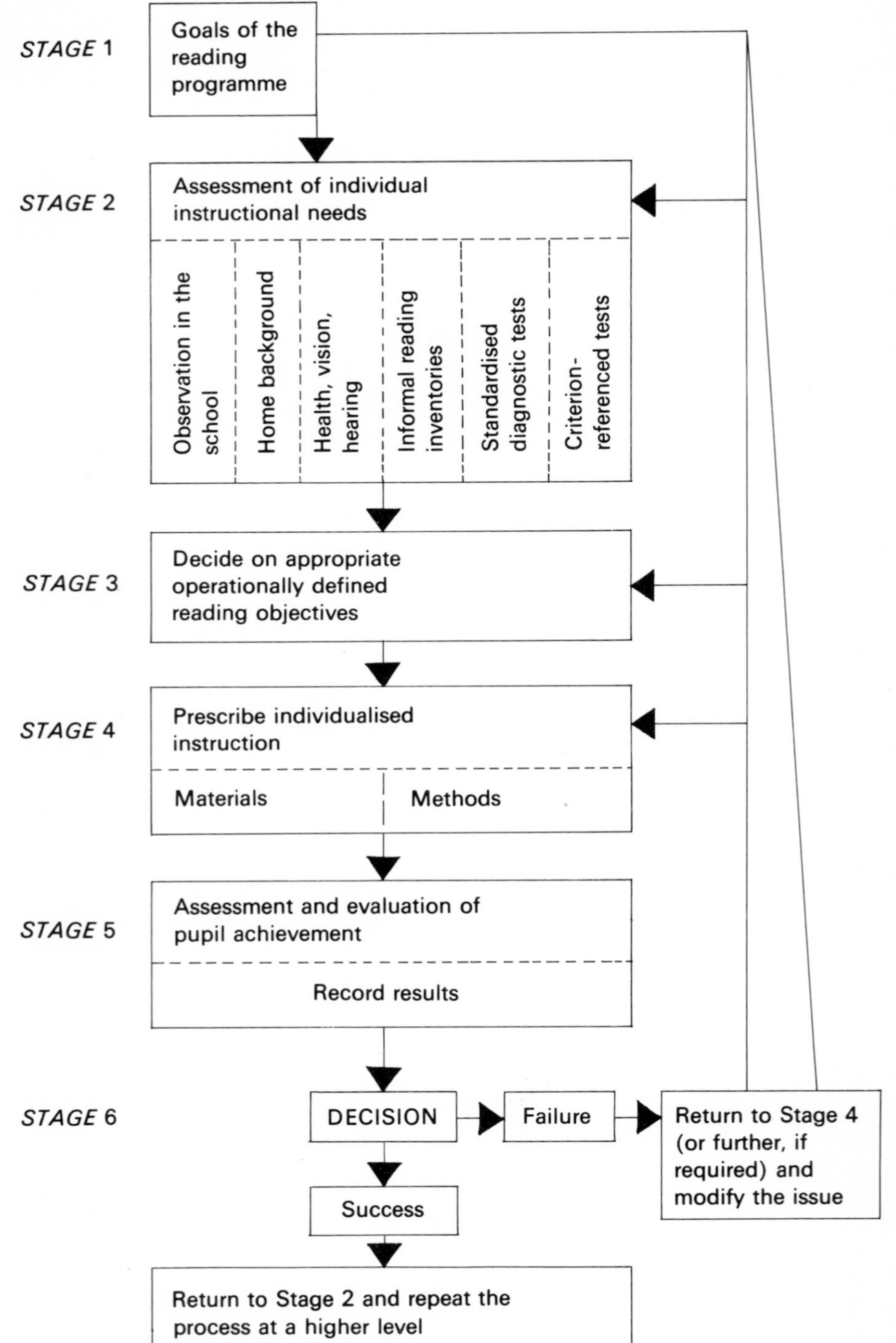

Figure 3 Model of diagnostic-prescriptive teaching of reading

mental, the diagnostic-prescriptive approach to the teaching of reading fits well with many teachers' beliefs as to how assessment and instruction can best be linked.

Important characteristics of reading tests

Once the teacher has decided on the *kind* of reading test needed to suit the particular purpose, the next task is to identify a suitable test. It is important, therefore, to understand certain characteristics of the tests themselves.

The three most important characteristics of any reading test are validity, reliability and practicability. The *validity* of a test indicates the extent to which it measures that which it is intended to measure. Its *reliability* describes the degree to which the instrument produces consistent results. Its *practicability* is concerned with the extent to which a particular instrument is of use to the teacher in her particular school situation.

It is possible to have a highly reliable reading test that is not valid for a particular purpose. For example, a test of reading comprehension can give very reliable results, but if the focus of the teacher's interest is on children's rate of reading a particular type of material, the comprehension test is unlikely to be a valid measure of her particular objective. High reliability does *not* guarantee validity. However, if a reading test can be shown to have high validity, it must have high reliability. By analogy, if I have a wrist watch which keeps excellent time, it is highly reliable. If, however, it stops and I wind it up without resetting the hands, it is still a reliable instrument but the information it provides concerning time is no longer valid. In selecting a reading test the first consideration should be its validity.

Strictly speaking, it is more accurate to talk about the validities and reliabilities of reading tests, although for convenience these terms are often referred to collectively. Each can be expressed with considerable precision in relation to the vast majority of standardised tests of reading but the concepts apply to information obtained from *any* source.

(i) *Validities*

The four types of validity most commonly mentioned in reading test manuals are *content*, *concurrent*, *predictive* and *construct* validity.

Content validity is indicated by the extent to which the items comprising the test form a satisfactory sample of items which actually tap the ability the test constructor wishes to measure. For example, if a test is of phonically regular three-letter words, does it adequately sample the universe of such words appropriate to the age level for whom the test is intended? The constructors of reading tests should give potential users evidence of the test's content validity. The responsibility is then on the teacher to decide whether the given test is appropriate for her particular purpose.

Evidence of *concurrent validity* is often presented by showing the extent to which the scores on a reading test relate to other measures of current reading performance by the same group of children. For example, the correlation between scores on an established and a newly constructed word reading test might be calculated to provide one index of concurrent validity for the new test. Thus, if children who do well on the new *Marino Graded Word Reading Scale* do well on the old *Burt (Rearranged) Word Reading Test*, and those who find difficulty with the new one also find the old test hard, this information could be presented as evidence of concurrent validity. Similarly the teacher's subjective ranking of children in word reading skill could be correlated with the same children's scores on a word reading test. A high relationship could be interpreted as further evidence of concurrent validity.

Information describing the validities of a reading test (other than content validity) is commonly presented as indices ranging from 0 to 1, the former indicating zero validity and the latter perfect validity. In practice no test is completely valid.

Predictive validity of a reading test is concerned with the extent that a test will predict children's future reading competencies. For example, children who are poor readers at the age of eight years as measured by a reading comprehension test are likely to remain *relatively* poor readers even at the end of their secondary school careers. Of course, there will be individual children who will not conform to this prediction. The aim of the teacher is firstly to recognise such predictive validity and secondly to seek to invalidate it. She can do this by diagnosing likely causes of a child's relative failure and attempting to reduce them by appropriate intervention. In some cases, the improvement of a child's reading competencies can be achieved without recourse to any reading material. This could occur if an extremely anxious child was helped, through therapy, to come to terms with his emotional problems. He could then channel his energies towards the mastery and enjoyments of reading.

Construct validity is concerned with the test constructor showing that the items of the test are an adequate sample of the behaviours included in whatever theoretical psychological attributes the particular reading test is designed to measure. If, for example, it is claimed that a test is measuring some kind of comprehension, the text constructor must provide reasonable grounds for supposing that such psychological processes exist and that the test provides a valid measure of them.

(ii) *Reliabilities*

To be valid, reading tests must be reliable. Indeed, test reliability puts a ceiling on the validity that can be expected. In general, no test can have a validity higher than the square root of its reliability. The reliability of a test is frequently expressed as a coefficient of the same kind as the correlation coefficient. It ranges from 0 to 1, where the former indicates complete unreliability and the latter complete reliability. The four major reliability coefficients pertinent to the selection of a reading test are those of *stability*, *equivalence*, *internal consistency* and a combination of *stability and equivalence*.

The *stability* of a reading test is estimated by administering it twice to a group of children. For this reason it is often referred to as 'test-retest reliability'. The agreement between the two sets of scores obtained is then calculated. If the children's scores do not vary greatly from one occasion to the next, the test-retest reliability is said to be high.

In some reading tests, for example the *Edinburgh Reading Test, Stage 3* (see Section II, p. 120), there are parallel forms of the tests. This makes it possible to test the same skill on *equivalent* but different material. The relationship between children's scores on the administration of two such parallel forms of a test is called the coefficient of equivalence.

When parallel forms are not available and it is not practical to test children twice on the same test, techniques have been devised enabling an estimate of reliability to be achieved from only one administration of a reading test. This is sometimes done by giving the test to a group of children and then dividing the items of the test into two sets, for example on the basis of odd and even items. Thus each child has a score on the odd items and another on the even items. The relationship between these sets of scores for the group can then be calculated. The resultant correlation is called a coefficient of *internal consistency*.

Finally, when a parallel form of a test is administered after a period of time, a coefficient of *stability and equivalence* can be calculated. Generally, such coefficients are rather lower than those obtained from other methods of calculating reliability.

Reading test manuals do not usually contain all of the above indices. The coefficient that is of interest to the teacher is the one that is most pertinent to her purpose in using the test. It is not necessarily the test with the highest coefficient of reliability that is the most appropriate. Because of this, it is difficult to prescribe arbitrary standards concerning the minimum acceptable reliabilities of reading tests. The NFER suggest that the minimum internal consistency reliability coefficients for attainment tests including tests of reading should be ·85 for stability and ·9 for internal consistency. However, there are different acceptable levels dependent on the type of decision one will have to make. Levels of reliability below those given here can be tolerated in certain circumstances (Pumfrey, 1977).

Another way of thinking about the meaning of reliability is in terms of the extent to which children's scores vary from time to time for any number of reasons. In one sense the score that a child obtains on a reading test can be considered as made up of two elements. There is that part which represents his 'true' score and a part representing the host of variables that can either raise or depress the score he obtains. This latter part is often referred to as 'error'. Illness, or having read some related material first before a test, could be chance influences that would affect the obtained score. In the first instance it would probably reduce the obtained score; and in the second increase it. If changes in reading test scores are not large between successive testings, the effects of extraneous variables are small and the test is reliable. If a child's score changed from say, a reading age of seven years to one of thirteen years on a test given twice over a period of a week and there appeared to be no valid reason for the change, one would have considerable doubts as to the reliability of such an instrument.

In fact, the extent to which a child's obtained score on a test is likely to differ from an estimate of his 'true' score can be calculated for any particular test. The extent of this variation in obtained scores is often expressed as the standard error of measurement. The smaller the standard error of a test, the more reliable it is. For example, in the NFER-Nelson *Reading Test AD* (formerly *Sentence Reading Test 1*), a standard error of 2·7 points is quoted for the age group 8 years 2 months to 9 years 1 month. This indicates that a child's obtained score will, by chance, only vary from his 'true' score by plus or minus twice the standard error of measurement once in twenty times. The test-retest reliability of this particular instrument is 0·97.

The most valuable source of information concerning any satisfactory reading test is the handbook which accompanies it. It should always be read carefully and critically before using any test. Many manuals contain relatively sparse details about validities, reliabilities and standardisation. Fortunately the situation is improving. Teachers are becoming more appreciative of the value of a good manual such as those usually produced by the NFER-Nelson. The content of manuals can be expected to improve in line with the criteria that have been spelled out by the British Psychological Society (1980a).

It is also useful to read critical reviews of reading tests and assessment techniques if one wishes to be aware of their weaknesses and strengths. An invaluable source of such reports is the series of *Mental Measurement Yearbooks*. The first of these was published in 1938. The latest available is the *Eighth Mental Measurement Yearbook* (Buros, 1978). The *Yearbooks* provide test users with factual information, critical reviews and comprehensive bibliographies on related test reviews. The editors aim to be comprehensive in the range of tests covered. A ninth *Yearbook* is in preparation and is likely to be published in 1985 (personal communication). Related to the *Yearbooks* are three smaller volumes. Each lists all tests in print at the time of publication. The most recent of these is *Tests in Print III* (Mitchell, 1983). Two other publications edited by Buros of particular relevance to teachers of reading are *Reading Tests and Reviews I* and *Reading Tests and Reviews II* (Buros, 1968; 1975). Others have produced comprehensive references to instruments used in various fields, including education (Sweetland and Keyser, 1983). At present the *Mental Measurement Yearbooks* are probably the best single source of test information and comment available. The founder of the series, Oscar Buros, died in 1978. The Buros Institute of Mental Measurements continues to operate and in future the University of Nebraska Press will distribute all publications of the Buros Institute. The preceding books are, however, usually only found in the reference sections of large libraries. Much more restricted in the range of reading tests covered, far less expensive and thus more accessible is a book containing detailed reviews of twelve of the most important diagnostic and criterion-referenced reading tests identified by a group of American authorities (Schell, 1981).

British authors have produced a number of books providing similar information. Probably the most substantial of these is *Tests in Education* (Levy and Goldstein, 1984). Less substantial but nonetheless valuable briefer reviews of reading and language tests are also available (Bate *et al.*, 1982; Vincent *et al.*, 1983).

The major disadvantage of such books, including the present one, is that they can never be completely up-to-date with new tests that are being produced. For evaluations of the most recent tests it is essential to consult periodicals produced by organisations such as the International Reading Association, the United Kingdom Reading Association (UKRA), the Irish Reading Association and the National Association for Remedial Education. Their addresses are given in Appendix 1, pp. 298–304.

(iii) *Practicability*

The most important characteristic of any reading test is that it must be suited to the particular purpose determined by the teacher. Within this limitation, for tests of similar validities and reliabilities, the following five practical considerations loom large:

1 Is the reading test readily available?
2 Am I able to administer the test?
3 Can I interpret the results?
4 How much time will its use entail?
5 Is it expensive to use?

These questions require considerable thought and in some cases result in a teacher making up her mind to acquire the knowledge and competencies needed if she is to use certain instruments (Pumfrey, 1977).

With reference to questions 1, 2 and 3, reading tests vary greatly in their complexity. Because of this, all reading tests are not openly available to all teachers. However, the vast majority of these instruments are available to teachers through their schools. The British Psychological Society has produced a system for classifying all psychological tests. Many publishers use the Society's recommended system. It is based on the following five levels (British Psychological Society, 1980b).

Level A – Attainment tests and inventories. This level includes any objectively scored instrument requiring limited technical knowledge for its use. The instruments are available to those professionally qualified and active in the field for which the instrument is designed. Level A covers the vast majority of commercially-produced reading tests.

Level P (T) – Group tests of ability. Tests requiring a level of expertise in administration, scoring and interpretation that will have been acquired by qualified teachers. Such instruments are available to teachers in schools and colleges.

Level P – Group tests of ability. Users of these tests are expected to meet one of the following three conditions:

(i) possess an honours degree in psychology recognised by the British Psychological Society;
(ii) completed satisfactorily a course of training in test administration and interpretation approved by the Society; or
(iii) had experience equivalent to either (i) or (ii) above under the supervision of a trained and qualified psychologist.

Level Q – Personality inventories or questionnaires and certain test batteries. These are available to individuals having a thorough knowledge of the theory of testing, considerable practical experience *plus* training in the particular instrument.

Level R – Individual tests of mental ability. At this level users require a very substantial background in the theory and practice of mental measurement at the post-graduate level.

Level K – Clinical instruments. Many of these require clinical judgment rather than the interpretation of objective scores. Users would typically be qualified educational psychologists, clinical psychologists, occupational psychologists, psychiatrists, or therapists who had undertaken special training.

The sequence A, P, Q, R, K indicates tests of increasing complexity. The tests described in Section II are classified in line with the above system.

Whilst some teachers might question the above restrictions in test availability, teachers sufficiently interested can acquire the testing and diagnostic expertise and knowledge required. Indeed, their initial training often contains a course on mental measurement and testing.

The vast majority of reading tests are available to most teachers. Not all test distributors are as restrictive (rightly or wrongly) as the British Psychological Society might wish.

The British Psychological Society has an active Standing Committee on Test Standards and, in 1984, two Working Parties on 'Competence in Psychological Testing' and 'Psychologists' use of Tests'. The Standing Committee has recommended that the publication 'Technical recommendations for psychological tests' (British Psychological Society, 1980a) be revised. Pamphlets such as 'Psychological tests: a statement by the British Psychological Society' outline the Society's position on test related issues. It and related documents can be obtained from the Society's Headquarters at Leicester.

In common with Psychological Associations in the United States of America, Canada, Australia, New Zealand and elsewhere, the British Psychological Society acts in the interests of users of psychological services and techniques. The content and organisation of test manuals are important fields. In them such organisations have been, and are, helping ensure that users of, for example, reading tests obtain the technical information that will enable them to evaluate the validity and utility of a given test for a specified purpose with individuals and or groups of pupils.

Records

Each school should have a recognised testing and assessment programme in which reading competencies figure prominently. Within the programme individual teachers can be encouraged to develop their individual testing and assessment expertise with the pupils for whom they have responsibility.

At both levels records should be kept so that both group and individual trends in reading progress can be identified. This information will enable such action as is deemed necessary to be taken on the basis of evidence rather than opinion.

For each individual child a cumulative record of his reading test results should be kept. There are good educational reasons for encouraging pupils to maintain these records themselves. Such records can be of great value to the teacher (and her pupils) in these days of rapid staff changes. The records should also be transferable to successive schools. In this respect the Armed Forces Educational Services are far ahead of their civilian colleagues.

References

AINSCOW, M. and TWEDDLE, D. A. (1979) *Preventing Classroom Failure: An Objectives Approach*. Chichester: Wiley.

BATE, M., SMITH, M. and JAMES, J. (1982) *Reviews of Tests and Assessments in Early Education (3–5 years)*. Windsor: NFER-Nelson.

BRITISH PSYCHOLOGICAL SOCIETY (1980a) 'Technical recommendations for psychological tests. Prepared by the Standing Committee on Test Standards'. *Bulletin of the British Psychological Society*, **33**, 161–4.

BRITISH PSYCHOLOGICAL SOCIETY (1980b) 'Notes for guidance in planning short courses in psychological testing.' *Bulletin of the British Psychological Society*, **33**, 244–9.

BUROS, O. K. (ed.) (1968) *Reading Tests and Reviews*. Lincoln, NE: University of Nebraska Press distributing for Gryphon Press.

BUROS, O. K. (ed.) (1975) *Reading Tests and Reviews II*. Lincoln, NE: University of Nebraska Press distributing for Gryphon Press.

BUROS, O. K. (ed.) (1978) *The Eighth Mental Measurement Yearbook*. Lincoln, NE: University of Nebraska Press, distributing for Gryphon Press.

DANIELS, J. C. and DIACK, H. (1958; 14th impression 1979) *The*

Standard Reading Tests. London: Chatto and Windus (later Collins Educational).

LEVY, P. and GOLDSTEIN, H. (eds) (1984) *Tests in Education*. London: Academic Press.

McNALLY, J. and MURRAY, W. (1984) *Key Words to Literacy and the Teaching of Reading*. Kettering: The Teacher Publishing Co.

MITCHELL, J. U., Jr (ed.) (1983) *Tests in Print III*. Lincoln, NE: University of Nebraska Press.

PUMFREY, P. D. (1977) *Measuring Reading Abilities: Concepts, Sources and Applications*. London: Hodder and Stoughton (obtainable from the author at the University of Manchester).

RYE, J. (1982) *Cloze Procedure and the Teaching of Reading*. London: Heinemann Educational.

SCHELL, L. M. (ed.) (1981) *Diagnostic and Criterion-Referenced Reading Tests: Review and Evaluation*. Newark, DE: International Reading Association.

SMITH, J. M., SMITH, D. E. P. and BRINK, J. R. (1977) *A Technology of Reading and Writing. Vol. 2: Criterion-referenced Tests for Reading and Writing*. New York: Academic Press.

SWEETLAND, R. C. and KEYSER, D. J. (1983) *A Comprehensive Reference for Assessments in Psychology, Education and Business*. Kansas City, KS: Test Corporation.

STOTT, D. H. (1971) *Programmed Reading Kit*. Edinburgh: Holmes McDougall.

VARGAS, J. S. (1977) *Behavioral Psychology for Teachers*. New York: Harper and Row.

VINCENT, D., GREEN, L., FRANCIS, J. and POWNEY, J. (1983) *A Review of Reading Tests*. Windsor: NFER-Nelson.

WULF, K. M. and SCHAVE, D. (1984) *Curriculum Design: A Handbook for Educators*. London: Scott, Foresman.

Further reading

See Section II, Appendix 2, pp. 305–33.
Books with the number 1 before the author's name are likely to be particularly helpful to any reader wishing to pursue further the topics touched on in this chapter.

3 The Informal Reading Inventory

Definition of reading levels

From the point of view of the teacher, each pupil can be considered as having not one but a number of reading age levels. A child's level of reading proficiency is related to his abilities, the nature of the reading task he faces and his interest in it. Following the work of Johnson and Kress, first published in 1965 and achieving its 16th impression in 1980, it is helpful to distinguish between four levels of reading skill:

Independent level: This is the level at which a child can read with fluency, understanding, accuracy and enjoyment. It is the level at which he can deal with reading material without requiring supervision or help. The material is seen by the child as 'easy to read'. The over-learning essential to proficient reading requires much experience at this level.

Instructional level: At this level the child can benefit from systematic instruction by a teacher. The material is seen by the child as presenting some difficulties with which he will need help but much of the material will be within his grasp.

Frustration level: Any material which is so difficult that the child makes many errors, is slow, hesitant, cannot readily understand the meaning and from which he can be easily distracted, can be considered as presenting him with a frustrating experience. At this difficulty level the chances of a child improving his reading skills and attitudes towards reading are virtually nil. The material is seen as distasteful and to be avoided.

Capacity level: Whilst the estimation of the level at which a child might be expected to read is exceedingly complex, a pupil's ability to listen to and comprehend orally presented material can form a useful index of reading potential. The child is tested to see whether when questioned on such material, he understands *and* shows an oral language level in line with the level of the material that has been read to him.

Estimates of these four levels can be obtained by administering an Informal Reading Inventory (IRI).

The concept of an inventory means that both attainments in and attitudes towards reading as well as any pertinent aspect of language development can be considered. It is an informal reading test in the sense that a wide variety of unstandardised materials can be used in an IRI, and there is no normative comparison with what other students can do. The child's performance is compared with a defined criterion of *mastery* of reading rather than by considering how much more or less capable he is than his peers. Such an inventory is *not* informal in its procedures. The central aim is to identify whether a text, from which a teacher wishes a child to work, is suited to the child's reading skills and is not too difficult for the child. *This applies irrespective of the subject concerned or the level of complexity of the material.* Thus the technique is of importance to *any* teacher of *any* subject at *any* level where the child's study involves dealing with textual material. The materials used are dictated by the purposes of the inventory.

The IRI is based on the assumption that reading attainments follow a developmental pattern analogous to aspects of physical development such as height, weight or size of feet. To determine whether a shoe 'fits', the common sense approach is to try it on. Similarly, to establish whether or not a book 'fits' a child, the child should try to read it. The IRI systematises the teacher's observation of how well particular reading material suits a child. To be able to recommend the appropriate book for a child, i.e. at either the Independent or Instructional level, is central to success in the teaching of reading.

The definition of the reading attainments appropriate to each of the levels described is given in Table 2. The figures presented are based on the consensus of expert opinion in the field. The percentages indicate the degree of success typifying the various levels in relation to different aspects of reading. These standards vary somewhat between advocates of IRIs. Empirical evidence of the validity of the levels is rarely given.

It is interesting to note that the class teacher *frequently underestimates* the difficulty level of the reading material with which her children are faced. The use of an IRI makes one immediately aware of discrepancies between teacher estimation of the difficulty level of textual material and the actual difficulty level experienced by the child. Too many pupils spend too much time with textual material which is at Frustration level.

The core of an IRI comprises a series of graded passages of writing which the child is asked to read aloud (or silently). After each passage he is questioned about it. It is usual to select passages from a graded basal reading series not known to the child, or from graded material such as that contained in a reading laboratory. If she so wishes, the teacher can use her own material.

In all instances it is important that the content of the material be pertinent to the child's interests, otherwise low achievement can be confused with poor effort. The lengths of the passages or block of words selected for reading should be about 20 words at the pre-primer level and gradually increased in length from more difficult texts by amounts which keep the calculation of the percentages given in Table 2 easy, i.e. use passages or blocks of 20, 40, 60, 80, or 100 words. In general, the longer the sample of reading obtained the more reliable is the assessment. Thus several passages can be used at a given level. The questions asked to test the child's understanding of the material should include different levels of comprehension. Questions concerning word meaning, questions of fact, questions concerning the main ideas contained in the passage and, where appropriate, questions concerning inferences and implications will be asked. Valmont (1972) gives a useful guide to the construction of suitable questions. The setting of questions poses many problems. It is known that the type of question asked can markedly affect the assessed level at which the child copes (Pikulski and Shanahan, 1982).

Thus the child might, for example, be asked to read aloud passages from graded material such as a series of basal readers beginning at an

Table 2
Suggested criteria for assessing some achievements using an Informal Reading Inventory

Reading Level	*Skills Tested*						
	Oral Reading Accuracy			Reading Comprehension		Rate of Reading	
	a. Words in isolation		*b.* Words in context	*c.* Definition of words out of context (text removed)	*d.* Answering questions using contextual cues (text available)	*e.* Oral	*f.* Silent
	i. flash presentation (i.e. ½″ exposure)	ii. untimed					
Independent Level	90%–100%	95%–100%	99%–100%	90%–100%	90%–100%	Oral reading about half the rate of silent reading for same level of comprehension	
Instructional Level	50%–89%	60%–94%	95%–98%	60%–89%	70%–89%	Oral reading rate equal to or not more than 15 words per minute *less* than silent reading	
Frustration Level	Below 50%	Below 60%	Below 95%	Below 60%	Below 70%	Oral reading faster than silent reading by up to 15 words per minute	
Capacity Level					Listening comprehension of 75% of material		

easy level (Independent) and continuing until the material is too difficult for the child according to the criteria given for Frustration level.

The teacher will need a prepared copy of the passages being read. The accuracy of the child and his ability to comprehend what is being read can be recorded. The child's errors can be easily recorded, analysed and (more difficult) their implications for reading instruction considered. An IRI can also be constructed from groups of 'out of context' words of progressively greater difficulty which can be read either orally and/or silently and the child's attainments summarised as in Table 3 (pp. 30–1).

The child's rate of reading can also be observed. If the child's rate of oral reading is very, very slow it is highly likely that the material represents a frustrating experience for the child, especially if the material is too lengthy. It has been argued that rate of oral reading itself does not *alone* determine that material is frustrating for a child unless his silent reading is much slower, given that the understanding of the material is equivalent under both conditions.

It should be noted that if *any one* of the skills tested is at the level of Frustration, then the material is Frustration level for the child even if the child's other indices all indicate higher levels. Many teachers question such an assertion as it could rule out, for example, the use of dictionaries and other reference materials.

Group IRIs

Informal Reading Inventories can readily be adapted for use with groups of pupils of any age and level of ability. A Group IRI may be used to assess the extent to which a child had understood a given passage of writing. It might also allow an appraisal of the extent to which the pupil was using appropriate techniques in situations requiring different reading skills.

The former consideration would necessitate the teacher devising questions on the meaning of the vocabulary used in the passage, as well as other aspects of reading comprehension. The first of these might be tested by requiring the child to select suitable synonyms or antonyms of given words, or to use a dictionary to establish the meaning of particular words. Other aspects of reading comprehension, such as the pupil's ability to identify the main ideas in a passage of writing, to note the sequence of ideas, to show understanding of particular points of explicit meaning, to comment on implicit meanings and to draw conclusions, could be tested by setting suitable questions. The second focus of concern, namely the pupil's ability to use differing reading techniques appropriately, could be examined by setting tasks that require the reader to use, for example, 'skimming' or other rapid reading techniques and other tasks that require close attention to detail.

An IRI can also be used by the teacher to check that readers are able to use the various parts of a book effectively. For example, the use of the table of contents, the subject index, the author index and the glossary can readily be tested by framing suitable questions. Attitudes to reading can be measured using IRIs by, for instance, getting a pupil to report on the extent to which he enjoys reading materials of various types using a simple five-point rating scale. The frequency with which a pupil uses the class, school or local library facilities can be recorded.

Thus both objective type comprehension questions about which there is no doubt as to the correct answer and subjective estimates

Table 3
Summarising children's responses to teacher-devised IRIs*

Name: John Smith *Date:* 21 September 1984 *Age:* 8 years *Examiner:* T. Cher

A. IRI Results

Material or Book Level	Oral Reading Accuracy			Reading Comprehension		Listening Comprehension	Rate of Reading	
	a. Words in isolation		*b.* Words in context	*c.* Definition of words out of context	*d.* Answering questions using contextual cues (silent reading)		*e.* Oral	*f.* Silent
	i. flash presentation (i.e. ½″ exposure)	ii. untimed						
Pre-Primer	100%	100%	99%	95%	95%		70	75
Primer	90%	95%	99%	90%	90%		60	65
Book 1	80%	85%	95%	80%	80%		50	50
Book 2	70%	65%	80% (F)	65%	85%	90%	40	30
Book 3	40% (F)	48% (F)	75% (F)	50% (F)	75%	85%		
Book 4						80% (C)		
Book 5						60%		

Table 3 *contd.*

B. Pupil's Reading Levels		*C. Significant Miscue Patterns* (Obtained from a consideration of John's responses to the IRI materials—see Table 6, page 36, for an example.)	*D. Action to be Taken* (Based on interpretation of B and C)
Independent	Primer		
Instructional	1		
Frustration	2		
Listening Comprehension (i.e. 'Capacity')	4		

* (i) Though here we are concerned mainly with attainments, *any* aspect of reading behaviour can be incorporated into an IRI, including rating of attitudes or other aspects of behaviour.
(ii) IRIs can be constructed from material at *any* level of difficulty from kindergarten to tertiary education.
(iii) IRIs are constructed by the teacher to suit her situation: thus it would be unlikely that all children in a normal class would be assessed on *all* the aspects of reading shown above.
(iv) The more competent the reader, the greater the emphasis in an IRI on various aspects of silent reading comprehension.

such as pupil and teacher ratings can be incorporated in the same IRI. Facts about reading comprehension can be compared with, say, the pupil's opinion of his own reading ability. The comparison by the teacher of her rating of the pupil on the same dimension can be most helpful in reducing misunderstanding between pupil and teacher. Currently, in writing end-of-term school reports, some schools include space for *both* pupils and teachers to record their comments on work done. Such a scheme has much to commend it. The approach can readily be built into an IRI as one part of the continuous assessment of a reading programme. All pupils can be encouraged to maintain, in part, their own records of reading progress.

The results of any Group IRI can be rapidly summarised by listing the reading skills tested at the head of a series of columns. The names of the children can be listed down the left hand side of the record sheet. If the teacher marks with a tick those aspects of reading in which each child is reaching a satisfactory criterion, her group summary sheet will provide a diagnostic pattern. This pattern will enable her to identify rapidly the reading skills in which, as a group, her pupils' need of instruction is greatest.

The scope of the IRI is virtually unlimited. Its flexibility is its greatest strength. A teacher-constructed IRI can include *any* reading programme objective that she considers important. As a technique the IRI allows the teacher to use her critical judgment and imagination in devising methods of monitoring the effectiveness of the reading programme that both she and her pupils find rewarding.

Many teachers find the IRI approach to assessment attractive. Its advantages appear considerable. IRIs can be tailor-made to pupils' specific situations using relevant pictorial and/or textual materials at any level from the pre-school to the post-graduate. IRIs provide a means of making explicit the teacher's assumptions concerning the nature of reading skills at a particular stage in their development. They encourage the analysis of miscues and the planning of educational interventions designed to alleviate difficulties and optimise skill acquisition. Additionally, the recording of behaviourally defined aspects of reading performances and the assessment of pupils' progress are integral to the approach. IRIs also sensitise teachers to both inter- and intra-individual differences in reading related skills between and within pupils. It helps teachers to become aware of the range of difficulties both within and between reading materials. The approach is frequently perceived by teachers as relevant to their professional concerns. Both primary and special school class teachers and secondary school subject specialists see the approach as having enabled them to effect a better match between pupils' reading abilities and reading materials, to the advantage of all concerned. It is also possible that the IRI approach appears not to require the teacher to understand the conceptual and statistical complexities (often seen as obfuscations) involved in conventional test theory. *Nothing could be further from the truth!* To use IRIs requires a technical awareness of their psychological and psychometric strengths and weaknesses. Ignoring such considerations does not make them disappear. An awareness of them will enable the teacher to use IRIs judiciously.

IRIs: a cautionary note

Critics and supporters of the flood of IRIs coming on to the market include reading experts who are sensitive to the psycholinguistic and psychometric bases of IRIs and of the empirical standing of the various criteria for 'Independent', 'Instructional', 'Frustration' and 'Capacity' levels that continue to be used (Spache, 1976, 1981; Harris and Sipay, 1979; Arnold, 1982). Spache's analysis is particularly well documented. He criticises assumptions that he considers to be naive and untenable. Chapter 10 in his 1976 publication and the review by Pikulski and Shanahan (1982) should be required reading for all actual and potential IRI users. Users of IRIs will find that an annotated bibliography produced by the International Reading Association gives an overview of the development of IRIs and the controversies that this has aroused (Johns *et al.*, 1977) (see Appendix 2 for further details). IRIs are neither as simple to use nor as practical as some proponents have suggested. 'Its scoring standards are subjective and probably invalid; its basal reader source is questionable; its testing procedure differs from that used in the research on which it is supposed to be based . . .' (Spache, 1976, p. 313). The reliabilities and validities of the associated methods of miscue (error) analysis have not been established and the relationships between the categories used in such analyses are frequently ignored. Despite such comments, IRIs have their defenders among reading experts and considerable support from teachers (Stauffer *et al.*, 1978; Senior, 1979; Arnold, 1982; Brown, 1982).

Some of the strengths and weaknesses of IRIs are summarised in Table 4, p. 33.

Oral miscue analysis

Goodman (1973) presented a valuable overview of this topic from a psycholinguistic viewpoint concerning the nature of the reading

Table 4
Some strengths and weaknesses of IRIs

	STRENGTHS	WEAKNESSES
1	Any teacher of any subject at any level can construct an IRI.	The validity of the criteria specifying levels of reading is suspect.
2	In using textual material available in the classroom, the assessment is related to the syllabus.	A reader's performances vary with the type of material presented.
3	If graded readers are used, the teacher is using text of a known difficulty level.	The readability levels of notionally similar graded readers vary considerably.
4	IRIs enable the teacher to identify the pupil's strengths and weaknesses in both word reading and comprehension thereby guiding instructional efforts.	To obtain valid diagnostic data, between 75 and 100 errors are required.
5	It provides a ready way of assessing reading comprehension.	Framing comprehension questions is a difficult task. To test the questions, item analyses would need to be carried out.
6	It is easy to devise, administer and interpret.	To record oral miscues accurately require considerable training and practice.
7	The technique has an appealing face validity and utility.	The information elicited by IRI contains an unquantified degree of error.
8	Its use sensitises the teacher to the child's reading strategies.	The interpretation of the data is largely subjective.
9	It costs little.	To appreciate the strengths and limitations of IRIs and to explore their utility is demanding of teachers' time.
10	It is popular with teachers.	It is treated with great caution by research workers.

process and its development. His emphasis is on the striving for meaning that characterises reading from continuous text by children. The reader's deviations from the printed material are construed as providing 'a window on the reading process'. Readers whose utterances deviate from the text may do so because they are concentrating on the meaning and the grammar rather than on decoding print to sound. Goodman considers that deviations often called reading errors are more appropriately thought of as miscues and should not be responded to negatively by labelling them 'wrong'. The taxonomy that he presents for the analysis of a child's oral miscues comprises twenty-eight categories. This type of miscue analysis is extremely time consuming although it is claimed that it has considerable potential in suggesting diagnostic procedures in both classroom and clinic. Since then simpler versions have been developed, one of the best known being the *Reading Miscue Inventory* (RMI) (Goodman and Burke, 1972). The extent to which the reader's miscues continue to make sense, coupled with the reader's success in retelling what he has read are central to the approach. Miscue analysis is primarily an aid to understanding the reading process. It has been argued that it is because miscue analysis is an integral part of most IRIs that the appeal of the latter has developed so markedly among the teaching profession.

British teachers wishing to find out more about miscue analysis have a number of readily available sources of information. The Centre for the Teaching of Reading at Reading University has published a manual which explains a simplified means of carrying out miscue analysis. It also includes an annotated bibliography of related research studies (Goodacre, 1979). The UKRA has published a monograph devoted to the topic of listening to children reading. The importance of this professional activity is well discussed and ways of ensuring that the time spent on it by pupils and teachers is used efficiently, are described. The longest chapter in the monograph (Chapter 4) is devoted to the use of miscue analysis in the classroom and includes a method for recording miscues devised by the author and used in in-service work with teachers (Arnold, 1982). This work has been further developed by Arnold and recently published (Arnold, 1984). Further details can be found under TRN 102, page 143.

Many teachers of reading hear children read orally and individually as one aspect of the reading programme. Frequently all that is recorded is a date and page number on a book marker. The child is merely given 'practice', with such help as seems appropriate at the time. With minimal effort on the teacher's part, a much greater return can be achieved from the session with the child.

On the reasonable assumption that a child's oral reading miscues are caused and are not fortuitous, the discrepancies between the child's observed oral response and the expected response (on the basis of 100 per cent accuracy) allows the teacher an opportunity of noting patterns of miscues and forming diagnostic hypotheses.

If the teacher systematises her observations of the child's reading and is able to record certain types of miscues, she is likely to see a pattern appear. From this *pattern*, appropriate remedial measures can be devised. For example, if the pattern of miscues showed a high level of reversals (e.g. 'no' for 'on'; 'was' for 'saw') various ways might be sought to help the child make the necessary discriminations. If, on the other hand, the teacher's observations had not been systematised, it is highly likely that the pattern of a child's miscues would never have become sufficiently clear to the teacher to enable her to plan appropriate learning.

In his research Christenson (1969) looked at the types and frequencies of deviations made by children using an IRI based on a graded reading series. The following seven types were considered:

omissions;
substitutions;
additions;
refusals;
repetitions;
reversals; and
gross mispronunciations.

It was found that the type of deviation produced was related to the reading level of the material. Errors of repetition occur more often at the Independent level. Mispronunciations, refusals and substitutions were more typical of the Frustration level. At the Frustration level, boys tended to substitute words but girls waited to be prompted. Characteristic differences also appeared between the Instructional level and the Frustration level. Thus miscue pattern is closely related to the level of difficulty of the material. (See also p. 39.)

A good ten-year-old reader will make virtually no errors when reading from say, *Wide Range Readers Green Book* 1 or 2. He will begin to make repetitions as the difficulty of the material increases. With reading material at the eleven to twelve-year-old level, he will begin to make substitutions and corrections but he will tend to correct these miscues. At the thirteen to fourteen-year-old level he meets unknown words, makes omissions, mispronunciations and does not correct his miscues spontaneously.

Miscue analysis is most usefully carried out with reading materials at the Instructional level for obvious reasons. The types of miscues and the patterns of miscues recorded by a teacher help her to link effective interventions with them, for children of given characteristics. Miscue analysis can thus result in (*a*) more rapid identification of patterns of miscues, and (*b*) effective help. To record a child's reading miscues requires the use of a shorthand such as that shown in Table 5 (p. 36). An arrangement of the IRI extract combined with the miscue categories in columns, as in Table 6 (p. 37), makes for easy recording and assignment of reading level of material.

Typically miscue analysis is less concerned with the quantification of miscues (i.e. counting their frequencies) than with a qualitative psycholinguistic interpretation of their significance in understanding a child's reading behaviours on specific textual material. However, a minimum number of miscues is required if any such analysis is to be made. Some authorities require that the text used generate at least 25 miscues. Followers of this approach emphasise the importance of the simultaneous yet independent use by readers of grapho-phonic, syntactic and semantic aspects of language when reading. Contextual cues are an important consideration. Cues are signs provided by a text enabling the reader to decode unfamiliar words and grasp meanings. Elsewhere I have presented a system for recording, analysing and interpreting the use made by the reader of the context cues available in a text. Suggestions are made concerning ways in which readers can be encouraged to use context cues in their reading (Pumfrey, 1977). Arnold's work is related (Arnold, 1984).

The analysis of children's oral reading errors, especially in the early stages of reading acquisition, can be of considerable importance to the teacher. However, it is necessary that the approach be kept in perspective. It can be argued that errors of oral reading are

Table 5
Coding for recording miscues

Sentence to be read	Miscue category	Method of recording miscue	Example
Which is the way to the house on the hill?	Substitution	Underline the word misread and write in word substituted	'home' Which is the way to the house on the hill?
	No response	If the child *waits* to be prompted or asks for a word, underline with a dashed line	Which is the way to the house on the hill?
	Addition	Use caret mark and write down word or part-word added	'go to' Which is the way to ^ the house on the hill?
	Omission*	Where words are omitted, circle them	Which is the way to the (house) on the hill?
	Self-correction	Where miscues are self-corrected, record by using initials 'S.C.' over the words	S.C. Which is the way to the house on the hill?
	Repetition	Record word/s repeated by putting '**R**' over appropriate section.	**R** Which is the way to the house on the hill?
	Mispronunciations	Indicate where stress is placed	
	Ignores punctuation	Circle punctuation ignored	Which is the way to the house on the hill (?) . . . . . .
	Reversals	This is a form of substitution, but may be of diagnostic significance if part of a regular pattern	'no' Which is the way to the house on the hill?

* Child does not wait for help.

Table 6
IRI and miscue analysis

Extracts from graded material forming basis of IRI	Miscue Categories: Substitution	No Response	Addition	Omission (words)	Self-Correction	Repetition	Mispronunciation	Ignores Punctuation	Reversals
'Come with me', said Peter to Mary.									
asked 'Where to?' she replied.	1								
our 'Over to the canal to get some frogspawn for ‸ school ⨀			1					1	
'I know (where) there is a lot and we can (easily) get it.'				2					
saw Mary was uneasy. 'The canal is (dangerous) ,' she replied. 'My mother has	1*			1					1*
told me not [to] go near it.'									

50 words to here

	Accuracy	*Comprehension*
(*a*) Miscues:	7 miscues	2/10 questions incorrect
(*b*) % Correct:	86% correct	80% correct
(*c*) Reading Level:	Instructional	Instructional level

* Refers to same miscues, but does *not* increase total number of miscues made.
N.B. In practice, several samples of text of known difficulty level would be used to obtain an estimate of the pupil's IRI levels and pattern of miscues.

Comment: Both accuracy and comprehension indicate Instructional level.
Reads rapidly and tends to omit words as a consequence.
If similar pattern of miscues occurs in other samples, will give help with extending sight vocabulary of certain words using flash-cards. Tape child's reading and get him to identify his own omissions.

unimportant provided that the child grasps the meaning of what he reads.

References

ARNOLD, H. (1982) *Listening to Children Reading*. London: Hodder and Stoughton in association with the United Kingdom Reading Association.

ARNOLD, H. (1984) *Making Sense of It. Miscue analysis during oral reading*. London: Hodder and Stoughton.

BROWN, D. A. (1982) *Reading Diagnosis and Remediation*. Englewood Cliffs, NJ: Prentice-Hall.

CHRISTENSON, A. (1969) 'Oral reading miscues in intermediate grade children at their independent, instructional and frustration levels.' In FIGUREL, J. A. (ed.) *Reading and Realism*. Newark, NJ: International Reading Association Proceedings, 13 (1).

GOODACRE, E. (1979) *Hearing Children Read*. Reading: Centre for the Teaching of Reading.

GOODMAN, K. (1973) 'Analysis of oral reading miscues: applied psycholinguistics.' In SMITH, F. (ed.) *Psycholinguistics and Reading*. New York: Holt, Rinehart and Winston.

GOODMAN, Y. M. and BURKE, C. L. (1972) *Reading Miscue Inventory*. New York: MacMillan.

HARRIS, A. J. and SIPAY, E. R. (1979) *How to teach Reading: A Competency-based Program*. New York: Longman.

JOHNS, J. L., GARTON, S., SCHOENFELDER, P. and SKRIBA, P. (eds) (1977) *Assessing Reading Behaviour – Informal Reading Inventories: An Annotated Bibliography*. Newark, DE: International Reading Association.

JOHNSON, M. S. and KRESS, R. A. (1965, 16th impression 1980) *Informal Reading Inventories*. Newark, DE: International Reading Association.

PIKULSKI, J. J. and SHANAHAN, T. (1982) 'Informal reading inventories; a critical appraisal.' In PIKULSKI, J. J. and SHANAHAN, T. (eds) *Approaches to the Informal Evaluation of Reading*. Newark, DE: International Reading Association.

PUMFREY, P. D. (1977) *Measuring Reading Abilities: Concepts, Sources and Applications*. London: Hodder and Stoughton (obtainable from the author at the University of Manchester).

SENIOR, J. (1979) 'Reading assessment in the classroom.' In RAGGETT, M. ST J., TUTT, C. and RAGGETT, P. (eds) *Assessment and Testing of Reading: Problems and Practices*. London: Ward Lock Educational.

SPACHE, G. D. (1976) *Investigating the Issues of Reading Disabilities*. Newton, MA: Allyn and Bacon.

SPACHE, G. D. (1981) *Diagnostic Reading Scales – Examiner's Manual*. Monterey, CA:CTB/McGraw-Hill.

STAUFFER, R. G., ABRAMS, J. C. and PIKULSKI, J. J. (1978) *Diagnosis, Correction and Prevention of Reading Difficulties*. New York: Harper and Row.

VALMONT, W. J. (1972) 'Creating questions for informal reading inventories.' In MELNIK, A. and MERRITT, J. (eds) *The Reading Curriculum*. London: University of London Press Ltd in association with the Open University.

Further reading

BETTS, E. A. (1957) *Foundations of Reading Instruction*. New York: American Book Co.

CARNINE, L., CARNINE, D. and GERSTEN, R. (1984) 'Analysis of oral reading errors made by economically disadvantaged students taught with a synthetic-phonics approach.' *Reading Research Quarterly*, **XIX**, 3, 343–56.

CARNINE, D., KAMEENUI, E. J. and COYLE, G. (1984) 'Utilization of contextual information in determining the meaning of unfamiliar words.' *Reading Research Quarterly*, **XIX**, 2, 188–204.

FUCHS, L. S., FUCHS, D. and DENO, S. J. (1982) 'Reliability and validity of curriculum-based Informal Reading Inventories.' *Reading Research Quarterly*, **XVIII**, 1, 6–26.

HOFFMAN, J. V. (1980) 'Weighting miscues in informal inventories — a cautionary note.' *Reading Horizons*, **20**, 135–9.

HOFFMAN, J. V., O'NEAL, S. F., KASTLER, L. A., CLEMENTS, R. O., SEGEL, K. W. and NASH, M. F. (1984) 'Guided oral reading and miscue focused verbal feedback in second-grade classrooms.' *Reading Research Quarterly*, **XIX**, 3, 367–84.

KIBBY, M. W. (1979) 'Passage readability affects the oral reading strategies of disabled readers.' *Reading Teacher*, **32**, 390–6.

Section II

Test Information

4 Reading Test Information and Comments

This chapter is divided into four parts, as follows:

1 Some screening and diagnostic tests of physical aspects of children's readiness for reading. These include tests of hearing, sight, visual-motor co-ordination, language, articulation and aural vocabulary;
2 Recognised tests of Reading-Readiness, usually with a diagnostic orientation;
3 Reading tests and batteries of tests, attainment and diagnostic; and
4 Attitude to reading scales.

Within each part, tests are presented alphabetically, British produced tests coming first, and tests produced in other countries next.

For each test the following pieces of information are given wherever possible:

(*a*) Test reference number (hereafter TRN) keyed to an alphabetic index of the tests presented, given on pages 47–51;
(*b*) Name of the test or battery of tests;
(*c*) Author;
(*d*) Country of origin of the test;
(*e*) Publisher;
(*f*) Year or years of publication;
(*g*) Type of test plus test user classification as employed by the British Psychological Society;
(*h*) Number and designation of parallel forms;
(*i*) Chronological age range of subjects for whom the test is intended. The convention used is that, for example, the range of from 5 years 1 month to 6 years 11 months is given as 5 : 01 to 6 : 11;
(*j*) Skills or other aspects of behaviour tested or rated;
(*k*) Average administration time and also whether or not the test is a timed one;
(*l*) Brief description of the test and comments on it. The comments given are not intended to provide a detailed critical evaluation, but draw attention to points the writer considers important.

Though this is not intended as an exhaustive survey of reading tests, the writer has included what he thinks are the most important reading tests currently in use in Great Britain. A few out-of-print British tests have been included because of their historical importance and interest. In general, the tremendous resources that have been devoted to the construction of reading tests in the USA in particular means that many of their instruments are superior to some of those produced in the UK. To give the reader an indication of the range of reading tests produced in other English-speaking countries, a limited number of non-British tests with interesting characteristics and possibilities is described.

Finding the appropriate test

Tables 7a and 7b and Tables 8a and 8b on pages 43–4 and 45–6 can be used to locate information in the book concerning tests suitable for a given purpose with a given age group of pupils. The numbers given in these four tables relate to the Index of Tests on pages 47–51. The Index of Tests is arranged alphabetically and, in addition, serially numbered from 1 to 199. These numbers are the Test Reference Numbers (TRNs).

Table 7a contains the TRNs of British instruments of use mainly at the descriptive level of interpretation. Table 7b contains the TRNs of similar tests that have been developed in other English speaking countries. Table 8a gives the TRNs of British instruments having a diagnostic orientation and Table 8b lists the TRNs of diagnostic tests that were originally constructed in other English speaking countries.

To identify the instruments most likely to be of use to her, the teacher needs to decide:

(a) the level of interpretation in which she is mainly interested, i.e. descriptive (Tables 7a and 7b) or diagnostic (Tables 8a and 8b);
(b) the goal with which she is concerned, i.e. attainments or attitudes;
(c) the source of information that she wishes to utilise, i.e. informal, standardised or criterion-referenced;
(d) the age level with which she is concerned; and
(e) whether she wishes to consider tests produced in Britain or those developed in other English speaking countries.

By looking at the appropriate cell in Tables 7a, 7b, 8a or 8b, the Test Reference Numbers of some potentially appropriate instruments will be found. By consulting the Index of Tests, the name of the test and its country of origin can be ascertained. The page number on which the test is described is also given. It is then possible to turn to the appropriate part of Section II, Chapter 4, and locate information concerning the instrument.

For example, the teacher might have decided that she is interested in the diagnostic level of interpretation in relation to reading attainment and that she wishes to use information from a standardised test produced in Britain. If the age level with which she is concerned is, say, Junior School, she will direct her attention to Table 8a and to the column headed *Standardised* under the goal of *Attainments* and identify the pertinent cell. In it TRN 60 might be of interest. Turning to the Index of Tests, it will be seen that the test referred to is the *Edinburgh Reading Tests, Stage 2*. Details of it can be found on page 119.

If this particular test is not suitable, the other tests indicated in the pertinent section of Table 8a can readily be located and considered. Alternatively, the teacher can look at the range of tests in the appropriate parts of Chapter 4.

Some blank test information sheets are printed on pages 292–7 for readers to record details of further reading tests as they come to their attention.

N.B. Because some tests can provide different types of information, TRNs may appear in more than one cell in the following four tables.

Table 7a
British tests and assessment procedures classified by age level according to goals (attainments or attitudes), source of information (informal, standardised, criterion-referenced) and level of interpretation (descriptive*)
(*The numbers refer to those given as Test Reference Numbers in the Index of Tests, pp. 47–51.*)

Source of information	Goals					
	Attainments			Attitudes		
	Informal	Standardised	Criterion-referenced	Informal	Standardised	Criterion-referenced
Pre-reading level		30, 64, 106, 161, 171, 191				
Infant	92	20, 30, 31, 32, 42, 64, 77, 78, 82, 85, 87, 90, 106, 109, 110, 126, 142, 144, 161, 169, 171, 175, 178, 181, 182, 188, 191, 194, 199	22, 91, 95	92		
Junior	92, 140	6, 20, 29, 30, 31, 32, 33, 36, 40, 42, 49, 59, 60, 61, 62, 64, 68, 69, 77, 78, 80, 81, 82, 85, 87, 100, 106, 109, 110, 112, 113, 114, 115, 116, 117, 118, 119, 120, 121, 125, 126, 128, 129, 130, 131, 135, 136, 142, 144, 160, 163, 167, 169, 170, 172, 175, 176, 178, 181, 182, 188, 194, 195, 199	95, 98, 99, 127	92	14, 16, 17, 56, 74, 196	
Secondary	92	6, 9, 20, 30, 31, 32, 33, 36, 62, 64, 69, 77, 78, 80, 82, 100, 106, 109, 110, 121, 122, 123, 124, 131, 132, 133, 134, 137, 141, 157, 163, 169, 170, 172, 174, 176, 178, 181, 194, 195	98, 99	92	15, 16, 17	
Tertiary	92	6, 9, 43, 64, 106, 137	86, 99	92		

* N.B. The above classification is a tentative and simplified one indicating a major emphasis of the tests.

Table 7b
Non-British tests and assessment procedures classified by age level according to goals (attainments or attitudes), source of information (informal, standardised, criterion-referenced) and level of interpretation (descriptive*)
(*The numbers refer to those given as Test Reference Numbers in the Index of Tests, pp. 47–51.*)

Source of information	Goals					
		Attainments			Attitudes	
	Informal	Standardised	Criterion-referenced	Informal	Standardised	Criterion-referenced
Pre-reading level	24, 83	71, 104, 107, 147, 184, 185	8			
Infant	24, 83, 92, 159	2, 34, 71, 103, 104, 107, 147, 148, 165, 166, 184, 185, 187, 193, 197	8, 25, 89, 93, 177, 197	92	149	
Junior	24, 39, 83, 92, 159	2, 3, 4, 34, 44, 53, 71, 103, 147, 148, 151, 152, 153, 154, 165, 166, 187, 197	8, 25, 89, 93, 177, 197	92	54, 55, 149, 168	
Secondary	5, 24, 39, 83, 92, 94, 159	3, 4, 34, 44, 53, 65, 71, 103, 148, 151, 152, 153, 154, 183, 187, 197	25, 89, 93, 177, 197	92	54, 55, 73, 105, 156, 162, 168	
Tertiary	92, 159	44, 65, 71, 183, 197	197	92	18, 73, 105, 168	

* N.B. The above classification is a tentative and simplified one indicating a major emphasis of the tests.

Table 8a
British tests and assessment procedures classified by age level according to goals (attainments or attitudes), source of information (informal, standardised, criterion-referenced) and level of interpretation (diagnostic*)
(The numbers refer to those given as Test Reference Numbers in the Index of Tests, pp. 47–51.)

Source of information	Goals					
	Attainments			Attitudes		
	Informal	Standardised	Criterion-referenced	Informal	Standardised	Criterion-referenced
Pre-reading level		138, 161, 171, 191	69, 91, 145, 150, 173, 180, 181, 198			
Infant	92, 102	87, 90, 109, 110, 138, 161, 169, 171, 191, 199	10, 12, 13, 22, 37, 38, 51, 66, 69, 91, 95, 101, 143, 145, 150, 173, 178, 180, 181, 198, 199	92		
Junior	92, 102	29, 35, 36, 49, 59, 60, 61, 62, 87, 109, 110, 131, 163, 169, 170, 172, 195, 199	10, 11, 12, 13, 21, 35, 37, 51, 63, 66, 95, 98, 101, 139, 140, 143, 145, 150, 155, 173, 178, 181, 189, 198, 199	92	74	
Secondary	92, 102	35, 36, 61, 62, 110, 131, 163, 169, 170, 172, 195	21, 35, 37, 45, 63, 98, 145, 178, 181	92		
Tertiary	92	43, 108	37, 86, 145	92		

* N.B. The above classification is a tentative and simplified one indicating a major emphasis of the tests.

Table 8b
Non-British tests and assessment procedures classified by age level according to goals (attainments or attitudes), source of information (informal, standardised, criterion-referenced) and level of interpretation (diagnostic*)
(The numbers refer to those given as Test Reference Numbers in the Index of Tests, pp. 47–51.)

	Goals					
		Attainments			Attitudes	
Source of information	Informal	Standardised	Criterion-referenced	Informal	Standardised	Criterion-referenced
Pre-reading level	24, 83	1, 13, 57, 67, 71, 76, 84, 88, 96, 104, 107, 184, 185, 186, 192	1, 8, 27, 41, 70, 75, 76, 97, 146, 147, 148			
Infant	24, 28, 83, 92, 159	1, 19, 41, 48, 50, 52, 57, 58, 67, 70, 72, 76, 79, 84, 88, 96, 104, 107, 184, 185, 186, 188, 192, 193	1, 7, 8, 25, 27, 28, 75, 76, 97, 146, 147, 148, 164, 177, 190	92		
Junior	24, 28, 39, 83, 92, 159	4, 19, 44, 46, 47, 48, 52, 57, 58, 67, 72, 76, 79, 88, 96, 153, 154, 179, 186, 188, 192	7, 25, 26, 27, 28, 44, 76, 147, 148, 164, 177, 179, 190	92		
Secondary	5, 24, 28, 39, 83, 92, 94, 159	3, 4, 44, 46, 47, 48, 52, 58, 65, 76, 79, 96, 153, 154, 179, 183, 188, 192	7, 23, 25, 26, 27, 28, 44, 76, 111, 148, 164, 177, 179, 190	92	156	
Tertiary	5, 39, 92, 94, 159	44, 46, 65, 76, 79, 179, 183, 192	7, 23, 26, 27, 44, 76, 158, 179, 190	92		

* N.B. The above classification is a tentative and simplified one indicating a major emphasis of the tests.

Index of Tests

Country of origin is shown in brackets as follows:
(A) = Australia
(B) = Britain
(C) = Canada
(E) = Eire (Republic of Ireland)
(J) = Japan
(NI) = Northern Ireland
(NZ) = New Zealand
(USA) = United States of America

* TRN – Test Reference Number as classified in Tables 7a and 7b, 8a and 8b, pp. 43–6.

* See chapter 3.

TRN	Name of Test	Page
170	Schools Council Oracy Project: Listening Comprehension Tests (B)	61
171	Sentence Comprehension Test (Experimental edition) (B)	62
172	Shortened Edinburgh Reading Test (B)	190
173	Simplified Colour Vision Test (B)	63
174	Slee 13 + Reading Test (B)	191
175	Southgate Group Reading Tests 1 and 2 (B)	192
176	SPAR (Spelling + Reading) Tests (B)	193
177	Standard Achievement Recording System (STARS) (USA)	261
178	Standard Reading Tests (B)	194
179	Stanford Diagnostic Reading Test (USA)	263
180	Stycar Hearing Tests (B)	64
181	Stycar Vision Tests (B)	65
182	Swansea Test of Phonic Skills (B)	195
183	Test of Adolescent Language (TOAL) (USA)	269
184	Test of Early Language Development (TELD) (USA)	73
185	Test of Early Reading Ability (TERA) (USA)	74
186	Test of Language Development (TOLD) Primary (USA)	271
187	Test of Reading Comprehension (TORC) (USA)	273
188	Test Your Child's Reading (B)	196
189	Testing Our Pupils (TOP) Tests Booklet (B)	197
190	Tests for Colour Blindness (J)	75
191	Thackray Reading Readiness Profiles (B)	81
192	Visual Motor Gestalt Test (USA)	76
193	Vocabulary Survey Test (USA)	77
194	Watts' Battery of Language and Reading Tests (B)	198
195	Wide-Span Reading Test (B)	199
196	Williams' Reading Attitude Scale (B)	281
197	Woodcock Reading Mastery Tests (USA)	274
198	Word Order Comprehension Test (B)	82
199	Word Recognition Test (B)	200

Abbreviations used in test reviews

N = number
p = probability
< = less than
r = reliability

1 Some screening and diagnostic tests of physical aspects of children's readiness for reading

Within the UK educational system, the majority of children have started to read by the age of about six years. However, there will be a considerable number of slow-learning children who will not have begun. These children are usually recognised by the teacher and a programme of pre-reading activities geared to their individual needs is devised. Amongst this group of children apparently requiring a further period of pre-reading experience there can be hidden a number of children who are unable to read, not because of dullness, but because of other reasons which may have been overlooked.

For example, although not deaf in the sense that his difficulties are clear to all, a child can suffer from impaired hearing. He may be failing to hear (unknowingly and unknown) certain parts of spoken language. A mild degree of high-frequency deafness would be one example of such a difficulty. The child's ability to discriminate between sounds or between certain similarly sounding spoken words will be diminished and some of his misunderstandings may be interpreted as typical of dullness when this may not be the case. The child's ability to match normally important sound discriminations to their visual presentation will also be adversely affected, e.g. matching sounds of letters or words to their visual representation. Hence reading will be a difficult task and the likelihood of failure to master necessary skills increased.

Similarly, the child with weakness of visual perception may be unable to discriminate certain written symbols such as letters and words and match these to their sounded or spoken equivalents. His failure to do so can in certain circumstances be wrongly attributed to dullness.

Both of the above paragraphs emphasise the importance of the child being able to receive the sensory stimulation on which he is to operate, and also to establish the equivalence of signs or symbols in more than one sense modality. There are many other physical disabilities frequently associated with difficulties in reading, for example, poor speech and articulation, and clumsiness in other aspects of coordination such as eye-hand. Such conditions may also mislead the teacher into thinking that a child's need for more pre-reading activities is attributable to general immaturity or dullness, rather than to a specific disability which might be alleviated. The situation is made doubly difficult for the teacher because the relationships previously mentioned between certain physical disabilities and immature reading skill attainments are not necessarily causal ones. A child with poor vision may or may not read adequately. Nevertheless, the *possibility* that a physical disability is responsible for a child's slow acquisition of reading skills should always be considered. If such a physical disability is found to exist, the implications for the child's programme of reading activities may be profound.

If a teacher suspects that a child's hearing, sight, coordination or articulation is in some way defective, the Community Physician (Child Health) will on request and with the parents' permission, carry out the necessary investigations. These may require diagnosis and treatment by audiologists, physiotherapists or speech-therapists concurrently with the child's educational programme if the effects of any disability on the acquisition of reading or any other skill are to be minimised.

In the majority of cases the regular screening surveys carried out by the Community Physician (Child Health) will identify children with the types of defect indicated above. However, children have been known to be absent at the times of such medical examinations or otherwise to have slipped through the net. The pressures of work on the Service are such that all children missing medical examinations are not necessarily followed up. In such a situation it is of value for the teacher to be aware of some relatively simple screening tests of hearing, vision and coordination.

Tests of articulation and some aural vocabulary tests have been included in this section. Although both of these aspects of language development underpin reading competencies, neither involves decoding a printed alphabet.

Pre-reading materials as screening tests

The majority of pre-reading material contains games intended to develop the young child's aural and visual discrimination and visual-motor coordination. These can be used as informal screening tests in many instances.

(a) British

TRN	Name of test	Author	Country	Publisher	Year
30	*British Picture Vocabulary Scale (BPVS)*	L. M. Dunn, L. M. Dunn and C. Whetton with D. Pintillie	B	NFER-Nelson	1982

Type	No. of forms	C.A. range	Skills tested	Time
Individual, attainment, standardised (level A)	2 (Long Form and Short Form)	3:00 to 17:11	Receptive (hearing) vocabulary	Untimed

Comments: Developed from the American *Peabody Picture Vocabulary Test*, each item in the *British Picture Vocabulary Scale* consists of a page containing four pictures. The tester says one word and the individual being tested responds by pointing to one of the four pictures. The *BPVS* can be used in either a Long or a Short Form dependent on the tester's purpose. It is an easily administered and scored test.

The test was standardised on a sample of 3 334 persons attending schools in fifteen LEAs. The sample was designed to be representative of the *school-attending* population. It is pointed out that at the nursery school, and at the post sixteen-year-old secondary stages of education, attendance at school is voluntary although determined by very different considerations for the two groups.

Raw scores for both the Short and Long Forms can be converted to standard scores and percentiles for each three months interval of chronological age. Raw scores can also be converted to age-equivalent scores.

Split-half reliability coefficients of the Short Form for the fifteen separate year groups range between 0·83 and 0·75 with the exception of the 17 : 00 to 17 : 11 group where it dropped to 0·41. As would be expected, for the Long Form these coefficients were higher, ranging from 0·70 to 0·95 with a median value of 0·91. Again, it was the oldest age group that had the lowest coefficient. Evidence for the validities of the scale is less adequate. It is admitted that there is no direct evidence for its concurrent or predictive validity. The history of mental measurement is considered to give considerable support as is work done on the vocabulary scales (of different format) of other major individual tests. Did exhaustion strike the constructors? Did time and/or money run out? Doubtless the establishment of the scale's validities – or otherwise – will now be under way. This test is likely to become popular with a wide range of professionals involved in the development of receptive vocabulary.

TRN	Name of test	Author	Country	Publisher		Year
37	*City University Colour Vision Test*	R. Fletcher	B	Keeler Instruments		1975
					2nd edition	1980

Type	No. of forms	C.A. range	Skills tested	Time
Individual, diagnostic, criterion-referenced (level K)	1	6:00+	Colour vision	3″ per page (about 5′)

Comments: The purpose of this test is to diagnose colour vision defects and their severity. The 2nd edition of the test contains ten plates (six used in the 1975 version, plus four new plates). Each plate provides an array of five coloured spots, one at the centre with the other four situated above, below, to the left and to the right of it respectively. The subject's task is to identify the spot whose colour most closely matches that of the central spot on the plate. The plate must not be touched by the subject. Evidence for the validity of the test has been reported and discussed (Fletcher, 1980; Fletcher and Voke, 1983).

FLETCHER, R. (1980) 'Second edition of the City University test.' *Colour Vision Deficiencies*, **V**, 195–6.

FLETCHER, R. and VOKE, J. (1983) 'A guide to colour vision tests – Part 2.' *The Optician*, **185**, 11–40.

TRN	Name of test	Author	Country	Publisher		Year
42	*Crichton Vocabulary Scale*	J. C. Raven	B	H. K. Lewis		1951
					Revised edition	1961

Type	No. of forms	C.A. range	Skills tested	Time
Individual, oral, normative (level P)	1	4:06 to 11:00	Oral definition	Untimed

Comments: This test was constructed for use with Raven's *Coloured Progressive Matrices*, a non-verbal test of intelligence. The scale consists of two parallel sets of forty words. The words are arranged in order of difficulty and the child's task is to define in his own words the stimulus word presented orally by the tester. The sample on which the norms are based is limited and the standardisation procedure is rather obscure. Satisfactory test-retest reliabilities are reported. These are given as 0·87 and 0·95 at the 6 : 06 and 9 : 06 levels. The correlations with other tests are also reported. The raw scores can be converted to percentiles for each six months of age between 4 : 06 and 11 : 00.

TRN	Name of test	Author	Country	Publisher	Year
64	*English Picture Vocabulary Tests 1–3*	M. A. Brimer and L. M. Dunn	B	Distributed by Educational Evaluation Enterprises, Bristol	1962 (1 & 2) 1970 (3)

Type	No. of forms	C.A. Range	Skills tested	Time
Test 1 Individual, oral, normative	1	3:00 to 4:11	Listening vocabulary (40 items)	Untimed
	1	5:00 to 8:11	Listening vocabulary (40 items)	
Test 2 Individual or group, oral, normative	1	7:00 to 11:11	Listening vocabulary (40 items)	
Test 3 Individual or group, oral, normative	1	11:00 to adult	Listening vocabulary (48 items)	
(level A)				

Comments: One important characteristic of this series is that it does not require the child to have any reading attainments. The items used to make Tests 1 and 2 are each a page of four pictures plus a spoken word. The child's task is to indicate the picture to which the spoken word refers. Test 1 has a pre-school and an infant age version. It is an individual test whereas Tests 2 and 3 can be given either individually or to a group. The format of Test 3 presents sixteen items on each of three pages of a printed record sheet. These tests are an adaptation of the American *Peabody Picture Vocabulary Test.* However, the authors have completely reconstructed the test for use with English children. For Tests 1 and 2, the standardisation procedure was carried out on samples of 3 240 and 5 084 Wiltshire children selected so as to ensure close agreement with national characteristics. Interestingly, boys scored consistently higher than girls at every age level tested. This difference is claimed to be due to differences in the functions being tested. Despite this, it is argued that the uses for which the tests are intended do not require that separate norms for boys and girls be prepared. The internal consistency reliabilities of the tests at each age level from 5 : 00 to 8 : 11 are fairly high (Test 1: from 0·87 to 0·89 for each group and 0·92 for the total 5 : 00 to 8 : 11 range; Test 2: 0·88 to 0·93 for each year group and 0·96 for the four-year range). Content validity seems adequate. Other evidence of validities is sparse and the intercorrelations presented are open to many interpretations. Test 3 in the series was standardised on 8994 subjects, representatively drawn from students and adults engaged in full or part-time education. The internal consistency reliabilities range from 0·88 to 0·94. Test-retest reliabilities are to be published shortly. A 'full range' edition of the above series of tests is now available. This covers the age range from 3 : 00 to 18 : 00 + and was based on further extensive test development and restandardisation.

TRN	Name of test	Author	Country	Publisher	Year
106	*Mill Hill Vocabulary Scale*	J. C. Raven	B	H. K. Lewis	1943

Type	No. of forms	C.A. range	Skills tested	Time
Individual and group, oral and written, attainment and diagnostic, normative	1 (Definitions Form)	4:06 to 14:00 70:00 to 85:00	1 Word definitions	Untimed (10′–20′)
	2 (Form 1 Senior and Junior)	11:06 to 60:00	1 Word definitions 2 Synonym selection	
(level P)	2 (Form 2 Senior and Junior)	11:06 to 60:00	1 Synonym selection 2 Word definitions	

Comments: Constructed as a complementary test to the non-verbal Raven's *Standard Progressive Matrices*, this scale consists of two parallel series of forty-four words known as sets A and B. In Form 1 of the scale, children able to read and write are asked to write down the meaning of words in set A and also to select a synonym from six alternatives for each word in set B. This procedure is reversed in Form 2. It is claimed that the oral administration of the scale gives similar results with such children. Children unable to write can be given the Definitions Form of the scale orally.

The standardisation both as individual and group tests for children was carried out on various samples of school children in Colchester, Essex. The test-retest reliabilities presented for the written form of the test seem acceptable, ranging from 0·87 to 0·98 for five age groups. Various groups of adults were tested during 1946 and 1947 and percentile equivalents for raw scores on the scale are presented for them. The major weakness of the scale is that relatively few items cover a vast range of vocabularies.

TRN	Name of test	Author	Country	Publisher	Year
145	*Picture Screening Test of Hearing*	M. Reed	B	Royal National Institute for the Deaf	1960*

Type	No. of forms	C.A. range	Skills tested	Time
Individual, oral, screening, criterion-referenced (level A)	1	5:00+	Aural discrimination	Untimed (10′)

Comments: The purpose of this test is to enable the teacher to establish whether or not a child has a slight hearing loss which could affect the child's ability to learn skills such as reading and to give the incorrect impression of being dull. The test is in the form of a spirally bound booklet consisting of eight cards. On each card is a coloured picture of four common objects. The names of the objects on a given card contain the same vowel sound, but different consonants; for example:

MOUSE : OWL : COW : HOUSE

The test depends on the fact that, in hearing impairment, consonants rather than vowels are the first elements of speech to be misheard. Having made certain that the child knows the names of the pictures on a given card, the tester stands *behind* the child to prevent lip-reading and asks the child to point to each object in turn. The child who points to a number of incorrect pictures is probably having difficulty in differentiating between certain sounds, According to the instructions, any child failing on two or more pictures on two or more cards should be referred for a full audiometric examination. No information is given concerning the reliability or validity of this screening test. However, it has the imprimatur of the Royal National Institute for the Deaf.

* The material is still supplied by the RNID in 1985, presumably because it meets a professional need.

TRN	Name of test	Author	Country	Publisher		Year
161	*Reynell Developmental Language Scales (RDLS)*	J. Reynell with M. Curwen	B	NFER-Nelson	Experimental edition Revised edition	1969 1977

Type	No. of forms	C.A. range	Skills tested	Time
Individual, attainment, diagnostic, normative, (level K)	1	1 : 00 to 7 : 00	Expressive language: Structure Vocabulary Content Verbal comprehension A (no speech by child required) Verbal comprehension B (adaptation of scale A for use with severely handicapped children)	Untimed

Comments: The promise of the Experimental edition led to the development of the revision published in 1977. It is designed to assess young children's receptive and expressive language abilities. After alterations made to improve the scales and to make them less complex in terms of the materials used, to give the tests higher 'ceilings', to make the scales more suitable for use with children with hearing difficulties and to increase the spread of early items in the Verbal comprehension scales, the unabridged scales were given to 903 children aged from 1 : 06 to 7 : 00 years. The subsequent refined scales were then standardised on 415 children aged from 1 : 00 to 7 : 00. 'After the necessary adjustments had been made to allow for the small modifications introduced after the item analysis, the two series were aggregated to form a total of 1318 children. It is from this total sample that the scores in the present volume have been compiled' (Manual, p. 11). Combining the scores of two groups on only items taken in common has dangers to the resultant reliability and validity of the norms that are not made explicit. Despite this point, the test has been extensively used. Internal consistency reliability coefficients are given for twelve six-monthly age groups for the three major scales. Of the 36 coefficients reported, in the Expressive Language Scale three were between 0·80 and 0·90 whilst the remaining nine were above 0·90; in Verbal Comprehension A, for the nine age groups 1 : 06 to 5 : 06, reliabilities exceeded 0·82 but fell somewhat for the older three age groups. A similar pattern occurred in Verbal Comprehension B. Sex and social class differences were analysed and the results presented. Raw scores can be converted to age equivalent scores and to standard scores. The latter conversion is based on children grouped into three monthly bands of chronological age. The scales have a developmental pattern based on normal language development. They also allow the user to make qualitative as well as quantitative assessments of expressive language and verbal comprehension.

TRN	Name of test	Author	Country	Publisher	Year
170	*Schools Council Oracy Project: Listening Comprehension Tests*	A. Wilkinson, L. Stratta and P. Dudley	B	Macmillan Education	1974

Type	No. of forms	C.A. Range	Skills tested	items in batteries A	B	C	Time*
Individual or group, attainment and diagnostic	3		*Listening comprehension*				
	A	10:00 to 11:00	i Test of content	15	12	12	59′
			ii Test of contextual constraint	15	19	15	
	B	13:00 to 14:00	iii Test of phonology	15	18		62′
			iv Test of register	15	15	17	
(level A)	C	17:00 to 18:00	v Test of relationships	15	15	18	78′

Comments: The three batteries are designed to measure subjects' listening comprehension of a variety of tape-recorded spoken materials. Each differs slightly in its composition. A and B each contain all of the above five sub-tests, whereas C does not include a test of phonology. Although in each battery each sub-test focuses on one element of listening comprehension, all the sub-tests are related. The batteries give a normative listening comprehension score indicating relative level of performance over the sub-tests. The profile of sub-test scores can be used for diagnostic purposes although such work is still in its infancy. Additionally, the taped stimulus materials are intended to provide ideas that can be adapted and developed by teachers for interesting language work in schools.

The tests have been standardised on samples of 180, 1 152 and 133 pupils for batteries A, B and C respectively. The internal consistency reliabilities of the batteries are 0·777, 0·827 and 0·838. Correlations with measures of intelligence, reading and aspects of personality are reported. The intercorrelations of the sub-tests in each battery are given. Sex differences in scores on the tests are reported. For battery B the large-scale testing enabled standard scores with a mean of 100 and a standard deviation of 15 to be calculated. Batteries A and C are less adequately standardised. The relationships between listening and reading comprehension could be explored by teachers using the above instruments to assess the former in their particular situation. In the authors' opinion, the test materials are seen '. . . as exemplifying features and functions of the spoken language which should be part of the knowledge of every teacher . . .'.

A research report on the Schools Council Oracy Project by the above authors is presented in *The Quality of Listening* published in 1974 by Macmillan Education.

* It is recommended that each battery be administered in two parts with a 30′ break. Thus the actual times for administration are: Battery A, $1\frac{1}{2}$ hr; Battery B, $1\frac{3}{4}$ hr; Battery C, $1\frac{3}{4}$ to 2 hr.

TRN	Name of test	Author	Country	Publisher	Year
171	*Sentence Comprehension Test (Experimental Edition) (SCT)*	K. Wheldall, P. Mittler and A. Hobsbaum	B	NFER-Nelson	1979

Type	No. of forms	C.A. range	Skills tested		Time
Individual, attainment, diagnostic (level K)	1	3:00 to 5:06 (or for handicapped children at comparable levels of language development)	*Sentence comprehension:* 1 Simple intransitive 3 Intransitive with adjective 5 Plural 7 Future tense 9 Simple negative 11 Comparative 13 Simple prepositions 15 Embedded phase	2 Simple transitive 4 Transitive with adjective 6 Past tense 8 Passive 10 Transitive negative 12 Superlative 14 Harder prepositions	Untimed (about 60′)*

Comments: Developed after extensive preliminary work, this test measures children's comprehension of sentences. This is done by using a booklet on each page of which there are four line drawings in a 2 × 2 matrix. Each drawing represents the correct match, plus three alternative grammatical interpretations of the sentence spoken by the tester. The child's task is to identify the picture illustrating the sentence. The grammatical structures tested are listed above (Sub-tests 1–15). Each sub-test contains four items of identical structure, thereby helping establish the child's ability to comprehend a given structure across a range of content. Scoring allows quantification (number of items correct and sub-tests passed) plus a qualitative appraisal of the types of misunderstanding displayed across the fifteen sub-tests.

Research on the *SCT (Experimental Edition)* is relatively limited as yet. A study of a sample of 50 five-year-old (5 : 00) children comparable to 100 children of the same age used in earlier work showed that mean *SCT* scores and number of sub-tests passed were very similar despite the problems of ceiling effect at this age level. Test-retest reliability was 0·78 for total score and 0·76 for number of sub-tests passed. In another study involving 160 3 : 00 to 5 : 00 year old children, mean scores and sub-tests passed were also similar to the original test results. For this sample test-retest correlation coefficients for total scores and sub-tests passed were 0·87 and 0·83 respectively. Internal consistency reliability coefficient of the scale was 0·90. Concurrent validity is supported by correlations with scores on the *English Picture Vocabulary Tests* (TRN 64). Intercorrelations between the sub-tests are presented. The pattern of mastery of sub-tests is presented for various age groups and provides an interesting normative indicator. This test appears to have considerable diagnostic and pedagogic potential. It demonstrates an interesting link between quantitative and qualitative analysis.

* Estimate based on clinical trial at a nursery school. Older pupils require less time.

NOTE: further comment is available on p. 175.

TRN	Name of test	Author	Country	Publisher	Year
173	*Simplified Colour Vision Test (SCVT)*	R. Fletcher	B	Hamblin (Instruments)	1983

Type	No. of forms	C.A. range	Skills tested	Time
Individual, diagnostic, criterion-referenced (level K)	1	Young children and older mentally handicapped subjects	Units I and III: Red-Green deficiencies Unit II: Blue-Yellow deficiencies	Untimed (about 3′)

Comments: Approximately 5% of boys and rather less than 1% of girls have inherited colour vision defects. The most frequent are red-green deficiencies. Defects of colour vision can be acquired. For example, illnesses such as diabetes, poisons and optical nerve disorders can lead to blue-yellow deficiencies. If learning to read involves exposure to materials using colour coding as a means of providing cues, it is possible that children with colour vision deficiencies may be at an unappreciated disadvantage unless identified.

Fletcher, an international authority in the field of colour vision, has developed a three-unit instrument that can be used as a screening test with young children and also with mentally handicapped adults. The three units each consist of a 4 × 4 matrix of sixteen equally sized square tiles of different or the same colours. The child's task is to touch tiles that are either the same as or different from a tile touched by the tester, as the tester instructs. Instructions are given concerning the illumination of the test situation. The interpretation and evaluation of the results are discussed. The issue of 'false negatives' and 'false positives' (children with deficient colour vision who are not identified and children with adequate colour vision incorrectly identified as having defective vision) is addressed. The importance of further testing of those children who do not pass the specified screening criteria is stressed whilst the need for the situation to be dealt with in a non-alarmist manner is rightly underlined. SCVT has been used extensively in various countries. Its strengths are its simplicity, robustness and validity.

There is a range of tests of colour vision. A useful review of these has been published by the developer of the SCVT (Fletcher and Voke, 1982; 1983).

FLETCHER, R. and VOKE, J. (1982) 'A guide to colour vision tests—Part 1.' *The Optician*, **184**, 43–50.

FLETCHER, R. and VOKE, J. (1983) 'A guide to colour vision tests—Part 2.' *The Optician*, **185**, 11–40.

TRN	Name of test	Author	Country	Publisher	Year
180	*Stycar Hearing Tests*	M. Sheridan	B	NFER-Nelson	1958 Revised 1976

Type	No. of forms	C.A. range	Skills tested	Time
			Baby tests:	Untimed
Individual,	1	0:06 to 1:02	(a) Voice and noise-making objects	
screening,		1:02 to 1:06	(b) Voice, noise-making objects and three toys	
diagnostic		1:06 to 2:00	(c) 5 toy test and 4 animal picture test	
		2:00 to 3:00	6 toy test, 1st cube test, 4 animal picture test	
		3:00 to 4:00	7 toy test, 2nd cube test, 6 high-frequency picture test	
(level K)		5:00 to 7:00	Picture vocabulary tests, word lists, 3rd cube test	

Comments: The author's aim was to produce an instrument capable of giving 'reliable information concerning the child's capacity to hear with comprehension in every-day situations'. The battery comprises a series of relatively simple clinical auditory screening tests. The play-like testing procedures and materials involve the subjects in enjoyable activities. The materials are also used in testing the hearing of mentally handicapped children.

The growth of sophisticated audiometric assessment procedures based on electronics has reduced the need for the Stycar test, although it can still provide the clinician with valuable insights.

TRN	Name of test	Author	Country	Publisher		Year
181	*Stycar Vision Tests*	M. D. Sheridan	B	NFER-Nelson		1960
					Revised edition	1969
					Revised manual	1976
					Repackaged	1983

Type	No. of forms	C.A. range	Skills tested	Time
Individual, screening, diagnostic	1	5:00 to 7:00	Vision: 9 letter key card and chart	Untimed
		2:06 to 4:00	Single-letter cards; Miniature toys test	
		0:06 to 2:06	Graded balls test	
		5:00 to 15:00 (For children with severe visual and often other handicaps)	Panda test	
(level K)				

Comments: Developed during her distinguished work as a School Medical Officer, the purpose of this battery is the early identification of visual defects in young and/or handicapped children. The battery comprises a series of relatively simple clinical tests that owe much to Sheridan's sensitivity and ingenuity. The manual contains details of the materials and their administration and the standards applied in interpreting a child's responses.

(b) Others

TRN	Name of test	Author	Country	Publisher	Year
7	*American Optical Pseudoisochromatic Plates*	L. H. Hardy, G. Rand and M. C. Rittler	USA	American Optical Co. (British-American Optical act as agents)	1957

Type	No. of forms	C.A. range	Skills tested	Time
Individual, criterion-referenced, diagnostic (level P)	1	5:00 +	Colour vision	Untimed (8′)

Comments: It is claimed that this test is an improvement on the Ishihara Test (see p. 75) as it enables a subject's degree of colour-vision defect to be more reliably quantified. Some evidence of validity is presented in the test manual. If a colour-coded reading scheme is in use, children with certain types of colour-blindness (usually boys) might be unwittingly presented with inappropriate material.

TRN	Name of test	Author	Country	Publisher		Year
19	*Auditory Discrimination Test*	J. M. Wepman	USA	Language Research Associates		1958
				Stoelting Co.	Revised edition	1973

Type	No. of forms	C.A. range	Skills tested	Time
Individual, oral, diagnostic (level A)	2 (I & II)	5:00 to 8:00 (approx.)	Auditory discrimination	Untimed (10′)

Comments: Wepman considers auditory discrimination to be highly related to the development of speech accuracy and, to a lesser degree, reading attainments. The forty-item test is an easily administered method of assessing the child's ability to distinguish certain fine distinctions between phonemes used in English speech. The child listens while the tester reads pairs of words from a given list. The child's task is to indicate either verbally or otherwise whether the words sound the same or different. When poor discrimination has been identified, remedial work can be planned. The standardisation of the test was initially on 533 unselected six- to eight-year-old children. Test-retest reliability is high (0·91) and evidence of validities is presented. The tester is asked to read the words *facing* the child. This could lead to a child using visual cues, i.e. lip-reading, rather than being concerned with auditory discriminations. Despite this reservation, the test is an accurate and easy to administer measure of auditory discrimination.

TRN	Name of test	Author	Country	Publisher	Year
67	*Frostig Developmental Test of Visual Perception*	M. Frostig	USA	Consulting Psychologists Press (NFER-Nelson act as agents)	1963

Type	No. of forms	C.A. range	Skills tested	Time
Individual, small group, diagnostic (level P)	1	3:00 to 10:00	1 Eye-motor coordination 2 Figure-ground discrimination 3 Constancy of shape 4 Position in space 5 Spatial relationships	30′–45′

Comments: This test claims to measure five important but relatively unrelated aspects of visual perception. Normative information is based on 2 116 normal children aged between four and eight years. This is reported in three-monthly chronological age intervals. The results are presented in profile form. The test-retest reliabilities of some of the sub-tests are well below 0·5. The theoretical basis of this test has been vigorously attacked and the relative independence of the sub-tests questioned by researchers. However, if visual perception is one component of reading ability, this test does begin to look closely at children's performances in an interesting way. Provided one exercises appropriate caution in interpreting the profiles for individuals, the test can give indications of children's strengths and weaknesses.

The training programme that Frostig has produced claims to improve children's visual perception. Whether the training programme is effective *because* it is similar to the various tests on the *Developmental Test of Visual Perception*, is currently being investigated. Earlier claims that, after identification of visual-perceptual weaknesses and strengths followed by appropriate training on the Frostig Programme, improvement in visual-perceptual *and* reading attainments occurred, have not been substantiated as yet.

TRN	Name of test	Author	Country	Publisher	Year
75	*Goldman-Fristoe Test of Articulation*	R. Goldman and M. Fristoe	USA	American Guidance Service, Inc. (NFER-Nelson act as agents)	1969

Type	No. of forms	C.A. range	Skills tested	Time
Individual, criterion-referenced (levels A and K)	1	2:00 +	1 Sounds in words 2 Sounds in sentences 3 Stimulability (the ability to produce a previously misarticulated phoneme when given maximum cues, both visual and oral)	Untimed (10′)

Comments: Errors in articulation are frequently found in groups of children with reading difficulties. This test enables a systematic assessment to be made of an individual's ability to articulate consonant sounds. If the ability to articulate correctly or not is to be assessed, a teacher could use the test. If each sound production is to be further judged for type of error, one needs to have had appropriate advanced training.

The materials are colourful and interesting to children. The test-retest and inter-rater reliabilities are acceptably high, though not expressed in conventional terms. The test is very well compiled and convenient to use.

TRN	Name of test	Author	Country	Publisher	Year
76	*Goldman-Fristoe-Woodcock Test of Auditory Discrimination*	R. Goldman, M. Fristoe and R. W. Woodcock	USA	American Guidance Service Inc. (NFER-Nelson act as agents)	1970

Type	No. of forms	C.A. range	Skills tested	Time
Individual, diagnostic, normative (level K)	1	3:08 +	Speech-sound discrimination: Training procedure Speech-sound discrimination test proper: 1 Quiet sub-test (no background noise) 2 Noise sub-test (controlled level of distracting background noise) Error analysis (consonant sounds):	 Untimed (about 5′) (about 7½′) (about 7½′)

	Plosives	Continuants	Nasals	
Voiced				Voiced Total
Unvoiced				Unvoiced Total
	Total Plosives	Total Continuants	Total Nasals	

Comments: The purpose of this test is to identify defects in speech-sound discrimination in a situation not confounded by the 'subject's vocabulary development, his familiarity with test materials, the memory tasks involved, and the variations of individual examiners in test administration' (Manual, p. 4). The training procedure is designed to familiarise subjects with the word-picture associations that are used in the two subsequent sub-tests and to allow the examiner to establish whether the child has mastered the associations. The administration of the test proper is presented using a tape and earphones, thereby standardising much of the administration. In the test the child responds to a stimulus word by pointing to one of four pictures. The pictures have been carefully selected on the basis of an explicit model of consonant classification involving voicing, stop, nasality and place of articulation. Each of the two sub-tests contains six words from the five categories shown above. The distractor words (shown as pictures) in each item were drawn from words in 'the same cell or else in the same row or column as that representing the test word' (Manual, p. 25). Thus a *clinical* error analysis by sound category is possible.

The test was standardised on 745 subjects from the general population and aged between 3:00 and 84:00 (!) years of age. No claim is made that the sample was representative. In twenty-nine age categories, with Ns ranging between 6 and 81, means and standard deviations of scores for each group under Quiet and Noise conditions are given. Internal consistency reliabilities for the standardisation sample are given for the three age groups 3:00 to 6:00, 7:00 to 11:00, 12:00 to 70 + and for the total sample. The coefficients range between 0·53 and 0·83 for the Quiet sub-test and between 0·52 and 0·68 for the Noise sub-test. Internal consistency coefficients are also given for three quite large clinic samples (Ns = 105, 99, 38) at three age groupings (4:00 to 6:00; 7:00 to 9:00 and 10:00 to 12:00). For the Quiet sub-test reliabilities were 0·86, 0·88 and 0·81; for the Noise sub-test they were 0·68, 0·63 and 0·66 respectively. Test-retest reliability using seventeen pre-school speech handicapped pupils was 0·87 on the Quiet and 0·81 on the Noise sub-test. The validities of the test are satisfactory. Evidence of concurrent validity includes agreement with the opinions of clinicians. Construct validity is supported by changes in performance with age, the levels of performance of selected groups and also low correlations with 'nonmeasures of auditory discrimination' (Manual, p. 21).

Raw scores can be converted to percentile rank norms and normalised T scores with a mean of 50 and a standard deviation of 10 for 32 different age groups. The stability of the associated figures should be borne in mind by users. The error analysis is intended only for clinical and research purposes.

TRN	Name of test	Author	Country	Publisher	Year
88	*Illinois Test of Psycholinguistic Abilities* (revised edition)	S. A. Kirk, J. McCarthy and W. Kirk	USA	University of Illinois Press (NFER-Nelson act as agents)	1968

Type	No. of forms	C.A. range	Skills tested	Time
Individual, diagnostic, normative (level P)	1	2:04 to 10:03	1 Auditory reception 2 Visual reception 3 Auditory association 4 Visual association 5 Verbal expression 6 Manual expression 7 Grammatic closure 8 Visual closure (timed) 9 Auditory sequential memory 10 Visual sequential memory 11 Auditory closure* 12 Sound blending* * Supplementary tests	45′ approx.

Comments: This test is designed to allow an analysis of children's psycholinguistic abilities. The three dimensions deemed important are: (*a*) Channels of communication (auditory-vocal; visual-motor), (*b*) Processes (reception; organisation; expression), and (*c*) Levels of organisation or complexity (automatic level; representational level). Results can be expressed as a Composite Psycholinguistic Age, an estimated Binet mental age and IQ, and as scaled scores for each of the sub-tests. This allows profile interpretation. The standardisation is satisfactory but was restricted to 'children of average intelligence, school achievement, and socio-economic status and of intact motor and sensory development'. The tests are generally acceptably reliable. The evidence on validities is extensive, but is not included in the test manual. The intercorrelations of the sub-tests are also not given, thus making profile interpretation unnecessarily difficult. Kirk and his colleagues have written several monographs, including one on the diagnosis and remediation of psycholinguistic abilities, based on the ITPA.

This is an extremely promising instrument. It is so, largely because the model of language on which it is based ensures that three major dimensions of information processing underlying reading abilities are systematically conceptualised and investigated.

The model on which the test is based and the test itself have been, and are, topics of controversy. A considerable number of researches have been carried out on and with the ITPA. Reference to one recent British study is given below.

NAYLOR, J. G. and PUMFREY, P. D. (1983) 'The alleviation of psycholinguistic deficits and some effects on the reading attainments of poor readers.' *Journal of Research in Reading*, **6**, 2, 129–53.

TRN	Name of test	Author	Country	Publisher		Year
184	*Test of Early Language Development (TELD)*	W. P. Hresko, D. Kim Reid and D. D. Hammill	USA	Pro-Ed		1981
					2nd impression	1982

Type	No. of forms	C.A. range	Skills tested	Time
Individual, attainment, normative, diagnostic (level A)	1	3:00 to 7:11	1 Overall language development 2 Item profile: MODE: Receptive, Expressive FEATURE: Semantic, Form	Untimed (about 15′–20′)

Comments: *TELD* is designed to identify children who are relatively retarded in their language development, to assist in recording progress over time and treatment, as a research tool and to provide suggestions for activities that will foster language development. The test is based on a two dimensional model of language. The dimensions are Language Mode—receptive; expressive; and Feature—content (semantics); form (phonology; morphology; syntax). Items were developed on the basis of the model. The original pool of 370 items was reduced to 38 as a consequence of two item analyses with different groups. A check using 500 protocols, 100 from each age level in the standardisation sample, is reported as confirming the appropriateness of the item analysis (Manual, p. 6). This seems an odd claim as the facility and discrimination values of items are affected by the total task within which they are elicited.

TELD was standardised on 1 184 children. Judged by the criteria of sex and place of residence, this sample is assumed to be representative of the population. This assumption is one that not all who consider using the test could accept without further supporting evidence. The internal consistency reliabilities (coefficient Alpha) for the five year groups range between 0·87 and 0·92. Test-retest reliabilities of 177 children tested over a two week period were 0·90 for the total group and, for each of the five constituent year groups, 0·84, 0·72, 0·86, 0·85 and 0·87. Concurrent validity of *TELD* is supported by significant correlations between *TELD* scores and scores on five pre-reading and early language development tests. Age differentiation is seen as supporting the construct validity of *TELD*.

Raw scores can be converted to a Language Quotient and percentiles for each six months' chronological age group between 3:00 and 7:11. Language Ages can also be calculated. The individual's responses to each item can be analysed in an item profile. Provided due caution is taken, this could be one way of generating diagnostic/instructional hypotheses.

TRN	Name of test	Author	Country	Publisher	Year
185	*Test of Early Reading Ability (TERA)*	D. Kim Reid, W. P. Hresko, and D. D. Hammill	USA	Pro-Ed	1981

Type	No. of forms	C.A. range	Skills tested	Time
Individual, attainment, diagnostic, normative (level A)	1	4:00 to 7:11	Early reading skills	Untimed (about 15′–20′)

Comments: *TERA* claims to be based on contemporary notions concerning the nature of early reading that have substantial empirical support. The purposes of the test are to identify children who are not keeping up with their age peers in learning to read, to record progress, to suggest instructional strategies and for use in research. The test consists of 50 items, the residue from an initial pool of 270 that were reduced to 76 and used with 150 three- to five-year-old (3.00–5.00) children. The appropriateness of the item selection was confirmed using a random sample of 500 subjects, 100 at each of the age levels 3:00 to 7:11, randomly chosen from the standardisation sample protocols. Oddly, it is not made clear whether this latter sample also took a test containing 76 items. From the comment in the manual, this appears unlikely. If this is the case, the claim seems somewhat unusual.

The test was normed on 1 184 children assumed to be representative of the population as a whole in the given age bands. At each age level the internal consistency coefficient of reliability was measured using Cronbach's coefficient Alpha. These ranged between 0·87 and 0·96, with a standard error of about two points of raw score. Using a sample of 177 three- to seven-year-old (3.00–7.00) children tested twice with a two week gap, test-retest coefficients of 0·85, 0·92, 0·94 and 0·82 are reported. The validity of the test is supported by age and group differentiation and by a series of concurrent validities calculated using small groups of between 30 and 50 pupils who had also been tested on five other language tests, Reading Readiness and an intelligence test.

Raw scores can be converted to deviation reading quotients (mean 100; standard deviation 15) for six monthly age groups between 3:00 and 7:11. The use of the norms with the youngest age group requires considerable caution and is not recommended. Percentiles and reading ages can also be obtained. Children's responses to individual items can also be recorded in an age-level × content matrix for clinical purposes. The three content areas specified, Meaning, Alphabet Knowledge and Convention, are not to be taken as specifying sub-test. As it stands, the test would not be suitable for use in Britain because of the content of certain of the items. These do, however, represent some novel approaches and could well be developed in other countries.

TRN	Name of test	Author	Country	Publisher	Year
190	*Tests for Colour-Blindness*	S. Ishihara	J	Kanehara Shuppan Co. (NFER-Nelson act as agents)	1971

Type	No. of forms	C.A. range	Skills tested	Time
Individual, diagnostic (level P)	2 (24-plate and 38-plate)	6:00 +	Ability to perceive colours and discriminate between colours	Untimed (10′)

Comments: If a child (usually a boy) suffers from one of the many forms of colour-blindness, it is possible that certain reading schemes using colour codes may confuse rather than assist the child to learn the discriminations apparent to children whose colour vision is normal. In such a case, a teacher may mistakenly assume that a child with a colour-vision deficiency is a slow-learner of the colour-coded material.

The above test can be used with children who know their number names or can match cards containing written numbers. Although the above date of publication is that of the most recent edition of the test, it has been in use for many years. The norms are elementary and details of standardisation are not given. The test can perhaps be considered as a mastery type test in which failure to cope with a prescribed number of items has important implications concerning the use of colour-coded reading schemes with a child.

The Ishihara Test was first published in Japan in 1917. The 10th edition appeared in 1951 and has been recommended by experts (Fletcher and Voke, 1982). In 1971 editions containing 24 and 36 plates were published in Britain.

FLETCHER, R. and VOKE, J. (1982) 'A guide to colour vision tests—Part 1.' *The Optician*, **184**, 43–50.

TRN	Name of test	Author	Country	Publisher	Year
192	*Visual Motor Gestalt Test*	L. Bender	USA	American Orthopsychiatric Association (NFER-Nelson act as agents)	1946

Test	No. of forms	C.A. range	Skills tested	Time
Individual, diagnostic (level K)	1	4:00 to 11:00 (and adults)	Used *clinically* as: 1 Test of visual motor-gestalt maturation 2 To explore retardation, regression, loss of function 3 To explore personality deviations where there are regressive phenomena	Untimed (15′)

Comments: In this test the subject is asked to reproduce a series of eight designs. The responses are interpreted in terms of Gestalt laws of perception and organisation.

The test manual gives nothing in the way of conventional psychometric information.

Studies of children and adults are to be found in Research Monograph Number 3 of the American Orthopsychiatric Association (1938) by Bender. Since then a wide variety of scoring systems have been devised. Those by Koppitz (1963, 1975) and by Pascal and Suttell (1951) attempt to quantify children's and adults' responses respectively.* The theoretical basis of the test is complex and the test is only available to psychologists of equivalent training and experience to qualify for Associate Membership of the British Psychological Society.

* KOPPITZ, E. M. (1963) *The Bender Gestalt Test for Young Children* New York: Grune and Stratton.

KOPPITZ, E. M. (1975) *The Bender Gestalt Test for Young Children: Research and Application, 1963–1973* New York: Grune and Stratton.

PASCAL, G. R. and SUTTELL, B. J. (1951) *The Bender Gestalt Test: Its Quantification and Validity for Adults* New York: Grune and Stratton.

TRN	Name of test	Author	Country	Publisher	Year
193	*Vocabulary Survey Test*	M. Monroe, J. C. Manning and J. M. Wepman	USA	Scott, Foresman	1971

Type	No. of forms	C.A. range	Skills tested	Time
Group, attainment and diagnostic (level A)	2 (A & B)	5:00 to 7:00	Comprehension of oral vocabulary 1 Nouns, mathematical terms 2 Place relationship terms, verbs, adjectives, pronouns, mathematical concepts	Untimed (2 sessions)

Comments: This test is designed to assess aspects of oral vocabulary. In both parts, the teacher dictates a word or a phrase and the child selects one of four picture options.

The standardisation sample is clearly described, but is hardly a typical one. Raw scores can be converted to standard scores and percentiles. The split-half reliability of the test is 0·93. The manual is very helpful concerning the interpretation of, and possible action based on, the children's responses.

2 Recognised tests of reading readiness

(a) British

TRN	Name of test	Author	Country	Publisher	Year
90	*Infant Reading Tests*	A. Brimer and B. Raban	B	Education Evaluation Enterprises	1979

Type	No. of forms	C.A. range	Skills tested		Time
Group, attainment, diagnostic	1	4:07 to 7:00	Pre-reading Test 1	Temporal-spatial coordination	Untimed*
			Pre-reading Test 2	Sound discrimination	Untimed
		(Age range of the sample on which the tests were developed)	Pre-reading Test 3	Shape discrimination	Untimed
			Reading Test 1	Word recognition	Untimed
			Reading Test 2	Sentence completion	Untimed
			Reading Test 3	Reading comprehension	Untimed
(level A)					(* not more than 20′ each)

Comments: This battery of tests is designed for use with any child attending infant school. The pre-reading tests aim to examine 'linguistic competence; the ability to use printed symbols; the recognition of speech sounds; and the discrimination of printed shapes varying in orientation' (Manual, p. 1). Each raw score is converted to a seven point equal interval scale only. Scores of two or less are claimed to indicate a high probability that the child has not yet developed the ability; scores of five or more indicate the converse. The tests were developed using both conventional and Rasch item analyses. The equal interval scale was constructed on the basis of the latter approach. The results are summarised in a profile. The internal consistency reliabilities of the scales as measured using Kuder-Richardson formula 20 are high, ranging between 0·88 and 0·95. For each of the tests, the *change* in raw score necessary to make the user reasonably confident that a real, as opposed to a chance, change has occurred, is given. Approximate reading ages for Reading Test 3 are given but considerable caution in their interpretation is (correctly) emphasised. Correlations between the tests are not provided. It would have helped profile interpretation if they had been given. In one sense, the statistical interpretation of a score on a scale is simple. However, the psychological processes involved in each test and the implications of their absence for the individual child's language programme are extremely complex. The brief guidance given on what each test measures and how this relates to the development of reading skills underlines the point. The sizes of the samples on which the tests were developed were between 130 and 183.

TRN	Name of test	Author	Country	Publisher	Year
91	*Infant Screening: A Handbook for Teachers*	P. Randall	B	Macmillan Education (for Humberside Local Education Authority)	1981

Type	No. of forms	C.A. range	Skills tested	Time
Group, screening, (level A)	1	5:00 +	Checklist 1: A Health B Self-help skills C Emotional/social development D Communication/language E Learning/attainment	Untimed
		5:10 to 6:03	Checklist 2: A Physical B Learning C Social development D Emotional/personality development	
			Initial screening tests: A Shape perception (2)* B Word-recognition (1) C Visual discrimination (1) D Auditory discrimination (1) E Auditory discrimination (1) F Numbers (1)	
			Diagnostic tests: Visual reception (decoding) (4) Auditory reception (decoding) (4) Association skill (1) Sequential skill (2) Expression (encoding) (2) Reading difficulties (7) 1 Pre-reading skills 2 Letter sounds, knowledge of 3 Sound blending 4 Silent 'e' rule 5 Initial consonant blends 6 Vowel digraphs 7 Consonant digraphs	

* Numbers of different sub-tests in each test are shown in brackets.

Comments: Although wider in scope than the measurement and remediation of reading difficulties, the latter figures prominently in this example of an LEA developed infant screening procedure. It aims to identify children who are educationally 'at risk', to pinpoint areas of particular difficulty and to suggest remedial procedures.

The model on which the system is based appears to owe much to Osgood's model of communication and to Kirk and McCarthy's well-known *Illinois Test of Psycholinguistic Abilities* (TRN 88), though also including other aspects of development of educational importance as can be seen by looking at the contents of the two checklists.

A developmental checklist is provided for use at age 5:00 +, for use after the first six weeks in the infant reception class. A second such checklist is presented for children aged 5:10 to 6:03 years. The battery of initial screening tests contains empirically tested cut-off points that are used to identify children 'at risk' of educational failure. The methodology is (commendably) based on a sequential hypothesis generation and testing approach to screening, diagnosis and remediation. The suggestions for remedial activities capitalise on the expertise of members of the East Riding Divisional Remedial Education Service and of the School Psychological Service.

A further battery of diagnostic tests related to the assessment model is given. Each test also has a cut-off score determined by use with 'many children aged between 5:10 and 6:03 years', below which a child is likely to be educationally 'at risk'.

The technical report of the construction and validation of the screening system is very brief (5 pages) for such an extensive battery. Discriminant function analysis was used to check the validity of the screening procedure, namely the accuracy with which it identified children already known to have problems. Regression analyses were used to determine the respective contributions of variables to overall predictive efficiency in relation to various criteria. It is somewhat baldly reported that the internal consistency reliability coefficients of the tests exceed 0·88 and test-retest coefficients exceed 0·85. Correlation with teachers' observations is deemed to support the validity of the screening procedure.

The system appears complex to the reviewer. The manual is so condensed that the evidence supporting the test construction and validation procedures is not as well explicated as one might wish. For example, chronological age is not used as a variable in the analyses presented, but the reason for its omission is not given. Evidence supporting the efficacy of the suggestions for remedial activities is not presented.

The concept of children educationally 'at risk' and the use of screening procedures highlights the degree of inter and intra-individual differences in, for example, reading and its related sub-skills that are acceptable and/or unavoidable at given stages of development. As yet this crucial issue remains almost entirely a matter of opinion.

The early identification of children with reading difficulties aims to provide early intervention with a greater likelihood of helping the child than if identification were deferred. Many LEAs have developed or are developing such systems. Evidence of their efficacy is eagerly anticipated.

TRN	Name of test	Author	Country	Publisher	Year
191	*Thackray Reading Readiness Profiles*	D. V. Thackray and L. E. Thackray	B	Hodder and Stoughton	1974

Type	No. of forms	C.A. range	Skills tested	Time
Group, diagnostic, normative	1	4:08 to 5:08 (approx.)	1 Vocabulary and concept development	20′
			2 Auditory discrimination	20′
			3 Visual discrimination	20′
(level A)			4 General ability	10′

Comments: Those who have read Dr Thackray's book *Readiness for Reading* (1971) (London, Chapman) will realise that he has made a long and intensive study of this area. The Thackrays have chosen to carry out pioneer work in an area which has previously been largely American-dominated. The profiles were the first reading-readiness test to be constructed in the UK. It is primarily intended for use with admission class pupils. If considered as a content criterion-referenced test, it could probably be used to some advantage with slightly older children. The aims of the test are to provide quick, reliable and valid measures of what the Thackrays consider the most vital reading-readiness skills. It comes in the form of an attractively presented sixteen-page individual booklet. The test has been standardised on 5 500 children aged from 4 : 08 to 5 : 08 drawn from 350 schools in urban and rural areas of Great Britain and Northern Ireland. The split-half reliabilities of the three reading-readiness scales are 0·80, 0·81, and 0·90 respectively. High content validity is claimed and evidence of acceptable predictive validities of the first three scales is given. The intercorrelations of the four scales are given. In addition, the manual contains information on the interpretation of the individual scales plus suggestions for developing reading-readiness skills in the areas of Language Development, Auditory Discrimination and Visual Discrimination.

The use of the Harris* revision of the Goodenough 'Draw-a-man' Test as a measure of general ability might be considered suspect by some teachers. The norms used for this scale are American. Perhaps of more concern, and despite the caveat entered, the guidance on the clinical interpretation of children's drawings given on page 22 of the manual suggests implications that require important qualification if unjustified overinterpretation is not to occur. Further research on the predictive validity of the profiles is in hand.

It should not be thought that there are no other British tests of reading-readiness skills available. The *Standard Reading Tests* (TRN 178) battery contains several criterion-referenced diagnostic tests. However, as yet there is no other British normative standardised objective test of reading readiness.

* HARRIS, D. B. (1963) *Children's drawings as measures of intellectual maturity. A revision and extension of the Goodenough Draw-a-Man Test*. New York: Harcourt Brace and World.

TRN	Name of test	Author	Country	Publisher	Year
198	*Word Order Comprehension Test*	G. Fenn	B	NFER-Nelson	1979

Type	No. of forms	C.A. range	Skills tested	Time
Individual, diagnostic (level A)	1	Children of any age	Understanding of simple sentence relationships Preposition *on* Preposition *under* Subject-Object *nouns* (1) Subject-Object *nouns* (2) Subject-Object *pronouns* Indirect Object *nouns* Indirect Object *pronouns* Indirect Object with prepositional phrase *nouns* Indirect Object with prepositional phrase *pronouns*	Untimed

Comments: Fenn has developed a clinical test intended primarily for the diagnostic assessment of children having problems of either language delay or disorder. She utilises the idea that the comprehension of simple sentences requires both a knowledge of vocabulary and an appreciation of the significance of word order. The strategy involves presenting two pictures, for example, a red brick on a black brick and a black brick on a red brick. Each picture can be described using the same words, but the order in which the words are presented determines the meaning of the sentence. The child has to indicate the picture matching the sentence. Presentation of sentences can be either spoken or signed. There is also a written presentation in which cards having sentences written on them must be matched to the appropriate picture. The pictures have been drawn with primary school pupils in mind.

Four sets of pictures cover the nine sub-tests. Each sub-test contains twelve items, two of which are practice ones. The order of presentation of the sub-tests is not prescribed. No age norms are provided. The only empirical data presented in the manual are of a pilot study with normal children aged from 4:00 to 5:06 years plus reference to results obtained from the use of the test with over a hundred deaf or mentally handicapped children whose characteristics are not otherwise indicated. In the pilot study, results on each sub-test from small samples are given (N ranging from 19 to 22). These data are broken down to show the scores for the 4:00 to 4:11 and 5:00 to 5:06 year groups respectively. With the handicapped children, scores on the *Word Order Comprehension Test* were not related to scores on other well-known tests of language development.

The central idea of the test is important. Weaknesses include a manual that does not give sufficient information concerning development of the test, its item selection and validation. The inclusion of an erratum slip to correct a crucial point relating to the presentation of the materials, does not inspire confidence. The author's blood pressure probably rose considerably when the printing error was eventually noted. Administration of the written presentation would be made easier if the sentence cards had been sequentially numbered within each sub-test. The colouring of some of the pictures could be improved. For example, a brick intended to be black is so shaded that much of it appears grey.

The criticisms are important, but despite them the test has considerable promise.

(b) Others

TRN	Name of test	Author	Country	Publisher	Year
1	*ACER Early School Series*	H. A. H. Rowe*	A	Australian Council for Educational Research	1981

Type	No. of forms	C.A. range	Skills tested	Time
Group, individual, normative, criterion-referenced, screening, diagnostic (level A)	1	6:00 + (and older pupils with reading difficulties)	Auditory analysis skills: Auditory discrimination Recognition of initial consonants and sounds Conceptual skills: Number Figure formation Language skills: syntactic structures Prepositions Verb tense Pronouns Negation Comprehension Word knowledge	Untimed (about 15′–20′ per test)

Comments: The ten paper and pencil tests in this battery each provide an estimate of a pupil's ability on an educationally important, operationally definable and modifiable cognitive skill in a specific curriculum-related field linked to later attainment in reading. The battery enables the teacher to identify the strengths and weaknesses of children starting school. The educational objective for *all* such pupils is complete mastery of all the ten skills assessed. Because the tests require no reading ability, the battery can also be used with older children experiencing reading difficulties. The author recognises the current absence of any agreed pattern of hierarchically sequential sub-skills providing a guide to a teaching programme. However, in this battery items in each skill area have been selected so as to be 'highly representative of teachable sub-skills' (p. 19). Their increasing level of difficulty gives the teacher guidance concerning the next instructional task that needs mastering by the pupil. It is acknowledged that the tests of syntactic structures and the comprehension test are 'less independent from each other conceptually than the others' (p. 68). It is claimed that results from the tests can be directly translated into individualised teaching procedures, and can also be used to monitor progress and enable programme efficacy to be readily evaluated. These are substantial claims.

The construction of the tests is based on the Rasch measurement model and involves two parameters: the ability of the individual and the difficulty of the item. Readers will find Chapter 10 in the manual a helpful introduction to the relationship between conventional test theory and the Rasch model, the latter gaining increasing popularity with many constructors of reading tests. It is claimed by Rowe that recent criticisms of the Rasch model were not empirically substantiated when tested during construction of the above battery. A ratio scaling of ability estimates and of item difficulty has been achieved, it is claimed, in this particular field. If this appears somewhat esoteric, the information given by such a scale is greater than that provided by the more commonly used interval scales. Not all workers accept the validity of the assumptions underpinning the Rasch model and have reservations concerning claims made for its educational utility.

The manual contains a detailed description of the sampling, item analyses, reliabilities and validities. Raw scores can be readily converted into ability estimates that are independent of the sample. In addition, comparative normative data are provided for each test.

It will be interesting to see whether this battery provides the link between assessment and instruction that is suggested.

* ROWE, H. A. H. (1981) *Early Identification and Intervention: A Handbook for Teachers and School Counsellors*. Hawthorn, Victoria: Australian Council for Educational Research.

TRN	Name of test	Author	Country	Publisher	Year
41	*Clymer-Barrett Readiness Test (CBRT)*	T. Clymer and T. C. Barrett	USA	Chapman, Brook and Kent	1983

Type	No. of forms	C.A. range	Skills tested	Time
Group, individual, attainment, diagnostic	2 (A & B)	5:00 to 6:11	*Visual discrimination*:	
			1 Recognizing letters (35 items) (no more than 8″ per item)	Short Form about 30′
			2 Matching words (20 items) (no more than 10″ per item)	
			Auditory discrimination:	
			3 Beginning sounds (20 items) (no more than 10″ per item)	Long Form 3 × 30′ sessions
			4 Ending sounds (20 items) (no more than 10″ per item)	
			Visual-motor co-ordination:	
			5 Completing shapes (20 items) (no more than 15″ per item)	
			6 Copy-a-sentence (1 sentence; 7 words; 27 letters)	(timed test 5′)
			Readiness survey:	
			1 Oral language	
			2 Vocabulary and concepts	
			3 Listening skills	
			4 Thinking abilities	
			5 Social skills	
			6 Emotional development	
			7 Attitudes towards learning	
(level A)			8 Work habits	

Comments: The *CBRT* is a revision of the *Clymer-Barrett Pre-Reading Battery* first published in 1967. The content of the *CBRT* remains virtually the same as does the data on which its reliabilities and validities are based. The changes that have taken place are largely cosmetic. The *CBRT* aims to provide teachers with information concerning a number of pre-reading skills plus an optional 'readiness survey' based on teacher ratings of a child on eight pupil characteristics important in early learning in general and in early reading in particular. The Short Form administration employs only sub-tests 1 and 3 and gives a useful score for screening and placement. The Long Form gives three diagnostic sub-scores and a total score. Raw scores can be converted to percentiles and stanines. The manual is helpful in interpreting the scores but fails to give adequate guidance concerning activities likely to facilitate improvement of underdeveloped or weak skills.

Standardisation is based on 5 565 pupils. The reliabilities of the sub-tests, their validities and intercorrelations are presented. These appear to be based on data that led to the first edition, though this is not made clear in the present

Continued at foot of p. 86

TRN	Name of test	Author	Country	Publisher	Year
70	*Gates-MacGinitie Reading Tests: Readiness Skills*	A. I. Gates and W. H. MacGinitie	USA	Teachers College Press, New York	1939 to 1968

Type	No. of forms	C.A. range	Skills tested	Time
Group, diagnostic, normative (level A)	1	5:00 to 6:00	1 Listening comprehension 2 Auditory discrimination 3 Visual discrimination 4 Following directions 5 Letter recognition 6 Visual-motor coordination 7 Auditory blending 8 Word recognition 9 Total score	4 × 30′ sessions

Comments: The child's scores on this test can be presented in a profile showing weaknesses and strengths in the areas tested. The Word Recognition sub-test is intended to help in the rapid identification of those children who have acquired some reading attainments. This score is *not* included in the total weighted score.

The test was standardised on a nationally representative sample. The reliabilities and validities presented in the Technical Supplement to the manual are satisfactory. Caution in interpreting differences between sub-test scores is emphasised. Raw scores can be converted to stanine scores and to percentiles. The scores from the sub-tests have been weighted so as to give the best prediction of later reading achievement. The total weighted scores of a group can be compared in terms of normalised standard scores called 'Readiness Standard Scores' and in 'Readiness Percentile Scores'.

The manual to the test gives helpful advice in interpreting the scores obtained.

---

manual. A potential user might think these data more recent than is the case. In Tests 3 and 4, the pictures on which the items are based have been slightly changed in a number of cases. In the absence of a further item analysis and restandardisation one cannot be certain that such changes have not affected the norms. There is a strong case for authors of test manuals to show quite clearly the dates when data used in standardisation, in support of reliabilities and validities, were obtained.

It has been reported that the earlier version of the test was at least equal to the *Metropolitan Readiness Tests* (TRN 104) in its ability to predict reading success on the *Gates-MacGinitie Vocabulary and Comprehension Reading Tests* (TRN 71) for children in grade 1, from a particular population. The two sub-tests that more accurately predict reading success are numbers 1 and 3. Presumably it is anticipated that this remains true for the revised test.

TRN	Name of test	Author	Country	Publisher	Year
84	*Harrison-Stroud Reading Readiness Profiles*	M. L. Harrison and J. B. Stroud	USA	Houghton Mifflin	1949 to 1956

Type	No. of forms	C.A. range	Skills tested	Time
Individual in part, but sections can be administered as a group test; diagnostic (level P)	1	5:00 to 6:00	1 Using symbols 2 Making visual discriminations (two parts) 3 Using context clues 4 Auditory discriminations 5 Using context and auditory clues 6 Giving the names of letters	Untimed Tests 1–5 about 1 hr 30′ (in groups) Test 6 3′ (individual)

Comments: The children's materials in this test are very attractively prepared. The only skills the child requires in order to cope with the first five tests are to be able, on instruction, to underline either a picture or a word or to draw a line joining a word to a picture. The sixth test is of naming letters and is almost entirely dependent on specific teaching, whether by parents or teacher. In this respect sub-test 6 differs from the other tests.

The results are summarised for each child in a profile giving a child's percentile rank for each of the tests. The authors discuss five characteristic profiles and indicate the type of programmes appropriate to children with such profiles. Typically, a profile presentation leaves little doubt in the mind of the observer as to a child's relative weaknesses and strengths in the skills tested. Unfortunately, no mention is made in the manual of the reliabilities of the tests or their intercorrelations. Yet such considerations are central if one is to interpret the differences between scores on different sub-tests. Whether the tests are satisfactorily valid is also open to some doubt. Despite such strictures, these tests have been found to be of value by many teachers.

TRN	Name of test	Author	Country	Publisher	Year
96	*Language Abilities Test (LAT)*	C. Wilson	A	Heinemann Educational (Australia)	1980

Type	No. of forms	C.A. range	Skills tested	Time
Individual,* group,† diagnostic, normative, oral administration (level A)	1 (response may be oral* or written†)	4:06 to 17:00+	The meaning of words: 1 Words in context 2 Word meanings The rules of grammar: 3 Grammatical reception 4 Sentence construction The sounds of speech: 6 Phonetic similarities 7 Auditory completion Sub-test 5, Listening comprehension, tests in all three of the above areas	Untimed

Comments: This test of semantic, syntactic and phonetic aspects of language is the result of more than seven years' development. To produce a test covering such a wide age-range, 36 items have been developed for each sub-test. Clients, however, take only a specified ten items per sub-test, the items taken being determined by the age group of the client. Oral responses require an individual administration. This is advocated for children aged seven or younger. Group administration is possible using written responses with children from the age of six years, provided that suitable precautions are taken. Each question carries two marks, thus all pupils' total scores are out of 140. Very simple normative data ('smoothed' mean scores) are provided for each of fourteen age levels on each sub-test based on trials with 12 000 students drawn from California and Victoria. No details are given in the administration manual of the composition of these samples. Data from 3 246 Australian pupils aged from 5 : 00 to 17 : 11 with means and standard deviations for each sub-test and age level are presented elsewhere in the manual. The internal consistency of total scores on *LAT* for each age level range from 0·651 to 0·855 using Kuder-Richardson formula 21. The intercorrelations of the sub-tests are not presented but are likely to be quite high. As a result of the Australian research, some unreliable items have been removed and it is suggested that the test reliabilities will be higher than those quoted as a result. Concurrent validity for the *LAT* is claimed by virtue of rank-order correlations with the *Illinois Test of Psycholinguistic Abilities* (TRN 88) of 0·75 for 'normal' and 0·63 for 'remedial' children. No description is given of the samples from which these figures derive. At any age level a score of twelve or less on any sub-test 'should be taken as a warning and ten or less as a clear indication, of problems in the relevant area' (Manual, p. iv). The frequency of false negative and false positive identifications is not mentioned. The simple rule-of-thumb seems peculiarly straightforward.

TRN	Name of test	Author	Country	Publisher	Year
97	*Linguistic Awareness in Reading Readiness (LARR)*	J. Downing, D. Ayers and B. Schaefer	C/B	NFER-Nelson	1983

Type	No. of forms	C.A. range	Skills tested		Time
Group, individual, screening, diagnostic	2 (A & B)	4:00 to 8:00 (and older children with reading difficulties)	1 *Recognising literacy behaviour*:		Untimed (about 45′–60′)
			Things that can be read		
			Act of reading		
			Writing tools		
			Act of writing		
			2 *Understanding literacy functions*:		
			Enjoying story	Obtaining information ('finding out')	
			Public announcement	Receiving private message	
			Telling story	Communicating information	
			Aid to memory	Sending private message	
			Giving directions	Leaving reminder	
			Communication in trade	Obtaining information ('finding out')	
			Recording observations	Social communication	
			3 *Technical language of literacy*:		
			Number	Letter	
			Printing	Writing	
			Line	Word	
			Capital letter	Punctuation	
			Letter in word	Sentence	
(level A)			Name		

Comments: In the belief, based on recent research findings, that learning to read and write is more closely associated with the child's understanding of linguistic concepts rather than with factors such as visual and auditory perception and letter-name knowledge, the above test was developed. *LARR* is a three part test designed to assess children's understanding of the concepts and vocabulary involved in both reading and writing, their awareness of the uses to which reading and writing are put and the child's understanding of words such as 'letter', 'word', etc., comprising essential aspects of the

Continued at foot of p. 90

TRN	Name of test	Author	Country	Publisher	Year
104	*Metropolitan Readiness Tests*	G. H. Hildreth, N. L. Griffiths and M. E. McGauvran	USA	Harcourt Brace and World	1933 to 1966

Type	No. of forms	C.A. range	Skills tested	Time
Group, diagnostic, normative (level R)	2 (R & S)	5:00 to 6:00	1 Word meaning 2 Listening 3 Matching 4 Alphabet 5 Numbers 6 Copying 7 Draw-a-man (optional)	Untimed (3 sessions)

Comments: This test has been used extensively since its first appearance. It has also undergone successive improvements as a result of its use. From the technical point of view this test is one of the better ones available. The manual contains clear instructions for administering and scoring, and stresses the care needed in the interpretation of a sub-test score for an individual. This is a counsel of caution to be welcomed. This test has produced evidence of being a valid predictor of children's later reading attainments. As such, it is potentially of value to the teacher hoping to maximise the chances of children making satisfactory reading progress.

---

technical language of literacy. The majority of items require the child to select and circle the correct answer, whether a picture or a word, from the alternatives provided on the child's test sheet. The scoring of a small minority of items requires the teacher to use her judgement in appraising a response. *LARR* is designed to enable teachers to monitor the development of and evaluate attempts at enhancing children's linguistic awareness and knowledge. A Class Evaluation Record is provided. This enables the performances of a class on all 75 items in the test to be recorded and analysed in terms of the patterns of linguistic awareness identified. The interpretation of the results is discussed in the manual and four books are suggested as providing useful ideas for developing the concepts and knowledge assessed by *LARR*.

The test was developed in British Columbia. Validation studies have involved some 300 pupils in three trials. Internal consistency reliability coefficients of the three parts of *LARR* are presented for each form of the test. These range from 0·76 to 0·95. Subsequent modifications are believed by the authors to have increased all reliabilities to above 0·85. The predictive validity of *LARR* was considered using pupils from the first try-out by looking at their scores on a reading attainment test one year later. Correlations between Parts 1 and 2 (Form A) and the reading test were 0·50, whereas for Part 3 (Form B) it was 0·60. Results from twelve classes show considerable inter-class differences. Part 3 is consistently the best predictor of later reading attainments, whereas Parts 1 and 2 failed to reach statistical significance in relation to later reading attainment in a number of cases.

No norms are presented, but guidance is given in the manual on a way of establishing somewhat basic criteria for below average scores. This test contains many promising ideas.

TRN	Name of test	Author	Country	Publisher	Year
107	*Murphy-Durrell Reading Readiness Analysis*	H. A. Murphy and D. D. Durrell	USA	Harcourt Brace and World	1965

Type	No. of forms	C.A. range	Skills tested	Time
Group and individual, attainment and diagnostic	1	6:00 to 6:11	1 Phoneme identification test (24 items)	Untimed
			2 Letter names test, upper and lower case letters (52 items)	Untimed
(level A)			3 Learning rate test (18 items) (words retained one hour after initial presentation)	Timed

Comments: This instrument is primarily intended to measure aspects of reading readiness that will help the teacher in grouping entrants to schools for reading instruction. The test was standardised on 12 231 grade 1 pupils from sixty-five school systems in twelve states of the USA. Scores can be converted to percentiles, stanines and quartile groupings.

The Learning rate test is a particularly interesting one. It involves presenting nine words, all meaningful and easily illustrated. Each word is presented in three modes: on the blackboard, in print on a flash-card, and in the test booklet. At each presentation the name of the word is said by the teacher and repeated by the pupils. An hour later, the pupils are required to identify the nine words under two different multiple-choice conditions (therefore 18 items). The first involves discrimination in the context of the other words taught. The second mode asks for identification in the presence of untaught words of similar form. This sub-test assesses the pupil's ability to learn, retain and later recognise a specified set of words. As a testing technique it has considerable potential.

The internal consistency reliabilities for the sub-tests are high, and the extent to which they predict later reading attainment is acceptable. The inter sub-test correlations are sufficiently low to suggest that differentially important components of pre-reading skills are being tested.

TRN	Name of test	Author	Country	Publisher	Year
146	*Pre-reading Assessment Kit*	Ontario Institute for Studies in Education	C	California Test Bureau/McGraw-Hill Ryeson Ltd, for Ontario Institute for Studies in Education	1972

Type	No. of forms	C.A. range	Skills tested	6 *y.o. Difficulty Level* *Easy* 65%–85%	*Moderate* 40%–65%	*Hard* 25%–40%	Time
Group and individual, diagnostic, criterion-referenced	*See* Skills tested	5:00 to 6:00	*Listening Unit*				Untimed (about 10′ per test)
			Rhyming 1	X			
			Rhyming 2	X			
			Beginning sounds		X	X	
			Ending sounds		X	X	
			Symbol Perception Unit				
			Visual discrimination 1	X			
			Visual discrimination 2	X			
			Recognition of letters		X		
			Recognition of words			X	
			Experience Vocabulary Unit				
			Experience vocabulary	X	X		
			Comprehension Unit				
			Classification	X	X		
			Emotional response	X	X		
(level A)			Cause-effect and prediction	X	X		

Comments: This battery was developed by a committee of teachers and members of the Ontario Institute for Studies in Education. The tests are intended to provide diagnostic indications of the specific skills, pertinent to reading, that the child has or has not acquired. The sub-tests are relatively short yet reasonably reliable. The correlations between the sub-tests are sufficiently low to suggest that relatively distinct abilities are being tested. The predictive validity of the instrument appears satisfactory. Suggestions for interpreting the results and for remedial activities are made in the handbook. This test has many possibilities, but its administration, scoring and interpretation is likely to be rather time-consuming if used with classes of children rather than with individuals.

3 Reading tests: attainment and diagnostic

(a) British

TRN	Name of test	Author	Country	Publisher	Year
6	*AH Vocabulary Scale*	A. W. Heim, K. P. Watts and V. Simmonds	B	NFER-Nelson	1978

Type	No. of forms	C.A. range	Skills tested	Time
Group, attainment, normative (level A)	6 (sets P to U)	P, Q: 9:00 to 11:11 Q, R: 12:00 to 14:11 R, S: 15:00 to 18:00 S, T: Students T, U: Graduates	Word knowledge	Untimed (up to 25′ per set of 40 items)

Comments: This test of word knowledge consists of six sets of 40 words. Two sets comprise one test. For younger pupils the use of one 40 item set is advocated, giving the possibility of parallel form testing by set. With older subjects, a two set (80 item) test is advised. Each item requires the subject to look at a question paper (reusable) containing a stimulus word and six response alternatives from which he is required to select a synonym. If the subject does not consider the alternative provided to be satisfactory, he may construct his own alternative. Answers are recorded on a separate consumable answer sheet. Within sets there is no gradient of difficulty. The six sets are, however, of increasing difficulty.

Norms are provided for 9:00 to 15:00+ pupils attending comprehensive schools for both 40 and 80 word sets. Means and standard deviations of raw scores are given for each year group. Raw scores are converted to a five point letter scale where the percentage in each category is as follows: A = top 10%; B = next 20%; C = central 40%; D = next 20% and E = the lowest 10%. Similar information is provided for Sixth Form pupils aged 16:00 to 18:00 years, for college of education students, for university students, graduates, miscellaneous adults and naval ratings. The sampling on which the norms are based appears to be mainly by convenience although the authors have tried to ensure that *some* of the samples are in certain respects similar to their notional populations. There is little doubt that the scale will rank-order individuals reliably on word-knowledge. The normative information should be used with considerable caution. Split-half coefficients of internal consistency reliability based on N = 100 for the six sets and five tests range from 0·54 to 0·86 for the former and from 0·74 to 0·90 for the latter. Understandably, the 80 item test tended to be the more reliable. Inter-set correlations ranged from 0·67 to 0·75. Kuder-Richardson formula 21 coefficients of internal consistency varied between 0·50 and 0·94 dependent on the sets and the sample.

TRN	Name of test	Author	Country	Publisher	Year
9	*APU Vocabulary Test*	S. J. Closs	B	Hodder and Stoughton 2nd impression	1977

Type	No. of forms	C.A. range	Skills tested	Time
Group, attainment (level A)	1	11:00 to 18:00	Vocabulary	15′

Comments: This 75-item test is designed to assess secondary school children's understanding of currently used vocabulary. The items take the form of synonym selection from a multiple-choice array, for example:

stimulus word	*options*
CHAIR	poor step seat thick mat

The test was standardised on a sample of 6 234 pupils. The internal consistency of the items based on item-total score correlations for a sample of 175 pupils aged from 15:00 to 16:00 was 0·954. Using 143 13:00 year old pupils tested on two occasions with a seven-day interval, a test-retest reliability coefficient of 0·831 was obtained. Concurrent validity is supported by a correlation of 0·778 between the scores of 142 13:00 year old pupils on the *APU Vocabulary Scale* and on the *Mill Hill Vocabulary Scale*. Predictive validity was examined by correlating scores with the grade obtained by pupils in leaving-certificate examinations. At Scottish O-level grade, coefficients for six language-oriented subjects ranged between 0·46 and 0·21. At Scottish H-grade, for four subjects, the coefficients ranged between 0·44 and 0·27. If the initial mean scores of groups on the *APU Vocabulary Scale* had been given also, these data might have been more illuminating.

The instrument is easily administered and scored. It is not recommended for use with pupils of either low ability or of high ability because of its psychometric characteristics.

Though currently out of print, the instrument has considerable potential for future development.

TRN	Name of test	Author	Country	Publisher	Year
10	*Assessing Reading Difficulties*	L. Bradley	B	Macmillan Education	1980
				2nd edition	1984

Type	No. of forms	C.A. range	Skills tested	Time
Individual, criterion-referenced, diagnostic, screening (level A)	2 (Tests 1 and 2)	5:00 to 8:00+ (and for older pupils with reading difficulties)	Nursery rhyme Speech Language Aural identification of 'odd word out': Condition 1 – Last sound different Condition 2 – Middle sound different Condition 3 – First sound different	Untimed (about 10′–15′)

Comments: Bradley's testing procedures are based on research evidence indicating that the ability of children to categorise sounds is an important predictor of both later reading and spelling attainments. It is claimed that training can improve sound categorisation skills and also attainments in reading and spelling. The assessment of children's ability to categorise sounds is carried out using, initially, an informal task based on nursery rhymes and leading to a word game in which the child is required to identify the 'odd word out' in sets of four orally presented words. The core of both tests consists of two preliminary trials followed by eight (Test 1) and ten (Test 2) further items under each of the three conditions listed above. The introductory work is used to check on the child's articulation and hearing. For Test 1, the numbers of errors under each of the three conditions are totalled separately. Acceptable levels of error scores under each condition are given for each yearly chronological age group for children of mixed abilities aged from 5:00 to 8:00 years. Children over seven years of age who are making normal progress are not expected to make errors under Conditions 1 and 2. Test 1 identifies 'young children and backward readers or non-readers of any age who need special help with sound categorisation'. Test 2 is designed for use with 'older backward readers'. Because it contains more items, it is likely that Test 2 is more reliable than Test 1, but no indices of reliability are reported for either test. No information is given on the intercorrelations between children's scores under the three conditions, thought the relative difficulties are discussed.

In Appendix II of the 45 page manual, norms for the sound categorisation Test 1 based on 83 young children in the early stages of learning to read and spell are presented. A further table gives scores on Test 2 for 264 five year old (non-readers) and 368 eight year old pupils.

The approach to assessment and remediation places considerable stress on the importance of the teacher's observational skills and knowledge of the individual child. Suggestions for remedial activities are presented in the manual. Bradley recognises that her concern has been with only one major group of possible causes of reading difficulties. Users of the tests should bear this important restriction in mind.

TRN	Name of test	Author	Country	Publisher		Year
11	*Assessment of Reading Ability (Revised edition)*	S. Baker and C. Macpherson (eds)	B	West Sussex County Council (Education Committee Psychological Service)	2nd edition	1975

Type	No. of forms	C.A. range*	Skills tested	Time
Individual, diagnostic, keyed to attainment criteria (level A)	1	7:00 to 11:00 (or older pupils with reading difficulties) * not specified in the manual	Schonell Graded Word Reading Test R1 Diagnostic tests: 1 Test of visual discrimination 2 Tests of auditory discrimination (a) Word pairs (b) Odd-man-out 3 Tests of Phonic Ability (a) Letter sounds (b) Two and three letter words (c) Consonant blends at beginning of words (d) Consonant blends at ends of words (e) Vowel digraphs (f) Consonant digraphs (g) Silent letters and word endings (h) Multisyllabic words	Untimed

Comments: The above battery of tests has been developed by Educational Psychologists, Remedial Advisory Teachers and Trainee Educational Psychologists working in West Sussex. It forms one part of a manual on the assessment of reading ability. The diagnostic tests are quick and easy to administer. It is claimed that they give the tester sufficient information to devise a teaching programme for an individual child. The tests are in an approximate order of difficulty. By assessing a child's reading age, the tester can then decide which diagnostic tests should be used initially by referring to a table in the manual. Guidance on interpreting the results of the diagnostic testing is given together with suggestions for remedial activities.

In the first edition of this battery, information was presented concerning the performance of 145 primary school pupils, most of whom were experiencing reading difficulties, on five of the diagnostic tests. Such information is not given in the current edition. In terms of conventional standardisation procedures and technical information on test reliabilities, validities and intercorrelations, no evidence is presented for the tests. This appears to be because the areas sampled are assumed to be used as 'mastery tests'. Thus to become competent readers all children need to master the skills tested at given levels. Not all professionals would agree without evidence stronger than is provided.

TRN	Name of test	Author	Country	Publisher	Year
12	*Aston Index (Revised)*	M. Newton and M. Thomson	B	Learning Development Aids	1982

Type	No. of forms	C.A. range	Skills tested	Time
Individual, diagnostic (level A)	1 (Levels 1 & 2 require different combinations of sub-tests from the battery)	5:06+ (Level 1) 7:00+ (Level 2)	General underlying ability and attainment: 1 Picture recognition (Level 1 only) 2 Vocabulary scale (Levels 1 & 2) *3 Goodenough 'Draw-a-man' Test (Levels 1 & 2) 4 Copying geometric designs (Levels 1 & 2) 5 Grapheme/phoneme correspondence (Levels 1 & 2) 6 Schonell Graded Word Reading Test R1 or other reading test (Level 2 only) *7 Schonell Graded Word Spelling Test B or other spelling test (Level 2 only) Performance items: 8 Visual discrimination (Levels 1 & 2) 9 Child's laterality (Levels 1 & 2) 10 Copying name (Level 1 only) *11 Free writing (Level 2 only) 12 Visual sequential memory (pictorial) (Levels 1 & 2) 13 Auditory sequential memory (Levels 1 & 2) 14 Sound blending (Levels 1 & 2) 15 Visual sequential memory (symbolic) (Levels 1 & 2) 16 Sound discrimination (Levels 1 & 2) 17 Grapho-motor test (Level 2 only) * Group administration, if required	Level 1 Untimed (about 45′) Level 2 Untimed (about 60′)

Comments: The major purposes of the *Index* are to assist classroom teachers in the early identification of children who are at risk educationally and to suggest constructive interventions. The *Index* can be used as a screening device for the first purpose, enabling teachers to assess an important range of skills shown by earlier research as necessary for literacy (Newton *et al.*, 1978). It can also be used to 'predict possible "barriers to learning" in the individual child' (Handbook, p. 1). Level 1 is intended for use after the child has been at school for about six months. Its purpose is to diagnose potential language problems. Level 2 is designed for use with older children who do not appear to be coping with reading, spelling and writing as adequately as the teacher might expect. No mention is made of those pupils who are doing better work than the teacher expected. There are usually some and the simultaneous consideration of both groups might be more illuminating than concentration on only one. The nature of a child's particular learning pattern can be *indicated* by the profile of results that represents the summary of the diagnostic testing, provided that information obtained from sub-tests not included in the profile together with an awareness by the teacher of (at least) six important general factors which may hinder learning, can be brought together. The profile of 'General underlying ability and attainment' uses chronological age plus sub-tests 2, 3, 6 and 7 together with measures of mental age and attainment. The 'Performance items' profile uses sub-tests 12, 13, 14, 15 and 16. It is suggested that eight types of learning patterns, four prefaced by the adjective "specific", may be identified. A list of materials designed to develop skills in the areas tested by the Index is provided. Thus testing is linked to teaching, although evidence on the efficacy of this particular diagnostic teaching approach is not provided in the Handbook. In this respect, a simultaneous consideration of the *Aston Index* and the *Aston Portfolio* (TRN 13) is recommended.

Those who have followed the development of the Index from its experimental edition in 1974 to the present, are aware of some of the research and development that has taken place. It is disappointing that the information given in the Handbook on the construction, standardisation and validation of the *Index* is so meagre. Brief reference is made to the use of the Level 2 battery with groups (sizes unspecified) of children succeeding and failing respectively in written language work at school. There is also a brief report on the follow-up of a group (size unspecified) of pupils aged initially 5:06 years. Mean scores for five of the sub-tests are given for each year group aged from 5:00 to 11:00. Again, the sizes of the samples and their characteristics are not given. The disclaimer that the norms 'should not be interpreted too rigidly' is correct, but hardly helpful. The discriminating power of some of the sub-tests are shown but the ones listed do not all match those listed above. Correlations between reading, spelling, writing and eleven Index scores are given for an experimental and a control group combined. Presumably the groups contained poor and competent performers in written language. A comparison of the correlation matrices for the two separate groups would have been more illuminating. The split-half reliabilities of six of the sub-tests whose reliabilities had not been established elsewhere, are given. These range between 0·86 and 0·95, but neither the size nor age of the group is specified. The advice on profile interpretation makes no mention of the need for a simultaneous consideration of both sub-test reliabilities and intercorrelations if the user is not to be misled by a visually presented profile of scores (Pumfrey, 1977). Interpretation is still largely dependent on the clinical skills and knowledge of the user of the *Index*. Whilst some progress has undoubtedly been made in meeting criticisms of earlier versions, a great deal of further work remains to be done if the Index is to fulfill its authors' intentions. 'The *Aston Index* represents just a beginning in awareness that certain neuropsychological correlates of "language and the brain" would need to be taken into account when trying to understand the individual differences in learning style of our school children' (personal communication, 1983).

NEWTON, M. J., THOMSON, M. E. and RICHARDS, I. R. (1978) *Readings in Dyslexia: A Study Text to accompany the Aston Index*. London: LDA Heinemann.

PUMFREY, P. D. (1977) *Measuring Reading Abilities: Concepts, Sources and Applications*. London: Hodder and Stoughton (obtainable from the author at the University of Manchester).

TRN	Name of test	Author	Country	Publisher	Year
13	*Aston Portfolio Assessment Checklist*	C. Aubrey, J. Eaves, C. Hicks and M. Newton	B	Learning Development Aids 2nd impression	1981 1982

Type	No. of forms	C.A. range	Skills tested		Time
Individual, diagnostic	1	5:06+	Spelling checklist:		Untimed
			Auditory, Letter/Word	(4)*	
			Visual, A Letters	(2)	
			B Words	(5)	
			Auditory-visual	(7)	
			Reading checklist:		
			Visual, A Letters	(4)	
			B Words	(6)	
			Auditory, A Letters	(5)	
			B Words	(3)	
			Visual-auditory	(4)	
			Advanced reading skills·	(3)	
			Written expression skills checklist:		
			Aston Index Vocabulary Scale	(4)	
			Handwriting skills		
(level A)			Comprehension skills		

Comments: The *Aston Portfolio Assessment Checklist* represents an attempt at making the diagnostic teaching of reading a reality for classroom teachers. It is packaged in a box about 230 × 135 × 110 mm. containing a 26-page manual, assessment cards, assessment checklists and teaching cards. The system is intended for use with children in the ordinary classroom 'with specific reading, spelling and writing problems (e.g. dyslexia)' (Manual, p. 4). To use the material it is suggested that one needs to identify children who, for no apparent reason, are underachieving in reading and spelling. A rule-of-thumb means of locating such children is given. It is based on the teacher's knowledge of the child's verbal and non-verbal skills and on the child's ability to grasp new concepts quickly. Attainments markedly below intellectual ability are the central focus for the teacher. By asking questions listed on the assessment cards an initial assessment of the child is completed. The teacher will have ringed numbers on the child's assessment checklist indicating skills that the child may not have acquired. These numbers link directly to sub-tests contained in the second part of the assessment checklist. The child is then tested on these. If he fails to meet the criterion specified, further references on the assessment checklist direct the teacher to teaching cards that may be used. The same end may be achieved by using the results obtained from administering the *Aston Index* (TRN 12).

The teaching programmes were developed during a small-scale experiment involving 'teaching sub-types of dyslexic children on different remedial programmes, in order to identify the most effective method' (Manual, p. 23) (Hicks, 1980). Four groups of six children were taught for two hours per morning for 20 weeks. The mean progress of the groups (gain scores) were compared. It was concluded that the use of 'a strength-orientated approach whenever possible as the basic teaching method and remediating the specific weakness areas in a continuing supportive programme' was the most promising approach (Manual, p. 24).

The validity of the assessment card-assessment checklist identification procedure is likely to receive considerable attention. The reliabilities and validities of the sub-tests are not reported. To date nothing is said about the identification of 'false positives' and 'false negatives'. Such issues are embedded in the controversy concerning the nature of underachievement. At present there seems no imminent professional agreement on how it should be measured. There are many teachers who question the importance of the ability-attainment disparity that is central to the assessment checklist. Despite such comments, both the *Portfolio* and the *Index* appear popular with teachers according to sales figures that have been given. In the crucible of the classroom and clinic, their metal will be tested.

HICKS, C. M. (1980) Modality preference and the teaching of reading and spelling to dyslexic children. *British Educational Research Journal*, **6**, 2, 175–87.

TRN	Name of test	Author	Country	Publisher	Year
20	*Ballard Reading Tests*	P. B. Ballard	B	University of London Press Ltd	1920

Type	No. of forms	C.A. range	Skills tested	Time
Individual, oral attainment	1	5:06 to 16:00	One Minute Reading Test (speed of reading simple words)	1′
Group or individual attainment	1	9:00 to 14:00	Silent Reading Test	3′
			Completion Test	Untimed
			Silent Reading (B)	15′
(level A)				

Comments: The above tests represent important approaches to the assessment of speed of reading and comprehension. The standardisation and normative data are relatively unsophisticated but allow cautious comparison of children's current attainments on these tests with those on whom the data was collected. The 'One Minute Test' might appeal to a teacher's sense of economy, but has some inherent weaknesses affecting its reliability and validity. The second and third tests employ what is currently called 'cloze' test procedure, in which the child must fill in missing words in a section of writing.

Ballard's books are now out of print, but are usually available in any library of books for teachers: *Mental Tests* (1920), *The New Examiner* (1923), *Group Tests of Intelligence* (2nd edition, 1923), all London: University of London Press Ltd.

This entry is left in both because of its historical interest and because of the unexplored potential in some of Ballard's ideas.

TRN	Name of test	Author	Country	Publisher	Year
21	*Bangor Dyslexia Test*	T. R. Miles	B	Learning Development Aids	1983

Type	No. of forms	C.A. range	Skills tested		Time
Individual, diagnostic (level A)	1	7:00+ (excluding children 'of limited ability')	1 Left-right (body parts) 2 Repeating polysyllabic words 3 Subtraction 4 Tables 5 Months forwards	6 Months reversed 7 Digits forwards 8 Digits reversed 9 b–d confusion 10 Familial incidence	Untimed

Comments: Professor Miles' involvement in the field of dyslexia is well known and documented (Miles, 1983). This test is the result of many years of clinical work with children, generally of above-average ability, who have experienced severe and prolonged difficulties in various aspects of literacy and numeracy. The instrument is offered as a way of advancing understanding of the child's difficulties. It is *not* intended as a 'means of definitive diagnosis' (Manual, p. 1). The scoring criteria for the sub-tests are intended only as a guide. It is suggested that after having used 'the test a few times you may prefer to rely on your overall impression rather than on the subject's precise score. Good sense is more important than numerical impression' (Manual, p. 1). The importance of 'incongruities' in performances on the sub-tests is seen as crucial in deciding whether a child is, is not, or is partially dyslexic. The significance of the incongruities is determined by the particular case. These points indicate that there are many unspecified sources of error variance that are likely to reduce the validity of any appraisal. It must be born in mind that the test is a clinical diagnostic instrument although anyone in the 'helping' professions can use the test. The contrasting performances of three samples of Dyslexic and Control pupils at ages 7 to 8 (N = 21), 9 to 12 (N = 80) and 13 to 18 (N = 31) are presented to show that significant differences exist between the mean number out of seven diagnostic indicators present. Age allowances in the marking system are given for only four of the sub-tests. The irrelevance of such an allowance in respect of other sub-tests is not established.

Technical details of the construction and validation of the test are not given in the manual. To find this one must turn to the book listed below. The reliabilities and validities of the sub-tests are not sufficiently reported in either the book or the manual.

The concentration on pupils of average and above ability poses many conceptual problems. One relatively small point that undermines further confidence in this test are the differences between the test and its scoring procedure given in the book and the separately published test and manual. It may be that dyslexia is usefully construed as a syndrome in which symptoms are regularly associated without the assumption that there is a particular causal relationship. It is possible that Miles' test begins to delineate the parameters of the syndrome. On the evidence presented, it is difficult to be convinced of this. Much more work needs to be done on the test.

MILES, T. R. (1983) *Dyslexia: The Pattern of Difficulties*. London: Collins Educational.

TRN	Name of test	Author	Country	Publisher	Year
22	*Barking Reading Project Test Battery*	Staff of Barking and Dagenham LEA Schools' Psychological Service in cooperation with University College, London	B	Barking and Dagenham LEA	1981/2

Type	No. of forms	C.A. range	Skills tested	Time
Individual, screening, diagnostic (level A)	1	6:00 to 7:00 (Provisional norms)	Word retention Concepts and vocabulary of reading instruction Letter knowledge Visual sequential memory Visual matching: (i) Word forms (ii) Orientation (iii) Detail Sounds in words Auditory sequential memory Sound blending Grapho-motor Attitude and motivation Early phonic knowledge: 1 Letter sounds; 2 Common digraphs; 3 Consonant-vowel consonant blends; 4 b/d confusion; 5 Double consonant endings; 6 'ee' and 'oo'; 7 End blends; 8 Magic 'e'; 9 Initial blends	Untimed

Comments: Screening techniques and supporting teaching materials for use by class teachers so as to provide 'individualised help directed at the children who need it' were developed in pilot work over several years. In recognition of its promise, the Department of Education and Science funded a research project under the joint directorship of G. Trickey, Principal Educational Psychologist of the LEA, and Dr R. Maliphant of University College, London. The following comments and the above details refer to the University College revision.

The system provides a continuous cycle of assessment and teaching. 'The assessment and programming elements of the scheme are fully integrated so that each child's individual pattern of strengths and weaknesses can be reflected in the learning experiences provided.' Significantly, attitude and motivation are specifically considered.

The battery of criterion-referenced tests assembled was determined by their utility in providing information helpful in designing a reading programme suited to children's needs. The battery encourages teachers to formulate and test successive hypotheses concerning a child's reading difficulties. A profile of a child's skills summarises his relative strengths and weaknesses on the first eleven of the above tests. The relationships between these were carefully considered, although as yet the empirical data obtained subsequently are not publicly available.

Provisional norms in the Assessment Manual are based on a number (unspecified) of children aged 6:00 to 7:00 years whose word-reading ages on the Carver *Word Recognition Test* (TRN 199) were below their chronological ages. Raw scores are converted to 'ability levels' on a five-point scale for each sub-test of the battery. Preliminary evidence suggests that the linking of assessment and instruction using the extensive materials developed has enhanced the reading attainments of the pupils involved.

The use of criterion-referenced tests is beset with conceptual problems. At this early stage the detailed technical data on standardisation of the tests, the empirical intercorrelations between the sub-tests, the reliabilities and validities of the sub-tests and the long-term effects of the system are not publicly available either. Doubtless they will be. 'We have a mass of statistical data on the procedures' (personal communication, 1982). Already the project, its test battery, teaching materials and rationale have aroused considerable attention. Papers have been presented at a number of meetings and have also been published in professional journals.

In a subsequent personal communication (14 September 1983), the Principal Educational Psychologist responsible for the project informed the reviewer that commercial publication of the battery and associated materials was under discussion. The demand for the materials is 'considerable'. Local publication of the materials is seen as an 'attractive alternative to commercial publication' and is likely to precede the latter. The demand has been such that the then current set of materials has been totally taken up by local demand. The description given in the preceding paragraphs is based on the set of materials available to the reviewer in 1982.

TRN	Name of test	Author	Country	Publisher	Year
29	*Bowman Test of Reading Competence*	A. J. Bowers and M. Mann	B	Science Research Associates	1980

Type	No. of forms	C.A. range	Skills tested	Time
Group, attainment, diagnostic (level A)	1	7:10 to 10:09	Reading comprehension Subscores: Semantic Syntactic	Untimed (about 20′)

Comments: The test is based on cloze procedure. Its novelty lies in the separate assessment of semantic and syntactic abilities in the context of a reading comprehension task. It aims to identify disparities between these two aspects of comprehension whilst still providing normative data on each. The deletion policy adopted in each of the four graded passages comprising the test was not random, but intended 'to represent as many areas of syntactic and semantic significance as possible' (Manual, p. 3).

The test was standardised on a sample of 2 393 pupils aged 7 : 07 to 11 : 04 drawn to provide a representative cross-section of attainments 'from inner-city, suburban and semi-rural communities' (Manual, p. 3). Eight LEAs and 25 schools were involved. Using a sample of 166 pupils retested after a two week interval, a test-retest reliability coefficient of 0·95 was obtained. Internal consistency reliability using Kuder-Richardson formula 21 on a sample of 2 331 was 0·94. The standard error of measurement at each of twelve age levels are given. These range between 2·9 and 3·5 points. Evidence of validity is limited, particularly in relation to the diagnostic function the test is designed to fulfill. Concurrent validity using the SPAR Reading Test (TRN 176) with a sample of 174 pupils gave a correlation of 0·86.

Marking is made quite easy by the use of templates. To position the template, extra 'windows' are provided. These show the title of the passage, the initial and the final words. On the stencil for page 4, there is no 'window' revealing the final word. Overall raw scores cán be converted to Reading Comprehension Ages or to reading quotients with a mean of 100 and standard deviation of fifteen for each three months chronological age group. The quotients allow comparisons with age peers only. The semantic and syntactic sub-scores can be converted to T scores. Tables are provided to allow the significance of any disparity to be evaluated, taking into account the reliabilities of the scales and their intercorrelations at each of six different age levels. The probability levels of 0·02 and 0·01 will seem insufficiently cautious to some users. If this test sensitises teachers to the importance of helping children to use different textual cues when reading, it will have served a useful purpose. Precisely what should be done about any semantic/syntactic disparity, even if one is reliably identified, remains controversial despite the suggestions in the manual for improving comprehension skills through contextual analysis.

TRN	Name of test	Author	Country	Publisher	Year
31	*Burt Reading Tests 1–5*	C. Burt	B	Staples Press	1921

Type	No. of forms	C.A. range	Skills tested	Time
Individual, oral	1	5:00 to 14:00	T(1) Graded Vocabulary Test (Accuracy) (110 items)	Untimed
Individual or group, oral	1	5:00+	T(2) Knowledge of Letters and Figures (52 and 46 items)	Untimed
Individual, oral	1	6:00 to 14:00	T(3) Two and three letter monosyllables (200 items)	Timed and Untimed
Individual, silent	1	5:00 to 14:00	T(4) Graded Directions Test (Comprehension) (17 items)	Untimed
Individual	1	7:00 to 14:00	T(5) Continuous Prose Test (Speed, Accuracy and Comprehension)	Timed
(level A)				

Comments: These were some of the earliest reading tests devised in Britain. The standardisation and norms are understandably not comparable in sophistication with many tests available today. Yet because Burt gives data concerning the performances of children on these tests in the 1920s, the tests can help the teacher of reading appreciate what was achieved in schools at that time. The insight into the nature of the reading process shown by Burt and the importance of particular aspects of it in the teaching of reading to children are worthy of any teacher's attention. The tests are available in *Mental and Scholastic Tests* published by Staples Press (4th edition, 1962). Almost any library of books for teachers will contain a copy.

TRN	Name of test	Author	Country	Publisher	Year
32	*Burt (Rearranged) Word Reading Test*	C. Burt, revised by P. E. Vernon	B	Hodder and Stoughton	1938 to 1975

Type	No. of forms	C.A. range	Skills tested	Time
Individual, oral	1	5:00 to 14:00	Word recognition	Untimed (10′)
(level A)				

Comments: In 1938 Vernon restandardised Burt's original word recognition test for use with Scottish children. It was found necessary to rearrange the order of some of the words. The 110-word 'rearranged' test was yet again restandardised in 1954 on 6 000 Edinburgh children aged from five to twelve years, and revised norms were published in 1967. The test is of doubtful value at its extremes as the initial and final ten words were arbitrarily selected to represent the ages, i.e. reading ages of four to five years and over fourteen years. The test's greatest weakness is the use of a relatively small number of items to represent a considerable change in reading attainments, one year of reading age being covered by only ten words. The ease with which raw scores can be converted to Reading Ages is a practice which appeals to teachers. Provided they are aware of the increase of variability of reading test scores from age group to age group, the inappropriate normative comparison of children can be avoided. The test manual produced by Vernon gives details of the test's revision and discusses the differences in reading attainments in English and Scottish schools.

In 1972, Eric Shearer, an educational psychologist in Cheshire, started work on updating the word order of the test. He has also produced new norms based on a representative sample of 6 000 children aged from just below five up to eleven years. These norms are currently available and according to Shearer should accurately represent contemporary national standards (Shearer and Apps, 1975).

In 1974 the Scottish Council for Research in Education undertook their own revision of the Vernon restandardisation (see TRN 33).

SHEARER, E. and APPS, R. (1975) 'A restandardisation of the Burt-Vernon and Schonell Word Reading Tests.' *Educational Research*, **18**, 1, 67–73.

TRN	Name of test	Author	Country	Publisher	Year
33	*Burt Word Reading Test 1974 revision*	Scottish Council for Research in Education	B	Hodder and Stoughton for the Scottish Council for Research in Education	1976

Type	No. of forms	C.A. range	Skills tested	Time
Individual, oral, attainment, normative (level A)	1	6:00 to 12:00	Word recognition	Untimed (about 10′)

Comments: This test is a revision of a restandardisation carried out thirty-six years before (Vernon, 1938). A representative sample of 2 200 Scottish primary school children was tested in June 1974. Pupils attending special schools, grant-aided and independent schools were excluded. The result was that the word order was revised and new norms were obtained for the test. Internal consistency reliability coefficients of 0·975 and 0·971 were obtained using Kuder-Richardson formula 20. The manual does not give the sizes of the samples from which the reliability estimates were calculated.

No reading ages below a raw score of 27 are given. Percentiles are presented for the end of each school year from Primary One to Primary Seven. Raw Scores above 27 can be converted into equivalent reading ages. Published in 1976, the *Burt Word Reading Test 1974 revision* supersedes all previous versions for use in Britain.

The most recent re-ordering and restandardisation of this test was published in New Zealand in 1981 (TRN 34).

VERNON, P. E. (1938) *The Standardisation of a Graded Word Reading Test.* Scottish Council for Research in Education Publication XII. London: University of London Press Ltd.

TRN	Name of test	Author	Country	Publisher	Year
35	*Cassell's Linked English Tests*	D. S. Higgins	B	Cassell Educational	1977

Type	No. of forms	C.A. range	Skills tested		Time
Group, attainment, normative and diagnostic (level A)	2 (A & B)	9:06 to 12:06	Spelling, Linguistics, Vocabulary, Punctuation, Comprehension	5 attainment tests 5 diagnostic tests	35′ untimed

Comments: The integration of assessment, diagnosis and instruction is the central aim of this set of materials. The system is devised so as to lead to an individually prescribed programme of instruction matched to the pupil's strengths and weaknesses. The attainment tests are used to determine whether pupils should take one or more of five diagnostic tests corresponding to the five areas tested. In turn, the diagnostic tests are linked to five workbooks. Dependent on the pupil's performance on a diagnostic test, he/she can be directed to specific sections of the workbooks.

The manual for the attainment tests includes advice on using a marking grid, which is printed on each pupil's test booklet, in order to identify strengths and weaknesses. A second manual accompanies the diagnostic tests. It includes a discussion of the skills involved in the tests and suggests instructional activities. The sections dealing with what the author has, with explicit reservations, called 'Linguistic' includes nine aspects of language: the use of tense, pronouns, compound sentences, stylistic features of language, syntax and construction.

Unfortunately, the standardisation of the attainment tests is not adequately described, nor are the reliabilities and validities of the attainment tests presented. No empirical evidence is given supporting the criterion scores used in the diagnostic tests to make decisions concerning instruction. The efficacy of the scheme in improving attainments is not substantiated. The system has considerable possibilities but further work is required before potential users can feel confident that it should be adopted.

TRN	Name of test	Author	Country	Publisher	Year
36	*Charteris Reading Test*	Moray House College of Education	B	Hodder and Stoughton	1985

Type	No. of forms	C.A. range	Skills tested	Time
Group, attainment (level A)	1	10:00 to 12:11	Reading comprehension	60′

Comments: These notes were written before full technical details of the above test were available to the reviewer. The test is designed to provide an assessment for pupils at the top of the primary school and in the early years of secondary education. In this respect, it complements the *Edinburgh Reading Test Stage 3* (TRN 61). Six passages of increasing length are presented. The content of these is described as Narrative/Fiction, Environmental Studies and Journalism. Each passage is accompanied by a series of various types of item testing aspects of reading comprehension. In all, the test contains 101 items.

The test has been standardised on a sample of 2 511 pupils attending schools in Scotland and on one of 2 533 attending schools in England and Wales. 'In each case the country or countries were divided into areas and representative samples of children were drawn from each area' (Manual, draft). Nine Scottish Regional Authorities were involved, and in England and Wales, one Greater London authority, two Metropolitan Borough areas and six county Education Authorities. The initial sampling was planned to use 3 000 pupils in Scotland and also in England and Wales. Absenteeism and papers returned for pupils whose ages were outside the limits of 10:00 to 13:00 years reduced the samples to the earlier figures specified above.

The differences between the scores of boys and girls were not statistically different in either sample but no figures are given for the separate age levels. Girls' mean scores were higher than those of boys. The implications when using the common set of normative tables for each of the two samples are discussed. Raw scores can be converted to standard scores with a mean of 100 and a standard deviation of 15 for three monthly bands of chronological ages. A rule of thumb method of estimating reading ages is described.

In the provisional manual to hand, the internal consistency reliability coefficients based on Kuder-Richardson formula 20 for boys and girls' scores separately and for the combined sexes in both samples are given as 0·94. The reviewer thanks the Project Director for making the above information available.

TRN	Name of test	Author	Country	Publisher	Year
38	*Classroom Observation Procedure (COP)*	Inner London Education Authority Schools Psychological Service Staff and Teachers	B	Inner London Education Authority (ILEA)	1982

Type	No. of forms	C.A. range	Skills tested		Time
Small group (N up to 5) and individual, attainments, personality, environment, combination of mastery scores and rating scales	1	6:00 to 7:00+ (for use during the first term of the child's *final* year in the infants' school; also suitable for certain older pupils with learning problems)	Writing name	Remembering groups of letters	Untimed
			Identifying shapes	Rhyming	
			Selecting colours	Initial sounds	
			Spatial arrangement	Dictation sentences	
			Pencil control	Letter names	
			Writing known words	Letter sounds	
			Auditory memory	Sound-symbol association	
			Letter formation	Word recognition	
			Figure drawings	Sound blending	
			Copying shapes	Language – structure	
			Eye-hand co-ordination	Language – expressive	
			Visual discrimination	Language – vocabulary	
			Visual memory	Reading page	
			Remembering 2 shapes	Reversals	
			Remembering 4 symbols		
			Child's personal data sheet		
		(the Behavioural observation checklists are recommended for use during the *first* years of infant education)	*Behavioural observation checklist (5 point rating scales)*		
			Motor (4 scales)	Language (3 scales)	
			Visual (2 scales)	Personality (9 scales)	
(level A)			Auditory (4 scales)	Environment (5 scales)	

Comments: The purpose of *COP* is to systematise, develop and capitalise on the class teacher's professional involvement with, observations and knowledge of her pupils in a particular group. *COP* provides data on a group's competence levels in various aspects of learning. It provides a profile of the individual pupil and also helps in identifying children who may require further assessment and extra help if their educational needs are to be met.

COP consists of four related elements. Firstly, the *COP* Workbook enables the teacher to collect and quantify objective performance data on the skills listed above. Secondly, important environmental/personal data are recorded (and some quantified). Thirdly, there is a series of Behavioural Observation Checklists using five-point rating scales. The information from all these sources is combined on a Marking Sheet covering twelve areas. These are further reduced to a ten-category Individual Learning Profile.

The result is not intended to be a normative one, but to indicate the pupil's pattern of skills, his approach to particular tasks and the strategies used. The information may provide insights that present opportunities for identifying and alleviating learning difficulties that might otherwise be overlooked. The fourth element is a set of Activity Cards loosely related to seven of the ten categories that comprise the Individual Learning Profile. These cards are a selection of ideas that have been found of value with individuals or groups by teachers who have considerable expertise in working with children having special educational needs.

COP can be criticised in that the rationale underlying the skills selected for inclusion is not spelled out. The reliabilities and validities of the scales and their inter-relationships are not discussed or presented other than in very general terms. No adequate justification is given for combining scores from five point rating scales with criterion-referenced scores. A major weakness is that a summer-born pupil whose *relative* attainments, allowing for age, equal those of an autumn-born child, receives no allowance for being younger. An *absolute* comparison by skills will show him to be less adequate than the latter. The link between the profiles and the efficacy of the suggestions contained in the Activity Cards should be empirically rather than clinically established.

On the positive side, the professional experience underpinning *COP* cannot be cast aside solely because of the preceding and important criticisms. The knowledge of experienced teachers and educational psychologists is of great importance. What is needed is a move to make public what is so often private to the clinician or remedial teacher. *COP* represents a step in that direction. As such it is to be welcomed, provided that users are sensitive to its many limitations.

TRN	Name of test	Author	Country	Publisher	Year
40	*Cloze Reading Tests*	D. Young	B	Hodder and Stoughton	1982

Type	No. of forms	C.A. range		Skills tested	Time
Group, attainment, normative (level A)	1 (at each of 3 levels)	8:00 to 10:06	(Level 1)	Reading comprehension	35′
		8:05 to 11:10	(Level 2)	Reading comprehension	35′
		9:05 to 12:06	(Level 3)	Reading comprehension	35′

Comments: The purpose of these three tests is to assess reading comprehension using cloze technique at the Junior 2, 3 and 4 levels. Each test contains 24 items.

Standardisation was based on nineteen schools collectively representative of national standards on other measures. The number of pupils used at Levels 1, 2 and 3 were N = 933, 929 and 968 respectively. Girls obtained higher median scores than boys at all three levels. The differences were 0·9, 1·5 and 1·4 points at Levels 1, 2 and 3. Young considers these differences of no practical importance for the purpose for which the tests were developed. A common set of norms for boys and girls was constructed for each age level. Within these, raw scores can be converted to standard scores having a mean of 100 and a standard deviation of 15 for each month of chronological age.

Using a sample of 93 Junior 1 pupils aged 7:06 to 8:06 years, the Level 1 test scores were calibrated using SPAR (TRN 176) reading ages. Level 2 and 3 scores of 121 secondary school pupils were calibrated using the children's scores on other (unspecified) tests, the latter providing median scores at the 13:00 year old level. Other sections of the age scale have been extended 'by means of equivalent scores . . .' (Manual, p. 15). Users are warned to be cautious in interpreting the age scales at 13:00 years and above. A similar caution is required when using the lower extension of the scale. Teachers find reading age scales understandable and of use.

Using Kuder-Richardson formula 20, internal consistency coefficients of reliability of 0·937, 0·936 and 0·941 are reported for Levels 1, 2 and 3 based on the data used in the item analysis. Reliability estimates based on a different sample would have been more appropriate. No information on test-retest reliability is given. Concurrent validity, the correlation between scores on the three levels of the *Cloze Reading Tests* and three other established tests of reading comprehension are given for two samples (N = 88, 87). All indices were above 0·81. Correlations with spelling tests are given for three samples (N = 87, 109 and 119). Indices are all significant and all above 0·729.

TRN	Name of test	Author	Country	Publisher	Year
43	*Comprehension Test for College of Education Students*	E. L. Black	B	NFER-Nelson	1962

Type	No. of forms	C.A. range	Skills tested	Time
Attainment mainly, but with diagnostic possibilities (level P)	1	18:00+	Reading comprehension	60′

Comments: The two main purposes of this test were to help in selecting students for entry to Colleges of Education and, secondly, to identify areas of weakness in which help might be provided to improve a student's skills. In the test, seven passages of reading are each followed by between seven and eleven questions, totalling sixty items in all. Multiple-choice type questions predominate.

The test was standardised in 1953 on a sample of 697 men and 911 women students in their first term at certain Colleges of Education. The internal consistency reliability of the test is high, $r = 0{\cdot}939$. Satisfactory evidence of predictive validity is presented.

Recent research has suggested that the scores of College of Education students have declined significantly since 1953. This is a matter of some importance which requires further study.

TRN	Name of test	Author	Country	Publisher	Year
45	*Development of Reading and Related Skills with pupils of Secondary age (DORRS)*	Inner London Education Authority Working Party (Chairman: M. C. Roe)	B	Inner London Education Authority Learning Materials Service	1981

Type	No. of forms	C.A. range	Skills tested		Time
Individual, diagnostic, criterion-referenced (level A)	1	11:00 to 18:00	*Checklist:* 1 Motor 2 Visual 3 Auditory 4 Language 5 Study skills	*Additional procedures:* 1 Informal reading inventory A Attitude to reading B Visual factors C Auditory factors D Language and understanding *2 Readability assessment *3 Cloze procedure	Untimed

Comments: *DORRS* is an observation-assessment-instruction system developed over three years by an ILEA Working Party. The system capitalises on the knowledge and experience of its members, their colleagues and the extensive resources of the ILEA (probably the best funded education authority in Britain). *DORRS* consists of three major elements: the Teacher's Manual, a Resource Materials Manual and a set of Activity Cards. The Teacher's Manual provides guidance on assessment of pupils' abilities, the planning of teaching activities related to a pupil's assessed difficulties, and the keeping of records. The Resource Materials Manual classifies, describes and grades a wide range of books and other resources pertinent to the development of reading and related skills. The Activity Cards provide teaching suggestions in various fields at four levels of complexity. *DORRS* is designed for pupils whose difficulties in reading, writing, spelling, language and related skills may be general or specific. Referring to the first of these, the pattern of assessment aims to (i) discover children who require special help in reading, (ii) suggest the type of help that the class teacher can provide and (iii) identify those pupils who may require more specialist help.

Initially, the use of a group test for screening is recommended, followed by individual assessments dependent on the child's level of attainment and field(s) of difficulty. Planning the remedial programme is based on a six areas by five levels taxonomy of developmental literacy skills. The teacher's observation and knowledge of the pupil is summarised by completing a checklist covering the five fields listed above but further divided into 29 separate four point scales. Using the Guide to the Activity Cards, the teacher can identify activities appropriate to the individual pupil's checklist profile. The system is easy to use and directly relates assessment to teaching.

No evidence is given concerning the reliabilities, validities and intercorrelations between the scales of the Checklist. The efficacy of the interventions suggested is not supported by empirical evidence. Presumably such information may be provided at a later date.

The 'Additional procedures' contain important approaches to the assessment of both pupils and materials. As such they will help widen the professional background of many teachers. *DORRS* is likely to become popular with many secondary school teachers. It represents a potential enhancement of their professional repertoire. Not the least of its advantages is that it is sufficiently flexible not to stifle teachers' imagination and ingenuity in facilitating pupils' learning.

* Appendix G, Teacher's Manual.

TRN	Name of test		Author		Country	Publisher	Year
49	*Diagnostic Spelling Test*		D. Vincent and J. Claydon		B	NFER-Nelson	1982
Type		**No. of forms**	**C. A. range**	**Skills tested**			**Time**
Group, attainment, diagnostic, normative (level A)		2 (Forms A & B)	7:08 to 11:08	Spelling: 1 Homophones 2 Common words 3 Proof-reading 4 Letter strings 5 Nonsense words 6 Dictionary use 7 Self-concept Dictation			Untimed (about 5′) (about 10′) (about 5′) (about 10′) (about 7′) Timed: 8″ per word Paced by Teacher No estimate given

Comments: The purpose of this test is to identify groups and individuals who are poor spellers and to assess the extent of their problems. It is claimed that a qualitative appraisal of performances on the various sub-tests is a first stage in understanding the nature of a child's spelling difficulties and in providing constructive interventions. This is an assertion rather than a fact.

The test was standardised on a sample of over 4 000 children aged 7:08 to 11:08. This group attended schools selected to approximate a national sample. A total raw score can be converted to a standard score with a mean of 100 and a standard deviation of 15 for each monthly chronological age group. Thus children's relative spelling performance is assessed against peers of the same age. The sub-tests intercorrelate quite highly with the exception of the Self-concept sub-test. The factor analyses reported are interpreted as confirming the unitary nature of spelling as measured by the spelling test. Internal consistency reliability coefficients obtained using Kuder-Richardson formula 20 with sub-tests 1–6 (combined) in Forms A and B were both 0·95. Test 7 was less internally consistent, with a coefficient of 0·77. A split-half analysis of the Dictation based on the number of errors in each half gave $r = 0{\cdot}93$ using a random sample of 400 scripts drawn from the standardisation sample. Corrected for length, this rises to 0·96. Test-retest reliability using ninety third-year junior school pupils tested in the morning and afternoon was 0·95. For sub-test 7 the coefficient was 0·72. Validity was tested using 422 pupils by correlating errors in free writing with scores from sub-tests in their original and unrefined form. For sub-scales 1–6 these ranged from 0·51 to 0·70. For sub-test 7 the coefficient was lower at 0·31. A much smaller study (N = 25) compared errors made in class exercise books, dictation and free-writing with scores on the *Diagnostic Spelling Test*. Correlations with sub-tests 1–6 ranged from 0·69 to 0·83. Self-concept correlated with the three indices cited earlier at 0·66, 0·72 and 0·66. Errors made in copying continuous prose showed no relationship with either combined score on sub-tests 1–6 or on sub-test 7.

Without further details of the factor analyses carried out on Form A and Form B, the meanings of the loadings presented are not as clear as the authors suggest. This is not unimportant. If spelling ability as measured by this test is unitary, what is the justification in giving teaching suggestions relating to the sub-tests? The case could, to advantage, have been more clearly made. There is a strong one.

TRN	Name of test	Author	Country	Publisher	Year
51	*Domain Phonic Tests and Workshop*	J. McLeod and J. Atkinson	B	Oliver and Boyd	1972

Type	No. of forms	C.A. range	Skills tested	Time
Group and individual, criterion-referenced, diagnostic (level A)	1	5:00 to 11:00	P1 Single consonants and single vowels P2 Single consonant followed by vowel blend P3 Consonant blends and single vowels P4 Vowel blends and consonant blends P5 Phonemic discrimination test	Untimed (about 10′ per test)

Comments: The aim of these tests is to enable the teacher to identify any difficulty a child might have with single-letter sounds, short and long vowels and with consonant and vowel blends. These tests are constructed by combining single vowels and consonants and the most frequently used vowel blends and consonant blends, such that each phonic unit is represented in several different words. Related to the tests is a series of exercises intended to remedy phonic weaknesses identified by the tests.

The tests appear to be based on a logical analysis of elementary phonics of importance in early reading. No evidence of reliabilities, validities or standardisation is given. In these respects the tests are similar to Jackson's *Phonic Skills* Tests. A claim based on experience rather than formal experiment is made for the effectiveness of the remedial exercises provided in the Workshop.

Performance is recorded on a grid that is keyed to the Workshop.

TRN	Name of test	Author	Country	Publisher	Year
59	*Edinburgh Reading Tests, Stage 1*	Godfrey Thomson Unit, University of Edinburgh	B	Hodder and Stoughton 8th impression	1977 1983

Type	No. of forms	C.A. range	Skills tested	Time
Group and individual, attainment, diagnostic, normative (level A)	2 (A & B)	7:00 to 9:00	Vocabulary Syntax Sequences Comprehension	'not crucial' (Manual, p. 4.) Working time about 30′ in two sessions Administration about 25′ per session

Comments: The test provides a general measure of reading comprehension. The empirical evidence presented shows that scores on all of the sub-tests are highly correlated. In such circumstances, the interpretation of a pupil's profile requires more than the visual inspection of a graph of results. The advice on profile interpretation is dealt with in a commendably clear yet appropriately cautious manner.

In standardising the test, the initial sampling was of 'representative educational authorities' (Manual, p. 28). From each of these, a random sample of schools was chosen and, within each school, a single class was selected. 2 500 children in Scotland and 3 013 in England and Wales attending state schools comprised the standardisation sample. Both administrative constraints and absenteeism affected the sampling. It remains unclear whether the standardisation sample was representative of the population of pupils attending state schools, especially if 'attending' means 'on the school roll'. Regional differences were found. The Scottish pupils scored higher, on average, than the English and Welsh pupils. Across both samples combined, the mean superiority of girls over boys was even more marked.

Separate tables of norms for boys and girls were constructed. Total raw scores on the test can be converted to standard scores with a mean of 100 and a standard deviation of 15 for each month of chronological age. Conversion of raw scores to reading ages can easily be obtained with separate norms for boys and girls. The sub-test scores can be converted to standard scores but these have no age allowance. The scores show a child's position on each sub-test in relation to the scores of the entire 7:00 to 9:00 age group.

Using Kuder-Richardson formula 20, the whole test has an internal consistency reliability coefficient of 0·946. The sub-test indices range between 0·776 and 0·842. No information on test-retest reliability, on parallel form reliability or on validities is presented. Mean scores on both forms are given, but not the correlations. Presumably the content of the test is considered adequate support for its validity as a measure of reading attainment. From the fact that an 8th impression has been printed, many members of the teaching profession must be finding it of value.

TRN	Name of test	Author	Country	Publisher	Year
60	*Edinburgh Reading Tests, Stage 2*	Godfrey Thomson Unit, University of Edinburgh	B	Hodder and Stoughton	1972
				2nd edition	1980
				6th impression	1983

Type	No. of forms	C.A. range	Skills tested	Time
Group and individual, attainment, diagnostic, normative	1	8:06 to 10:06	Practice Test (untimed)	(30′)
	1		Part 1	
			A Vocabulary	12′
			B Comprehension of sequences	12′
			C Retention of significant detail	12′
	1		Part 2	
			D Use of context	12′
			E Reading rate	2′
			F Comprehension of essential ideas	16′
(level A)			Total Score	

Comments: This was the first of the proposed four tests in the series to become available. Its purpose is to provide the teacher with information concerning children's reading attainments that will help her in adapting methods and materials to facilitate children's acquisition of reading skills. The test constructors consider reading to be a unified ability which most children tend to be good or bad at as a whole. Thus the handbook stresses great caution in the interpretation of the profiles obtained: 'most children need help right across the board, and not in one ability more than in any other' (Manual, p. 29). The test manual advocates that, for children with low scores on any sub-test (except E), the teacher can go through the test individually with the child in an attempt to discover what it was that the child found difficult: 'if he gets an answer wrong, ask him why he thinks his answer is right' (Manual, p. 29). The danger of 'teaching the test' would appear very near in such a situation. If the test were a mastery or criterion-referenced test, this might not matter. In a normative test, such an approach, if used extensively, could make future interpretation of the scores difficult.

As would be expected of the Godfrey Thomson Unit, the standardisation on both English and Scottish children is clearly reported. The total score and the sub-tests all (excepting E) have high internal consistency reliabilities. Sex differences and nationality differences in scores are discussed and reported. The manual allows conversion of raw scores into standard scores for *Total* scores only, for each month of age between 8:06 and 10:06. For the sub-tests, scores are awarded *only* to allow comparison between the different aspects of a given child's performance. Hence no age allowance is included on sub-test conversion tables. This distinction must be borne in mind by test users, or else unjustified inter-individual comparisons on sub-test scores might be made between children of different age groups. The manual is helpful on the content of the sub-scales and the interpretation that is suggested when certain items are failed.

The administration of the test requires considerable care and accurate timing.

The test is a valuable one and has been used extensively in the UK, in particular by teachers concerned with identifying and helping children with reading difficulties. The second edition (1980) consolidates the pupil's three booklets into one.

TRN	Name of test	Author	Country	Publisher		Year
61	*Edinburgh Reading Tests, Stage 3*	Moray House College of Education	B	Hodder and Stoughton	Stage 3A	1973
					2nd edition	1981
					3rd impression	1982
					Stage 3B	1982

Type	No. of forms	C.A. range	Skills tested	Time
Group and individual, attainment, diagnostic, normative	2 (3A & 3B)	10:00 to 12:06	Practice Test (untimed)	(about 35′)
			Part 1	
			A Reading for facts	10′
			B Comprehension of sequences	10′
			C Retention of main ideas	10′
			Part 2	
			D Comprehension of points of view	15′
(level A)			E Vocabulary	10′

Comments: As can be seen from the publication dates listed above, this test has a long history. Originally it was intended to give an overall measure of a child's general reading competence and also a profile for each child in the five areas indicated above. The 1973 test has been standardised on random samples of 2 865 children in Scotland and 2 793 in England and Wales, excluding children in special schools containing pupils of very low reading ability. The 1973 manual gives data on total score and sub-test reliabilities (internal consistency). Total score reliability was 0·97 and sub-test reliabilities ranged from 0·81 to 0·95. No information on test-retest reliability is given. No evidence on validities is available other than that the content validity rests on the judgment of reading experts. The second edition of 3A consolidates all test items within a single book. This is more convenient than having separate sections.

It was decided that a parallel form of the test would be valuable. Form 3B, published in 1982, was the outcome. Typically, parallel forms of a test are standardised on the same population. Clearly this could not be done with Form 3B. A separate sampling, described in some detail in the Supplementary Manual to Test Booklet B, involved 3 000 Scottish and 2 446 English and Welsh pupils. Significant differences between the mean scores of boys and girls on four of the five sub-tests were found, boys scoring higher on sub-tests A, C and E and girls on B. Scottish pupils obtained consistently and significantly higher mean scores on the five sub-tests than English and Welsh pupils. The pattern of regional differences is very similar to that obtained when Form 3A was standardised, though more marked for the girls in the 1982 test. No parallel form reliability evidence is presented. The coefficients of internal consistency using Kuder-Richardson formula 20 with scores from 283 Scottish and 301 English and Welsh pupils' scores were both 0·97. Sub-test reliabilities were, as is to be expected, somewhat lower within the range 0·83 to 0·91. The basis of the test's validity is the same as for Form 3A.

On both forms, children's raw scores can be converted to reading quotients with a mean of 100 and a standard deviation of 15. Because of the regional differences noted earlier, separate norms are provided for Scottish and for

Continued at foot of p. 121

TRN	Name of test	Author	Country	Publisher	Year
62	*Edinburgh Reading Tests, Stage 4*	Godfrey Thompson Unit, University of Edinburgh	B	Hodder and Stoughton 7th impression	1977 1983

Type	No. of forms	C.A. range	Skills tested		Time
Group and individual, attainment, diagnostic, normative (level A)	1	12:00 to 16:00	(Session 1)	Skimming	8′
				Vocabulary	12′
				Reading for facts	10′
			(Session 2)	Points of view	15′
				Comprehension	15′

Comments: The five sub-tests require an hour's on-task time. This is divided into two sessions. The test provides an overall score plus a profile. The test was standardised using a multi-stage sampling procedure described in the manual. This involved 2282 Scottish and 2216 English and Welsh pupils. The final sample was not as large as originally intended and two authorities refused to collaborate. Whether this has affected the representativeness of the standardisation sample is not made clear.

Girls score slightly higher than boys on the test, especially at the lower end of the ability range. Scottish pupils obtain significantly higher mean scores than English and Welsh pupils. Separate tables of norms are provided for the two groups. A combined but considerably condensed table of norms is given in an appendix. Raw scores can be converted to standardised scores with a mean of 100 and a standard deviation of 15 for each monthly age group of Scottish and of English and Welsh pupils. Reading ages can also be obtained. Standardised scores can be obtained for the sub-test scores. The reliability of the whole test, based on Kuder-Richardson formula 20, was 0·956. For the sub-tests these indices ranged between 0·732 (Comprehension) and 0·911 (Vocabulary). The relatively high intercorrelation of the sub-tests requires that profiles be interpreted with considerable caution. Appropriately cautious yet constructive suggestions are given in the manual as to how this can be done. An analysis of the content of the items is given together with suggestions concerning the interpretation of particularly high or low scores.

English and Welsh pupils. Reading ages can also be obtained. Raw scores on sub-tests can be converted to standard scores but without any age allowance. Advice is given on the interpretation of the profiles. The high intercorrelations between the sub-tests on both forms suggest that a common core of reading abilities is sampled by them. The problems of interpretation that this poses are dealt with in the manual.

In conclusion, the format of 3A and 3B are identical. It is interesting to note changes in the content used. Paragraphs on Astronomy and Bees are replaced by ones about Oil and Steel. Lest it be thought that the changes were all in the same direction, a paragraph on Local Politics in the 1973 Form 3A is replaced in the 1982 version by one on Orpheus and Eurydice.

TRN	Name of test	Author	Country	Publisher	Year
63	*Edwards' Reading Test*	P. Edwards (UK edition prepared by R. Nichols)	B/A	Heinemann Educational	1980

Type	No. of forms	C.A. range	Skills tested	Time
Individual, attainment and diagnostic (level A)	1	6:00 to 13:00	Quick word screen test (accuracy) Oral reading: comprehension accuracy speed Silent reading: comprehension speed Listening comprehension Word list (100): reading spelling	Not specified

Comment: First published in Australia in 1976, the UK version of this test appeared in 1980. The authors claim that it will 'enable the teacher to evaluate reading skills in different situations in oral and silent reading'. By establishing a child's reading level, the selection of suitable material for the child's reading programme is facilitated.

The terminology of the Informal Reading Inventory is used. Children's performances on four of the five tests can be related to Instructional and, for some indices, Independent reading levels. For each of the first four tests, 'satisfactory' scores are given indicating performances at Instructional levels. The final test comprises the 100 most frequently found words in English prose. The pupil's ability to read and spell these provides indices of what is known and what needs to be learned. It is suggested in the manual that children having an uneven profile for comprehension, accuracy and speed of reading can be identified. However, the criteria for an uneven profile are not made clear. Nor are the implications for remedial instruction clearly linked to the profile information. Reference is made to a separate book by Edwards in which it is claimed that this is dealt with. Evidence for the efficacy of such procedures is not presented in the test manual.

The test manual can be criticised on two major counts. Firstly, no technical data are given on how and why the tests were selected and constructed. Admittedly, references are provided for those wishing to know more and having the time and energy to follow-up the references. Omitting such information from the manual itself can be seen as a somewhat cavalier attitude towards the professional development of teachers of reading if it is considered that they should become increasingly informed and critical in selecting reading tests for particular purposes. Secondly, no mention is made of trials with British pupils to ascertain the validity of the criteria specified for the 'acceptable' scores on which the teacher is encouraged to make important pedagogic decisions.

Finally, in the reprinted (1981) manual before me, pages 5 to 8 are duplicated. It is not assumed that this is necessarily so in all copies of the manual. A further minor detail eroding confidence is that in the Introduction to the manual, test administration page references are all incorrect (by 1).

TRN	Name of test	Author	Country	Publisher		Year
66	*Framework for Reading*	J. Dean and R. Nichols	B	Evans		1974
				Bell and Hyman	2nd edition	1985

Type	No. of forms	C.A. range	Skills tested	Time
Individual, group, diagnostic (level A)	1	Not specified (apparently for the primary age range and also for any children experiencing difficulties in reading)	Check List 1:* A The language of instruction (4) B Reading skills, Level 1 Word-recognition (3) C Handwriting Skills (2) D The analysis of word patterns (2) Phonic knowledge, Level 1 (5) E Development of reading skills, Level 2 (4) F Phonic knowledge, Level 2, spelling (8) Check List 2: G Motivation and attitudes (1) H Child's understanding of language (1) I Child's own use of language (1) J Auditory factors (6) K Vision and visual-motor factors (7) * Figures in brackets indicate the number of sub-checklists contained within each section	Untimed

Comments: The notes in the next three paragraphs are based on the first edition published by Evans. Paragraph 4 indicates the difference between the first edition and the revised edition to be published by Bell and Hyman.

This is a developmentally based approach to assessment and teaching that acknowledges the interactive effects of all aspects of language involved in the initial stages of learning to read. It utilises observational strategies and individual and group testing. By using 22 spirit masters, sufficient copies of the checklists for a considerable number of pupils can be quickly and economically produced.

The first Check List details the basic knowledge and skills that the authors consider are required if a child is to master the beginnings of reading. The Check List helps to structure the teacher's observation of children and simultaneously provides a means of monitoring progress and planning instruction. The section ends with a scheme for summarising the types of difficulties identified and links this with teaching suggestions whilst always emphasising the autonomy of the teacher. The second Check List is intended for use with children failing to make 'normal progress'. It, too, is followed by teaching suggestions.

One major strength of these check lists is the extensive body of experience and knowledge on which its authors draw concerning the development of

Continued at foot of p. 124

TRN	Name of test	Author	Country	Publisher	Year
68	*GAP Reading Comprehension Test*	J. McLeod and D. Unwin	B/A	Heinemann Educational	1970

Type	No. of forms	C.A. range	Skills tested	Time
Constructed response, attainment, normative (level A)	2 (B & R)	8:00 to 12:00	Reading comprehension	15′

Comments: The GAP test presents a series of seven short passages of writing with certain words omitted. The child has to *construct* his own response. The correctness of the response is judged against the criterion of the response of 'good readers'. No penalty is exacted for spelling a semantically correct response incorrectly.

The test was originally standardised in Australia on a sample of 2029 children aged from 7:00 to 12:00. The test has been used on over 1 000 children attending schools in Great Britain with results comparable to those obtained in Australia. The norms presented are based on the British sample and provide reading ages ranging from 7:08 to 12:06. Australian evidence of test-retest reliability and concurrent validity is presented. A concurrent validity coefficient of 0·73 showing the correlation between the GAP test score and *Schonell Reading Test B* for the British sample is reported. The details of the standardisation and of the test's reliabilities and validities are meagre.

Some teachers might have reservations about penalising children who produce a plausible response rather than the one(s) prescribed by the authors on the basis of 'good readers'' responses. Despite this comment, the simplicity of the test will appeal to many teachers requiring an assessment of a child's reading comprehension of continuous prose.

---

early language abilities and the realities of classroom pressures on teachers. Its weakness is an absence of an explicit theoretical and empirical justification of the type of progression the check lists monitor and the failure to provide evidence for the efficacy of the educational interventions indicated.

The revised edition of the above assessment system will contain almost all of that included in the first edition together with some new materials. These include a new section on 'The teacher's role in encouraging the participation of parents in the child's literacy programme'. There will also be an additional Check List, 'Developing Literacy Skills', followed by a new chapter with the same title in which suggestions for teachers are made. Reflecting the increasing interest in the new technologies, an appendix has been added called 'Development of work with computers'. This appendix focuses on the use of computer software in reading. Finally, the reading list will be updated. (Personal communication from the publisher's editor, July 1984.)

TRN	Name of test	Author	Country	Publisher	Year
69	*GAPADOL Reading Comprehension Test*	J. McLeod and J. Anderson	A/B	Heinemann Educational	1973

Type	No. of forms	C.A. range	Skills tested	Time
Constructed response, attainment, normative (level A)	2 (G & Y)	7:03 to 16:11	Reading comprehension	30′

Comments: The GAPADOL test consists of six passages of writing with certain words omitted. The child has to construct responses that fit the gaps, of which there are 81 and 83 in Forms G and Y respectively. The adequacy of a child's response is judged against the criterion of the response of 'good readers'. Incorrect spellings are not penalised.

The manual is extremely brief. It refers readers wanting information concerning the construction and standardisation of the test to other sources. The evidence of reliabilities presented is presumably based on Australian children. Internal consistency reliabilities and the standard errors of measurement are given for each year of chronological age, with the exception of the age range 8 : 03 to 9 : 03 which appears to have been (inadvertently?) omitted. The coefficients presented range from 0·84 to 0·92. No evidence of validities is presented in the manual.

Raw scores can be converted directly to reading ages. For each month of chronological age from 7 : 03 to 16 : 11 raw scores indicating the norm for the age group and also of the 90th and 10th percentile ranks are presented. The latter is interpreted as showing 'retardation' in reading.

As with the *GAP Reading Comprehension Test*, some teachers would have reservations about penalising a child who produced a response that was semantically correct but not precisely that response produced by 'good readers'. Despite this reservation, the simplicity of the test is likely to appeal to many teachers. Presumably English norms will be developed in time, though the twelve years that have passed since its first publication in the UK suggests that this is unlikely.

TRN	Name of test	Author	Country	Publisher	Year
77	*Graded Word Reading Test*	P. E. Vernon	B	Hodder and Stoughton	1938

Type	No. of forms	C.A. range	Skills tested	Time
Individual, oral, attainment, normative (level A)	1	6:00 to 18:00	Word reading	Untimed (10′)

Comments: In Glasgow, Vernon devised a word reading test of 130 words producing reading ages ranging from five years (raw score of 0) to twenty-one years (raw score of 130). Both the first fourteen and the last thirty words of the test are particularly suspect. Bearing in mind the year when it was produced, the manual gives considerable details of the standardisation procedure and of the test's reliabilities and validities. Vernon points out how weaknesses in the standardisation procedure at various age levels and in the selection of words causes difficulty in interpreting the test results. Not the least of these arises from the use of 'reading ages'. It is likely that his openness in this respect has resulted in the test's relatively infrequent use by teachers. Reading ages have an appealing simplicity that can be misleading.

TRN	Name of test	Author	Country	Publisher	Year
78	*Graded Word Spelling Test*	P. E. Vernon	B/C	Hodder and Stoughton 5th impression	1977 1983

Type	No. of forms	C.A. range	Skills tested	Time
Group, individual, attainment (level A)	1	5:06 to 17:06+	Spelling	Untimed (in groups, about 25′ to 30′, Individually, takes less time)

Comments: Based on 80 words arranged in average order of difficulty, the test has about six words for each age group. Each child or class with whom it is used takes only a section of words in an appropriate difficulty range. A table in the manual links age-group to the sub-set of words to be used. Administration involves saying the word to be spelled, reading a specified short sentence containing the word, and then repeating the word.

Initially 228 words were selected covering the range from top infants to Sixth Form levels or, in Canadian terms, from Grades 1 to 12. Thirty-six tests containing thirty words were tried out on 1 169 English and 968 Canadian pupils. Scores in the two countries were comparable with the exception of the youngest age level where the earlier start of English children in formal education gave them some advantage. The items selected to form the final test were standardised on 3 313 English and 1 909 Canadian pupils. The uncertainty about the representativeness of these samples is acknowledged by the author. It follows that the norms must be treated with caution.

Raw scores can be converted to spelling quotients with a mean of 100 and standard deviation of 15 for three month chronological age groups. Separate norms are provided for English and Canadian children up to the age of 8 : 06 years after which a common set of norms is provided. Scores can also be converted to spelling ages.

The only evidence on reliability is from corrected split-half internal consistency coefficients of 0·943 and 0·933 obtained from samples of Canadian 7th Grade pupils on a 40 item test and 4th Grade pupils on a 25 item test. The validity of the scale depends on the initial selection of items from a large corpus of graded words selected to sample a wide variety of spelling difficulties. Precisely what these difficulties are is not specified.

TRN	Name of test	Author	Country	Publisher	Year
80	*Group Literacy Assessment (GLA)*	F. A. Spooncer	B	Hodder and Stoughton	1981

Type	No. of forms	C.A. range	Skills tested	Time
Group, attainment	1	10:06 to 12:06	Efficiency of pupils with written materials	
			1 Proof-reading	8′
(level A)			2 Reading comprehension and spelling (cloze test)	8′
				(about 30′ in all)

Comments: *GLA* is intended for use with final year junior school pupils and first year secondary school pupils. For the former, it monitors children's attainments at the end of primary education, enables the LEA to take an overview of standards and assists liaison between primary and secondary schools. For the latter, it allows an objective comparison between the attainments of successive intakes to a given secondary school, helps in grouping within the school and allows the LEA to monitor standards.

The first 36 item section is an 'in context' spelling test. It involves the students in identifying and correcting errors, for each of which activities he can obtain a mark. The second section consists of a 32 item cloze test in which the pupil has to spell the inserted word correctly to gain marks. Scores on both sections are totalled to give one overall score on the *GLA*.

Standardisation involved all first year secondary school pupils (N = 2 544) and all fourth year junior school pupils leaving for secondary schools in the Waltham Forest LEA. The two groups were tested in the autumn of 1979 and June of 1980 respectively. One cannot tell whether the standardisation sample was representative of other populations. The Godfrey Thomson Unit for Academic Assessment situated at the University of Edinburgh constructed one table of norms for the two groups. The table allows raw scores to be converted to standard scores with a mean of 100 and a standard deviation of 15 for each monthly chronological age group. Raw scores can also be converted to percentiles and to Reading Age Equivalents.

Internal consistency reliability coefficients of 0·91 and 0·92 for Parts 1 and 2 and of 0·95 for the full test, based on a sample of 188 scripts, are reported. Concurrent validity is supported by correlations of 0·81 and 0·78 between *GLA* and scores on the Daniels and Diack *Standard Reading Test 12* (TRN 178) for boys and girls (independently) in the standardisation sample. Correlation of *GLA* with *Group Reading Assessment* (TRN 81), *Sentence Reading 1* (now *NFER Reading Test AD*, TRN 129) and *Primary Reading 2* (now *NFER Reading Test BD*, TRN 130) were 0·81, 0·82 and 0·86 respectively for samples of N = 595, 93 and 93. With a sample of N = 78, correlations with the *Blackwell Spelling Test* (presumably this refers to the Test Cards that form part of Blackwell's *Spelling Workshop*) and the sub-tests of the *Richmond Tests of Basic Skills* (TRN 163) ranged between 0·50 and 0·78.

Potential users might wonder whether a total time-on-task of 16′ under timed conditions is the best way of making an assessment of literacy. Without doubt, the test is economical of teachers' and pupils' time. That could be one of its most appealing points.

TRN	Name of test	Author	Country	Publisher	Year
81	*Group Reading Assessment*	F. A. Spooncer	B	Hodder and Stoughton	1964
				2nd edition	1980

Type	No. of forms	C.A. range	Skills tested	Time
Group, attainment	1	7:08 to 9:00	Word recognition Sentence reading	30′
(level A)				

Comments: The test consists of three parts. In the first sixteen items, the teacher says a word contained in a suggested sentence and the child has to draw a line under one of five words in the printed test booklet. The twenty-five items in part 2 are sentence completion from multiple-choice. In part 3 the children are presented with rows of words in which at least two words, although spelt differently, sound the same. The task is for the child to underline the words which have the same sound as the first word in the row, e.g. 'too: two, low, ton, to, chew'. There are sixteen of these items. This test is intended to assess the reading level of children at the end of their first year in the junior school. Its content was determined after discussions with teachers as to which aspects of reading they considered important. Thus both mechanical aspects of reading and reading comprehension were sampled. The validity data presented suggests that the test fulfils its primary aim of testing mechanical reading rather than comprehension. The reliability (internal consistency) of the test is high, 0·969 for the whole test. Test-retest reliability after an eight-month interval was 0·91. It is suggested by Spooncer that the test should not be used during the autumn term of the first year in the junior school as some children find difficulties in following the instructions at that stage.

TRN	Name of test	Author	Country	Publisher	Year
82	*Group Reading Test*	D. Young	B	Hodder and Stoughton	1968
				2nd edition (Manual)	1980
				4th impression	1984

Type	No. of forms	C.A. range	Skills tested	Time
Multiple-choice, group, attainment (level A)	2 (A & B)	6:05 to 12:08	1 Word-picture matching	4′
			2 Reading comprehension (sentence completion)	9′
				(practice items untimed; total time 20′)

Comments: This is the second edition of a test originally published in 1968. Each form comprises forty-five items. In fifteen of these items *one* of between three and five words must be selected to match a picture. In the next thirty items the child is looking for synonyms in multiple-choice sentence-completion format. Although in two distinct parts, it is the total score only that is used in assessing reading attainment.

Between 1974 and 1979 surveys were carried out in three (unspecified) different areas of Britain. 21 711 infants, 5 560 first year juniors and 1 867 second year junior and older pupils aged between 8:00 and 12:10 were tested. Score distributions in each area were calibrated by means of nationally standardised tests. Data were combined to provide separate norms for Infants aged 6:05 to 7:10, for first year juniors aged 7:00 to 8:10 and for 'below-average second-year juniors and older pupils aged 8:00 to 12:10. For each of these groups, raw scores can be converted to standardised scores with a mean of 100 and standard deviation of 15 for each monthly age group. Raw scores can also be converted to reading ages. A table links scores on the *Group Reading Test* to four other well-known instruments. Evidence is presented from a variety of samples concerning the test's reliabilities. This appears acceptable, as is the evidence for validities that is presented. The test's predictive validity is shown using a sample of 130 pupils. Concurrent validity is supported by high and significant correlations with other reading tests and with teachers' scaled order of merit.

A major weakness of the test lies in trying to cover reading attainment over such a large age range with such a small number of items. The author himself acknowledges the problems of standardisation and the construction of the reading age scale. Use of the lower end of the latter requires particular caution. One of the major appeals of this test is that it does not take long to administer. Some critics would argue that a 13′ sample of a child's reading behaviour is insufficient – but there are even briefer tests.

TRN	Name of test	Author	Country	Publisher	Year
85	*Holborn Reading Scale*	A. F. Watts	B	Harrap (now distributed by the Test Agency)	1948

Type	No. of forms	C.A. range	Skills tested	Time
Individual, oral (word recognition), silent (comprehension) (level A)	1	5:06 to 11:00	Word recognition Comprehension	Untimed (20′–30′)

Comments: The scale comprises thirty-three sentences in increasing order of difficulty in terms of word recognition and comprehension. Each sentence represents a reading age three months higher than the preceding sentence. A child's mechanical reading ability can be rapidly assessed, but there are no norms for comprehension; hence the comparison between a child's mechanical reading and comprehension cannot be made as meaningfully as is suggested in the manual. There is no mention of reliability or validity in the manual. The norms are dated. This test has achieved popularity perhaps because of its ease of administration and the apparently simple interpretation of scores. It also offers the possibility of comparing a pupil's oral reading and silent reading comprehension of the same sentence by answering related questions. The reading ages of the sentences range from 5 : 09 to 13 : 09 years.

The appeal of the approach used in this test led to the later development of the *Salford Sentence Reading Test* (TRN 167).

TRN	Name of test	Author	Country	Publisher	Year
86	*How's It Going?*	M. Good and J. Holmes	B	Adult Literacy Unit (Interprint Graphic Services Ltd act as agents)	1978

Type	No. of forms	C.A. range	Skills tested		Time
Individual, checklist, diagnostic	1	Adults with reading difficulties	*Reading*:	*Writing*:	Untimed
			*A Reading as communication	A Writing as communication	
			A Reader's job (voice)	A Voice	
			SK Alphabet	SK Form letters	
			SK Social sight	SK Grammatical conventions	
			SK 'Key' words	AK Purposes	
			ASK Context cuing	AK Drafts	
		*KEY:	SK Visual features	AS Editing	
		A = Attitude	SK Letter names	ASK Failure technique	
		S = Skill	SK Phonics	SK Memorising	
		K = Knowledge	ASK Failure technique	SK Dictionary	
			AK Idea of strategy	ASK Noticing	
			AK Purposes	AK Concept of strategy	
			K Print 1: L & R	SK Writing letters	
			SK Print 2: structure	AK Importance of practice	
			ASK Grammatical jargon	ASK Knowing about the language	
			SK Dictionary	SK Note taking	
			ASK Study skills	SK Essays	
			ASK Skim/scan	ASK Writing for speech	
			ASK Library	SK Thesaurus	
(level A)			SK Speed		

Comments: In a booklet addressed to both tutors and learners, the authors present an alternative approach to the assessment of reading and writing for use with adults who have decided that they wish to work at becoming literate (see Appendix 2). The approach is based on the use of checklists developed from the work of Kohl who suggested that reading developed through four levels which he called, in a typically jargon-free manner, 'Beginning', 'Not bad', 'With ease' and 'Complex' (Kohl, 1974). The aim is to provide both tutor and student with insights (metacognitions) into the nature of literacy and its development whilst simultaneously providing a means of cooperatively developing, recording and evaluating the student's progress.

The Reading checklist covers the first three of Kohl's four levels for each of 20 aspects of reading categorised as attitudes, skills or knowledge, or a combination of these. The meaning and importance of each item is presented in the manual. Student performances are graded on a three point scale: 'knows it', 'is working at it' or 'starting off'. Users of the system are encouraged to develop their own extensions and modifications of the checklists to suit the student's needs. A similar structure is presented in the Writing checklist.

No evidence is presented concerning the reliabilities, validities or utility of the system. The relationships between the items included in the two checklists are not quantified, nor does the ASK classification have empirical support. Despite these serious reservations, the approach contains some innovations that could hold considerable promise. The importance of being able to 'fail well' and to develop a range of strategies are but two among many. It is to be hoped that some empirical work will be done to develop and refine the approach as well as integrating it with other more conventional assessment techniques, despite the authors' explicit rejection of the latter.

KOHL, H. (1974) *Reading – How To.* Harmondsworth: Penguin.

TRN	Name of test	Author	Country	Publisher	Year
87	*Hunter-Grundin Literacy Profiles (HGLP)*	E. Hunter-Grundin and H. Hunter-Grundin	B	Test Agency	1980

Type	No. of forms	C.A. range†	Skills tested	Time
Individual,* group, attainment, attitude, diagnostic	1 (five levels)	Level 1 6:04 to 8:05	Reading for meaning (Reading age and standard score)	10′
		Level 2 7:10 to 9:03	Attitudes/interests	3′
		Level 3 8:10 to 10:03	(i) Attitude scale (Pupil ratings)	
		Level 4 9:10 to 11:05	(ii) Profile of personal interests (Pupil ratings)	
		Level 5 10:10 to 12:07	Written language	
			(i) Spelling (Standard score)	10′
		†Taken from the tables at the back of the reference book at each level	(ii) Free writing (Teacher ratings)	10′
			(a) Legibility	
			(b) Fluency	
			(c) Accuracy	
			(d) Originality	
			*Spoken language (Teacher ratings)	about 5′
			(a) Confidence	
			(b) Enunciation	
			(c) Vocabulary	
			(d) Accuracy	
(level A)			(e) Imagination	

Comments: The purposes of the *HGLP* are to help the teacher monitor the progress of individuals and to encourage diagnostic teaching by providing both normative and qualitative assessments of various aspects of written and spoken language. There are two normed tests, 'Reading for meaning' and 'Spelling'. The former is in 'maze' test format, a modified multiple-choice in which the alternatives are arranged vertically in a text. The spelling test involves the completion of gaps within a narrative passage that is read aloud by the teacher. Free writing and spoken language are assessed using rating scales. To use such scales reliably and consistently requires a considerable amount of practice and conference with colleagues. At Levels 1 and 2 an attitude scale is included in the battery. At Levels 4 and 5 a 'Profile of personal interests' is provided. These devices enable ratings by pupils on five and four point scales respectively to be made indicating their attitudes to or interests in specified activities.

Potential users should note that the reading age tables at each Level provide a wider range of age-equivalent scores than the standardised score tables. Thus Level 1 has reading ages from 6:00 to 9:00+ years; Level 2, 6:00 to 10:09+ years, Level 3, 6:06 to 12:00+ years, Level 4, 6:06 to 13:07+ years and Level 5, 6:09 to 15:10+ years.

The standardisations of the five Levels are based on samples of children drawn from between 21 and 23 LEAs, attending from between 50 and 70 schools and involving between 2400 and 2600 individuals. It is stated that the schools were chosen so as to be representative of the variation of schools in each area. The internal consistency reliability coefficients of the reading tests are very high, ranging from 0·97 to 0·98. Correlations with other reading test scores provide evidence of concurrent validity and range from 0·74 to 0·87 over the five Levels. The internal consistency reliability coefficients of the spelling tests range between 0·92 and 0·94. The sizes of the groups on which these data were obtained are not given, nor is their composition specified. Statistical evidence concerning the reliabilities and validities of the various rating scales are not provided. Supplementary information concerning differences between schools in relation to pupils' socioeconomic background is given at Levels 1 to 3.

Separate manuals are provided for each Level. A cumulative record of a child's profiles can be kept in a Record Wallet on the cover of which the results of successive administrations can be recorded. Whilst easy to administer, the profiles require a considerable investment of time and effort in scoring and interpretation. On the positive side, they offer some interesting approaches to assessment and instruction. Information on the intercorrelations between variables at each of the five levels would have been a helpful addition to judicious profile interpretation.

The *HGLP* have been used in an important research project in Coventry (Widlake and MacLeod, 1984).

WIDLAKE, P. and MacLEOD, F. (1984) *Raising Standards: Parental Involvement Programmes and the Language Performance of Children.* Coventry: Community Education Development Centre.

TRN	Name of test	Author	Country	Publisher	Year
95	*Key Words Attainment and Diagnostic Test*	J. McNally	B	Teacher Publishing (previously Schoolmaster Publishing)	1962

Type	No. of forms	C.A. range	Skills tested	Time
Content criterion-referenced, group and individual	1	5:00+	A Word recognition (group)	Untimed
			B (i) Word recognition (individual)	1′
			(ii) Timed reading of first ten lines of list	timed
			C Word recognition: comparison of speed of reading and word attack on phonically regular and irregular words respectively	
(level A)				

Comments: The above test is based on the 200 words most frequently in common use, as identified by McNally and Murray (1962; revised edition 1984).* Early incorporation of these words into a reader's sight vocabulary is considered vital by these authors. McNally describes three major ways in which the specially devised test card can be used. Variations in the administration of tests A, B and C of diagnostic importance are described. Because the test is content criterion-referenced, none of the norms or indices of reliability and validity typically provided with normative tests, are given. It is suggested that in tests B and C, teachers can establish their own norms for subsequent use. Because the test is a mastery test, the teacher is perfectly justified in teaching to her pupils such of the words in the test as she considers appropriate to her pupils' needs. The success of the teaching and of the pupils' learning will be reflected in changes in pupils' raw scores on the tests.

The publication has been extremely popular since its first publication in 1962. In part, this is because the central word list is directly linked to a reading scheme that has been widely used in British schools, thereby providing a close link between the teaching and testing of reading. There are many experts in reading who are somewhat suspicious of the validity of the *Key Words* approach.

* MCNALLY, J. and MURRAY, W. (1984) *Key Words to Literacy and the Teaching of Reading* (revised edition). Kettering: The Teacher Publishing Company.

TRN	Name of test	Author	Country	Publisher	Year
98	*Literacy Schedule*	J. Dean	B	Centre for the Teaching of Reading, University of Reading	1979

Type	No. of forms	C.A. range	Skills tested	Time
Individual, criterion-referenced, diagnostic, checklists	1	9:00+	*Section A Finding Out* I Finding out by observation (a) Looking and watching (b) Listening II Finding out from other people (a) Asking questions (b) Making judgments about speech III Finding out from pictures, film and television IV Finding out from books and print (a) Library skills (b) Using reference books and material (c) Ways of reading and studying (d) Making judgments about what you read (e) Newspapers and magazines V Following directions and instructions VI Finding out from symbols, charts, diagrams and maps VII Using maps and plans *Section B Sorting things out and making decisions* I Sorting things out and putting them together II Making decisions III Solving problems IV Making and testing hypotheses V Planning skills (a) Personal planning (b) Planning with others *Section C Presentation* I Knowledge of language	Untimed

Literacy Schedule continued

(level A)

Skills tested

II Speaking

III Writing
- (a) Handwriting
- (b) Writing correctly
- (c) Spelling
- (d) Writing in different ways
- (e) Making notes
- (f) Form filling

IV Graphic skills
- (a) Using symbols
- (b) Making plans and maps

Section D Working with other people

I Knowing what to do

II Discussion skills

III Running meetings

IV Explaining and teaching

Comments: The *Schedule* consists of 18 pages containing checklists of sets of skills. In the author's considered opinion, based on extensive experience in this field as an LEA Adviser and Inspector, the skills covered by the schedule will 'help teachers ensure that children acquire sufficient of the skills of literacy for adult life, sufficient of the skills of study to continue learning after they leave school, and sufficient social skills to feel at ease in a wider variety of social situations . . .' (p. 1). The *Schedule* is neither a syllabus nor 'a policy document about language'. Users are required to develop operational definitions of many of the skills listed. The checklists can be used as an individual record by pupils. As such they could have a beneficial motivational effect on both pupils and teachers. The strength of the *Schedule* is that it is not a professional straightjacket restricting both teacher and child but a stimulus to the *development* of explicit statements concerning the objectives of a literacy programme, their integration into a developmental programme and the formation of clear links between objectives, assessment and instruction.

TRN	Name of test	Author	Country	Publisher	Year
99	*Literacy Tests for Schools*	H. Diack	B	Hart-Davis Educational	1975

Type	No. of forms	C.A. range	Skills tested	Time
Group, attainment (level A)	50	8:00 to 18:00	Comprehension of words	Untimed (about 15′–20′)

Comments: A major purpose of this battery of 50 (presumably) parallel tests is to enable a rapid estimate to be made of the extent of a child's vocabulary. The tests are apparently based on a corpus of 18 000 words. This is considered sufficiently large to include 'all school pupils except a proportion of sixth formers and an occasional budding polymath or potential lexicographer'.

Each test consists of four sets of ten words. The first set is not scored but is designed to engage even poor readers and provide their teachers with information concerning commonly used (in writing) words that these pupils may have difficulty in reading and understanding.

The words in the final three sets of ten words in each test are numbered. The pupil reads the words to himself. If he does not understand the meaning of a word, he records the number and proceeds to the next word. This is done until ten failures are recorded. The pupil then has to provide evidence that he understood the meaning of the last five words that he claimed to have read and understood. No guidance is given as to whether this should be done by the pupil orally or in writing. By multiplying the words out of 30 that he did understand by 600, an estimate of the pupil's vocabulary can be obtained. Because there are 50 apparently parallel tests, it is easy to adopt the advice given and use the average of three tests as the basis for the multiplication. In addition, the test materials can be used for word-study and for spelling practice and testing.

Although it is not mentioned, an oral presentation of the words by the tester would enable an estimate of the understanding of words, independent of any decoding difficulties, to be obtained.

No details of the manner in which the 18 000 word corpus was obtained are given in the manual. No information on the reliability and validity of the estimates of individuals' vocabularies obtained using the Literacy Tests is presented. There must be many children (and adults) who genuinely consider that they understand the meaning of a word but who, when required to explain its meaning, show clearly that they did not understand. The tests provide opportunities for exploring such issues, as does virtually any word list. However, the tests are now out of print and will not be reissued in their present form.

TRN	Name of test	Authors	Country	Publisher	Year
100	*London Reading Test*	M. Biscoe, C. Bradshaw, S. Clarke, M. Halliwell, D. Morgan, T. Nunn, H. Quigley and I. Zelickman	B	NFER-Nelson	1980

Type	No. of forms	C.A. range	Skills tested	Time
Group, attainment (level A)	2 (Forms A & B)	10:07 to 12:04	Reading comprehension	About 1 hr

Comments: At the request of the ILEA Central Consultative Committee of Headteachers, a Working Party was set up to construct a 'survey/screener' test that would reduce problems of communicating information about children's reading when transferring from primary to secondary schools.

Each of the two parallel forms consists of three passages of prose. The first two of these are accompanied by pictures and comprehension of the passages is tested by close technique. The third passage has no associated picture and comprehension is tested by questions requiring a constructed response. The prose passages were written bearing in mind the city's urban multi-racial population. The test was designed to be particularly discriminating at the lower end of the ability range.

Standardisations were obtained for final year primary school and first year secondary school age groups within the ILEA on stratified random samples of 1 000 pupils. In addition, the tests were standardised on samples representative of England and Wales at the same two age levels using 5 000 pupils in each group. Primary pupils were tested during their final term in the primary school and the secondary school pupils were tested during their first term at the secondary school.

Raw scores can be converted to standard scores with a mean of 100 and a standard deviation of 15 on each of the four tables derived from the above samples. In the primary school groups this can be done for each monthly age group from 10 : 07 to 12 : 01 years and from 10 : 11 to 12 : 04 years in the secondary school age group.

The internal consistency reliability (Kuder-Richardson formula 21) for the ILEA sample was 0·95 and for the national sample was 0·93. The validity of the instrument is supported by highly significant correlations between both Forms A and B and six other well-established tests using samples ranging from N = 44 (*Neale Analysis of Reading Ability*, TRN 109) and N = 293 (*Holborn Reading Scale*, TRN 85).

TRN	Name of test	Author	Country	Publisher	Year
101	*Macmillan Diagnostic Reading Pack*	T. Ames	B	Macmillan Education	1980

Type	No. of forms	C.A. range	Skills tested	Time
Individual and group, diagnostic (level A)	1	Primary Reading Skills (no C.A. specified) Stage 1 R.A. 5:00 to 6:00 Stage 2 R.A. 6:00 to 7:00 Stage 3 R.A. 7:00 to 8:00 Stage 4 R.A. 8:00 to 9:00	*Stage 1* A 32 Key words A1 Letter-matching A2 Upper & lower-case matching A3 Visual memory (recognition) A4 Visual memory (reproduction) B Transcribing sounds B1 Sound value of letters B2 Auditory discrimination B3 Short-term auditory memory C Blending 2/3 letter words C1 Auditory blending *Stage 2* D 68 Key words A 32 Key words E Final consonant blends, consonant diagraphs and initial consonant blends E1 Consonant and vowel sounds F Consonant blends and digraphs C Blending 2/3 letter words B Transcribing sounds H Reading strategies (Stage 2) H1 Accuracy H2 Comprehension *Stage 3* D 68 Key words A 32 Key words J Long vowels and vowel digraphs E Final consonant blends, consonant digraphs and initial consonant blends K Vowel digraphs F Consonant blends and digraphs M Spelling short vowel words containing consonant blends and digraphs H Reading strategies (Stage 3) H1 Accuracy H2 Comprehension *Stage 4* J Long vowels and vowel diagraphs E Final consonant blends K Vowel digraphs F Consonant blends and digraphs O Spelling of regular single syllable words M Spelling of short vowel words containing consonant blends and digraphs H Reading strategies (Stage 4) H1 Accuracy H2 Comprehension	Untimed

Comments: Ames has produced a package aimed at enabling teachers to diagnose 'surface' primary reading skills and to link diagnosis to instruction.

The package includes a Teachers' Manual entitled *Teach yourself to diagnose reading problems*. This explains the rationale underpinning Ames' approach, test administration instructions and four decision flow-charts related to the postulated four stages of reading development on which the diagnostic process is predicated. There are also four checklists, based on selections from 28 test items, on which a pupil's performances are recorded together with fifteen test cards. The diagnostic process begins with an assessment of the child's reading age. The decision charts for each stage help the teacher decide on the instruction the child requires and/or further testing.

The testing programme appears to be based on Ames' (and his colleagues in Leeds) informed opinions concerning the nature of primary reading processes and their 'surface' sub-skills. The idea seems to be a development of the *Assessment of Reading Ability* (TRN 11). It suffers from the same technical limitations.

Unfortunately, the theoretical basis of the battery is not well explicated. The reliabilities, intercorrelations and validities of the tests are given very little attention. The empirical bases of the decision points in the charts are not presented. The interpretation of the profiles obtained is largely based on intuitions rather than on known probabilities. It should be stressed that this weakness is not an uncommon one even in widely used diagnostic batteries.

Despite the above reservations, the package represents the results of a considerable amount of work based on the experience of practising teachers. As an approach to diagnosis, it contains promise. It does help the teacher to adopt a sequential hypothesis testing approach. More development and research needs to be done to establish the validities of the tests, their interpretation and utility.

TRN	Name of test	Author	Country	Publisher	Year
102	*Making Sense of It*	H. Arnold	B	Hodder and Stoughton	1984

Type	No. of forms	C.A. range	Skills tested	Time
Individual, informal, diagnostic (level A)	1	6:00 plus	Analysis of miscues at grapho-phonic, syntactic and semantic levels: 1 Non-responses or refusals 2 Substitutions 3 Omissions 4 Insertions 5 Reversals 6 Self-correction 7 Hesitation 8 Repetition Comprehension ratings via 'retelling': A Straight recall B Structure and shape C Appreciation	Untimed

Comments: Listening to children's oral reading is seen by many teachers as a valuable means of assessing the progress of individuals and of identifying difficulties experienced by the reader in reading accuracy and, by appropriate questioning, reading comprehension. Arnold's argument is that less frequent but better organised observation of children's oral reading by the teacher can provide valuable diagnostic information. The rationale, together with an earlier account of the technique, is contained in a recent book (Arnold, 1982).

The technique is based on a series of 30 passages of increasing lengths from about 200 to 300 words, graded for readability. There are ten passages in each of the three content fields of autobiography, narrative and information. The pupil is required to read a passage in which a minimum of 'about 20' miscues, required for a 'fair analysis', are identified. The oral reading is tape-recorded, as is the child's retelling of the story. Oral reading miscues are identified as positive or negative. The former represent a reasonable and logical use of the information whereas negative miscues indicate a restricted and unhelpful use by the child of the cueing systems that fails to capitalise on the child's knowledge of language and life. Typically, only miscues 1–6 are used in these analyses. Miscues are coded on an analysis sheet and related to the three levels of miscue. From these data, process difficulties are inferred and instructional strategies for the individual are derived. The child's understanding of the material is further rated on a three point scale in relation to the three levels A, B and C shown above.

In part, because the assessment procedure is largely qualitative in its nature, no information is given concerning the reliability or validity of it. Whilst such a task would be difficult, it is not impossible. Oral miscues and comprehension of textual material depend on passage difficulty, content and the child's experience, as Arnold recognises. Although the procedure is untimed and 'appears time-consuming at first, it (the analysis) can be completed in about ten minutes with experience' (Manual, p. 11). This does not include initial taping of the material. Having tried the system, the reviewer has concluded that he would need very considerable practice in order to attain the level of proficiency indicated by Arnold. If Arnold had demonstrated that the investment of teacher time entailed leads to a more efficient use by children of the cueing systems in text and language, to enhanced attainments and more positive attitudes towards reading, her interesting case would have been considerably strengthened. The field is one in which more research in Britain is needed. It is likely that Arnold's initiative will stimulate this.

The great appeal of the approach is that it sensitises teachers to qualitative aspects of children's reading development and to the complexities of the reading process.

ARNOLD, H. (1982) *Listening to Children Reading*. London: Hodder and Stoughton.

TRN	Name of test	Author	Country	Publisher	Year
108	*National Adult Reading Test (NART)*	H. E. Nelson	B	NFER-Nelson	1982

Type	No. of forms	C.A. range	Skills tested	Time
Individual, attainment, diagnostic (level K)	1	Adults (20 : 00 to 70 : 00)	Word reading	Untimed (about 10′–15′)

Comments: The test is designed for the 'assessment of pre-morbid intelligence in patients with dementia'. The rationale underpinning the use of a word-reading test for such a purpose is discussed in the manual. When intellectual abilities have been assessed pre-morbidly, then deterioration of abilities can readily be estimated. In most cases, such pre-morbidity assessments are not available. Because word-reading ability is generally well-maintained in the presence of dementing processes, then word-reading ability can be used to estimate pre-morbid intelligence.

NART consists of 50 words arranged in increasing order of difficulty. These 50 were selected from an original pool of 120 using a group of 25 non-demented patients. Each word is 'irregular' in the sense that the effectiveness of phonemic decoding is deliberately minimised. From the number of errors made in oral reading, by substituting in regression equations, it is possible to estimate a subject's pre-morbid Full-scale I.Q. as measured by the *Wechsler Adult Intelligence Scale (WAIS)*, the *WAIS Verbal Scale I.Q.*, and *WAIS Performance Scale I.Q.* For poor readers, additional information based on the patients' errors when completing the *Schonell Graded Word Reading Test* (Form A) is used.

The *NART* was standardised on an unselected series of 120 patients aged from 20 : 00 to 70 : 00 years. Seven sub-tests of the *WAIS* plus the *Schonell Graded Word Reading Test* (Form A) were completed by the sample. From these data the regression equations were derived. The sampling hardly justifies the use of the word 'National' in the test title. Validation is based on small sample work with 45 demented and 98 control group patients. The author indicates some of the limitations of the test when used with groups having distinctive characteristics. These limitations underline the care that must be taken in interpreting *NART* results.

NELSON, H. E. and O'CONNELL, A. (1978) 'Dementia: the estimation of pre-morbid intelligence levels using the new adult reading test.' *Cortex*, **14**, 234–44.

TRN	Name of test	Author	Country	Publisher	Year
109	*Neale Analysis of Reading Ability (NARA)*	M. D. Neale	B	Macmillan Education	1957–8 2nd edition 1966

Type	No. of forms	C.A. range	Skills tested		Time
Individual, oral, attainment, diagnostic, normative (level P)	3 (A, B & C)	7:00 to 11:00	Main test: Reading accuracy i. Mispronunciations ii. Substitutions iii. Refusals Reading speed Reading comprehension Subsidiary tests: Names and sounds Of letters Auditory discrimination Syllable blending and recognition	 iv. Additions v. Omissions vi. Reversals	Untimed* (about 25′) *Time taken is recorded in order that the pupil's rate of reading can be calculated

Comments: *NARA* is designed to assess the child's 'difficulties, weaknesses, types of errors, persistence and attitudes . . .' (Manual, p. 3). Normative information can be obtained from the Main test. Patterns of errors (currently viewed as 'miscues') can be identified. The optional supplementary tests allow the teacher to explore other skills that are important in the reading process.

Each of the three parallel forms of the *NARA* contains six short stories of increasing length. Each story is illustrated by a picture designed to provide a context increasing the appeal of the material. The test materials are well-organised and the instructions for its use are clear. However, because of the complexity of the test and the need to record in six error categories, users are advised to practise the administration a number of times before using the results for individual decision-making.

The test was standardised on a sample of over 2 000 pupils selected from thirteen schools. No details are given of the sample other than that the 'size, area, social background, age and sex' of the sample were controlled. It appears that the children in the standardisation sample were all primary school pupils. The parallel form reliability for the accuracy scores is high, 0·96 being the lowest of the coefficients presented for samples from four year groups. For the same groups, the lowest parallel form reliability for the comprehension scores was 0·92. No information is given concerning the reliability of the rate of reading scores. Absence of the standard deviations and inter-correlations of the three scales makes profile interpretation a clinical procedure. The validity of the *NARA* was assessed by correlating a pooled score for rate, accuracy and comprehension with a pooled score on a similar battery. With samples of 200 nine year olds and 200 eleven year old pupils, coefficients of 0·95 are reported for each age level. Separate validations of the three major scales would have been more informative. The validity of simultaneously testing rate, accuracy and comprehension has been questionned. The instrument has been extensively used in many studies throughout the English-speaking world. The test is seen of value by clinicians and remedial teachers of reading in particular. A more detailed review of *NARA* has been published that may be of interest to readers requiring fuller and more technical details than are given here (Pumfrey, 1984).

It has been said that the content of some of the paragraphs have dated and that the use of the information from the analysis of errors could be improved on in the light of work that has taken place since the *NARA* was devised. Currently the author is engaged in a revision of *NARA* in Australia. A contemporary British version or development would be welcome.

PUMFREY, P. D. (1984) 'Review of the Neale Analysis of Reading Ability.' In LEVY, P. and GOLDSTEIN, H. (eds) *Tests in Education*. London: Academic Press.

TRN	Name of test	Author	Country	Publisher	Year
110	*Neale Analysis of Reading Ability* (NARA) adapted for use with blind children	J. Lorimer	B	NFER-Nelson	1977

Type	No. of forms	C.A. range	Skills tested	Time
Individual, diagnostic (level A)	3 (A, B & C)	7:06 to 13:05	Main test: Reading accuracy; Reading comprehension; Reading Rate; * Supplementary tests: Names and sounds of letters; Auditory discrimination; Syllable blending and recognition	Not specified in the manual, but likely to take between 35′ to 50′

Comment: Lorimer has produced a braille version of the *NARA* for use with blind children. Users need to be familiar with the original *NARA* and also to be experienced teachers of the blind who have taught braille and are aware of the difficulties this medium presents to the reader. Because blind readers using braille are considerably slower than sighted readers using the normal form of the *NARA*, the administration of the test in its braille form has different limits concerning, for example, the time allowed for recognition of a word. Additionally, verbal instructions replace the pictures used in the conventional *NARA*. The recording of six types of errors is required during the administration of the test. Facility in administering, recording and scoring require considerable practice.

Standardisation of the braille version posed many difficulties, particularly in identifying a suitable sample. This issue and its resolution is clearly discussed in the manual. The standardisation sample included all children meeting specified selection criteria aged between 7:06 and 13:06 years attending special schools for the blind. The sample comprised 55% (N = 299) of the entire population in such schools.

Age norms for reading accuracy, comprehension and rate are obtained. Percentile points for each of these indices is provided for each of the six year groups on which the test was standardised. Parallel form reliability coefficients for each of the six age levels are presented for all pairs of comparisons of forms A, B and C. The accuracy coefficients range from 0·9903 to 0·9974, comprehension coefficients from 0·9593 to 0·9960 and the rate coefficients from 0·9526 to 0·9979.

Evidence of validities is yet to be explored but Lorimer claims that, for the blind, this test is as valid as the original version was for the sighted. Despite its relatively recent arrival on the educational scene, the test is being widely used with visually handicapped pupils in this country. Links between the patterns of reading behaviours revealed by the test and instruction of benefit to a pupil remains mainly a matter of clinical judgement.

* These three supplementary tests are contained in the pupils' record form but no reference is made in Lorimer's manual to their use.

TRN	Name of test	Author	Country	Publisher	Year
112	*NFER English Progress Test A*	A. F. Watts	B	NFER-Nelson	1953

Type	No. of forms	C.A. range	Skills tested	Time
Group, attainment (level A)	1	8:00 to 9:00	English language: Common combinations of words Class names Reading comprehension Answering questions	Untimed (about 45′)

Comments: This forty item test samples various aspects of English language. The reason for selecting the particular skills is not discussed. The test was standardised on a representative sample of 3 199 children aged 8:00 to 9:00 years. Kuder–Richardson formula 20 coefficient of internal consistency of 0·96 is reported. This is based on a sample of unspecified size.

The test enables one to assess inter-individual differences in relation to a total score only. The point that the *same* total score could be made up by different children who scored differently on the four sections of the test poses problems of interpretation. The test is still in the publisher's current catalogue (1984–5). One wonders why.

TRN	Name of test	Author	Country	Publisher	Year
113	*NFER English Progress Test A2*	B. Barnard	B	NFER-Nelson	1966

Type	No. of forms	C.A. range	Skills tested	Time
Group, attainment (level A)	1	7:03 to 8:11	Reading comprehension with particular emphasis on aspects of English Language useage	Untimed (about 50′)

Comments: Intended for junior schoolchildren, this 42 item test contains a range of items testing a somewhat heterogeneous collection of skills including plurals, rhyming, opposites, spelling, tense and other aspects of grammar. The curricular provenance of this content is not made clear. In this respect the test reflects the state of the art of test construction at that time. However, provided that the content matches a school's curricular objectives, the test may have some limited value.

The limitations are added to by the standardisation on 4 776 children in two Borough Education Authorities. There was no sex difference in the *rate* of score increase with age. The regression coefficients of score upon age calculated separately for boys and girls did not differ. Hence only one combined table for converting raw scores to standard scores (mean 100; standard deviation 15) is provided despite the fact that girls in the sample typically score higher than boys by about 3·6 standard score points. It is therefore suggested that, for comparison purposes, the scores of boys and girls should be considered separately.

A Kuder-Richardson formula 20 coefficient of internal consistency of 0·973 based on the scores of 368 pupils is reported. There is no other evidence of reliabilities or validities.

The normative utility of a test standardised on children from two Boroughs, but of different age groups in each Borough, is questionable. Possibly the fact that the test appears, on the face of its content, to be one of English accounts for the absence of evidence on validity. The absence from the publisher's catalogue of the original date when the test was constructed and published does not help potential purchasers to make wise decisions. This fault is not the prerogative of NFER-Nelson.

TRN	Name of test	Author	Country	Publisher	Year
114	*NFER English Progress Test B2*	NFER Staff	B	NFER-Nelson	1961

Type	No. of forms	C.A. range	Skills tested	Time
Group, attainment (level A)	1	8:06 to 10:00	English useage	Untimed (about 40′)

Comments: Intended as a measure of the attainments of second year primary school pupils, the test was constructed by the NFER in cooperation with the Surrey Educational Research Association. The content is grouped and includes sections on rhymes, opposites, tense, reading comprehension, capitalisation, sentence completion, plurals, spelling and punctuation. This presumably reflected curricular concerns at the time. Do these still hold today?

Standardisation was on a representative sample of 5458 children aged 8:09 to 9:09 years. The norms were extrapolated in both directions to the limits shown above. Using a random sample of 246 scores from the standardisation sample, an internal consistency coefficient of reliability, Kuder–Richardson formula 20, of 0·969 is reported. No other indices of reliability or validity are presented.

Raw scores can be converted to standard scores with a mean of 100 and a standard deviation of 15 for children in each monthly age group. The test contains 46 items and the maximum score obtainable is 50. The norms relate only to the total raw score. The problems of interpretation and the educational significance of the same score having been obtained in markedly different ways by different children is not discussed.

TRN	Name of test	Author	Country	Publisher	Year
115	*NFER English Progress Test B3*	NFER Staff	B	NFER-Nelson	1970

Type	No. of forms	C.A. range	Skills tested	Time
Group, attainment (level A)	1	8:07 to 9:09	English language	Untimed (about 45′)

Comments: The 40 items in this test sample a range of English language skills. The manual says nothing about these, but an examination of the test booklet suggests that these include reading comprehension, collective nouns, syntax, synonyms and sequencing. The curricular bases of the item generation and selection is not made explicit.

The test was standardised on 3 789 children tested in 1972. Total raw scores on the test for each monthly chronological age group can be converted to standard scores with a mean of 100 and a standard deviation of 15. The six pages of duplicated papers that comprise the 'manual' contain no information concerning the test's reliabilities, validities or any suggestions as to the educational implications of the information the test elicits.

It is difficult to see why this test should still be published.

TRN	Name of test	Author	Country	Publisher		Year
116	*NFER English Progress Test C2*	V. Land	B	NFER-Nelson		1961
					36th impression	1979

Type	No. of forms	C.A. range	*Skills tested	Time
Group, attainment (level A)	1	9:06 to 11:00	Reading comprehension Vocabulary Punctuation Spelling Sentence construction	Untimed (about 40′–45′)

Comments: The skills listed above* are not specified in the manual but are derived from an inspection of the pupil's test booklet and the manual together. The purpose of the test is to provide a normative inter-individual comparison of attainments on a group of English language skills. Only total scores on the test are used. The test contains 54 items.

The curricular justification of the content of the test is not given. Despite this, the test has (surprisingly) reached a 36th reprint in 1979. Is it still meeting some valid educational purpose? Or is it that habit dies hard? The test was standardised on a representative sample of 5 499 children aged 9 : 09 to 10 : 09 years. The norms were extrapolated to the limits specified in the table above.

Raw scores can be converted to standardized scores with a mean of 100 and a standard deviation of 15 for children of each monthly chronological age group. Thus children are compared with others of virtually the same age only. Using 222 scripts from the standardisation sample, the internal consistency reliability coefficient was found to be 0·969 using the Kuder-Richardson formula 20.

TRN	Name of test	Author	Country	Publisher	Year
117	*NFER English Progress Test C3*	NFER Staff	B	NFER-Nelson	1977

Type	No. of forms	C.A. range	Skills tested	Time
Group, attainment (level A)	1	9:07 to 10:10	Reading comprehension Sequencing Comprehension of a poem Punctuation Comprehension of a prose passage	Untimed (about 40′–45′)

Comments: 'The test consists of 50 items which include two comprehension passages and a series of questions which test basic punctuation and other language skills' (Manual, p. 2). This is a somewhat imprecise specification of a test's content. Listed in the above table is an analysis based on an inspection of the pupil's test booklet and the test manual. The curricular relevance of a test's content is a crucial consideration when selecting any measure of attainment.

A printed form of the test appeared in 1970. The manual was completed by December 1976 and published in 1977. In standardising the test a representative sample of 5 747 pupils aged from 9 : 09 to 10 : 08 was used. Data for this purpose were collected during the summer term, the time in the school year when it is suggested that the test be used. Girls scored higher on average than boys by 4·5 points of raw score. Separate tables of norms were produced for boys and girls. The norms were extrapolated in both directions to the age limits shown above. A Kuder-Richardson reliability coefficient of 0·964 is specified (N = 408).

Raw scores can be converted to standard scores with a mean of 100 and a standard deviation of 15 for each month of chronological age covered by the test. Only inter-individual comparison of total scores is possible.

TRN	Name of test	Author	Country	Publisher		Year
118	*NFER English Progress Test D2*	J. Henchman	B	NFER-Nelson		1964
					23rd impression	1977

Type	No. of forms	C.A. range	*Skills tested	Time
Group, attainment (level A)	1	10:06 to 12:00	Spelling Sequencing sentences Vocabulary Reading comprehension Sentence construction Punctuation Active-passive	Untimed (about 40′–45′)

Comments: The content of this 75-item test is not analysed in the manual. An indication only of the content is given above on the basis of an inspection of the pupils' test booklet and the manual. The curricular relevance of a test's content is a key issue for any potential user to consider. The validity of the inter-individual comparisons that can be made requires that the test samples educationally important aspects of English language.

The sample of 4 096 pupils aged from 10:07 to 11:08 on which the test was standardised is not claimed to be representative. In preparing the tables for converting raw scores to standard score (mean 100; standard deviation 15), the constructors extrapolated upwards and downwards from their data in order to provide for a wide age range of pupils. The internal consistency coefficient of reliability based on a sample of 241 scripts drawn randomly from the standardisation sample was 0·97, based on Kuder-Richardson formula 20. No other data on reliabilities or validities are given.

Raw scores based on a pupil's total score on the test can be converted to standard scores for each month of chronological age. Thus young children in a year group, e.g. those born in August where the school-year starts in September, are not compared with older children in the same year group. Children in each of the twelve monthly age groups who obtain the same standardised score will obviously have different raw score on the test, the younger age groups having the lower raw scores. The difference between raw scores and standardised scores in the assessment of inter-individual differences on a test such as this must always be born in mind.

* The following are not specified in the manual, but are derived from an examination of the manual and booklet.

TRN	Name of test	Author	Country	Publisher	Year
119	*NFER English Progress Test D3*	NFER Staff	B	NFER-Nelson	1977

Type	No. of forms	C.A. range	Skills tested	Time
Group, attainment (level A)	1	10:00 to 11:08	Use of contextually correct words Punctuation Sequencing sentences Comprehension of a poem Comprehension of a prose passage	Untimed (about 45′)

Comments: Development of this test appears to have begun in 1970. Its 50 items sample various English skills. No curricular analysis is presented to justify the selection.

Standardisation was completed by 1975. A sample of 7813 was used. Internal consistency reliability is reported as being 0·96 using Kuder-Richardson formula 21 and based on the standardisation data. No other information on reliabilities or validities is presented. The manual was completed by December 1976 and published in 1977. This does seem rather a lengthy time to take between the initiation and conclusion of the exercise.

Raw scores can be converted to standard scores with a mean of 100 and a standard deviation of 15 for each month of chronological age covered by the test.

TRN	Name of test	Author	Country	Publisher		Year
120	*NFER English Progress Test E*	M. A. Brimer	B	NFER-Nelson		1956
					11th impression	1978

Type	No. of forms	C.A. range	Skills tested		Time
Group, attainment	1	10:00 to 11:00	*Use of English*:		Untimed (about 40′–45′)
			Vocabulary	Reading comprehension	
			Expression	Grammatical usage	
			Punctuation	Spelling	
(level A)					

Comments: Although Brimer's name as author of the test appears in the NFER-Nelson catalogue for 1984–5, his name does not appear on either the manual or the pupil's form. Although the manual specifies the above six skills as being tested, pupils are only compared in relation to total scores. The weighting of the six areas is not discussed.

The test remains only 'provisionally' standardised on a small sample of unspecified size and representativeness. As the manual points out, in such circumstances any normative interpretation of the results obtained by pupils can only be a rough estimate. An internal consistency coefficient of reliability estimated by using Kuder–Richardson formula 20 on a sample of 185 scripts is reported as being 0·95. In its present form, the most constructive use to which it could be put would be to place pupils in a rank order. The conversion of raw scores to standardised scores, including age-allowances, is of questionable use.

The curricular content is justified as being '. . . an array of tasks which are common to many schemes of work and which are part of more liberally conceived programmes' (Manual, p. 2).

TRN	Name of test	Author	Country	Publisher		Year
121	*NFER English Progress Test E2*	S. M. Unwin	B	NFER-Nelson		1974
					8th impression	1977

Type	No. of forms	C.A. range	Skills tested		Time
Group, attainment	1	11:00 to 12:09	Transformations	Sentence writing	Untimed (about 40′–45′)
			Vocabulary	Spelling	
			Punctuation	Comprehension	
			Language experience	Organisation	
(level A)					

Comments: Although Unwin's name as author of the test appears in the 1984–5 NFER-Nelson catalogue, the name does not appear on either the manual or the pupil's test form. The content of the test is analysed by items in relation to the above eight areas. It is pointed out that 'there is no statistical evidence to show that psychologically separate or discrete skills are being tested. Test scores should be taken as unitary measures of attainment . . .' (Manual, p. 3). The test is intended to assess globally inter-individual differences in attainment. It is not intended as a basis for teaching, but a point of departure. It can be used to identify pupils in need of remedial help in basic literacy. Although teaching and exercises in the type of activities tested is not advocated as a panacea, some such tasks could be incorporated into certain remedial education programmes, according to the author. The test was first printed in 1963!

During 1971 and 1972 the test was standardised on 8 709 pupils aged from 11:00 to 12:09 years in three LEAs, using complete age groups. This does not necessarily mean, nor is it claimed, that the sample was a nationally representative one. On average, girls obtained a higher mean score than boys. As, however, the rate of increase of score with age did not differ between the sexes, only one table of norms based on the combined data was provided. Using a random sample of 257 scripts from the standardisation sample, the internal consistency coefficient of reliability obtained using Kuder-Richardson formula 20 was 0·96. No other evidence of reliabilities or validities is presented.

Raw scores can be converted to standard scores with a mean of 100 and a standard deviation of 15 for each month of chronological age covered by the test.

TRN	Name of test	Author	Country	Publisher	Year
122	*NFER English Progress Test F2*	J. Henchman and E. Hendry	B	NFER-Nelson	1977

Type	No. of forms	C.A. range	*Skills tested	Time
Group, attainment (level A)	1	12:03 to 13:08	Reading comprehension Punctuation Sequencing sentences Spelling Comprehension of prose passages Grammatical usage	Untimed (about 40′–45′)

Comments: The purpose of the test is to estimate pupils' relative attainments in English. There is no analysis of the test content in the manual. The test booklet before me is copyright 1963. The standardisation data were obtained in 1971 and 1972. The manual that the reviewer has was completed in December 1976, and published in 1977. Test content does date. Does the content of this test still match the language concerns of secondary school teachers?

Two distinct samples of children were used in the standardisation. Thus separate norms are available for the Non-industrial Midlands based on 4 759 pupils aged 12:03 to 13:09 and for the Urban North-West based on 1 295 pupils aged from 12:06 to 13:02. The only reliability estimate presented is based on the second sample. The Kuder–Richardson formula 20 coefficient of internal consistency for this group is reported to be 0·95.

It is difficult to see why this test has not been revised. The considerable thought that went into devising various types of items could have led to interesting developments.

* The following are not specified in the manual, but are derived from an examination of the manual and booklet.

TRN	Name of test	Author	Country	Publisher		Year
123	*NFER English Progress Test F3*	NFER Staff	B	NFER-Nelson		1963
					4th impression	1977

Type	No. of forms	C.A. range	*Skills tested	Time
Group, attainment (level A)	1	12:09 to 13:08	Reading comprehension Syntax Comprehension of a poem Punctuation Synonyms Sentence construction Vocabulary	Untimed (about 40′–50′)

Comments: The curricular content of the above test is neither analysed nor listed in the very brief duplicated manual. Standardisation data were collected from a sample of 1 563 boys and girls in December 1969. Raw scores based only on the total score on the test can be converted to standardised scores with a mean of 100 and a standard deviation of 15 for each monthly age group. No evidence of reliabilities, validities or utility is presented. Either the test should be revised and restandardised in the light of current English Language objectives, or it should be deleted from the publisher's catalogue. The items contained in the test may be of value as starting points for further developments.

* The following are not specified in the manual, but are derived from an inspection of the pupil's booklet and the manual.

TRN	Name of test	Author	Country	Publisher		Year
124	*NFER English Progress Test G*	S. M. Unwin	B	NFER-Nelson		1962
					Standardisation	1975
					5th impression	1976

Type	No. of forms	C.A. range	*Skills tested	Time
Group, attainment (level A)	1	13:01 to 14:04	*English language*: Grammatical usage Reading comprehension Transformation from direct to indirect speech Sequencing Vocabulary Verb to noun transformations Punctuation	Untimed (about 35′–40′)

Comments: The test consists of 60 items presented in a continuous form, together covering grammatical usage, vocabulary, comprehension, punctuation and spelling, through the medium of four different exercises' (Manual, p. 2). This is a somewhat imprecise specification of a test's content. Listed in the above table* is an analysis based on an inspection of the pupil's test booklet and the manual. The curricular relevance of a test's content is a crucial consideration when selecting any measure of attainment. The manual gives no indication as to how the content of the test was determined.

A printed form of the test appeared in 1962. The manual on which this report is based is dated 1976, as is the pupil's booklet. Standardisation involved a sample of 3 061 pupils aged between 13 : 04 and 14 : 02 years drawn from one Midlands urban LEA during 1975. It was not possible to obtain a group that could be deemed nationally representative, hence the manual advises caution when using the norms. Presumably the conversion tables were extended to a wider age range by extrapolation. The internal consistency of the test based on the standardisation sample yielded a Kuder–Richardson formula 21 reliability coefficient of 0·92. The standard error of measurement of the test is reported as 4·3 points. There is no other evidence on reliabilities or validities other than the support that the latter gains from the test's content. No mention is made of sex differences on the test.

Raw scores can be converted to standard scores with a mean of 100 and standard deviation of 15 for each month of chronological age covered by the test. Only inter-individual comparison of total scores is possible.

TRN	Name of test	Author	Country	Publisher	Year
125	*NFER Prawf Darllen Brawddegau 1* (Welsh Sentence Reading Test)	G. J. Evans	B	NFER-Nelson	1959

Type	No. of forms	C.A. range	Skills tested	Time
Group or individual, multiple-choice sentence-completion, attainment (level A)	1	8:00 to 10:11	Reading comprehension	20′

Comments: This test is in Welsh. It consists of thirty-five graded sentences presented as multiple-choice sentence-completion items. The test was standardised in 1959 on a sample of 2 693 Welsh-speaking school children. It is an acceptably reliable instrument, its internal consistency reliability being 0·93 and the standard error of measurement being 4·0. One would need to be a Welsh-speaking curriculum expert to assess whether the test's content is still educationally appropriate.

TRN	Name of test	Author	Country	Publisher	Year
126	*NFER Primary Reading Test*	N. France	B	NFER-Nelson	1979

Type	No. of forms	C.A. range	Skills tested	Time
Group, attainment (level A)	2	6:00 to 12:00	Level 1 Word-recognition Reading comprehension Level 2 Reading comprehension	Untimed (about 20′–30′)

Comments: Developed in cooperation with LEAs throughout the UK, this test enables the same material at Level 1 to be used, dependent on the mode of presentation, as either a word-recognition or a reading comprehension test. Level 2 material is used only as a test of reading comprehension having a five-option multiple-choice format. Parallel forms of both levels are available.

Raw scores can be converted to reading ages, standard scores for each six monthly chronological age group, stanines and percentiles. Separate tables of norms are provided for the word-recognition administration of Level 1 and also for Levels 1 and 2 as separate reading comprehension tests, for representative samples of children from (a) England, Wales and Northern Ireland combined and (b) Scotland.

The construction, validation and standardisation involved 20 000 children. Initially over 250 items were administered to a representative national sample of UK children aged from top infants to junior 3 (6:04 to 10:09 years). Satisfactory evidence of the reliabilities and validities of the tests is reported. At the validation stage, items were chosen to minimise sex differences and consequently a common set of norms for boys and girls is provided. The issue of sex differences in scores is discussed in the manual and the extent of these, despite the previously mentioned item selection strategy, is indicated.

This is a well-constructed, reliable, valid and easily administered instrument based on conventional test theory. It has the added advantage of a well-prepared manual that is likely to help teachers' professional development. The manual is clearly written, technically sound yet easily understood.

TRN	Name of test	Author	Country	Publisher		Year
127	*NFER Reading Level Tests (Experimental version)*	NFER Staff	B	NFER-Nelson		1977*
					2nd impression	1980

Type	No. of forms	C.A. range	Skills tested	Time
Group attainment, criterion-referenced	1 (Part 1)	7:06 to 9:06	Reading comprehension (cloze procedure)	Untimed
	(Part 2)	9:06 to 11:06	Reading comprehension (cloze procedure)	(about 20′–25′)
(level A)				

Comments: It is difficult to establish the history of this test.* The manual before me gives a 1961 copyright date. The content of the manual refers to the preparation of the sixteen cloze passages printed in Parts 1 and 2 and their testing on children in 1974. The copyright date on the Parts 1 and 2 that I have are 1970 and 1977.

Sixteen cloze passages were written to meet a range of readability levels from below the 6:06 to the 10:06 year level using the Fry Readability Chart (Fry, 1968; 1969). A one in ten deletion policy was used although it was not applied automatically. The passages were tried out on about 740 junior school pupils. Correlations between mean cloze scores and syllable length and sentence length of the passages were 0·7 and 0·8 respectively. Eight of the passages were selected to form the present test. The first four comprise Part 1 and the second four Part 2. The former are intended for use with Junior 1 and 2 and the latter for Junior 3 and 4 pupils. A table in the manual gives criterion scores for each of the eight passages indicating whether a child's score shows his reading of a passage to be at the Independent, Instructional or Frustration levels. Teachers using the test are advised to familiarise themselves with the ideas of cloze procedure, text readability and of reading levels (Harrison, 1980; Robertson, 1981).

Whilst the internal consistency reliability of the test is reported as 0·96 using Kuder–Richardson formula 21, the very tentative nature of the values chosen provisionally to represent the three levels of readability is acknowledged and the user of the test advised to be cautious in interpreting a pupil's scores. The validity of the categorisation provided by the test has yet to be established.

FRY, E. B. (1968) 'A readability formula that saves time.' *Journal of Reading*, **11**, 513–16.

FRY, E. B. (1969) 'The readability graph validated at primary levels.' *The Reading Teacher*, **6**, 534–8.

HARRISON, C. (1980) *Readability in the Classroom*. Cambridge: Cambridge University Press.

ROBERTSON, C. G. (1981) 'Cloze procedure: a review.' *Educational Research*, **23**, 2, 128–33.

TRN	Name of test	Author	Country	Publisher	Year
128	*NFER Reading Test A*	NFER Guidance and Assessment Service	B	NFER-Nelson	1970

Type	No. of forms	C.A. range	Skills tested	Time
Group or individual, multiple-choice sentence-completion, attainment (level A)	1	6:09 to 8:09	Reading comprehension	Untimed (20′–30′)

Comments: This test is comprised of thirty-eight simple sentence-completion type items printed in an eight-page booklet. The child has to select the correct word or phrase from four alternatives. The test is preceded by four practice items.

The test was standardised on five samples totalling 7 249 pupils and the results were pooled. Although girls scored higher than boys on this test by an average of about three points of raw score, only one set of norms is provided. Appropriate cautionary advice concerning the use of the norms for comparing the reading attainments of boys and girls is given. Raw scores can be converted to standard scores with a mean of 100 and standard deviation of 15 for each monthly chronological age group. Based on scores from a random sample of 272 pupils, a Kuder–Richardson formula 20 coefficient of internal consistency reliability of 0·96 is reported. The manual indicates that the test is less reliable at the extremes of the range covered. No evidence of validities is presented. However, the face validity of such a test of reading comprehension will appear high to the majority of teachers. It is to be hoped that more substantial evidence of the test's validities will be forthcoming.

TRN	Name of test	Author	Country	Publisher	Year
129	*NFER Reading Test AD*	A. F. Watts	B	NFER-Nelson	1954 1978

Type	No. of forms	C.A. range	Skills tested	Time
Group, attainment, normative (level A)	1	8:00 to 10:07	Reading comprehension	15′ plus 5′ practice

Comments: The purpose of this test is not explicitly stated in the manual. In practice it is typically used as a means of obtaining a global measure of a particular type of reading comprehension for screening, grouping pupils and monitoring progress. The test consists of 35 multiple-choice sentence-completion items printed in a four-page booklet. The test proper is preceded by four practice items. As can be seen from the dates given above, the test has been on the educational scene for a long time. The following comments relate to the information contained in the 1978 edition of the manual and the 1977 standardisation work.

Standardisation in 1977 involved a nationally representative sample of 9 363 pupils aged between 8:06 and 10:07. The conversion tables include extrapolations downward to make them suitable for use at any time during the school year. Users are warned of the likely higher degree of error in extrapolated scores. Although girls, on average, scored higher than boys on the test, the increase in test score with age did not differ. On this basis only combined conversion tables are provided. Raw scores can be converted to standard scores on a scale having a mean of 100 and a standard deviation of 15 for each age group. A correction for 'Chance' scoring that is shown to increase the discrimination of the test is included in the marking directions.

The Kuder–Richardson formula 20 internal consistency reliability coefficients were calculated for second- and third-year junior school pupils respectively using random sample of 411 and 474 scripts. Coefficients of 0·92 and 0·92 are reported. The manual also specifies the test's standard error of measurement at each age level and gives guidance on the interpretation of scores. No evidence of validities is presented. In earlier editions of the manual test-retest reliabilities of a high order (0·91 to 0·97) were given. Although reading experts continue to debate the pedagogic value of such sentence completion reading tests, such instruments remain popular with many teachers. In part, this is because they are easy to administer and mark, are reliable and valid for some purposes. Such tests were used to monitor national reading standards among 11:00 and 15:00 year old pupils before the setting up of the Assessment of Performance Unit of the Department of Education and Science. A Welsh version of the above test is available (see *NFER Prawf Darllen Brawddegau*, TRN 125).

TRN	Name of test	Author	Country	Publisher	Year
130	*NFER Reading Test BD*	NFER Staff	B	NFER-Nelson	1969 1971

Type	No. of forms	C.A. range	Skills tested	Time
Group, attainment, normative (level A)	1	7:00 to 10:04 10:00 to 11:04* *(Provisional norms only)	Reading comprehension	20′ plus 5′ to 10′ practice

Comments: This is a 44 item test of reading comprehension. Its multiple-choice format leaves a gap in the middle of a sentence, the pupil having to identify the correct response from a five-option choice given at the end. The test was standardised on a sample of 19046 pupils in Oxfordshire, Portsmouth, Preston and Surrey. Provisional norms are also available for ages 10:00 to 11:04. A decision to make no correction for guessing is justified on the basis of empirical research. This represents a different conclusion from that reached in relation to *NFER Reading Test AD* (TRN 129). Raw scores can be converted to standard scores on a scale with a mean of 100 and a standard deviation of 15 for each monthly age group. Combined tables for both sexes are given because the age allowances for boys and girls did not differ significantly despite the fact that, on average, the girls obtained higher scores than the boys. The need for caution when comparing boys and girls using the test is emphasised.

Kuder–Richardson formula 20 internal consistency reliability coefficients were calculated for each of three age groups and for all pupils. Sample sizes were 128, 107, 102 and 337 respectively and the resultant coefficients of reliability were 0·91, 0·92, 0·92 and 0·92. Test-retest reliabilities for second, third and fourth year pupils based on samples of 211, 219 and 241 pupils were 0·94, 0·94 and 0·95. Validity was studied by comparing test scores for various methods of marking with teachers' estimates of pupils' reading abilities as part of the investigation into the effects of guessing. The age and representativeness of the standardisation sample makes normative comparisons problematic. The development of local norms is one way forward, provided that the skills tapped and the information provided by the test are of pedagogic value.

TRN	Name of test	Author	Country	Publisher		Year
131	*NFER Reading Comprehension Test DE*	E. L. Barnard	B	NFER-Nelson		1967
					Manual	1976

Type	No. of forms	C.A. range	Skills tested	Time
Group, diagnostic and attainment (level A)	1	10:00 to 12:10	1 Reading comprehension (Global Understanding) 2 Extraction of facts from a relatively complex sentence or series of sentences (Detail) 3 Ability to make inferences from the facts presented (Inference) 4 Understanding of the use of individual words or phrases	Untimed (about 50′)

Comments: The purpose of the test is to assess pupils' understanding of complete passages rather than only of single sentences. The test is made up of eight varied passages of writing of increasing complexity, each on a separate page. Between four and eight questions are asked after each passage, some of them being open-ended. There are fifty questions in all.

It is emphasised that the four categories of Skills tested overlap to an unspecified degree. A table classifies questions in a Skills tested by passage matrix. Apart from the use of the pupils' total scores to determine their relative attainment on the test, it is suggested that the pupils' individual scripts can usefully be studied to see which of the four skills are dealt with most adequately. 9/50 questions relate to 'Global Understanding', 23/50 to 'Detail', 10/50 to 'Inference' and 8/50 to the 'Understanding of the use of individual words or phrases'. Users should appreciate that any such interpretation of a pattern of scores will be a clinical one because the reliabilities and intercorrelations of the four scales are not given.

The test was standardised on a total sample of 13 949 pupils of whom 7 076 were boys and 6 873 were girls. Of these, 13 070 were in the 10:02 to 12:01 age range in four different LEAs. There were 879 pupils aged from 11:09 to 12:08 drawn from a city area in the north-west of England. No significant sex diffferences in the age allowances for boys and girls were identified and therefore a combined conversion table for both boys and girls is provided. Despite this, a significant difference in the mean raw scores of boys and girls, with the latter scoring significantly higher than the former, in the sample of 13 070 pupils is reported. Raw scores can be converted to standard scores with a mean of 100 and a standard deviation of 15 for each monthly chronological age group.

The only evidence of reliability presented is based on 317 scripts drawn from one of the areas in the standardisation sample. A Kuder–Richardson formula 20 internal consistency reliability coefficient of 0·96 is reported. It is to be hoped that greater evidence of both reliabilities and validities will be reported. Whilst such evidence will be relatively easily obtained in relation to the total score on the test, it will be more difficult to obtain it in relation to the diagnostic aspect implicit in the four skills to which the comprehension questions are directed. It is this latter area that has the greater pedagogic significance and, hence, appeal to teachers.

TRN	Name of test	Author	Country	Publisher		Year
132	*NFER Reading Test EH 1*	S. M. Bate	B	NFER-Nelson		1961 1965
					Manual	(1975)

Type	No. of forms	C.A. range	Skills tested	Time
Group, attainment, normative (level A)	1	11 : 00 to 15 : 11	Vocabulary : reading comprehension	Untimed (about 20′)

Comments: The test is a 60 item sentence-completion multiple-choice test. As can be seen from the dates listed above, the test was eventually standardised after a lengthy period of development – and delay. The standardisation sample consisted of 21 390 pupils aged between 11 : 00 and '14+'. There were 11 301 boys and 10 089 girls. The pupils were not evenly distributed over the year groups; the bulk (13 278) was in the youngest age group, 4 508 were in the oldest group and the remaining 3 604 were in the two central age groups. The pupils attended schools in four areas of the country but there is no claim that the sample was nationally representative, despite its size.

Because the age allowances for boys and girls did not differ significantly, one conversion table for both was constructed for each age level. In each of these, raw scores can be converted to standard scores with a mean of 100 and a standard deviation of 15 for each monthly age group. Internal consistency reliability coefficients were calculated on random samples of scripts drawn at each age level. Sample size ranged between 219 and 312. The Kuder–Richardson formula 20 coefficients obtained were 0·90, 0·92, 0·94 and 0·93 at successive age levels. No other evidence of reliabilities or validities is presented.

Interpretation of such norms is difficult in that it is uncertain what population they represent. If a school or an LEA built up its own norms, the test could provide information of value in relation to some educational decision making.

TRN	Name of test	Author	Country	Publisher		Year
133	*NFER Reading Test EH 2*	S. M. Bate	B	NFER-Nelson		1961 1965
					Manual	1975

Type	No. of forms	C.A. range	Skills tested	Time
Group, attainment, normative (level A)	1	11:00 to 15:11	Comprehension	Untimed (25′ to 45′)

Comments: The purpose of this test is to assess the pupil's ability to understand prose passages. There are seven paragraphs of writing each followed by five questions mainly, but not exclusively, multiple-choice in format. As can be seen from the dates listed above, the test was finally standardised after a lengthy period of development and delay shared with the other two tests in the battery (*EH 1* and *EH 3*, TRN 132 and 134 respectively).

The standardization sample consisted of 17 117 pupils aged between 11:00 and '14+'. There were 8 781 boys and 8 336 girls. The pupils were not evenly distributed over the year groups; the bulk (9 049) was in the youngest age group, 4 442 were in the oldest group and the remaining 3 626 were unevenly spread over the two central age groups. The pupils were drawn from four areas of the country. Despite its size, there is no claim that the sample is representative nationally.

Girls scored higher than boys, on average, at each of the four age levels. However, 'In no case did the age allowance for boys and girls differ significantly and consequently one conversion table was constructed for each group (boys and girls)' (Manual, p. 4). Four separate conversion tables are provided for successive age groups. A pupil's raw score can be converted into a standard score on a scale with a mean of 100 and a standard deviation of 15. Internal consistency reliability coefficients were calculated on random samples of scripts drawn at each age level. Sample sizes ranged between 254 and 430. The Kuder–Richardson formula 20 internal consistency reliability coefficients obtained were 0·88, 0·85, 0·81 and 0·84 at successive age levels. No other evidence of reliabilities or validities is presented.

Although the test constructors used pupils' performances on other tests to enable national norms to be projected, the procedure is only briefly mentioned. As with the *EH 1*, interpretation of such norms is difficult because one is uncertain of the population represented. The development of local norms could provide information of value in relation to some educational decision making.

TRN	Name of test	Author	Country	Publisher	Year
134	*NFER Reading Test EH 3*	S. M. Bate	B	NFER-Nelson	1961 1965 1973

Type	No. of forms	C.A. range	Skills tested		Time
Group, attainment, normative (level A)	1	11:03 to 15:07	Rate of reading comprehension	Years 1 & 2 Years 3 & 4	7′ $4\frac{1}{2}$′

Comments: This is the third test in the *NFER Reading Test EH* series. It aims to test what is called 'rate comprehension'. The test consists of two extracts, one from *Aku-Aku* by Heyerdahl and the other from *The Story of San Michele* by Munthe. In *EH 3*, a series of multiple-choice items is inserted into the extracts. The last point that the child has underlined is used as the basis on which his speed of reading is assessed.

EH 3 was provisionally standardised in 1973 using 2 511 boys and 1 841 girls attending schools in a predominantly rural county in the North West of England. No claim is made for the representative nature of the sample. At the 11:00 to 11:11 and the 12:00 to 12:11 year old age levels respectively, girls obtained significantly higher mean scores than boys. Despite this, only one common set of conversion tables is provided.

Raw scores can be converted into standard scores with a mean of 100 and standard deviation of 15 for each month of chronological age. No evidence of reliability or validity studies is given in the 12-page duplicated typescript manual.

Rate of reading comprehension is an important aspect of literacy and varies with the type of material being read. *EH 3* has a literary bias. This, together with its age and the existence of only provisional norms after such a long time, suggests that the information it elicits is of limited utility.

TRN	Name of test	Author	Country	Publisher	Year
135	*NFER Reading Test SR-A*	B. Pritchard	B	NFER-Nelson	1970
				Revised Manual	1979

Type	No. of forms	C.A. range	Skills tested	Time
Goup, attainment (level A)	1	7:06 to 11:11	Reading comprehension (Sentence completion)	20′

Comments: This 48 item test is designed to estimate junior school pupils' relative reading comprehension attainments using a multiple-choice sentence-completion format. Devised in 1970, a major standardisation took place in 1978 involving 13 886 first to fourth year junior school pupils representative of the population in England and Wales. Girls scored higher than boys, on average, in all four age groups. The mean differences from first to fourth year in terms of raw scores on the test were 0·74, 0·82, 0·52 and 0·05 respectively. Only the first two of these were significantly different ($p < \cdot 01$; $p < \cdot 05$). The increase in score with age did not differ significantly between the sexes at any age level. Because of this, only combined conversion tables are provided.

Separate tables of norms are provided for each age group. Raw scores can be converted to standardised scores with a mean of 100 and a standard deviation of 15 for monthly chronological age groups within each year. The Kuder–Richardson formula 21 coefficient of internal consistency for the four age groups ranged between 0·85 and 0·88. No other evidence on reliabilities or validities is given in the manual.

The use of only 48 items to discriminate between the entire range of reading comprehension characteristic of children aged between 7 : 06 and 11 : 11 years means that the grading tends to be rather coarse. Users of the test need to know when, in the school year, the standardisation data were collected if the normative results are to be interpreted correctly. This information is given in the 1979 manual. Both *SR-A* and *SR-B* (TRN 136) share the same manual and have an identical format.

TRN	Name of test	Author	Country	Publisher	Year
136	*NFER Reading Test SR-B*	B. Pritchard	B	NFER-Nelson	1979

Type	No. of forms	C.A. range	Skills tested	Time
Group, attainment (level A)	1	7:06 to 11:11	Reading comprehension (Sentence completion)	20′

Comments: This 48 item test is designed to estimate junior school pupils' relative reading comprehension attainments using a multiple-choice, sentence-completion format. The standardisation took place in 1978. The norms were obtained using data from a sample of 3 099 first to fourth year junior school pupils who took both this test and a very similar one, *SR-A* (TRN 135) which had been standardised on a large and nationally representative sample. A method of adjusting the raw score distribution in the first test utilised all this information. From the adjusted raw scores on *SR-B*, tables of norms for each of the four age groups were constructed. It is stated that because the calibration sample was relatively small, no firm statement can be made concerning sex differences on this test, but that a difference favouring girls in Junior 1 and 2 is likely on the basis of the similarities between *SR-B* and *SR-A*. It is a pity that the actual mean scores of boys and girls for each of the four year groups are not given in the manual. Separate tables of norms are given for each of the four year groups. Using a child's raw score and chronological age, his relative attainment is compared with that of other pupils born in the same month. Internal consistency coefficients of reliability were calculated using data from the standardisation sample, a practice of which many workers would not approve. Using Kuder–Richardson formula 21, the coefficients ranged between 0·85 and 0·7 for the four year groups.

The use of a relatively small number of items to discriminate between the range of reading ability encompassed in the junior school means that the grading tends to be rather coarse. In using the normative scores it is important for users to know when, during the school year, the standardisation data were collected. This information is in the manual. Both *SR-B* and *SR-A* share the same manual and have an identical format.

TRN	Name of test	Author	Country	Publisher		Year
137	*NFER Senior English Test*	NFER Staff	B	NFER-Nelson		1964
					Standardisation	1975
					Published	1976

Type	No. of forms	C.A. range	Skills tested	Time
Group, attainment (level A)	1	16:00 to 18:00	English language: Reading comprehension, Vocabulary, Grammatical skill, Ability to summarise	60′

Comments: Designed long ago with the assistance of teachers in technical education, this test was intended as one of 'basic knowledge of English for general entry groups in Technical Colleges' (Manual, p. 2). It is suggested that college staff could use the results to discover the individual strengths and weaknesses in various aspects of English of the entrants. The complementary institutional decision-making function served by the test is course allocation.

The test was standardised in late 1975 on 1 370 boys at Technical Colleges. The internal consistency of the test, as measured by Kuder–Richardson formula 20, yielded a reliability coefficient of 0·92 using a sample of N = 374. The standard error of measurement was 3·0 points. No other statistical evidence of validities, reliabilities or utility is presented.

Total raw scores are converted to standardised scores with a mean of 100 and a standard deviation of 15 for each monthly chronological age group. The suggestion that the test can be used to identify strengths and weaknesses is suspect to say the least. Without much more detail concerning the item characteristics, the cohesion of the sub-scales and their intercorrelations, such a diagnostic function can only be carried out at an intuitive level. Is this sufficient for a profession?

TRN	Name of test	Author	Country	Publisher	Year
138	*NFER Sentence Comprehension Test (Experimental edition)*	K. Wheldall, P. Mittler and A. Hobsbaum	B	NFER-Nelson	1979

Type	No. of forms	C.A. range	Skills tested		Time
Individual, diagnostic level A)	1	3:00 to 5:06 (or for handicapped children at comparable levels of language development)	(i) Simple intransitive (iii) Intransitive with adjective (v) Plural (vii) Future tense (ix) Simple negative (xi) Comparative (xiii) Simple prepositions (xv) Embedded phrase	(ii) Simple transitive (iv) Transitive with adjective (vi) Past tense (viii) Passive (x) Transitive negative (xii) Superlative (xiv) Harder prepositions	(about 60′)

Comments: Ten years of development culminated in the publication of the experimental version of this test. Its purpose is to enable the user to understand how a child deals with spoken sentences of varying complexity. The test can be used to screen nursery and infant classes, or be used with handicapped children at a similar level of language development, to study both inter and intra-individual differences in children's apparent understanding of sentences. The user is alerted to possible difficulties that a child may have with receptive language, thereby indicating where pedagogic (or other) attention might be needed.

In the test the child is required to point to one of four pictures representing the stimulus sentence. Each of the 15 sub-tests contains four sentences of different grammatical form or sentence type. If necessary the testing can be spread out over a number of sessions. There are 60 sentences in the test but interest is focused on a child's profile in the 15 sub-tests rather than on a total score out of 60.

The manual presents evidence from small-scale studies supporting the reliability and validity of the current version using a representative sample of 50 five year old pupils. The test-retest reliability coefficient on total score was 0·78, despite ceiling effects, and a coefficient of 0·76 for number of sub-tests passed. A split-half internal consistency coefficient of 0·88 was obtained (presumably on all 60 items). Using a sample of 160 three to five year old pupils, test-retest correlations for total score and for sub-tests passed were statistically significant at 0·87 and 0·83 respectively. Internal consistency coefficient of 0·90 is reported. Correlations with other tests of receptive language are presented as evidence of concurrent validity. Good discrimination between pupils of different ages and stages of language development is obtained.

Whilst the empirical relationships between the sub-tests is presented, a theoretical integration of these data remains elusive. The test has considerable potential for development. In its present form it can usefully identify a child's ability to comprehend an important range of sentence structures although the reliability of sub-tests comprised of four items only must be borne in mind. Users will almost certainly find their appreciation of conventional grammatical structures enhanced.

TRN	Name of test	Author	Country	Publisher		Year
139	*NFER Tests of Proficiency in English*	National Foundation for Educational Research	B	NFER-Nelson		1973
					2nd impression	1977

Type	No. of forms	C.A. range	Skills tested	Levels of Linguistic Analysis *(i)*	*(ii)* 1	*(iii)* 2	*(iv)* 3	*(v)*	Time
Group, individual, diagnostic		7:00 to 11:00							Some timed, some not
	1 (3 tests)		Listening comprehension skills		*(33)	*(28)	*(30)		
	1 (3 tests)		Speaking skills (individual test)		*(25)	*(15)	*(12)		
	1 (3 tests)		Reading skills		*(33)	*(28)	*(30)		
	1 (3 tests)		Writing skills		*(25)	*(20)	*(11)		
(level A)			(* Levels at which tests are available: no. of items in brackets)						

Comments: The above tests, with colour-coded booklets for ease of identification, were originally designed for use with immigrants whose native tongue or dialect differed from the English used in schools. Such children may require special placement and instruction. The tests can also be used with native English children. The tests have been constructed on a linguistic analysis of language as sets of five hierarchically-related skills in the four areas shown above, level (i) being the most elementary. There are three main tests in each area, tapping approximately those parts of the language model shown by asterisks. These tests are labelled 'Listening 1, 2 and 3', etc. The first tests in all areas use a common core of twelve nouns and eight verbs. Listening 2 and Reading 2 share ten common items. Taped instructions are used in Listening 2 and 3. The child's individual responses to Speaking 1, 2 and 3 are tape-recorded.

The use of a content criterion-referenced testing model is interesting, but as there is no evidence from a native English speaking group, one has some doubts concerning the validity of the criteria of mastery given for each test. Internal consistency reliability coefficients for Listening 2 and 3 and for Reading 1, 2 and 3 range between 0·63 and 0·75. Inter-rater reliabilities on the Writing and Speaking tests range between 0·85 and 0·98 based on 50 scripts and two markers. The intercorrelations between the tests are not given.

These tests sample a wide range of elementary language patterns and may well have value in identifying the language difficulties of any child. However the need to key such tests to educational programmes that are shown to be effective is of paramount importance. These tests could well achieve considerable popularity with teachers of immigrant pupils and of British-born children of immigrant parentage. The considerable amount of time needed to administer and mark the battery, especially the Speaking tests, is a disincentive to their use. The linguistic content of the tests is analysed in Appendix 1 of the Manual. The interpretation of the results is also discussed in relation to this analysis.

TRN	Name of test	Author	Country	Publisher	Year
140	*NFER Transitional Assessment: English*	Sumner, R. and Bradley, K.	B	NFER-Nelson	1978 2nd impression 1979

Type	No. of forms	C.A. range	Skills tested	Time
Group, attainment, criterion-referenced	1	10:00 to 11:00	1 Autobiographical (Essay)	No time limit. Allow at least 1 hr.
			2 Descriptive (Essay)	No time limit. Allow at least 1 hr.
			3 Explanatory/Factual (Essay)	No time limit. Allow at least 1 hr.
			4 Story-writing (Essay)	No time limit. Allow at least 1 hr.
			5 Sentence-writing	Allow about 30′
			6 Punctuation	
			7 Reading comprehension (Cloze technique)	
(level A)			8 Reading comprehension (Passage and questions)	

Comments: In cooperation with the London Borough of Hillingdon LEA, the authors carried out a joint project. Its purpose was to improve the quality of the information available when children transferred from primary to secondary education. Each of the eight modules is assessed on a four point scale. This enables the pupil's overall performance to be summarised in a profile. The four essays are marked by 'impression' marking but criteria for marking each are suggested in order to produce a more structured approach to the assessment. For each of the other four modules, marking criteria of different types are specified. No details of the reliabilities, validities and utility of the procedures are given in the Manual. Those wanting further details are referred to a report published by the NFER: SUMNER, R. and BRADLEY, K. (1977) *Assessment for Transition: A Study of New Procedures.*

At present (1983) some LEAs use the modules as published but others, whilst keeping the framework, have modified the content on advice from teachers (personal communication).

TRN	Name of test	Author	Country	Publisher	Year
141	*Northern Ireland Council for Educational Research Reading Test BTW1*	J. A. Wilson, J. Bill and K. Trew	NI	Northern Ireland Council for Educational Research	1974

Type	No. of forms	C.A. range	Skills tested	Time
Group, normative, attainment (level A)*	1	14:06 to 15:05†	Reading comprehension	15′

Comments: *BTW1* is a 55 item test of reading comprehension using sentence-completion multiple-choice format. Each item contains five possible answers. The test was constructed because other available similar instruments had too low ceilings. The present test is suitable for even the most able 14:00 to 15:00 year old pupils. A first version was constructed in 1971. Using a sample of 231 pupils, an internal consistency coefficient of reliability of 0·94 was obtained. The test was to be standardised on a sample of some 3 000 14 year old pupils in 51 secondary schools in Northern Ireland in connection with the *Enquiry among 15-year-olds, their teachers and parents in the year preceding the raising of the school leaving age to 16* (Northern Ireland Council for Educational Research, 1974). In the Report of that Enquiry, normative information on the test is given based on a sample of 2 995 pupils. The samples comprising this group were '. . . not strictly proportionate by sex and type of school to the parent population' (p. 330).

Subsequently, item analysis on representative samples of 400 boys and girls with a mean chronological age of 14:11† was carried out. Internal consistency as measured by Cronbach's alpha coefficient was 0·95. Raw scores against percentiles are presented for the sample. Evidence of the test's reliabilities (other than its internal consistency) is sparse. Data on its validities are also limited, although some are presented from an earlier version in the form of a matrix of correlations between pupils' scores on various tests. The test will certainly spread pupils out along the dimension it measures and is not time-consuming in its administration.

'The test has not been used since then by ourselves or anyone else. It is most useful as a research or survey instrument and as such could be made available to accredited researchers. The copyright resides with the NICER' (personal communication, 1983).

NORTHERN IRELAND COUNCIL FOR EDUCATIONAL RESEARCH (1974) *Early Leaving in Northern Ireland: Report of an Enquiry among 15-year-olds, their teachers and parents in the year preceding the raising of the school leaving age to 16*. Social Science Research Council Project HR 919/1.

* Although a relatively simple instrument, its availability is limited to accredited research workers through the publisher.

TRN	Name of test	Author	Country	Publisher	Year
142	*Parallel Spelling Tests*	D. Young	B	Hodder and Stoughton	1983

Type	No. of forms	C.A. range	Skills tested	Time
Group, attainment, normative (level A)	12*	6:04 to 12:11	Spelling	Untimed (about 15′–20′)

Comments: The purpose of this test is to allow continuous normative assessment of spelling attainments from the infants to the secondary school levels of education. Two banks of words, A (276 words) and B (300), were obtained mainly from a 1957 research on children's vocabularies. Bank A is intended for use up to Junior 2 level and Bank B for older pupils up to first year secondary level. Each bank is divided into sections containing six pairs of words. To construct a test, one *pair* of words is selected from each of the sections in the bank. A table gives the number of words to be used at each age level. The system allows twelve matched tests with no overlap in item use to be constructed.* If overlap between tests is allowed, many more tests can be made up. The content of the two banks are assumed to 'achieve an unbiased proportional representation of the common spelling structures' (Manual, p. 34). Whilst the orthographic characteristics of the overall lists may be equivalent, the spelling tasks each presents at different levels is equivalent only in terms of whether children could, or could not, spell them correctly. The use of individual items was almost entirely determined by whether these had adequate discriminating power and appropriate facility values when used with English children in 1981 and 1982. Short sentences are provided for each word. Administration involves saying the word to be spelled, reading a sentence containing the word and instructing the pupils to write the word.

Raw scores can be converted to quotients with a mean of 100 and standard deviation of 15 for each two-monthly chronological age group. Spelling ages can also be obtained. The tests were standardised using 3 904 pupils representative of national standards on other measures. An extensive array of evidence on reliabilities and validities from various small-scale studies supports the acceptability of the tests. The manual contains advice on interpreting the results, extending assessments and the teaching of spelling. Appendices provide advice on examining spelling errors, assessing spelling in children's written work and on identifying relative weakness in spelling in comparison with an expectation based on an average of a child's attainments in reading, mathematics and intelligence.

TRN	Name of Test	Author	Country	Publisher	Year
143	*Phonic Skills (P.S.) Tests*	S. Jackson	B	Robert Gibson	1971

Type	No. of forms	C.A. range	Skills tested	Time
Individual and group, diagnostic, criterion-referenced (level A)	1	5:00 to 10:00	1 Sounds, names, initial sounds, final sounds (lower-case letters, group test) 2 Sounds, names (upper-case letters, group test) 3 Individual letters (lower case, individual test) 4 Individual letters (upper case, individual test) 5 Two- and three-letter words 6 Final consonant blends 7 Initial consonant blends 8 Vowel digraphs 9 Consonant digraphs 10 Word endings 11 Multi-syllabic words	Untimed

Comments: Jackson has devised a series of eleven reading tests of the phonic skills he considers important in reading. These tests enable the teacher to identify the skills with which a child has difficulties. The results of whichever tests are administered are recorded on a Phonic Skills Record Card. Guidance is given in the interpretation of test results and in developing individual remedial programmes for each child. These suggestions are based on Jackson's considerable experience and knowledge. This series of tests is apparently based on a logical analysis of the component phonic skills involved in reading. It has much in common with the Stott *Programmed Reading Kit* (1971). Jackson's series of tests can be looked upon as a checklist of important skills or as a series of mastery tests. There is no evidence given at all concerning standardisation (one suspects that none was carried out), reliabilities and validities. No evidence is presented for the efficacy of the remedial treatment he suggests. It is a pity that such information is not provided. The major reason for including this series of tests is that they represent an interesting analysis of the possible phonic skills involved in reading. The tests are likely to be of value to the teacher who is concerned with diagnosing and rectifying the weaknesses in phonic skills of her children. Jackson's suggestions for remedial work, in *Get Reading Right: a handbook for remedial teachers*, have been favourably received by many teachers.

TRN	Name of test	Author	Country	Publisher	Year
144	*Picture Aided Reading Test (PART)*	N. W. Hamp	B	N. W. Hamp (with support from The National Deaf Children's Society, the Northampton Branch of the NDCS and The Spastics Society)	1975

Type	No. of forms	C.A. range	Skills tested	Time
Individual, attainment, normative (level A)	1	6:00 to 11:00*	Word reading Picture identification	Untimed (between 2′–6′)

Comments: *PART* was primarily designed to test the reading attainments of deaf and partially-hearing pupils. The test contains two practice items followed by 55 items in the test proper. Each item contains two stimuli: on one side of a card, a printed word (capable of being illustrated) and on the other, four illustrations including one of the preceding printed word. The pupil's task is to read the word and then, with the word removed from sight, select its pictorial representation.

The test is standardised on a random sample of 2 279 *hearing* pupils aged from 5:00 to 11:00 plus. The representativeness of the sample is not specified.

In a very readable manual of 24 pages, the author has packed a great deal of information. He presents substantial evidence supporting the reliability and validity of the test with deaf, partially-hearing and children with normal hearing. An extensive empirical basis to the instrument is well-summarised from his research (Hamp, 1971).

The test should only be used with hearing-impaired children with a reading age of 7:02 years or more.

Whether or not the correction for guessing is needed is very much open to question, as is his decision to use different criteria for correct responses from hearing-impaired and normal pupils. The former needed only to get the picture correct; the latter are *required* to read the word correctly in order to be *allowed* to select the picture, yet both word-reading and picture selection had to be correct if the child was to be credited with passing the item.

Raw scores can be converted to reading ages in preference to standard scores as the author considers the former to be more meaningful to teachers who use the test. A case could be made for both being provided. Despite such comment, the test has many important strengths and has already been found of value with other children having linguistic difficulties. The retardation of deaf and partially-hearing pupils' reading attainments in relation to the standardisation sample are, as would be anticipated, very considerable. Comparisons between the samples can be made in several ways using the tables provided.

It is surprising that the test has not been commercially published. Presumably Hamp's sampling and also his discussion of the reasons why precise norms are not set out for hearing impaired pupils may have contributed. The need for caution when interpreting *PART* results that he also rightly stresses for such pupils could have been a further deterrent.

* The test has a ceiling reading age of 11:00 years for hearing pupils. The mean reading ages of deaf and partially-hearing pupils aged 15:00 years are respectively, on this scale, approximately 8:06 and 9:08 years respectively.

HAMP, N. W. (1971) 'Reading attainment and some associated factors in deaf and partially hearing children.' M.Ed. thesis: University of Leicester.

TRN	Name of test	Author	Country	Publisher	Year
150	*Profion Bangor* *(The Bangor Tests)*	P. Williams *et al.**	B	Gwasg Gomer	1984

Type	No. of forms	C.A. range	Skills tested	Time
Individual (I), group (G), criterion-referenced, diagnostic (level A)	1	5:00 to 9:00	(I) Reading Readiness: Checklist and observation schedule	Untimed
			(I) Visual Discrimination / (I) Auditory Discrimination } 4 tests of matching skills	,,
			(I) Phonic Checklist	,,
			(I) Word Recognition: list of 50 graded words	,,
			(G) Spelling Competence: list of 160 graded words	,,
			(G) Comprehension	,,

Comments: This battery of diagnostic tests was designed for use with first language Welsh pupils learning to read in Welsh. It is anticipated that the battery will also be of value with pupils learning Welsh as a second language. The tests are presented in book form and individual test cards are also available. A specially devised record book directs the teacher's attention to the need for intervention following testing by including space for recording the action taken following each test entry. The tests are deliberately criterion-referenced and prescriptive. They help the teacher identify strengths and weaknesses and initiate remedial interventions. The battery is designed to allow a systematic analysis of a pupil's progress and to assist in developing individual programmes of instruction. Comprehension is assessed by 6 tests based on the first six readers of a Welsh reading scheme (*Cunllyn y Canllaw*).

The utility of the battery was examined by involving a sample of teachers dealing with pupils having learning difficulties. Twenty schools throughout Wales were involved in this aspect of the work. The content validity of the sub-tests is supported by evaluations in project schools across Wales. Analyses of children's responses supported the internal consistency reliabilities of the tests where this technique was appropriate.

(The reviewer is indebted to Professor P. Williams, Dr G. Lowden of the University College of North Wales at Bangor and to Ms G. Sturgess of the Schools Council for their help in providing the information used in compiling this entry. Any misrepresentation is the reviewer's sole responsibility.)

* P. Williams, G. Lowden, C. Lloyd Griffith, A. Waddon, G. Wyn Jones, M. Thomas, C. Baker, A. Roberts and E. Jones.

TRN	Name of test	Author	Country	Publisher	Year
155	*Quest Screening, Diagnosis and Remediation Kit*	A. H. Robertson, A. Henderson, A. Robertson, J. Fisher and M. Gibson	B	Arnold-Wheaton	1983

Type	No. of forms	C.A. range	Skills tested	Time		Time
Group (screening), individual (diagnostic), attainment	1	7:00 to 7:11 (end of infant school)	*Reading Screening Test* Part 1 Word identification 2 Reading comprehension *Pre reading* *Diagnostic Reading Test* about 30′ Test 1 Auditory discrimination Part A (Words-same or different?) B (Initial, medial and final sounds) Test 2 Visual discrimination Part A (Drawings) B (Letters) Test 3 Auditory sequential memory Part A (Word sequences) B (Digit span retention) Test 4 Visual sequential memory Test 5 Visuo-motor co-ordination Part A (Mazes) B (Shapes) C (Read and copy sentence) *Word attack skills* Test 6 Sight vocabulary Test 7 Letter recognition (sounds) Test 8 Simple blends	Untimed (30′–40′)	*Number Screening Test* *Diagnostic Number Test* *Pre number* Test 1 Visual perception Part A Pattern B Shape Test 2 Visuo-motor co-ordination Part A Completing and copying shapes B Copying numbers Test 3 Auditory sequential memory Part A Word sequences B Digit span retention *Early number concepts* Test 4 Sorting Test 5 Conservation Test 6 Ordering Test 7 Addition: union and counting Test 8 Subtraction Part A Take away B More: how many more? C Less: how many less? D Difference *Number skills* Test 9A Ordering: oral	Untimed (30′–40′) (about 30′)

Quest Screening, Diagnosis and Remediation Kit continued

(level A)

Skills tested

Test 9 Beginnings and endings
Test 10 Digraphs and the silent 'e' rule
Test 11 Reversals

Part (a) Oral counting
(b) Number 'before' and 'after'
Test 9B Ordering: written
Part (a) Notation
(b) Ordering numbers
Test 10A Computation: oral
Part (a) Addition
(b) Addition
(c) Subtraction
(d) Subtraction
(e) Subtraction
Test 10B Computation: written
Part (a) Within 10
(b) Within 20

Comments: *Quest* was developed as a co-operative venture between a College of Education and a Child Guidance Service in East Kilbride. Its aims were to produce (i) screening tests for use at the end of infant education to identify children failing in reading and/or number, (ii) diagnostic tests identifying a profile of a child's abilities, and (iii) suggestions for remedial techniques based on the profile. In commenting on this kit, both the reading and number tests have been described above. Comments following are deliberately restricted to the Reading Screening Test, the Diagnostic Reading Test and the suggestions for remedial activities.

The screening test was designed to spread out pupils with low attainments and not to discriminate between pupils with high attainments. It appears to do this well. On the basis of work with over 6 000 pupils, cut-off points were established identifying the 5% of pupils having serious difficulties. Children obtaining scores below the cut-off point '. . . should be given the Diagnostic Reading Test so that a remedial reading programme can be constructed' (Manual, p. 30). This particular cut-off point contains no age allowance. Anomalies can arise because this approach takes no consideration of attainment relative to age in the group. Later on in the appendix the possibility of making age allowances is presented. A matrix is presented of chronological age against test score. The matrix presents five chronological age bands in the range from below 6 : 09 to above 7 : 05 years and test scores in ten bands from 0 to 30. The numbers and cumulative percentages are given for pupils in each of the 50 cells. Hence the unusualness of a score can be appreciated in relation to the appropriate age band in the group of 2 046 pupils from which the data were derived. This helps the user to avoid the problems that arise if a single cut-off point is used irrespective of age, a suspect suggestion that is unfortunately made earlier in the manual. This is an example of simplicity being bought at too high a price in terms of valid decision making.

No evidence of the validities or reliabilities of the screening test is given. There is no evidence of the reliabilities, validities or intercorrelations concerning the sub-tests of the Diagnostic Reading Test. Some small scale

Continued at foot of p. 185

TRN	Name of test	Author	Country	Publisher	Year
157	*Reading Comprehension Test for Personnel Selection*	L. R. C. Haward	B	Hodder and Stoughton	1965

Type	No. of forms	C.A. range	Skills tested	Time
Group or individual, attainment (level A)	1	15:00 +	Extraction of information from a technical text	15′

Comments: This twenty-five-item test is intended to help in the selection of students over fifteen years of age wishing to take further courses of training that depend upon an extensive use of textbooks. To this end it has been used in the selection of 'nurses, technical apprentices and foreign immigrants as well as in the field of further education'. The test comprises a passage from a textbook followed by twenty-five questions which test students' ability to obtain information from a technical text.

The standardisation of the test is based on a very small sample. In calculating the item characteristics, only item facility appears to have been considered; no attention was apparently paid to item discrimination. The test is reported as having high split-half and test-retest reliabilities. The data for the test's predictive validities are not impressive although concurrent validity appears rather higher. The data on which suggested cut-off points for predictions of future course success, partial failure and failure are based appear rather slender.

---

studies were carried out and much (unreported) data from computer analyses were collected (personal communication). The efficacy of the remedial procedures was not evaluated. Indeed, the link between the pupil profile and the remediation suggested appears to be logical/intuitive and probably based on teaching experience, rather than being empirically established. *Quest* represents an important initiative, but it has many weaknesses. Some of the technical issues should be dealt with in a technical supplement to the manual. If the profession is to develop its competence, members cannot avoid their consideration. It is hoped that the utility and efficacy of the kit will be explored further and some of the weaknesses indicated above progressively eliminated or otherwise answered.

TRN	Name of test	Author	Country	Publisher	Year
160	*Reading Vocabulary Tests*	A. Brimer and H. Gross	B	Education Evaluation Enterprises	1979

Type	No. of forms	C.A. range	Skills tested	Time
Group, attainment (level A)	2 (A & B)	6:11 to 12:02	Reading comprehension (sentence-completion, multiple-choice)	30′

Comments: Each form of the test contains 36 items. Each item is of sentence-completion, multiple-choice format. The test is one of reading comprehension. Raw scores can be converted either to scale scores or to standardised scores. The scale scores range from one to twenty with intervals of equal size. This scale is one against which the reading levels of children of different ages can be compared. It is based on Rasch theory. Raw scores can also be converted to standardised scores with a mean of 100 and a standard deviation of 15 for each six monthly chronological age group.

After pilot work, the test was standardised on about 500 junior school children drawn from an unspecified number of primary schools. The internal consistency coefficients of reliability for younger and older pupils, for boys and girls and for the resultant four cross-classifications and the total group range between 0·85 and 0·92 for Form A and between 0·80 and 0·88 for Form B with samples of between N = 96 and N = 500. Parallel form reliability coefficients varied between 0·71 and 0·87 for different groups. The standard error of measurement of both Forms A and B is about two and a half points of raw score. The construct validity of the scale is largely dependent on the acceptability of the assumption concerning the relationship between person ability and item difficulty underpinning the Rasch model.

The test is easily administered and marked. A possible weakness is that a scale of 20 points covering the development of the ability tested over a period of about five years seems somewhat crude.

TRN	Name of test	Author	Country	Publisher	Year
163	*Richmond Tests of Basic Skills (RTBS)*	A. N. Hieronymus and E. F. Lindquist (UK edition compiled by N. France and I. Fraser)	B	NFER-Nelson	1975 1981

Type	No. of forms	C.A. range	Skills tested		Time
Group, attainment, normative, diagnostic	6 (1 to 6 for successive year groups from Junior 2 to Secondary 3)	7:00 to 15:06	Test V	Vocabulary	17′
			Test R	Reading comprehension	55′
			Test L	Language skills	
				L-1 Spelling	12′
				L-2 Use of capital letters	15′
				L-3 Punctuation	20′
				L-4 Usage	20′
			Test W	Work-study skills	
				W-1 Map reading	30′
				W-2 Reading graphs and tables	20′
				W-3 Knowledge and use of reference materials	30′
			Test M	Mathematics skills	
				M-1 Mathematics concepts	30′
				M-2 Mathematics problem solving	30′
(level A)				Working time: 4 hr 39′. Total about 5 hr spread over four sessions	

Comments: Developed form the *Iowa Tests of Basic Skills*, the *Richmond Tests of Basic Skills (RTBS)* comprise eleven separate instruments organised into six levels. The 1975 edition of the *Teacher's Guide* relates these levels to approximate age ranges from 8:01 to 14:00 at 30 September, thus covering Junior School years 2 to 4 and Secondary School years 1 to 3. In the Tables of Norms published at the same time, tables are provided at six-monthly chronological age levels from 7:00 to 15:06 years. The publisher's catalogue recommends Level 1 for the eight- to nine-year-old group and Level 6 for the 13:00 to 15:06 year-old group.

All test materials for all levels are contained in one re-useable book (96 pp.). The content has been modified to represent the curricular concerns of British education. Provided that the sub-tests are a valid reflection of key curriculum areas, the battery provides a useful means of successively testing attainments in these and therefore monitoring the progress of individuals and

Continued at foot of p. 188

TRN	Name of test	Author	Country	Publisher	Year
167	*Salford Sentence Reading Test*	G. Bookbinder	B	Hodder and Stoughton	1976

Type	No. of forms	C.A. range	Skills tested	Time
Individual, oral, attainment (level A)	3 (A, B & C)	6:10 to 11:09	Sentence reading	Untimed (5′)

Comments: This test consists of thirteen progressively more complex sentences. The child's task is to read these aloud to the tester until six errors have been made. The test is easily and quickly administered.

Standardisation was carried out on a sample of 250 children whose reading attainments were equivalent to national standards. Inter-form reliability is high. Evidence of concurrent validity is given via correlations with scores on well-known tests of reading, spelling and English. The manual provides details of construction and standardisation. It also gives percentile scores for chronological ages 6 : 10 to 11 : 09. *All* children with reading ages of less than six years are classed only as 'below six years'. The ceiling of the test is a reading age of 10 : 06 years.

This test is similar to the *Holborn Reading Scale* (TRN 85) but has the advantages of parallel forms.

---

groups. The battery is included here as at least six of the sub-tests concern aspects of literacy. For each field, except that of Vocabulary, there is a detailed specification of the skills tested by each item, together with suggestions for improving pupils' performances.

After a pilot study and consequent amendments, the tests were tried out on a sample of 17 000 pupils representative of a national population (Teacher's Guide, p. 6). In the Tables of Norms booklet, it appears that only 12 000 pupils' results were used in constructing the tables provided (p. 7).

Using a child's basic score on a test, together with his chronological age, a standard score with a mean of 100 and a standard deviation of 15 can be obtained. Thus children's relative scores in relation to a group containing a six months' age span is readily obtained from the tables of norms. Percentiles and stanines can also be obtained. The results of successive testing over the six levels covered by the tests can be cumulated. For each use of the battery, a profile of the pupil's attainments can be obtained. Circular profiles provide an alternative form for displaying such results. The test can be scored either by hand or by computer, provided the appropriate answer sheets are used.

Evidence of internal consistency reliability using Kuder–Richardson formula 21 is presented for each of the 11 sub-tests at each of eight year groups from Junior 1 to Secondary 4. The samples used ranged from 1 667 to 2 290. All the coefficients were statistically significant and ranged between 0·709 and 0·928. Tests 3 and W-1 and 2 had the lowest coefficients. Many of the reliability coefficients in the other sub-tests were above 0·85 and a considerable proportion above 0·90. There is no evidence of validation studies carried out on the final British edition of the battery.

The use of the test results in improving instruction and learning is described with due caution. A criterion-referenced interpretation of items is advocated. Skills can be taught. The effects of such teaching on the meaning of the norms remains obscure. Despite this comment, the many reprints of the UK edition since its initial publication suggests that teachers find the information provided by the battery of value in their work.

TRN	Name of test	Author	Country	Publisher	Year
169	*Schonell Reading Tests*	F. J. Schonell and F. E. Schonell	B	Oliver and Boyd	1942 to 1955

Type	No. of forms	C.A. range	Skills tested	Time
Individual, oral	1	5:00 to 15:00	R1 Graded Word Reading	5′–15′
Individual	1	6:00 to 9:00	R2 Simple Prose Reading Test ('My Dog')	3′–8′
Group	1	7:00 to 11:00	R3 Silent Reading Test A	15′
Group	1	9:00 to 13:00	R4 Silent Reading Test B	20′
Individual	1		R5 Analysis and synthesis of words containing common phonic units	5′–15′
Individual	1		R6 Directional attack on words	5′–10′
Individual	1		R7 Visual Word Discrimination Test	10′–15′
(level A)				

Comments: These tests form a battery for the assessment of reading attainment (R1 to R4) and for the diagnosis of aspects of failure in some of the mechanics of reading (R5 to R7). The last three tests have no norms. Information on the standardisation, reliability and validity of the tests is noticeable by its absence. The norms of tests R1 to R4 are dated but those for R1 were revised in 1972. The diagnostic tests do not include a number of aspects of reading now considered important, e.g. auditory discrimination between words, matching written and heard forms of words.

The battery was designed for use by teachers and specialists in the teaching of reading. It proved a useful tool in its day. Teachers who have built up the necessary experience for the interpretation of the results from tests R5 to R7 will doubtless continue to use them.

Test R1, the *Schonell Graded Word Reading Test*, is one of the most widely used in the UK. The publishers issued new norms in 1972 based on 10 000 children aged from 6:09 to 11:09 years attending schools in Salford. The norms were appropriately adjusted to have national validity. Recently Eric Shearer, an educational psychologist working in Cheshire, has administered the test to a nationally representative sample of 6 000 children aged from below five up to eleven years attending Cheshire schools. He has been able to revise the order of difficulty of the words and to restandardise the norms for the test. Shearer claims that the new norms are remarkably similar to those produced by Schonell over thirty years ago, but are very different from those given in the 1972 norms issued by the publishers. There is currently some controversy as to which set of norms has the more general validity.

TRN	Name of test	Author	Country	Publisher	Year
172	*Shortened Edinburgh Reading Test*	Godfrey Thomson Unit for Educational Research, Moray House College of Education, and the Child Health and Education Study, University of Bristol	B	Hodder and Stoughton	1985

Type	No. of forms	C.A. range	Skills tested	Time
Group, attainment, screening and diagnostic (level A) (Availability may be restricted in some LEAs)*	1	10:00 to 12:00	Vocabulary Syntax Comprehension Retention of significant detail	Untimed (about 40′)

Comments: These notes are written before the final form of the *Shortened Edinburgh Reading Test* and its manual are available. From the 624 calibrated items included in Stages 1 to 4 of the *Edinburgh Reading Tests* (TRN 59, 60, 61 and 62), 71 items were identified providing a wide range of difficulty levels for children of average ability in the specified age range. A deliberate bias in favour of easy questions means that the test can be used for screening.

A child's results can be recorded as a profile on the four sub-tests. The recording diagram is marked in standard error units. This enables the user to identify statistically significant differences between sub-test scores easily and then to consider their educational significance. Existence of the former does not necessarily imply the latter. The first three sub-tests each contain more items and are more reliable than the fourth sub-test. Scores on all four sub-tests can be summed and converted to a General Reading Quotient.

Whilst no information concerning the reliabilities and validities of the test is currently available to the reviewer, the reputation of the institutions involved in this development is such that one can be confident that the psychometric characteristics of the instrument will be presented in the test manual and that they will meet stringent standards.

* Details can be obtained from the Test Department of Hodder and Stoughton.

TRN	Name of test	Author	Country	Publisher	Year
174	*Slee 13 +Reading Test*	F. W. Slee	B	Learning Development Aids	1982

Type	No. of forms	C.A. range	Skills tested	Time
Group, attainment, normative (level A)	1	13:00 to 14:06	Reading comprehension	20′

Comments: The test consists of 35 very short passages from fiction and also from non-fiction text books used in secondary school subject areas. Each passage is followed by one, two or three questions with answers in multiple-choice format.

It is claimed that the test makes demands on 'knowledge of word meanings, literal comprehension, the drawing of inferences, the interpretation of metaphor and the use of the pupils' own knowledge of the subject of the extract'. Insufficient detail concerning item generation, selection and analysis is given in the rather slight manual accompanying the test to allow the potential user to judge the validity of such an assertion. No information is given concerning the effectiveness of the distractors in the multiple-choice responses.

Raw scores can be converted to standard scores with a mean of 100 and a standard deviation of 15 for each monthly C.A. group. Thus a global score of relative reading comprehension is obtained. As no sex difference in attainment on the test was found, only one set of combined norms for boys and girls is provided. The test was standardised on a sample of over 1 600 thirteen-year-old pupils representative of a particular Metropolitan District (unspecified). Internal consistency reliability coefficient (Kuder–Richardson formula 20) is reported as 0·88, the standard error of measurement being 2·43. No information on test-retest reliability is presented. Correlations with NFER-Nelson *Reading Tests EH1* and *EH2* (TRN 132 and 133) of 0·81 and 0·71 respectively indicate concurrent validities although the samples on which these were obtained are specified only by size.

Unfortunately, the dates when the standardisation data were collected and that when the test was first published are not given in the manual or on the pupils' test form. The date presented in the above table was provided at my request by the publisher.

TRN	Name of test	Author	Country	Publisher	Year
175	*Southgate Group Reading Tests 1 and 2*	V. Southgate	B	Hodder and Stoughton	Test 1, 1959 Test 2, 1962

Type	No. of forms	C.A. range	Skills tested	Time
1 Group, oral administration, attainment	3 (A, B & C)	6:00 to 7:06	1 Word selection	Untimed
2 Group, attainment	2 (A & B)	7:00 to 8:11	2 Sentence-completion (comprehension)	15′–20′
(level A)				

Comments: Test 1 is a thirty-item test specially devised for use with children in the early stages of reading acquisition. It was standardised on a group consisting of every child aged from 5:08 to 8:01 in Local Education Authority schools in Worcester in 1957. The test is contained in an illustrated booklet. Sixteen of the thirty items involve selecting a word to match a picture named by the tester. In the other items the children have to underline, from sets of five, one word dictated by the tester. Testing in groups of no more than fifteen to twenty children is advised. It is also claimed that the test can be used with older children having difficulty with reading. The results are expressed in reading ages from 5:09 to 7:09.

Test 2 is a test of reading comprehension and can be administered to classes. Form A is printed in white and Form B in blue, hence cheating can readily be minimised. Each form consists of forty-two sentences with a choice of five words of which the child must choose one to complete the sentence. Norms are given for reading ages from 7:00 to 9:07 and in percentiles. The accompanying manuals give clear instructions and also evidence of satisfactory reliabilities and validities. These tests have been extensively used in national and local surveys. A restandardisation of these useful tests would be welcomed by many teachers.

TRN	Name of test	Author	Country	Publisher	Year
176	*SPAR (Spelling and Reading) Tests*	D. Young	B	Hodder and Stoughton	1976

Type	No. of forms	C.A. range	Skills tested	Time
Normative, group, attainment and diagnostic	Spelling: a number of parallel forms can be constructed	7:00 to 15:11	Spelling (30 items)	Untimed
	Reading: 2 (A & B)	7:00 to 15:11	Reading: picture-word matching	4′
			sentence completion	9′
(level A)				

Comments: The SPAR tests are intended to assess the progress towards literacy in both spelling and reading of the majority of junior school pupils and of less able secondary school pupils.

From two item banks, each of 150 words, the teacher can construct ten parallel spelling tests without any overlap in content, and a far larger number with partial overlap.

The reading test follows the same format as the author's *Group Reading Test* (TRN 82). Raw scores on both the spelling and reading tests can be converted to attainment ages and quotients. The standardisation of the tests at the junior school stage is on pupils in schools known to be representative of national attainment standards on various NFER and Moray House tests. At this age band, 1 864 and 3 797 pupils were involved in the standardisation of the spelling and reading tests respectively. At the secondary level the norms are based on the same 936 pupils for each test, but the norms are derived by an undescribed method of calibration from nationally standardised tests. Various indices of reliability and validity are presented for various groups of pupils, mostly for the junior groups.

It is particularly useful to have at the secondary-school level tests of spelling and reading based on the *same* group of slow-learning pupils. This allows a more adequate consideration of intra-individual differences in attainments on these two important aspects of literacy. Despite reporting sex differences in attainments in these tests, Young has decided to present combined norms as these '. . . are of greater practical value to the practising teacher than separate tables of norms . . .'.

TRN	Name of test	Author	Country	Publisher	Year
178	*Standard Reading Tests*	J. C. Daniels and Hunter Diack	B	Chatto and Windus Since 1983 Collins Educational 14th impression	1958 1979

Type	No. of forms	C.A. range	Skills tested	Time
Test 1, individual, oral,	1	5:00 to 9:00*	1 The standard test of reading skill	Untimed
attainment	1	initial stages	2 Copying abstract figures	Untimed
Tests 2–10, individual,	1	of reading	3 Copying a sentence	Untimed
diagnostic	1		4 Visual discrimination and orientation	Untimed
Test 11, group or individual	1		5 Letter recognition test	Untimed
diagnostic and attainment	1		6 Aural discrimination test	Untimed
Test 12, group attainment	8		7 Diagnostic word-recognition tests	Untimed
	1		8 Oral word-recognition tests	Untimed
	1		9 Picture word-recognition tests	Untimed
	1		10 Silent prose-reading and comprehension test	Untimed
	1	5:00 to 12:03*	11 Graded spelling test	Untimed
	1	6:00 to 14:00*	12 Graded test of reading experience	20′
(level A)				

* Reading attainment ages covered by the test norms.

Comments: The twelve tests come in a convenient book form. Only Tests 1, 11 and 12 have norms. Test 1 is made up of thirty-six sentences in question form but is only scored for accuracy of reading. The items are arranged in a statistically derived order of difficulty which also reflects increasing content difficulty from the point of view of a logical analysis of reading.

The reading age range covered is from 5:00 to 9:00. Test 11 is a spelling test giving spelling ages from 5:00 to 12:03. Test 12 is a multiple-choice sentence-completion group test giving reading ages from 6:00 to 14:00, although norms above the ten-year-old level are unreliable. The manual contains no details of the standardisation procedure or of the test reliabilities or validities, which makes it difficult to interpret the results. The nine diagnostic tests cover a wide range of abilities underlying reading attainments. The instructions for administration of the tests are clear and the interpretation of results indicated in the handbook seem to have been of value. Despite serious limitations in the technical aspects of the handbook, many teachers have found this battery of tests a great help in individual diagnostic work. It is now in its fourteenth impression, which gives an indication of its popularity. After over twenty-seven years one suspects that the norms on Tests 1, 11 and 12 may have altered.

TRN	Name of test	Author	Country	Publisher	Year
182	*Swansea Test of Phonic Skills* (experimental version)	P. Williams, with the assistance of P. Congdon, M. Holder and N. Sims	B	Basil Blackwell Schools Council	1972 1981

Type	No. of forms	C.A. range	Skills tested	Time
Group or individual, diagnostic (level A)	1	5:09 to 7:09 (standardisation sample)	1 Short vowels 2 Long vowels 3 Initial letter blends 4 Final letter blends 5 Miscellaneous: (*a*) vowel combinations (*b*) consonant digraphs, initial position (*c*) consonant digraphs, final position	40′

Comments: This test was developed as one aspect of the Schools Council Research and Development Project in Compensatory Education centred at Swansea University. The test is primarily intended for children having reading ages of below 7 : 06. The phonic skills tested are seen as of particular interest to those teaching reading to children from low socio-economic backgrounds. The authors also recommend its use with children in remedial reading groups, in slow-learning classes and with top infant and young junior school children whose reading is causing concern. The test consists of sixty-five items. Each item is a *nonsense* word placed with four alternatives. The child has to ring the printed nonsense word when the tester utters it. The manual has some weaknesses. For example, the instructions for administration give no reference to the appendix listing the specified stimulus words. In view of the specific focus of the study which resulted in these tests, the rather sparse information on standardisation and reliability is understandable. Evidence of validities is presented and further studies are in hand. The information on interpretation of the results, which are in effect profiles, is kept extremely simple. The reliabilities and inter-correlations of the sub-test scores are not given. The scores are used to see whether a child has mastered a series of definable reading skill objectives. Raw scores can also be related to *Southgate Group Reading Test* scores.

It is accepted that, although reissued in 1981 by the Schools Council, this test is still in an experimental stage. It looks as if it has some promise.

TRN	Name of test	Author	Country	Publisher	Year
188	*Test Your Child's Reading*	Not given	B	Hodder and Stoughton (produced exclusively for W. H. Smith)	1982

Type	No. of forms	C.A. range		Skills tested	Time
Individual, attainment	1	6:00 to 11:06	1	Reading words aloud (6:00 to 7:00 yrs.)	Untimed
			2	Word-picture matching (6:00 to 7:00 yrs.)	
			3	Putting words together (7:00 to 11:00 yrs.)	
			4	Reading sentences aloud (6:00 to 9:00 yrs.)	
			5	Reading sentences aloud (7:00 to 11:00 yrs.)	
			6	Sentence completion (7:00 to 11:00 yrs.)	
			7, 8, & 9	Reading comprehension – sentence completion, multiple choice (8:00 to 11:00 yrs.)	
			10 & 11	Reading comprehension – cloze (8:00 to 11:00 yrs.)	
			12	Words in context (8:00 to 11:00 yrs.)	
			13	Words on their own (8:00 to 11:00 yrs.)	
(level A)			14	Spelling– "Spot the mistake" (8:00 to 11:00 yrs.)	

Comments: This battery of tests is intended for parents and teachers. The instruments presented are claimed to highlight '. . . some of the many skills which come together in the smooth reading of the mature reader'. The individual tests are similar in content and format to many currently in use in schools. Brief instruction on the administration and marking of each test is given. It is explicitly stated that the tests are *not* designed to give a precise 'Reading Age'. A Rating Chart is provided that indicates the '. . . normal range of scores likely to be achieved by average children at the beginning of each year group' from 6:00 plus to 11:00 plus.

No technical information is given on the construction of the tests in the battery or on the standardisation that forms the basis of the Rating Chart. Presumably such information is unlikely to interest the majority of parents. Teachers coming across this battery might well expect such information to be available, possibly in an extended manual.

Critics might see the battery as a parasitic commercial exploitation of concerned parents able to afford the material. It could lead to parents developing a dangerously oversimplified view of reading. Others might see the pack as a positive contribution enabling parents to become more informed about and involved in their children's reading development and simultaneously encouraging a more informed dialogue between parents and teachers.

TRN	Name of test	Author	Country	Publisher	Year
188	*Testing Our Pupils (TOP) Tests Booklet*	D. Moseley	B	The Open University*	1976

Type	No. of forms	C.A. range	Skills tested	Time
Individual, diagnostic, criterion-referenced (level A)	1	7:00 to 8:05	English Picture Vocabulary Test Finding visual patterns: Problems of Position (POP) Immediate memory for L-R order of pictures: Please Avoid Wrong Sequences (PAWS) Immediate memory for a series of spoken letters: Letter Memory Span (LMS) Hearing Sounds in words: Discrimination of Phonemes (DOP) Blending sounds in words: Blending of Phonemes (BOP) Learning sight words: Word Retention (WR)	Untimed

Comments: Moseley's aims in developing the *TOP* battery included linking diagnostic testing with educational prescription and involving practising teachers in the process. Initially 3 373 top infant school pupils were tested on the Carver *Word Recognition Test* (TRN 199). The 405 (12 %) poorest readers were identified and given a further assessment. A means of scoring the Carver Test that enabled four types of errors to be identified was developed. The seven diagnostic tests in *TOP* were then given to the children. Three of the above tests were developed especially for the project. Each test in the battery is claimed to assess 'skills and abilities which underlie or are pre-conditions of learning to read' (*TOP* Tests Booklet, p. 3). A child's scores on the battery reveal a profile of individual strengths and weaknesses. Each test is linked to a list of suggestions concerning ways in which the child's performance might be enhanced.

A provisional scoring guide is based on the 400 backward readers' responses. (In passing, where did the other five go?) Within this group, POP, PAWS, LMS and BOP all had statistically significant predictive validity over a twelve month period. With a sample of N = 207, the coefficient of internal consistency of the POP test was 0·93. No other reliabilities are given. The scores of the top 25 % of the backward readers, the middle 50 % and the bottom 25 % for different age groups within the year are given for POP, PAWS, LMS and WR. Less detailed information is given on DOP and BOP. The validity of such screening tests and the efficacy of the treatments indicated by individual diagnostic testing is of crucial concern.

* Educational Studies: A Second Level Course. Personality and Learning. E201 Block 10 Folder Material. *Testing Our Pupils* (*TOP*) *Tests Booklet* and *Remedial Activities Booklet*.

TRN	Name of test	Author	Country	Publisher	Year
194	*Watts' Battery of Language and Reading Tests*	A. F. Watts	B	Harrap	1944

Type	No. of forms	C.A. range	Skills tested	Time
Group, attainment			Vocabulary tests:	
Group, attainment	1	10:00 to 15:00	1 One hundred common names	50′
Group, attainment	1	10:00 to 15:00	2 One hundred common class names	50′
Group, attainment	1	10:00 to 15:00	3 One hundred common verbs	50′
Group, attainment	1	10:00 to 15:00	4 One hundred common adjectives (List A)	50′
Group, attainment	1	10:00 to 15:00	5 One hundred common adjectives (List B)	50′
Individual, oral	1	4:03 to 8:03	6 A vocabulary test for young children	Untimed
Group, attainment	1	11:00 to 15:00	7 Words with more than one meaning	Untimed
Group, attainment	1	11:00 to 15:00	8 Ideational addition	Untimed
Group, attainment	1	10:00 to 13:00	1 A sentence completion test	Untimed
Individual, oral	1	4:00 to 10:00	2 An English language scale	Untimed
Group, attainment	1	8:00 to 12:00	3 Sentence patterns	Untimed
Group, attainment	1	8:03 to 10:08	4 Connecting words and phrases	40′
Group, attainment	1	8:06 to 11:06	5 A reported speech test	Untimed
Group, attainment	1	6:06 to 11:00	1 Sentences for a reading scale	Untimed
Group, attainment	1	7:00 to 11:00	2 Questions on the reading scale for infants and juniors (reading comprehension)	Untimed
Group, attainment	1	11:00 to 15:00	3 Reading tests for seniors	Untimed
Group, attainment	1	9:00 to 14:00	4 Sentence-arrangement tests	Untimed
Group, attainment		10:00 to 15:00	5 Time-relation tests:	
Group, attainment	1		(*a*) Related actions	Untimed
Group, attainment	1		(*b*) Common time relation words	Untimed
Group, attainment	1	10:00 to 14:00	6 (1) Paired qualities test	Untimed
(level A)			(2) An Aesop's Fables Test for older children	Untimed

Comments: These tests are contained in Watts, A. F. (1944) *The Language and Mental Development of Children*, now out of print. Despite their technical limitations by today's standards, within Watts' tests are some excellent ideas worthy of development.

TRN	Name of test	Author	Country	Publisher	Year
195	*Wide-span Reading Test*	M. A. Brimer and H. Gross	B	NFER-Nelson	1972

Type	No. of forms	C.A. range	Skills tested	Time
Group, attainment and diagnostic	2 (A & B)	7:00 to 15:00	*Attainment*	
			1 Silent reading comprehension	30′
			Diagnostic indicators	
			1 Decoding	
			2 Linguistic	
(level A)			3 Vocabulary	

Comments: This eighty-item test in reusable booklet form asks the child to complete a sentence having one word missing. The word to be entered is selected from another sentence to the left of the incomplete one. Responses are recorded on separate answer sheets.

e.g. A. Clear the table and wash up the dishes.
We   with soap and water.

The test is arranged in eight levels, four each for the junior and secondary schools respectively. The standardisation claims to be on a sample of children in schools representative of the national distribution of schools. Test-retest reliabilities are satisfactory. No data are presented concerning validities. The Diagnostic Indicators are 'valid' only if there are at least ten incorrect responses within the range given, presumably in a given diagnostic indicator category. A number of important qualifications are made concerning the use of this part of the test. This seems the least valuable part of the test to the reviewer. Whether it is desirable to use only eighty items to cover such a wide age and ability range is a point which the test user must decide in the light of his purposes in testing reading.

TRN	Name of test	Author	Country	Publisher	Year
199	*Word Recognition Test*	C. Carver	B	Hodder and Stoughton	1970

Type	No. of forms	C.A. range	Skills tested	Time
Group or individual, attainment and diagnostic, multiple-choice (level A)	1	4:06 to 8:06	Word recognition Patterns of errors (*a*) Initial letters (*b*) Mid vowel sounds (*c*) Distortions of letters (*d*) Distortions of words (*e*) Reversals (*f*) Word endings (*g*) Initial multiple consonants (*h*) Combined vowels (*i*) Sight/regular words (*j*) Other errors	Untimed (15′-30′)

Comments: This test, developed by an experienced remedial teacher in the Manchester area whilst taking an advanced course of study in Educational Guidance at the University, contains fifty items. Each item consists of a row of five or six words, only one of which is the correct answer. The teacher gives the stimulus word orally in a sentence specified in the manual. The child underlines the word he believes the tester has spoken. Raw scores are converted to reading ages and Word Recognition Ability levels. Sex differences in the skills tested are ignored. The test is intended to assess the early stages of word recognition and to provide the opportunity for the analysis of individual error patterns. Carver claims that the test can be used with four to five-year-old children in small groups. For children who are clearly non-readers in the sense that they cannot cope with any of the first ten items, an alternative activity is allowed for in the test booklet. According to Carver, the test reveals both the child's knowledge of the visual presentation of sounds and words, and also the child's ability to analyse sounds themselves. The aural analysis of words is considered a crucial pre-requisite for word recognition and the alternatives in the multiple-choice are 'systematic and structured alternatives' to the correct answer.

The manual provides a brief analysis of ten stages in word recognition ability ranging from the level of virtually no knowledge to that appropriate to a word recognition ability level of about 8:06. The original sample on which the items were tested was a very small one and the work was carried out in 1962. However, the evidence in the manual indicates that the test is both reliable and valid.

This test has been used extensively for screening purposes in the Manchester area. Its use with individual children as a source of diagnostic information is less popular, possibly because of the time required.

(b) Others

TRN	Name of test	Author	Country	Publisher	Year
2	*ACER Primary Reading Survey Tests, Levels AA & BB*	G. P. Withers and M. L. Clark	A	Australian Council for Educational Research	1972
				Manual	1979

Type	No. of forms	C.A. range		Skills tested	Time
Group, attainment, normative	2 (R & S)	6:00 to 6:11	Level AA	Word recognition	16′
		7:00 to 7:11	Level BB	Word knowledge	16′
				Comprehension	20′
(level A)					

Comments: The tests are intended to enable teachers to achieve more adequately eight desirable educational ends (Manual, p. 6). These include identifying inter-individual differences between pupils in the abilities tested, grouping pupils for instructional purposes, matching materials to pupils' attainments and identifying children with special educational needs. The Word Recognition test consists of 16 multiple-choice picture-stimulus recognition items. Word Knowledge is tested using twenty multiple-choice synonym items and Comprehension by twenty-three multiple-choice items.

Normative data in table form based on 1 217 and 573 test results are presented. These tables enable raw scores to be converted to stanines for April and November entries in two States at both age levels for each form of the tests. Users are advised of the benefits of constructing local norms and are shown how this can quite easily be done. An example of the process is given in the test manual. The importance of recognising the inherent unreliability of test scores is discussed.

The AA tests have internal consistency reliability coefficients of 0·67, 0·75, 0·76 and 0·79 for Forms R and S April and November norms respectively. These are rather low. This is probably due, in part, to the brevity of the test. The two BB tests have internal consistency reliability coefficients ranging between 0·79 and 0·86. Word Knowledge and Comprehension are shown to be related to a considerable extent. Forms R and S correlate at 0·792 and 0·783 in this respect.

TRN	Name of test	Author	Country	Publisher		Year
3	*ACER Primary Reading Survey Tests A-D*	Australian Council for Educational Research	A	Australian Council for Educational Research	Manual	1971 1976

Type	No. of forms	C.A. range	Skills tested	Time
Group, attainment	1 (R)	8:00 to 9:00	A Word knowledge (40 items, multiple-choice synonyms)	20′
	2 (R & S)		Comprehension (35 items, multiple-choice)	30′
	1 (R)	9:00 to 10:00	B Word knowledge (45 items, multiple-choice, synonyms)	20′
	2 (R & S)		Comprehension (38 items, multiple-choice)	30′
	1 (R)	10:00 to 11:00	C Word knowledge (45 items, multiple-choice, synonyms)	20′
	2 (R & S)		Comprehension (39 items, multiple-choice)	30′
	1 (R)	11:00 to 12:00	D Word knowledge (40 items, multiple-choice, synonyms)	20′
(level A)			Comprehension (34 items, multiple-choice)	30′

Comments: This series of reading tests is designed to assess two aspects of the reading skills of primary school pupils. Standardisation is based on representative samples of Australian children. The need for the compilation of local and state norms is stressed. The tests have high internal consistency coefficients. For Word Knowledge these range between 0·76 and 0·89 over the four levels while for Comprehension the figures are between 0·88 and 0·92. The intercorrelations are also given. Evidence on validities is less apparent.

Raw scores can be converted to stanines (abridged from 'standard nine') which has a nine-point scale (1–9) with the high score indicating very good relative attainment.

TRN	Name of test	Author	Country	Publisher	Year
	ACER Spelling Test Years 3–6	ACER Staff	A	Australian Council for Educational Research	1976–81

Type	No. of forms	C.A. range	Skills tested	Time
Group, normative, attainment, diagnostic level A)	2 (X & Y)	9:00 to 12:00	Written spelling Spelling error types: C Conforms to spelling precedent (include homophones) NC Does not conform to spelling precedent P Perservation A Auditory discrimination U Unclassifiable error	Untimed (about 20′–30′)

Comments: The purpose of this test is to provide a normative assessment of pupils' spelling attainments, to identify pupils requiring further help and to elicit information concerning the types of spelling error made in order that an appropriate remedial intervention might be devised. There are fifty words for each of the four years covered by the test. Each selection was made according to the same criteria from a specified corpus of words. Standardisation is based on 'proportionate stratified cluster sampling' (Manual, p. 6) of children attending schools in New South Wales and initially involving 324 and 340 children respectively, in clusters of four and five from 81 and 68 schools where testing was done in April and October. Altogether 4 605 children were involved. In 1979 further data were obtained from schoolchildren in the state of Victoria (N = 3 903). The test manual also contains the facility values of the 50 words at each age level for the various standardisation groups. Internal consistency reliability coefficients from nineteen samples ranged (if that is the right word) between 0·95 and 0·97.

Raw scores can be converted to percentile rank norms for each of the standardisation samples in each of the four years. Advice is given on the use of percentile rank ranges in order to sensitise users to the extent of unreliability present in such data. The method of error analysis appears suspect on many counts. The psychometric and/or psycholinguistic relationships between the error types are not explored adequately. Reference is, however, made to other books that deal with such considerations and with the central issue of remedial strategies. The advice given on such strategies in the manual itself is too general to be of much utility. One novelty is the provision of a Class Analysis Chart to which pupils' answer sheets can be attached. This provides a basis for various group and individual comparisons with the normative data contained in the manual.

TRN	Name of test	Author	Country	Publisher	Year
5	*Advanced Reading Inventory (ARI)*	J. L. Johns	USA	Wm C. Brown	1981

Type	No. of forms	C.A. range	Skills tested	Time
Individual, group, diagnostic, criterion-referenced (level A)	2 (A & B)	Grade Seven through College (13:00 to 19:11)	Word recognition: Isolation (word lists) Context (graded passages) Comprehension and rate: Oral reading (graded passages) Silent reading (graded passages) Cloze tests (graded passages)	Mainly untimed other than to assess rate

Comments: The *ARI* is an extension of the author's *Basic Reading Inventory (BRI)* (TRN 24), but designed for older pupils. It consists of graded word lists, graded reading passages and cloze tests based on the latter. Its major purposes are to help teachers match reading materials to the pupil's reading skills and also to provide teachers with a diagnostic means of studying reading behaviour. A system for recording oral reading miscues is described. The reading comprehension questions are intended to allow various aspects of reading comprehension to be assessed through the pupil's ability to cope with these. The *ARI* comes in two forms allowing a variety of uses such as pre- and post-testing, individual and group administration of parallel materials and also oral and silent reading of the graded passages. Criteria are given enabling a pupil's performance to be assessed as at 'Independent', 'Instructional' or 'Frustration' levels on a given set of materials. The criteria used to determine these levels are controversial, as is the general notion of informal reading inventories. A selected annotated list of articles and research studies bearing on the controversy is given in Appendix A of the manual. No claims are made concerning the reliabilities or validities of the data elicited in terms of conventional test theory. The interpretation of the information is, in essence, clinical. This is not to imply that such data are of no value, but to indicate that no evidence on this matter is presented. Users of this or any other informal reading inventory need to be aware of the grounds on which such instruments continue to be legitimately criticised (see Chapter 3).

TRN	Name of test	Author	Country	Publisher	Year
	Ann Arbor Learning Inventory: Tests and Remediation	W. B. Bullock and B. Meister	USA	Ann Arbor Publishers	1978

Type	No. of forms	C.A. range	Skills tested	Time
Group, individual, diagnostic	1	4:00 to 6:11	Section A: Body image (Test 1) Section B: Visual discrimination skills (Tests II to VII) Section C: Visual motor coordination skills (Tests VIII to XII) Section D: Visual sequential memory skills (Tests XIII to XV) Section E: Aural discrimination skills (Tests XVI to XVII) Section F: Aural sequential memory skills (Tests XVIII to XIX) Section G: Aural conceptual skills (Test XX)	Untimed
(Level A)		7:00 +	Section A: Visual discrimination skills (Tests I to II) Section B: Visual motor coordination skills (Tests III to VII) Section C: Sequential memory skills (Tests VIII to XI) Section D: Aural skills (Tests XII to XIII) Section E: Comprehension skills (Tests XIV to XV)	

Comments: These two batteries of 20 and 15 tests respectively have been developed over many years. They were originally devised to replace sub-tests from a number of different tests. The batteries (referred to in the singular in material reaching the reviewer) were used in 'an Early Learning Programme in Florida'. The linked programme was field tested for three years before publication. The teacher's manuals give criteria for each test whereby the child's need, or otherwise, for remediation may be established. Clear guidance is given as to what should be done to remediate low performances on the tests. This includes a quite heavy reliance on commercially produced materials (many of these also being published by Ann Arbor). The pupils' booklets are re-usable provided that a 'Chem Rite' pen (price 80p) is available as suggested. The claim (personal communication) that the tests can be used with groups of 15 to 20 children at a time is one that teachers of top nursery and lower infant school pupils will probably have reservations about.

Of even greater concern is the absence of sufficient technical data to enable potential users to evaluate the tests and remedial suggestions. Nothing is said about the reliabilities and validities of the scales, the justification of the criteria specified for mastery of a test, and the relationships between the tests. One is not asking for the application of conventional test theory to criterion-referenced tests; there are alternative ways of evaluating such instruments. It is quite reasonable to expect teachers to be provided with the information that will allow them to make a professional judgment concerning the merits of any inventory. Work *has* been done. The battery was 'refined for use in an Early Learning Programme in Florida. The program was field tested for three years before its publication.' Why is this important information not presented in sufficient detail to allow a critical appraisal? It might be that to do so would require a bulky technical manual. Despite the fact that not all teachers would consult such a publication, it should be available for the increasing proportion of the profession that wishes so to do. In the absence of such information it is not easy to accept the claim that 'The *Ann Arbor Learning Inventory* pinpoints breakdowns in skills underlying reading, writing and spelling' (1983 catalogue, p. 2).

TRN	Name of test	Author	Country	Publisher	Year
23	*Basic English Skills Test (BEST)*	Staff of the Centre for Applied Linguistics	USA	Centre for Applied Linguistics	1982

Type	No. of forms	C.A. range	Skills tested	Time		Time
Individual,* group,† attainment, diagnostic, criterion-referenced (level A)	1	Adults with limited command of English	* *Core section*: Listening comprehension Communication Pronunciation (rating scale) Fluency (rating scale) Reading/Writing	(about 10′–15′)	† *Literacy skills section*: 1 Personal background form 2 Calendar 3 Food labels 4 Clothing labels 5 Rent check 6 Envelope 7 Telephone directory 8 Train schedule 9 Time and number 10 Composition 11 Reading passage 12 Newspaper–Bulletins	Untimed (about 45′)

Comments: *BEST* was designed to assist in the assessment and teaching of basic English language skills included in non-academic English as a second language (ESL) curricula for adults, frequently immigrants/refugees. *BEST* is an approach towards a 'standardized criterion-reference test'. It will enable learning needs to be identified and met.

BEST tests elementary listening comprehension, speaking, reading and writing skills of adults whose English language is limited. An individually administered 'Core' section is followed by a 'Literacy skills' section which can be administered to either groups or individuals. The 'Core' section consists of 'simulated real-life listening comprehension and speaking tasks' including telling the time, asking directions, using money and other aspects of basic social language. The 'Literacy skills' section includes reading and writing in the twelve areas listed above.

The development of *BEST* involved cooperation between ESL teachers and test constructors. Item selection was based on the results of a SCALAR analysis programme. Preliminary versions were tried out on seven different native language groups involving 318 students. Refining the test reduced the 'Core' section from 62 to 49 items and the 'Literacy skills' section from 104 to 70 items. The internal consistency reliabilities of the four scales in the 'Core' section range from 0·95 to 0·98; that of the reading and writing scores obtainable from the 'Literacy skills' section being 0·93 and 0·58 respectively. For this particular field and 'population' these are encouraging findings.

Continued at foot of p. 208

TRN	Name of test	Author	Country	Publisher	Year
24	*Basic Reading Inventory (BRI)*	J. L. Johns	USA	Kendall Hunt	1981 2nd edition

Type	No. of forms	C.A. range	Skills tested	Time
Individual, diagnostic, criterion-referenced (level A)	3 (A,B,C)	Pre-Primer to Grade 8 reading levels (5 : 06 to 14 : 06)	Word recognition: isolation (timed & untimed) context Comprehension: oral reading silent reading listening Rate of reading	Mainly untimed

Comments: The main purposes of the *Basic Reading Inventory (BRI)* are to identify the level of various materials at which the pupil can work to advantage and to identify a pupil's strengths and weakness thereby establishing a link between testing and teaching. The *BRI* comes in three forms. Each is based on graded word lists that can be given under timed or untimed conditions, plus graded passages of prose that can be read either aloud or silently by the pupil. The pupil's comprehension of the passages is tested using questions provided in the manual. A pupil's rate of reading can be assessed and the author also provides a system for recording a pupil's oral reading miscues. Criteria are given enabling a pupil's performance on a given set of materials to be specified as at 'Independent', 'Instructional' or 'Frustration' levels. The assessment of listening comprehension is seen as an index of the highest level of material read to the pupil that he is capable of understanding. (Some texts refer to this as 'Capacity' or 'Reading Potential' level.) The criteria used to determine the four reading levels are controversial, as is the whole idea of informal reading inventories. The *BRI* makes no claims for reliabilities or validities as understood in conventional test theory. Claims *are* made for its classroom and clinical utility in devising reading programmes sensitive to the unique characteristics of individual readers. The changes included in the second edition reflect comments made to the author by users who have found this approach of value.

Inter-rater reliabilities on the rating scales used ranged between 0·81 and 0·97 in the 'Core' section. In the 'Literacy skills' section, on the far less subjective assessments of reading and writing, inter-scorer reliabilities were 0·99 and 0·93 respectively.

Validity rests largely on the test's content. Few would disagree that it covers essential aspects of basic communication. Concurrent validity is supported by correlations between tutors' ratings and students' scores. In the 'Core' section these range between 0·49 and 0·71. For reading and writing scores in the 'Literacy skills' section the indices are 0·51 and 0·54 respectively, based on a sample of 217 students. Inter-scale correlations are also presented. These demonstrate the links between the various sub-tests. They also show that the instrument is not adversely affected by the student's native language.

This test appears to have considerable promise. Its approach could well be adapted by any country receiving immigrants/refugees whose ESL skills are minimal. Additionally, the content has in parts some important lessons for minimum skills testing and teaching of native tongue speakers.

TRN	Name of Test	Author	Country	Publisher	Year
25	*Basic Sight Word Test*	E. W. Dolch	USA	Garrard Publishing	1942

Type	No. of forms	C.A. range	Skills tested	Time
Group or individual mastery test (level A)	1	Mainly primary school, but also poor readers at any age	Word recognition	Untimed (4 × 15′ sessions)

Comments: This word recognition test presents the complete Basic Sight Vocabulary, comprising the 220 words which are the content of 70 per cent of first readers and up to 65 per cent of second and third readers in graded reading series.

Dolch argues that competent reading requires that the child be able to recognise these 220 words immediately on sight if he is to become an effective reader. Thus the test is a 'mastery' test of a particularly important content.

No norms are given for the test, the raw score of words correct being seen as a valid index of the child's mastery of the skill tested. The aim is for all children to master all of these words as soon as possible, consistent with individual differences. There are numerous English Word Lists which teachers can adapt to act as 'mastery' tests.

Despite its age, this test is still popular, probably because the words in it have retained their currency and importance.

TRN	Name of test	Author	Country	Publisher	Year
26	*Bishop Diagnostic-Teaching Oral Reading Programme (BD-TORP)*	B. K. Bishop	A	Harcourt Brace Jovanovich Group (Australia)	1979

Type	No. of forms	C.A. range	Skills tested		Time
Individual, attainment, criterion-referenced, diagnostic	1	Not specified other than as appropriate for 'children and adults who have oral reading problems'	*Screening Test*: Words Sounds		Untimed (about 10′)
			Full Tests: Short vowel sounds Consonant sounds Consonant-vowel beginning sounds Words 1 – regular Words 1 – nonsense Oral reading passage 1	Long vowel sounds Two-consonant single sounds Words 2 – regular Words 2 – nonsense Oral reading passage 2	Untimed
			Two-vowel single sounds Vowel-consonant single sounds Words 3 – regular Words 3 – nonsense Oral reading passage 3	Sounds requiring three or more letters Words 4 – regular Words 4 – nonsense Oral reading passage 4	
(level A)			Letters and letter combinations with more than one sound Syllabication Irregular words		

Comments: The *BD-TORP* emphasises diagnostic teaching in order to identify and alleviate oral reading problems experienced by children and adults. Initially the Screening Test is given. This enables *unlearnt* skills to be identified. A further examination of these can be carried out using the appropriate sections of the Full Test. The results are recorded on graph sheets. The specific unlearnt skill is taught using ' . . . your own methods and materials or those provided in the Program' (Manual, p. 8). This is followed by re-testing to check that the instruction has been effective.

This test will probably only appeal to teachers who wholeheartedly support the 'bottom-up' approach to the teaching of reading and who accept that 'the teaching of specific word attack (phonic) skills is the most logical method to remediate oral reading problems' (Manual, p. 86). The final two and a half pages of the manual are devoted to specifying the assumptions on which the material is based.

No evidence is given concerning the reliabilities, validities, interrelationships between the variables or of the efficacy of either the Screening Tests or the Full Tests to identify pupils who might benefit from the programme. The problem of false negative and false positive identifications is not explicitly dealt with. The effects of the programme of remediation are not supported by any empirical evidence at all. If such evidence is available, it should be presented in a technical manual for the benefit of potential users. Task analysis is a legitimate approach to diagnostic teaching. Having said that, in the absence of evidence in the manual, Bishop's assumptions will not be ones that all reading teachers will be able to accept.

TRN	Name of test	Author	Country	Publisher	Year
27	*Boder Test of Reading-Spelling Patterns*	E. Boder and S. Jarrico	USA	Grune and Stratton	1982

Type	No. of forms	C.A. range	Skills tested	Time
Individual, criterion-referenced, diagnostic (level A)	1	6:00 to Adult	1 Sight vocabulary (*flash* presentation – up to 1″ allowed per word) 2 Sight vocabulary (*untimed* presentation – up to 10″ allowed per word) 3 Spelling (words from correctly read *flash* presentation) 4 Spelling (words not correctly read on *flash* presentation)	up to 30′

Comments: Based on extensive clinical work over at least sixteen years, a paediatric neurologist and a research psychologist have developed a test of reading-spelling patterns. It is claimed that the instrument allows sub-types of reading disability to be identified. 'Specific reading disability, or developmental dyslexia' can be differentiated from non-specific reading disability by comparing a student's reading and spelling performances on words that are 'known' and 'unknown', phonetically regular and otherwise.

On the basis of the pattern of performances obtained, three sub-types of developmental dyslexia can be identified. These are called 'dysphonetic', 'dyseidetic' and 'mixed dysphonetic-dyseidetic'. It is stressed that a diagnosis of developmental dyslexia for children aged between five and eight years of age should only be made with great caution. The test materials include thirteen word lists graded for both reading and spelling. In each of the lists of 20 words, one half are phonetically regular. Where needed to clarify the diagnosis, a further eight additional diagnostic indicators are described. Implications for remediation are presented.

Adequate administration of the test requires considerable practice even though the record forms and summary sheets are well-designed and easy to use. For example, in assessing a student's responses to the spelling tests, the tester has to be able to identify 'good phonetic equivalents' (GFEs). Despite the appendix of guidance provided, this introduces some problems. Evidence of high inter-rater reliability in recognising GFEs is presented.

The differential diagnosis of reading-spelling patterns is determined by empirically derived critical cut-off performance scores on the tests. Test-retest reliabilities for 50 students aged between six and fifteen years for Reading Level, correctly spelled known words and GFEs range between 0·76 and 0·97. For sub-groups of this sample, reliabilities range between 0·56 and 0·99. Evidence for the validities of the differential diagnostic power of the test is provided and includes work from four Ph.D. theses. The claim is made that 'the three clinical dyslexic subtypes represent three distinct neuropsychological syndromes identified on the basis of reading and spelling performance alone' (Manual, p. 105).

The test can be criticised technically in relation to item selection and cut-off criteria on which little information is provided. The instrument's general validities and utility require further research based on the crucibles of clinic and classroom. Despite such legitimate reservations, the approach to differential diagnosis developed by Boder and Jarrico has aroused considerable interest among clinicians and research workers.

TRN	Name of test	Author	Country	Publisher		Year
28	*Botel Reading Inventory*	M. Botel	USA	Modern Curriculum Press		1966
				Follett	Revised edition	1978

Type	No. of forms	C.A. range	Skills tested	Time
Group and individual, content	2	6:00 to 18:11		Untimed
criterion-referenced	(A & B)		1 Phonemic inventory test	
	(A & B)		2 Word recognition test	
(level A)	(A & B)		3 Word opposites test (reading)	
			4 Word opposites test (listening)	

Comments: On the assumption that 'standardised testing methods have not been successful in determining proper placement' of pupils to levels of reading books, Botel claims to have capitalised on the informal testing procedures used by effective reading teachers. His tests are content criterion-referenced. The results are interpreted in terms of the children's levels of mastery of the skills tested.

The Phonemic inventory test assesses ten skills. For students at the 10:00 year old level or above, a test using nonsense words is given. Success on this task means that the other phonics tests are not given. The Word recognition test has twenty words at each reading level from 5:00 to 10:00 years. The first of the Word opposites tests measures comprehension. The second is intended to measure reading potential.

No evidence of reliabilities or validities is given, nor is the content the tests sample clearly specified. The tests apear to be based on Botel's analysis of the skills comprising the reading process. Whilst his ideas may be valid, and whilst content criterion-referenced measurement and testing are important in the assessment of reading, to use the *Inventory* is, on the evidence presented, an act of faith in Botel's claims.

The *Botel Reading Inventory* provides more detailed data on word identification than many informal reading inventories. It is useful for estimating instructional levels. It is open to criticism on theoretical grounds, in particular, in relation to the estimation of reading potential. The general criticisms of IRIs given in Chapter 3 (p. 32) are also pertinent.

TRN	Name of test	Author	Country	Publisher	Year
34	*Burt Word Reading Test, New Zealand Revision*	C. Burt Revision by A. Gilmore, C. Croft and N. Reid	NZ	New Zealand Council for Educational Research (NZCER)	1981

Type	No. of forms	C.A. range	Skills tested	Time
Individual, attainment, oral (level A)	1	6:00 to 12:11	Word-recognition	Untimed (about 10′)

Comments: Following a survey carried out in 1977 by the NZCER, it was established that the word-difficulty order and the norms published by the Scottish Council for Research in Education (TRN 32) were not entirely appropriate for use with pupils in New Zealand. To obtain national norms for New Zealand, the re-ordered test was given to approximately 400 pupils at each of the seven class levels in the 6:00 to 12:11 years age range attending 120 primary and intermediate schools. A representative sample of pupils with some 200 in each half-year chronological age group provided the necessary data. The means and standard deviations of pupils' scores on the test for boys and girls separately and for the combined groups are provided. Girls obtain higher mean scores than boys at all age levels.

An innovation in scoring the test is the abandonment of converting raw scores to reading ages. It is argued that this common practice is an unjustified oversimplification and gives a misleading sense of precision in measuring a child's word-recognition attainment. Raw scores are therefore converted to Equivalent Age Scores based on the mean scores of children by monthly chronological age group. To sensitise teachers to the inherent unreliability of test scores and to encourage test users to think of a child's score as indicating attainment in a range rather than at a specific point in a continuum, the norms are given in terms of Equivalent Age Bands. These bands are based on the ages of children obtaining raw scores at one standard error of measurement below and above the mean raw score. Because of the consistent sex differences indicated earlier, Equivalent Age Band norms are given for boys and girls separately and for the groups combined. No norms are given for raw scores below 20 or higher than 80.

The test-retest reliability coefficients, based on seven groups of 30 pupils of different age groups tested on two occasions a week apart, ranged between 0·95 and 0·99. The provision of the mean scores on each occasion would have been of interest in relation to practice effects. Using three different age groups, internal consistency coefficients obtained using Kuder–Richardson formula 20 were 0·96, 0·97 and 0·97. The standard error of measurement at each age level was about three raw score points. The concurrent validity of the test is supported by high correlations with the *Schonell Graded Word Reading Test* (see under TRN 169) and the *Oral Word Reading Test*

(Fieldhouse, 1952). Criterion-related validity is supported by 14 correlations with *Progressive Achievement Tests: Reading Comprehension and Vocabulary* (TRN 152) and the *Test of Scholastic Abilities* (Reid *et al.*, 1981).

The manual for test users is very well organised, reflecting the contribution of the practitioners who contributed to its construction. The great strength of the test is the use of the Equivalent Age Band norms and the heightened awareness of the variability in a test score that these encourage.

FIELDHOUSE, A. E. (1952) *Oral Word Reading Test*. Wellington: New Zealand Council for Educational Research.

REID, N., JACKSON, P., GILMORE, A. and CROFT, C. (1981) *Test of Scholastic Abilities*. Wellington: New Zealand Council for Educational Research.

TRN	Name of test	Author	Country	Publisher		Year
39	*Classroom Reading Inventory (CRI)*	N. J. Silvaroli	USA	Wm C. Brown (Transatlantic Book Services act as UK agents)	5th edition	1982

Type	No. of forms	C.A. range	Skills tested	Time
Individual, group,* diagnostic, criterion-referenced (level A)	4 (A,B,C,D)	8:00 to 14:00 (Forms A,B,C) 'mature students in high school and adult programs' (Form D)	Part 1 Graded word lists reading (a) accuracy (b) error analysis (i) consonant consonant sounds, diagraphs, compounds, blends endings, contractions. (ii) vowel long vowels, short vowels, long/short, vowels plus 'r', 'a' plus 'l' or 'w', dipthongs, lacks vowel rule understanding, vowel combinations. (iii) syllable visual syllable problems, prefix, auditory syllable problems, suffix.	About 4′
			Part 2 Oral reading of graded paragraphs (a) accuracy (b) comprehension: (i) fact, (ii) inference, (iii) vocabulary. (c) hearing comprehension (d) rate of reading (e) error analysis repetition, insertion, substitution, omission, needs assistance. Part 3 Spelling survey*	About 8′

Comments: Forms A, B and C of the *CRI* are intended to be individually administered diagnostic instruments designed to identify 'minimum level reading skills' in word-recognition and comprehension. *CRI* is based on the assumption that if the pupil can read independently at the 12:00 level, the skills typically acquired in the primary school will have been mastered. The spelling test elicits additional related data bearing on that obtained in Parts 1 and 2. Form D is for mature students in tertiary education. Form D does not include a spelling survey. The scoring criteria provided enable a performance on material to be assessed as being at the 'Independent', 'Instructional' or 'Frustration' level. The various means of error analysis suggested allow specific difficulties to be identified. It is claimed that the teacher should be able to test one pupil in about 12′. The manual gives no evidence of the reliability or validity of the procedures involved in the *CRI*, other than that relating to the readability measures used. In this context, to find the august name of George D. Spache misspelled came as a shock to the reviewer. There is reference to work by doctoral degree students in the development of the *CRI*. Details of related publications could have been presented to advantage. The interpretation of the *CRI* deserves more attention than is given in the manual. It is claimed that the information elicited by the *CRI* should 'enable the teacher to develop independent and instructional reading programs for the students'. It will almost certainly help the teacher become sensitive to intra-individual differences in a range of skills, but the educational pertinence of the data obtained is less public than the data themselves.

TRN	Name of test	Author	Country	Publisher	Year
44	*Degrees of Reading Power*	M. W. Kibby	USA	The College Board	1981

Type	No. of forms	C.A. range	Skills tested	Time
Group, attainment, normative, criterion-referenced (level A)	2 (A series; B series)	8:00 to 20:00	Comprehension of non-fiction prose	CPIA 75′ * PA2 75′ PA4 70′ PA6 70′ PA8 65′

Comments: *The Degrees of Reading Power (DRP)* programme comprises a range of tests to assess a student's ability to understand prose linked to an assessment of the readability of instructional materials. The central notion is to measure a student's reading attainment (comprehension of prose) on the same scale as is used to measure the reading difficulty level of prose.

Written passages can range from easy to read to difficult. Developing Bormuth's mean cloze formula, the *DRP* scale of prose difficulty was produced ranging from 15 (easy) to 100 units (very difficult). Test passages were then constructed. These *look* somewhat like cloze tests but do not embody a mechanical deletion procedure. Each *DRP* test consists of a series of passages of about 325 words in length arranged in ascending order of difficulty. *DRP* tests allow predictions to be made about the difficulty level of prose that the student can read.

A student's raw score can be converted, by machine or manually, to *DRP* units and linked to predictions concerning the student's ability to read with understanding prose material having different readability values. For any raw score on a particular test, the 'Independent', 'Instructional' and 'Frustration' levels of material are given in *DRP* units. Clearly, the *DRP* rating of material with which the student is likely to cope with a 0·90 likelihood of success (Independent level) will be lower than the *DRP* ratings for Instructional level (0·75 likelihood of success) and Frustration level (0·50 likelihood of success).

The regular availability of Readability Reports specifying the *DRP* rating of materials facilitates the matching of individual and material insofar a difficulty level is concerned. Coupled with an extensive range of optiona supporting services, the *DRP* programme is most impressive.

DRP tests are based on the assumptions underlying the Rasch model, latent trait model using the two parameters of person ability and iten difficulty. This model has been the topic of considerable academic con troversy in the UK. If required, *DRP* scaled scores can also be obtained.

Extensive traditional reliability and validity studies have been carried out Non-traditional reliability and validity studies are also reported in the Users Manual. The amount of development and research work is impressive. A reasonably accessible review of the *DRP* test worth the attention of anyon considering developing such a battery for use in another culture is availabl (Kibby, 1981).

KIBBY, M. W. (1981) 'Test Review: The Degrees of Reading Power.' *Journal o Reading*, **24**, 416–27.

* Odd numbered PA forms are available to States for large-scale testin programmes.

TRN	Name of test	Author	Country	Publisher	Year
46	*Diagnostic Analysis of Reading Errors (DARE)*	J. Gillespie and J. Shohet	USA	Jastak Associates	1979

Type	No. of forms	C.A. range	Skills tested	Time
Group, attainment, diagnostic (level A)	1	12:00 to 20:00+	Spelling (correct score) Error scores: Sound substitution errors Omission errors Reversal errors	Untimed (for groups 20′–30′)

Comments: Based on an explicit position concerning the nature of effective reading, *DARE* claims to test the auditory-visual transcoding process efficiently and accurately. The student is given a sheet containing 46 items. Each item consists of a word correctly spelled and three variations. The student's task is to listen to a word and circle the correct spelling. A strength of the test is that the information contained in a student's errors is used to produce three error scores that, in relation to the correct score, are considered to have diagnostic and remedial implications. A raw score can be converted to a grade level score, standard scores and percentiles. The results are summarised on a profile sheet. A table of error expectancies for each correct score is intended to help in identifying atypical functioning. The intercorrelation between the four scores are not given together with their reliabilities at the age levels at which standardisation data and conversion tables are provided. This reduces the diagnostic value of the error scores. Despite the guidance given on interpreting error scores, for each category to 'be considered separately' is of suspect simplicity (Manual, p. 7). The ipsative scores present many difficulties whichever approach to interpretation is adopted.

A major purpose of the test is to identify learning disabled students. It can be used as a criterion-referenced and a normative test. Standardisation appears to have been based largely on convenience samples although efforts have been made to make them representative of defined populations. The population characteristics need to be considered carefully by users. Evidence of split-half reliability is based on a sample of only 39 students of one age group. Test-retest reliability evidence is based on only nineteen students' scores. *DARE*'s validity is supported by its ability to discriminate between various groups of special education students. Evidence from a variety of small-scale studies provides some limited support for its predictive and concurrent validities. The growth characteristics of the *DARE*'s four indices support its claim to construct validity. Ten individual profiles are used to show the way in which individual profiles provide pointers to remedial programmes.

TRN	Name of test	Author	Country	Publisher		Year
47	*Diagnostic Reading Scales (DRS)*	G. D. Spache	USA	CTB/McGraw-Hill		1963
					2nd edition	1972
					3rd edition	1981

Type	No. of forms	C.A. range	Skills tested	Time
Individual, oral, diagnostic (level A)	2 (Set R & Set S)* 1 elsewhere	6:00 to 13:00	A Word recognition lists (3) B Reading selections and comprehension questions (Set R & Set S)* C Word analysis and phonics tests: 1 Initial consonants; 2 Final consonants 3 Consonant digraphs; 4 Consonant blends 5 Initial consonant substitution; 6 Initial consonant sounds recognised auditorily 7 Auditory discrimination; 8 Short and long vowel sounds 9 Vowels with 'r'; 10 Vowel diphthongs and digraphs 11 Common syllables or phonograms; 12 Blending D Word analysis checklist E Use of graphic clues and context clues F Checklist of reading ability	About 60′

Comments: One major purpose of the *DRS* is to assess the Instructional, Independent and Potential reading levels of individual students using graded reading selections. The first, Instructional, measures oral reading and comprehension. The second measures silent reading comprehension and the third is based on listening comprehension. It should be noted that Spache does *not* define these levels as currently used in Informal Reading Inventories. Spache has been an outspoken critic of the Informal Reading Inventory approach to assessment advocated by Betts and his followers. The manual explains and documents the reasons for this divergence. His case is a powerful one.

The 1981 revision of the *DRS* took into account the opinions of over 200 users. The reading levels assigned to the reading selections and the word recognition lists were updated and twelve new and revised tests of word analysis and phonics skills were incorporated. A 90′ sound cassette provides training in the use and administration of the *DRS*. The importance of non-standard English dialects is taken into account in respect of certain minority groups.

Word recognition lists are used as a pre-test indicating the entry level for the reading selections and also allowing an assessment of the student's sight vocabulary together with the strategies used in decoding out-of-context words. Uses of the graded reading selections and associated comprehension questions include identifying the nature and degree of oral reading errors and determining the level of classroom instructional materials appropriate to the individual. Additionally, students likely to benefit from remedial instruction can be identified. The word analysis and phonics tests are optional and supplementary. They are intended for use only up to about the ten-year-old level. In connection with the 1981 revision, the author refers to a national study involving 250 users of the *DRS* and performance data from 534 students aged from 6 : 00 to 14 : 00 years. The performance data obtained were used in reappraising the difficulty levels of the reading selections and in establishing the reliability of the *DRS*. In addition, the internal consistencies of the word analysis and phonics tests were calculated. Details of these and other related researches are presented in a technical report supplementary to the *DRS* Manual.

The manual itself contains relatively little statistical detail. It presents a series of questions likely to be asked by a perceptive user, followed by Spache's answers. Typically these are based on research, concise and to the point. Critics will say that some of these answers merit qualification. The greatest value of the *DRS* is as a means of structuring the sampling, assessment and analysis of an individual student's reading skills. The data derived indicates how pupil and materials can, to advantage, be matched. It also encourages the generation of remedial hypotheses.

TRN	Name of test	Author	Country	Publisher	Year
48	*Diagnostic Reading Tests (DRT)*	Committee on Diagnostic Reading Tests	USA	Committee on Diagnostic Reading Tests Inc.	1947 to 1966 1982 (new norms for some tests)

Type	No. of forms	C.A. range	Skills tested	Time
Group, individual,* attainment, diagnostic			*DRT*: Kindergarten through 4th Grade	
	2 (A, B)	5:00 to 9:11	SURVEY SECTION (K-4)	Untimed (variable)
	1 (B)	5:00 to 6:11	Reading Readiness: 1 Relationships 2 Eye-hand coordination 3 Visual discrimination 4 Auditory discrimination 5 Vocabulary	Untimed (variable)
	1 (A)	5:00 to 6:11	Booklet 1: (Grade 1) 1 Visual discrimination 2–5 Auditory discrimination (3 sub-tests and total) 6–9 Vocabulary (3 sub-tests and total) 10–12 Story reading (2 sub-tests plus total)	Untimed (about 30′)
	2 (A, B)	7:00 to 7:11	Booklet 2: (Grade 2) 1 Word attack 2 Comprehension 3 Total	Untimed (about 30′)
	2 (A, B)	8:00 to 10:11	Booklet 3: (Grades 3 to 4) 1 Word attack 2 Comprehension 3 Total	Untimed (about 30′)
	2 (A, B)	6:00 to 14:11	SECTION IV: (Grades 1–8) Word attack Part 1 (Oral)*	Untimed (about 20′)
			DRT: Lower level (Grades 4–8)	
	4 (A, B, C, D)	10:00 to 14:11	SURVEY SECTION (Grades 4–8)	
	4 (A, B, C, D)	10:00 to 14:11	Booklet 1: Part 1 1 Word recognition 2 Comprehension (i) Literary (ii) Scientific (iii) Social Studies	Untimed (about 30′)

Diagnostic Reading Tests continued

	No. of forms	C.A. range	Skills tested		Time
	4 (A, B, C, D)	10:00 to 14:11	Booklet 2: Part 2 Vocabulary Booklet 2: Part 3 Rate of reading		Untimed (about 30′)
		6:00 to 14:11	SECTION IV: (Grades 1 to 8) Word attack Part 1 (Oral)* Part 2 (Silent)		
			DRT: Upper level (Grades 7–13)		
	8 (A, B, C, D, E, F, G, H)	13:00 to 18:11	SURVEY SECTION 1 Rate of reading 2 Comprehension check	3 Vocabulary 4 Total comprehension	40′
	2 (A, B)		SECTION I: Vocabulary (revised) 1 English grammar and literature 2 Mathematics	3 Science 4 Social studies 5 Total vocabulary score	40′
	4 (A, B, C, D)		SECTION II: Comprehension		
			Part 1: Silent		Untimed (about 40′)
			2: Auditory		Untimed (about 60′)
	4 (A, B, C, D)		SECTION III: Rates of reading		
			1 General		Untimed (about 30′)
			2 Social Studies		Untimed (about 20′)
			3 Science		Untimed (about 30′)
			SECTION IV: Word attack		
	2 (A, B)		Part 1: Oral*		Untimed (about 30′)
	4 (A, B, C, D)		2: Silent		Untimed (about 30′)
(level A)					

Comments: This was a comprehensive endeavour over many years to produce an all-embracing series of diagnostic reading tests based on long-term planning and continuing study of the reading process. The tests are organised in three batteries covering the age range from kindergarten to the year of entry to college. Each battery includes a survey test intended to assess the pupil's general reading proficiency, plus a host of supplementary tests.

The above outline indicates the structure and major content of the *DRT* and was derived from information and materials provided for the reviewer by the publishers. Interested readers can readily obtain further details from Buros or from the Committee.

The laudable aim of the Committee was to produce tests that could be scored in areas of reading instruction rather than in terms of 'pure factors'. Teachers of reading were consulted right from the start of the project. Of the three batteries, that for the older pupils was produced first. The production of the material that the reviewer has inspected is of variable quality. The manuals have been criticised by reviewers for lack of detail on technical aspects of construction and validation. This is not to say that such evidence is not provided at all. The scope of the series is wide. This does not mean that the tests are the best available for the diagnosis of reading failure.

Changes in the content and organisation of the *DRT* over time, coupled with too brief descriptions of the battery and a far from clear order form, make it difficult to know in detail what is *currently* available. Nonetheless, the series is one of which teachers should be aware.

Inevitably, the passage of time, coupled with recent research findings give much of the material a dated air. Despite this, the concept of the *DRT* was, and remains, a challenging one. It also faced up to the difficult task of linking testing and teaching in a manner that was acceptable to the teaching profession. The latest information to hand (1983) was that the norms of the Survey Sections had been updated on the basis of data collected in 1980–1.

More confidence in the work of the Committee on Diagnostic Reading Tests would be generated if references to recent and proposed research and development initiatives were specified in the literature they distribute.

TRN	Name of test	Author	Country	Publisher		Year
50	*Diagnostic Survey*	M. M. Clay	NZ	Heinemann	2nd edition	NZ 1979
						UK 1981
					2nd impression	1982

Type	No. of forms	C.A. range	Skills tested	Time
Individual,	Can be different for each child	6:00 +	A record of reading behaviour on books	Untimed
diagnostic	1		Letter identification	
	2 (SAND & STONES)*		Concepts about print (SAND & STONES Tests)	
	3		Word tests	
			Other reading tests	
			Writing samples	
(level A)			Writing vocabulary	10′

Comments: The *Diagnostic Survey* is integrated with what are termed 'recovery procedures' (Clay, 1979). The survey battery aims to identify at an early age children for whom the process of learning to read is going awry. It is suggested that the techniques can be used also with older failing readers by those teachers familiar with the administration and interpretation of the survey with younger children.

Initially a running record of reading behaviour on books at three levels of difficulty is required. The results are analysed for various categories of errors (miscues). The test of Letter Identification is accompanied by normalised scores, to which the raw scores can be converted, based on 320 urban children aged 5:00 to 7:00 and 282 aged from 6:00 to 7:03 in 1968 and 1978 respectively. The split-half reliability based on the scores of 100 urban 6:00 year old pupils is 0·97 and the correlation with word reading 0·85. The Concepts about Print test known as SAND has a parallel form STONES. Norms as for the Letter Identification test are given. Test-retest reliability coefficients in the range 0·73 to 0·89 and split-half internal consistency coefficients of 0·84 to 0·88 are reported from a small sample of kindergarten pupils. The 'Ready to Read' Word test comprises three lists of fifteen words taken from the 45 most frequently occurring words in the early part of a graded series. Norms as for the Letter Identification test are provided. With 6:00 year old pupils (N = 100) the internal consistency coefficient of reliability was 0·90. Correlation with the *Schonell Word Reading Test R1* was 0·90 at 7:00 for a group of 87 children. A rating technique for written stories is provided. In addition, a test of writing vocabulary with norms based on 282 urban children aged 6:00 to 7:03 is included. Its test-retest reliability using a sample of 34 children aged 5:06 was 0·97. Its correlation with reading using 50 children of the same age was 0·82.

Details of the Reading Recovery procedures to be used with 10% to 20% of children requiring them are provided. The result of a three year research programme capitalised on the skills of competent teachers to develop teaching procedures. The results show that the extensive field trials were effective. The recovery programme integrated all four aspects of language.

CLAY, M. M. (1979) *The Early Detection of Reading Difficulties: A Diagnostic Survey with Recovery Procedures* (2nd edition). Auckland: Heinemann (published in UK by Heinemann Educational in 1981).

* SAND was first published in 1972; STONES followed in 1979. Both are now available only as a double pack. All the other test materials are contained in the book referred to above.

TRN	Name of test	Author	Country	Publisher	Year
52	*Doren Diagnostic Reading Test of Word Recognition Skills*	M. Doren	USA	American Guidance Service Inc. (NFER-Nelson act as agents) Revised edition	1956 to 1964 1973

Type	No. of forms	C.A. range	Skills tested		Time
Group, diagnostic	1	6:00 to 15:00	1 Letter recognition	7 Blending	3 × 60′ sessions
			2 Beginning sounds	8 Rhyming	
			3 Whole-word recognition	9 Vowels	
			4 Words within words	10 Discriminate guessing	
			5 Speech consonants	11 Spelling	
(level A)			6 Ending sounds	12 Sight words	
			(Each of the sub-tests 1 to 11 comprises two or more sections)		

Comments: The content of the eleven sub-tests is based on an analysis of the word recognition skills required to cope with the initial three books in five extensively-used series of graded readers. Doren's stated purpose is to identify the students' mistakes, thus specifying the skills towards which remedial work might profitably be directed. The reliability coefficients of the sub-tests range from 0·53 to 0·88, thus great care is required in interpreting the profiles. A concurrent validity coefficient of 0·90 for total score with reading attainment in the first four school grades is given. Validity coefficients based on small samples for each grade level range from 0·77 to 0·92. Some of the sub-test items appear suspect; for example, 'Beginning Sounds', at some levels, seems to tap skills requiring the use of context and of sight vocabulary as much as the skill it purports to measure.

Suggestions for remedial activities are given. These appear to be based on sound teaching principles, but no evidence is given of the efficacy of the practices with children having particular difficulties.

TRN	Name of test	Author	Country	Publisher	Year
53	*Drumcondra Attainment Tests – English (DATE)*	V. Greaney (Project Director)	E	Educational Research Centre, St Patrick's College	1978

Type	No. of forms	C.A. range		Skills tested	Time			Time
Group, attainment, normative	2 (A & B)*	7:00 to 15:00	*Level I*	Vocabulary	8′	*Level II*	Vocabulary	12′
				Word analysis	12′		Spelling	8′
				Comprehension (A) (Passages)	15′		Language	19′
				Comprehension (B) (Definitions)	10′		Capitalisation	
							Punctuation	
							Usage	
							Comprehension	25′
			Level III	Vocabulary	22′	*Level IV*	Vocabulary	15′
				Spelling	12′		Comprehension	21′
				Language	40′		Language	26′
				Capitalisation			Capitalisation	
				Punctuation			Punctuation	
				Usage			Usage	
				Parts of speech			Parts of speech	
				Comprehension	28′		Spelling	6′
			Level V	Vocabulary	15′	*Level VI*	Vocabulary	14′
				Spelling	8′		Spelling	8′
				Language	21′		Language	22′
				Capitalisation			Capitalisation	
				Punctuation			Punctuation	
				Usage			Usage	
				Grammar (Parts of speech)			Grammar (Parts of speech)	
				Comprehension	43′		Comprehension	49′
				Passages			Passages	
				Prose			Prose	
(level A)				Poetry			Poetry	

Comments: *DATE* is one part of a coordinated set of standardised measures in basic curricula areas developed for use with pupils in the last five years of primary and the first three years of secondary school education in Eire. The tests were developed in a cooperative project involving practising teachers and staff of the Educational Research Centre with expertise in the theory and practice of test construction. *DATE* is designed to allow an assessment of the range of attainments in a class, to facilitate the grouping of pupils by attainments, to allow the *initial* identification of individual pupils with learning difficulties and to assist teachers in reporting the pupils' progress to parents.

The manuals accompanying each level of the battery contain a content area by intellectual behaviour specification matrix. The various national samples on which the six levels were standardised are clearly described. Normative data on reliabilities and validities are presented. Of considerable interest are the intercorrelation matrices between the sub-tests in the battery. These are essential if profile interpretation is to be approximately cautious. The magnitude of the correlations raises important pedagogic issues.

Raw scores can be converted to percentile ranks, indicating the percentage of pupils in the standardisation group scoring lower than a given raw scor and standardised scores with a mean of 100 and a standard deviation of 15 fo the beginning, middle and end of the school year for successive year groups c pupils.† Some users might have also liked to have monthly age allowanc tables.

The complete *Drumcondra Attainment Tests Battery* includes assessmen of pupils' attainment in mathematics at Levels I to VI and of Irish at Levels I to VI, together with standardisations using the same pupils who took *DATE* The *Drumcondra Attainment Tests – English* are the major instrumen available for the normative appraisal of reading and related skills available i Eire. The *Marino Graded Word Reading Scale* is the only other nationall normed reading test available and covers the individual testing of wor recognition only (**TRN** 103).

* Initially the normative data for Form B will be only for beginning of schoo year attainments.

† At Level VI, only beginning of year norms are currently provided.

TRN	Name of test	Author	Country	Publisher	Year
57	*Durrell Analysis of Reading Difficulty (DARD)*	D. D. Durrell and J. H. Catterson	USA	The Psychological Corporation	1933 2nd edition 1955 3rd edition 1981

Type	No. of forms	C.A. range	Skills tested	Time
Individual, diagnostic (level A)	1	Pre-reading to 12:00	*Reading analysis tests*: 1 Oral reading (comprehension, reading errors, speed) 2 Silent reading (recall, speed) 3 Listening comprehension 4 Listening vocabulary 5 Word recognition (flash presentation) 6 Word analysis (untimed) 7 Spelling *Sounds in isolation*: 1 Letters 2 Blends and digraphs 3 Phonograms 4 Affixes (initial) 5 Affixes (final) *Other additional tests*: 1 Phonic spelling of words 2 Visual memory of words (primary) 3 Visual memory of words (intermediate) 4 Identifying sounds in words *Pre-reading phonics abilities inventories*: 1 Syntax matching 2 Identifying letter names in spoken words 3 Phonemes in spoken words 4 Writing letters from dictation 5 Writing letters from copy 6 Naming letters (lower case) 7 Naming letters (upper case) 8 Identifying letters named (upper case) 9 Identifying letters named (lower case) *Check list of instructional needs* (non-reader or pre-primer level; Primary grade reading level; Intermediate grade reading level) *General history data* 1 Pre-school record 2 School record 3 Recent medical record 4 Psychological factors/Home history	About 30′–90′

Comments: The purposes of this battery of tests are to estimate a pupil's general level of reading attainment and also to identify weaknesses and faulty habits that can be corrected. This test has been in use and under continuous development for over fifty years; its first clinical use was in 1932. The 1981 revision provides new normative data, an updating of content and the addition of two new tests recommended to the authors by users. Checklists for recording observations of children's difficulties are central to the *DARD*. 'While norms are provided for most of the tests, an analytic record of the difficulties the child displays is critical if specific help is to be given . . . ' The items in the checklists are claimed to be those 'of highest frequency and greatest significance in remedial work'.

Norms for the oral and silent reading tests are based on *time* taken to read a passage and on *comprehension* of the content. These are provided for each school grade from 1 to 6, based on convenience samples of about 200 pupils of average reading ability at each age level. Using a random sample of 200 pupils, the reliability of time taken to read two paragraphs was shown to be 0·85 for oral and 0·80 for silent reading. Some readers will have reservations concerning the validity and utility of reading time as one of the two indices used to identify Instructional, Independent and Capacity levels of reading. In passing, it must be stressed that the definition of these terms differs from that typically associated with Informal Reading Inventories. The amount of technical information contained in the manual is relatively meagre in relation to reliabilities and validities although internal consistency coefficients ranging from 0·70 to 0·97 are presented for thirteen tests based on samples of at least 200 pupils. The relationships between selected tests based on 210 pupils' scores are also given. Collecting data from a test that is individually administered presents any test constructor with formidable problems, even when as eminent a worker as Durrell is involved.

TRN	Name of test	Author	Country	Publisher	Year
58	*Durrell Listening-Reading Series*	D. D. Durrell	USA	Harcourt Brace Jovanovich	1970 (Primary, Intermediate) and 1969 (Advanced)

Type	No. of forms	C.A. range	Skills tested	Time
Group or individual, diagnostic and attainment	2 (D & E) Primary	6:00 to 9:06	1 Vocabulary (listening comprehension)	20′
			2 Sentence (listening comprehension)	15′
			3 Vocabulary (reading comprehension)	20′
			4 Sentence (reading comprehension)	15′
	2 (D & E) Intermediate	9:06 to 12:00	1 Vocabulary (listening comprehension)	20′
			2 Paragraph (listening comprehension)	23′
			3 Vocabulary (reading comprehension)	20′
			4 Paragraph (reading comprehension)	23′
	2 (D & E) Advanced	12:00 to 15:00	1 Vocabulary (listening comprehension)	20′
			2 Paragraph (listening comprehension)	20′
			3 Vocabulary (reading comprehension)	20′
(level P)			4 Paragraph (reading comprehension)	20′

Comments: The aim of these tests is to compare the child's understanding of equivalent material presented orally and requiring no reading attainments, with his ability to read and understand. In one part of the test he listens and responds whereas in the other section he reads and responds. The manual presents details of an extensive standardisation programme and also gives evidence of satisfactory reliabilities and validities. Intercorrelations between parts of the tests and correlations with other tests are presented. The authors argue that listening comprehension is a most satisfactory measure of a child's 'potential' for reading. However, it is also noted that some children's reading scores exceed their listening scores. Thus whilst listening scores indicate the extent to which a child can understand spoken language, it is not necessarily the level at which the child *should* be reading. Neither does it set an upper limit to reading attainment: 'Actually, a higher score in either of these abilities indicates a "potential" level for the other' (Primary Manual, p. 16). Whilst care has been taken to make the content of listening and reading tests equivalent though different, one could see interpretation being easier in some respects if the material was identical but the order different. The interpretation of the differences between scores on the listening and reading tests requires some sophistication, but is within the capabilities of any interested teacher. The manual contains helpful comments on the translation of results into remedial programmes.

This test is a most interesting approach to differential diagnosis.

TRN	Name of test	Author	Country	Publisher	Year
65	*English Skills Assessment*	Australian Council for Educational Research	A	Australian Council for Educational Research	1982

Type	No. of forms	C.A. range		Skills tested	Time
Group, individual, diagnostic, attainment	1	16:06 to 19:06	Part I	Spelling	12′
				Punctuation and capitalization	20′
				Comprehension I	18′
			Part II	Comprehension II	10′
				Usage	15′
				Vocabulary	10′
				Sentence structure	15′
(level A)				Logical relationships	10′

Comments: In response to requests by teachers and school counsellors, the above battery of tests of basic English and reading skills was developed using material from previously well-validated instruments. Its major focus is diagnostic, aiming to identify strengths and weaknesses and to indicate content for remedial programmes. The battery can, however, also be used to assess the relative attainments of students.

Test construction involved the use of item analyses based on conventional test theory and on Rasch models. Items selected for the final form of the test showed good discrimination and test fit by both procedures. The norms in the Interim Manual are based on a pilot study involving 197 students aged 16:06 to 17:06 and on 210 first year college entrants. Thus the norms are only tentative. Currently, data for more adequate norms are being collected. The manual (wisely) advocates that local norms be developed and informs the reader how this can be done for each of the eight sub-tests, Part totals and Overall total. In addition, a method of calculating a provisional passing score on a scale is presented.

Based on the pilot study, internal consistency reliabilities (Kuder–Richardson formula 20) of the eight sub-tests range from 0·52 to 0·80 at the younger and from 0·54 to 0·82 at the older age level. These reliabilities are not particularly high in terms of conventional test theory. For Parts I and II respectively, reliabilities are higher, ranging from 0·83 to 0·89. The overall reliabilities of the battery at the younger and older age-levels are given as 0·92 and 0·88 respectively. The inter-correlations between the sub-scales are presented. Users are warned that small differences between a pupil's scores on two sub-tests must be interpreted with great caution. The use of percentile ranges derived from the standard error of measurement of the scales is suggested as one way of enabling the test user to exercise appropriate caution. It can be argued that the simultaneous consideration of sub-test reliabilities and intercorrelations would have been preferable.

The content validity of the sub-scales appears high in that English specialists would have little difficulty in recognising the skills being tested. The provenance of the test items suggests that other indices of validity are likely to prove satisfactory when eventually reported. More central to both teachers and pupils will be the utility of the battery in enabling weaknesses to be identified and alleviated. On this issue, evidence is awaited with interest.

TRN	Name of test	Author	Country	Publisher	Year
71	*Gates-MacGinitie Reading Tests* (2nd edition)	A. I. Gates and W. H. MacGinitie	USA	Houghton Mifflin (NFER-Nelson act as agents)	1978

Type	No. of forms	C.A. range*	Skills tested	Time
Group, attainment	2 (Level R)	5:00 to 7:00	Reading readiness and early reading skills	Untimed
	2 (Level A)	5:00 to 7:00	Vocabulary	20′
			Comprehension	35′
	2 (Level B)	7:00 to 8:00	Vocabulary	20′
			Comprehension	35′
	2 (Level C)	8:00 to 9:00	Vocabulary	20′
			Comprehension	35′
	2 (Level D)	9:00 to 12:00	Vocabulary	20′
			Comprehension	35′
	2 (Level E)	12:00 to 15:00	Vocabulary	20′
			Comprehension	35′
(level A)	2 (Level F)	15:00 to 18:00	Vocabulary	20′
			Comprehension	35′

Comments: The seven levels of this test allow continuous and cumulative assessment of the reading attainments and progress in reading of pupils aged between 5:00 and 18:00 years. Except for Level R, all levels of the test contain a vocabulary and a comprehension sub-test. Level R has a more heterogeneous content of what seems to be reading readiness and early reading items including letter sounds, vocabulary, letter recognition, comprehension, word analysis, word families and letter matching. The manual indicates items assessing the first four only of these seven skills.

Standardisation was on a national (USA) sample of approximately 100 000 students. It is weakest at Level F where the smallest sized group was used (N = 2400). Internal consistency coefficients measured by Kuder–Richardson formula 20 and parallel form reliability coefficients range from 0·88 to 0·95. The approach to validity emphasises the match between the school's curricular objectives and the content and skills in the tests. The manual provides the user with a series of questions that assist him in making a decision on this issue.

Raw scores can be converted to grade equivalent, percentile and stanine scales. Normal Curve Equivalent Scores, a variant of the percentile scale but having equal units, is available. Extended Scale Scores allow the assessment of progress over time on a continuous scale. The publishers provide a wide range of scoring services. The Decoding Skills Analysis Report based on the Vocabulary sub-tests of Levels A and B gives a diagnostic analysis of the major decoding skills involved.

* The chronological ages quoted are those given by NFER-Nelson. They do not relate exactly to the Grade Levels given in the manual at the bottom end.

TR	Name of test	Author	Country	Publisher		Year
72	*Gates, McKillop, Horowitz Reading Diagnostic Tests*	A. I. Gates, A. S. McKillop and E. C. Horowitz	USA	Teachers College, Columbia University	2nd edition	1981

Type	No. of forms	C.A. range	Skills tested	Time
Individual, diagnostic	1	6:06 to 11:00 (selected tests may be used with older students who have reading difficulties)	*Oral reading Analysis of oral reading errors: 1 Omissions of words 2 Additions of words 3 Repetitions 4 Analysis of mispronunciations: (a) Directional errors (b) Wrong beginnings (c) Wrong middle (d) Wrong ending (e) Wrong in several parts (f) Accent errors	Untimed with one exception (about 1 hr if all tests are used)
			Reading sentences	
			*Words: flash presentation (card tachistoscope provided)	$\frac{1}{2}''$ per word
			*Words: untimed Knowledge of word parts – word attack: Syllabication Recognising and blending common word parts Reading words Giving letter sounds Naming capital letters Naming lower-case letters Recognizing the visual form of sounds: Vowels Auditory tests: Auditory blending Auditory discrimination Written expression: * Spelling Informal writing sample	
(level A)				

Comments: The above battery of tests is designed to help the teacher diagnose the causes of reading deficiencies 'in terms of the child's unique weaknesses' (Manual, p. 3). By identifying specific strengths and weaknesses, a programme of instruction can be more adequately planned, it is claimed. Not all pupils will need to be given all the diagnostic tests and the tests themselves can be given in any order. Normative comparisons of an unsophisticated nature are possible on the four tests marked by asterisks above. It is the study of the individual child's unique pattern of responses that is considered most important for diagnostic and remedial purposes.

This revised version of the test was restandardised on 3 600 pupils in 1979 and 1980, 60 at each age level. Whilst the characteristics of the sample are specified, it is not claimed to be representative. Only limited information is presented on reliabilities and validities. A test-retest reliability coefficient of 0·94 is reported from a sample of N = 27 on the Oral Reading Test. A study of marker agreement on the classification of word errors on the Oral Reading Test using 50 protocols showed agreement levels for different sections of 94 % and 91 %, but only two markers were involved. No information is given on the intercorrelations between the tests. Checklists included in the Pupil Record Book allow a record to be made of qualitative aspects of the pupil's test performance to be readily recorded for three of the asterisked tests. The importance of recording a pupil's responses whenever an error is made is stressed.

It is surprising that in a 1981 revision the term 'errors' has not been replaced by 'miscues'. The interpretation of errors is discussed and for some tests minimum levels are specified. What is lacking is guidance on remediation strategies and, consequently, evidence of the efficacy of the interventions suggested by the use of the battery or parts of it. The need for a simultaneous diagnosis of silent reading ability leads to a recommendation that the *Gates-MacGinitie Reading Tests* be used (TRN 71).

TRN	Name of test	Author	Country	Publisher	Year
79	*Gray Oral Reading Test*	W. S. Gray and H. M. Robinson	USA	Bobbs-Merrill	1963 to 1967

Type	No. of forms	C.A. range	Skills tested	Time
Individual, attainment and diagnostic (level P)	4 (A, B, C & D)	6:00 to 18:00	1 Oral reading achievement 2 Types of errors (*a*) aid (*b*) gross mispronunciation (*c*) partial mispronunciation (*d*) omission (*e*) insertion (*f*) substitution (*g*) repetition (*h*) inversion	The time taken to read a passage is measured

Comments: These tests are designed to measure oral reading using thirteen passages of increasing complexity ranging from pre-primer to college level, although it is difficult for beginning readers. It is claimed that the results of the test will provide a quick and valid means of placing a child at a level of work suited to his reading skills. The standardisation and norms are based on rather small and restricted samples. Separate norms for boys and girls are provided. The standard error of measurement of the tests increases markedly as the more advanced levels are reached. Nonetheless, the test compares favourably with other oral tests of reading. Claims for the test's validity are based on its construction and content. The availability of four equivalent forms is a considerable asset.

TRN	Name of test	Author	Country	Publisher		Year
83	*Handbook in Diagnostic Teaching: A Learning Disabilities Approach*	P. H. Mann and P. Suiter	USA	Allyn and Bacon		1974
					6th impression	1977

Type	No. of forms	C.A. range	Skills tested	Time
Some individual, some group, diagnostic, criterion-referenced	Various, as listed	Not specified. Intended for use with 'learning handicapped' pupils	*Developmental spelling inventories*: Developing a spelling inventory Screening procedures Spelling errors Mann-Suiter Developmental Spelling Inventory *Developmental Reading Inventories*: Developing your own word reading inventory Word reading errors Checking oral language development Developing your own developmental paragraph reading inventory Screening procedures for the developmental paragraph reading inventory Silent reading comprehension Listening comprehension level Reading errors Mann-Suiter developmental paragraph reading inventory, Forms A & B *Developmental screening*: (all of the following 20 instruments were devised by Mann and Suiter) Primary developmental checklist Visual-motor screen Visual discrimination screen Visual memory for objects Auditory closure (blending) screen Alphabet speech screen Visual language association screen Auditory language association screen Developmental screening Figure-ground screen Visual closure screen Auditory discrimination screen Auditory memory (sentences) screen Visual language classification screen Auditory language classification screen Manual language expression screen	Mainly untimed; a few tests require flash presentation of items

Handbook in Diagnostic Teaching continued

Skills tested

		Time
Speech screen	Verbal language expression screen	Mainly
Written language expression screen	Non-verbal language screen	Untimed

Supplementary evaluation and special forms

Deficit level curriculum (process oriented) checklists:

Auditory channel	Visual channel
Motor	Language
Control factors	Motivational and emotional factors

Comments: This handbook of tests is intended to assess the learning needs of children and to facilitate appropriate instruction in the basic subjects. Individual differences in pupils' learning styles is a central tenet of the approach. The assessment and instructional techniques described have been developed and tested in practical teaching situations. Using a task-analysis orientation, the authors have tried to identify the skills and abilities children require if they are to cope adequately with the basic subjects. A criterion-referenced approach to assessment and the curriculum means that both are linked in a manner likely to appeal to many teachers. The final section of the manual (Chapter 7) on *Task Level Curriculum* provides suggestions for alleviating difficulties in reading, spelling, handwriting, language and arithmetic.

The manual is good at providing suggestions for developing assessment procedures especially for teachers interested in developing Informal Inventories appropriate to their unique classroom circumstances. Relatively little technical information is given concerning the validities of the assessment procedures or the efficacy of the interventions, though some is provided in connection with the instruments developed by Mann and Suiter. Evidence in support of the importance of the skills specified by the authors can be obtained by reference to the researches listed in an eight-page bibliography. Having only recently come across this manual, the reviewer can understand why it had already reached a sixth printing in 1977.

TRN	Name of test	Author	Country	Publisher	Year
89	*Individual Pupil Monitoring System – Reading*	J. L. Laffey (Editorial adviser)	USA	Houghton Mifflin	1974

Type	No. of forms	C.A. range	Skills tested	Time
Group, attainment (level A)	2 (A and B)	6:00 to 12:00	Word-attack Vocabulary and comprehension Discrimination/study skills	Untimed

Comments: *Individual Pupil Monitoring System–Reading (IPMS-R)* is a group and individual means of criterion-referenced assessment providing a continuous record of pupil progress. It is based on a detailed analysis of the reading behavioural objectives most commonly used in the USA. These objectives were placed in ascending difficulty in six levels approximating the first six years of elementary school. Items were then written to test pupils' achievement of the objectives. The items were validated on a national sample of children.

For each of the three areas of reading skill tested at each grade level, there are two parallel tests. Each test booklet contains between eleven and twenty-nine individual tests. Each test of a specified objective contains five items. The behavioural objectives to be tested are listed at the front of each test booklet. The objectives are classified using three digit numbers in which the first number identifies the grade level and the next two the specific skill. Pupils can keep a graphic record of their progress on all the tests they have taken.

An extensive array of behavioural objectives is listed in the *IPMS-R* system. The publishers have a Customized Objectives Monitoring Service. Under certain conditions this allows educational agencies to select those objectives appropriate to its needs. The publishers will then construct tests based on these selected objectives using the item bank from which the *IPMS-R* system was developed. Additionally, the *IPMS-R* objectives are cross-referenced to a range of basal reading programmes thereby enabling the teacher to link instruction to assessment.

In many respects this is an interesting system although the brevity of the individual tests (only five items) may cause some concern. Users may also have reservations about the extreme degree of flexibility concerning a 'satisfactory' score on a test. This is left almost entirely to the user's discretion.

TRN	Name of test	Author	Country	Publisher	Year
93	*Instant Words Criterion Test*	E. Fry	USA	Jamestown Publishers	1980

Type	No. of forms	C.A. range	Skills tested	Time
Individual, group,* attainment, diagnostic (level A)	1	Not specified (suitable for learners of any age in the early stages of learning to read)	Word-recognition Knowledge of suffixes Spelling *	Untimed

Comments: The test is based on the most common 300 words in the English language. These words, together with their common suffixes, make up approximately 65% of all written material. Mastery of these words as an instant sight vocabulary is considered by Fry as essential for fluent reading and adequate comprehension.

Each of the three pages of the test contains 100 words. Each page begins with a Quick Survey Test of twelve items. The complete Diagnostic Test requires the pupil to read aloud the listed words. This establishes which ones are known and which ones have yet to be mastered. At the bottom of each page there is an eight-item test of common suffixes. By asking the student to listen to and then spell the words, the test can be used as a diagnostic spelling test. The utility of the test for self-study or home study is advocated as is repeated use in order to assess progress. Reference is made to three books which contain teaching suggestions. The attraction of such a test to many teachers is that the items not known can, indeed, should, be taught provided one accepts Fry's assumptions concerning the importance of an instant sight vocabulary in the development of efficient reading.

The validity of the test rests on the extent to which one is certain that the 300 words in it represent the proportion of all written material that is claimed. The test can be used with readers at almost any chronological age. The earlier the child's stage of reading development, the fewer the items he will master. It would be possible to establish for children of different chronological ages from a defined population the percentage likely to have mastered each word at a given age. The most frequently used words in writing are not necessarily the most readily mastered.

RN	Name of test	Author	Country	Publisher	Year
4	*Johnston Informal Reading Inventory (JIRI)*	M. C. Johnston	USA	Educational Publications	1982

ype	No. of forms	C.A. range	Skills tested	Time
iroup, ndividual, lacement, diagnostic, riterion-referenced evel A)	3 (B, C, L)	12:00 to 18:00+ (Junior High to Adult)	1 Word opposites test (to identify starting paragraph) 2 Silent reading comprehension (a) main ideas (MI) (d) vocabulary (V) (b) factual details (D) (e) inference (I) (c) cause and effect (CE) 3 Oral reading of paragraphs 4 Synonyms	Untimed

omments: A major aim of the *JIRI* is to use an adapted group testing rocedure to assess the highest level of silent reading comprehension of tudents based on their responses to a series of carefully graded, high interest vel, prose paragraphs. It is a practical approach to placing students on uitable materials provided that the reading programme includes the type of igh interest material used in the *JIRI*. A group administered Word)pposites test is used initially to determine the starting silent reading aragraph for each individual. Forms B and C are parallel in paragraph ngths; Form L is a longer version designed to serve as an extra check on omprehension levels. It can also be used for individual oral reading (miscue) nalysis using the teacher's preferred system.

The revised Fry Readability Formula was used to establish the readability vels of the paragraphs, but no technical details are given. The reading levels of the paragraphs range from about 8:00 to 16:00 years. The number of questions per paragraph varies between seven and nine, and are of the five types specified above. It is claimed that the flexibility of the *JIRI* is one of its major strengths. Evidence of the utility of the information elicited is represented by a brief reference to several years of experimental use in a range of educational settings. The strengths of this instrument include the high interest level of the paragraphs used and the attempt to develop a system that can be used with classes of students rather than only with individuals. Absence of research-based evidence of the validity of the evaluation and of the follow-up procedures is a weakness. For example, evidence of inter-rater reliability in assessing students' responses to the comprehension questions could have been provided. The diagnostic significance of the information provided by the *JIRI* could have been more adequately explicated.

TRN	Name of test	Author	Country	Publisher	Year
103	*Marino Graded Word Reading Scale*	J. Sullivan	E	Longman, Browne and Nolan, now Educational Co. of Ireland	1970

Type	No. of forms	C.A. range	Skills tested	Time
Attainment, individual, oral (level A)	1	5:00 to 15:00	Oral word reading	Untimed (10′)

Comments: This is a 130-item word recognition test. It is intended for the age range 7:00+ to 12:00+ years in particular. However, reading ages can be obtained, ranging from a base of five years (no words read correctly) to twenty years (130 words read correctly). The extremes of the scale are likely to be suspect, especially the upper end.

The test was standardised on a sample of 3 930 children aged between five and fifteen years. Raw scores can be converted to reading ages only and this would be considered a weakness by some test constructors. The manual is clearly written and provides satisfactory evidence of validities and reliabilities. The account of the test construction procedure given in the appendix to the manual manages to combine brevity with lucidity.

This test has become quite popular in Eire but is relatively unknown in Britain. It could well find uses here after some comparative investigations have been carried out.

TRN	Name of test	Author	Country	Publisher	Year
111	*Newman Language and Mathematics Kit (NLMK)*	A. Newman	A	Harcourt Brace Jovanovich Group (Australia)	1983

Type	No. of forms	C.A. range	Skills tested	Time
Group,* individual,† attainment, diagnostic, criterion-referenced (level A)	1	10:06+	*A Screening Test (10 items) *B Follow-up Test (15 items) †C Error Analysis Guidelines used in a diagnostic interview: *Strategies* 1 Reading recognition: Words, Symbols 2 Comprehension: (a) Specific terminology understanding; (b) General meaning 3 Transformation 4 Process skills: Numerical, Spatial, Logic items: (i) Random response; (ii) Wrong operation; (iii) Faulty algorithm; (iv) Faulty computation; (v) No response; Other errors 5 Encoding ability: Words, Symbols 6 Carelessness 7 Motivation 8 Task form	Untimed

Comments: The above instrument is brought to readers' notice as children's comprehension of the language of mathematics raises important issues for teachers of reading, teachers of mathematics and teachers of children. Using the *NLMK*, the identification of specific difficulties in dealing with mathematics problems is facilitated, an understanding of the individual pupil's strategies is obtained thereby allowing remedial activities to be prescribed. The author is interested in *why* children fail.

All pupils take a screening test containing 10 items. Pupils scoring 6 or less are deemed 'at risk'. They take a 15 item follow-up test. The teacher then conducts individually a diagnostic interview focused on the items failed in both the screening and follow-up tests. The diagnostic interview is based on the Error Analysis Guidelines which includes the eight 'Strategies' listed above. The information elicited enables the Initial Error Cause for the item to be identified. A diagnostic profile is prepared and from this remedial activities can be prescribed. The intention is laudable.

The author emphasises the importance of matching the readability of mathematics texts and problems with the reading ability of the pupil and gives advice on how this can be achieved. Even then children still have difficulties. The background to and rationale underpinning her approach is explored in a 57-page booklet. The potential of the diagnostic interview using a structured approach to identifying the strategies the child employs, is considerable and the author is to be congratulated on her endeavours.

Unfortunately, the absence of empirical information concerning the item selection for the screening and follow-up tests, the validity of the 'cut-off' criterion in the former, the failure to consider 'false positive' and 'false negative' identifications, the absence of any established links between the profile, the remediation and its efficacy means that anyone adopting the system does so on its logical appeal alone. Further work to determine the efficacy of the approach would be worth while.

TRN	Name of test	Author	Country	Publisher		Year
147	*Prescriptive Reading Inventory (PRI)*	CTB/McGraw-Hill Authorship Staff	USA	CTB/McGraw-Hill	1st edition	1972
						1977

Type	No. of forms	C.A. range	Skills tested	Time
Group, individual, diagnostic, criterion-referenced, normative	1 (six levels)		The *PRI* assesses pupil mastery of behaviourally defined reading objectives. These objectives are classified under seven process groups at Levels I and II and Levels A to D as shown below.	Untimed
	Level I	5:00 to 7:00		(LI about 75′)
	Level II	5:06 to 8:00		(LII about 75′)
	Level A/Red	7:06 to 8:06		(LA about $3\frac{1}{4}$ hrs)
	Level B/Green	8:00 to 9:06	Levels I and II: Auditory discrimination	(LB about 3 hrs)
	Level C/Blue	9:00 to 10:06	Visual discrimination	(LC about 3 hrs)
	Level D/Orange	10:00 to 12:06	Alphabet knowledge	(LD about $2\frac{3}{4}$ hrs)
			Language experience	
			Comprehension	
			Attention skills	
			Initial reading	
			Levels A to D: Recognition of sound and symbol	
			Phonic analysis	
			Structural analysis	
			Translation	
			Literal comprehension	
			Interpretive comprehension	
(level A)			Critical comprehension	

Comments: The *PRI* is designed to allow the diagnostic teaching of reading by identifying pupils' strengths and weaknesses in pre-reading and reading skills. The analysis of the results is directly linked to the prescription of appropriate activities likely to develop the skills that have not been mastered. *PRI* Teacher Resource Files give information on teaching each of the 102 reading objectives covered by the *PRI* system. The system is keyed to the most widely used basal and non-basal reading schemes. If needed, norm-referenced information on pupil attainment can also be obtained. Accurate and reliable diagnosis is claimed by virtue of the extensive research and development programme on which the system is based. Although the *PRI* can be scored by hand, the process is very time consuming. A computer scoring system is provided by CTB/McGraw-Hill at a low cost. The following information can be obtained using the system:

1 *Individual Diagnostic Map* Specifies the objectives that a pupil has mastered, needs to review, or has been unable to cope with.

2 *Class Diagnostic Map* Summarises for a class the results on each objective tested.
3 *Pre-post Matched CRT Report* Evaluation of progress over time on specific objectives.
4 *Individual Study Guide* Identifies each individual child's reading strengths and weaknesses and provides an educational prescription linked to the reading programme in use in the school.
5 *Class Grouping Report* Identifies common needs of students and provides a record keeping system summarising the group's performances on specific objectives.
6 *Programme Reference Guides* For each reading programme linked to the *PRI*, these guides list the pages in the textbooks, the teacher's manual and pupil workbooks where work related to each of the objectives measured by the *PRI* is to be found.

The *PRI* represents a systems approach to the diagnostic teaching of reading that utilises the latest in information processing technology. Although such developments are only just beginning to affect the assessment and teaching of reading in the UK, it represents an approach that cannot be ignored. The scope and promise of the *PRI* is impressive. It will be interesting to receive reports on the efficacy with which its use alleviates children's reading difficulties and raises standards of literacy. **CTB/McGraw-Hill** have already built on this work (see **TRN** 148).

It should be noted that within the system there is still considerable scope for the teacher's ingenuity in devising remedial materials and techniques.

TRN	Name of test	Author	Country	Publisher	Year
148	*Prescriptive Reading Inventory Reading Systems 1 and 2 (PRI/RS)*	CTB/McGraw-Hill Authorship Staff	USA	CTB/McGraw-Hill	1980

Type	No. of forms	C.A. range
3roup, ndividual, liagnostic, riterion-referenced, normative	1 (five levels)	
	Level A	5:00 to 7:00
	Level B	7:00 to 8:00
	Level C	8:00 to 9:00
	Level D	10:00 to 12:00
	Level E	13:00 to 15:00+
level A)		

Skills tested

The PRI/RS are based on a grade-related selection taken from 171 behaviourally defined reading and language objectives covering the 5:00 to 15:00+ age levels.

Skills	A	B	C	D	E
I *Oral language*:					
Oral language	*	*			
Oral comprehension	*	*			
II *Word attack & usage*:					
Word analysis	*	*	*	*	
Vocabulary		*	*	*	*
Word usage		*	*	*	*
III *Comprehension*:					
Literal comprehension		*	*	*	*
Interpretive & critical comprehension		*	*	*	*
IV *Applications*:					
Study skills			*	*	*
Content area reading			*	*	*

Time

Untimed

(Objectives inventory
Level A about 80′
Level B about 4 hr. 25′
Level C about 4 hr. 23′
Level D about 2 hr. 44′)
Level E about 2 hr. 22′)

Comments: The *PRI/RS 1 and 2* are a development of the company's xperience with the *Prescriptive Reading Inventory (PRI)* (TRN 147). The ystems, or combinations of elements from both, provide information for lecision-making at both the individual and institutional levels. *PRI/RS* rovides education authorities with a set of programmes that can provide 'continuing daily information about student reading skills'. Both criterion-referenced information for teachers and normative information for evaluating programmes and systems can be obtained. Each of the two systems provides information on the following six elements in the diagnostic-prescriptive teaching of reading: (i) placement, (ii) diagnosis, (iii) prescription, (iv) teaching, (v) monitoring and (vi) enriching and reinforcing behaviours.

RS 1 is 'a graded approach to the assessment of *skills by level*'. It utilises the Instructional Objectives Inventory. *RS 2* is a 'multigraded approach to the assessment of *skill clusters across levels*'. Each system is separately packaged. Instructional materials directly linked to the assessment procedures are provided.

Related to the six headings listed above, *RS 1* will provide the following: (i) Locator test; (ii) Instructional objectives inventory, Category objectives test, Skills areas survey, Individual diagnostic map, Objectives mastery report, Class grouping report; (iii) Master reference book; (iv) Teacher resource files; (v) Mastery tests, Continuous progress monitoring log, Estimated norms class record sheet; and (vi) Tutor activities and Student worksheets.

RS 2 provides the following: (i) Placement test; (ii) Skills area diagnostic tests, Individual diagnostic map, Class grouping report; (iii) Master reference book; (iv) Teacher resource files; (v) Mastery tests, Continuous progress monitoring log; and (vi) Tutor activities and Student worksheets

Any reader unfamiliar with the system who has read this far may well b breaking out into a cold sweat at the thought of the testing and recordin involved in operating it. Fortunately, a comprehensive computerised scorin system is available – at a price. In addition, software programmes are bein developed (some are already available) to enable schools to use their ow computing facilities. 'The coming of the microcomputer provides a uniqu opportunity to reduce the paperwork load and provide more consistent an timely monitoring of student progress.'

PRI/RS combines the latest developments in information processin technology with an objectives/skills-mastery approach to the diagnostic prescriptive teaching of reading. As such it is a *tour de force*. The validity o the model of the reading process on which it rests is one that man professionals would question as they would also question the relate pedagogy. However, one crucial issue will be the efficacy of the systems i improving children's reading attainments. Quite clearly the investment in thi project is testimony to the conviction of its developers.

RN	Name of test	Author	Country	Publisher	Year
51	*Progressive Achievement Tests: Listening Comprehension*	W. B. Elley and N. A. Reid	NZ	New Zealand Council for Educational Research (NZCER)	1971 1978

Type	No. of forms	C.A. range	Skills tested	Time
Oral, group, attainment and diagnostic (level A)	2 (A & B at each of the eight levels)	7:00 to 15:00	Listening comprehension	Times in which tester must read passages are prescribed

Comments: In this test the teacher reads passages, related questions and four alternative answers after each question. The child's task is to select the correct answer from those read aloud. His response is recorded by a letter, i.e. A, B, C or D. Like the *Progressive Achievement Tests of Reading Comprehension and Vocabulary,* this test is intended to be used early in the school year in order to give information helpful to the teacher in planning a programme of instruction.

Standardisation is based on representative samples of 1 000 pupils at each age level. Reliabilities and validities are acceptably high. The manual is excellent. Raw scores are converted to percentiles for each six months of age range covered. One possible weakness is that there are relatively few test items per level or year.

The uses of a listening comprehension test to provide an estimate of a child's 'reading expectancy' is interestingly and cautiously discussed. Teachers in New Zealand are fortunate to have the series of *Progressive Achievement Tests* available to them.

In 1978 the norms were checked by the Test Development Division of NZCER. Sixteen out of twenty-one comparisons showed no significant differences. The report on this study states: 'In terms of educational decisions made by classroom teachers using these tests, the results of this analysis indicate that the published norms can be used with complete confidence as there has been virtually no change in pupil performance over the seven-year period since the tests were first standardised.' Concern was also expressed that standards had not risen.

TRN	Name of test	Author	Country	Publisher	Year
152	*Progressive Achievement Tests: Reading Comprehension and Vocabulary*	W. B. Elley and N. A. Reid	NZ	New Zealand Council for Educational Research	1969 1974 1981

Type	No. of forms	C.A. range	Skills tested	Time
Group, attainment	3 (A, B & C)	8:00 to 15:00	Vocabulary (125 items)	30′
			Reading comprehension (97 items)	40′
(level A)			(A series of 7 sub-tests of these scales appropriate to particular age levels of pupils has been prepared)	

Comments: This series of seven tests is designed to enable teachers to assess their pupils' levels of achievement in terms of a reading content and of reading objectives measured by the tests. In the vocabulary tests, the underlying content scale is based on the most frequently known 10 000 words in the English language, according to the Wright* (1965) list. Scores are recorded in ten levels and equivalent average ages of children performing at that level for both the vocabulary and comprehension tests are given. Thus the test gives both a content mastery score and a percentile rank for each six-month age group from 8:00 to 15:00, if required. The level scores place a child's reading attainments on a ten-stage developmental scale ranging from illiteracy to the competence of the adult.

The test is available in three parallel forms, A, B and C, but the C form is reserved for research purposes only. The reusable test booklets contain the complete test in either vocabulary or comprehension for Forms A, B or C and the separate answer sheets are prepared for *each* of the seven sub-sections of the scale. The split-half reliabilities and the equivalent form correlations for both aspects of reading tested are satisfactory. Evidence of concurrent validities is also presented. Content validity is clearly defined. The handbook contains extremely helpful suggestions on the use of reading tests and the interpretation of the results. One weakness is that the uses of the tests a indicators of mastery of content criteria depend on rather few items for eac level of achievement. On balance, this is a well-designed and well-constructe test with a most useful manual describing what any test user needs to know

A set of *Listening Comprehension Tests* have also been developed to b used in conjunction with the above reading tests so that some indication o level of expectancy in reading attainment by a child can be estimated by th teacher (see TRN 151, p. 249).

Checks on the norms of this test were carried out in 1974 and 1981. Th 1981 report notes an overall small but fairly even raw score decline in bot reading comprehension and vocabulary. However, very few of the difference were greater than one point of raw score. The report comments: '. . . in term of the educational decisions made by classroom teachers using these tests, th results of this analysis indicate, as did the 1974 check, that the publishe norms can continue to be used with confidence.'

* WRIGHT, C. W. (1965) *An English Word Count*. Pretoria, South Afric National Bureau of Educational and Social Research.

TRN	Name of test	Author	Country	Publisher	Year
153	*Progressive Achievement Tests: Study Skills*	N. A. Reid, A. C. Croft, and P. F. Jackson.	NZ	New Zealand Council for Educational Research	1978

Type	No. of forms	C.A. range		Skills tested	Time
Group, attainment, diagnostic	1 (Booklet I for 9:00 to 10:11 Booklet II for 11:00 to 15:11)	9:00 to 15:11	Series 1	*Knowledge and use of reference materials*: Using reference sources; Using the library; Alphabetical order; Using an encyclopaedia; Using a Table of Contents; Using an index; Using a dictionary; Using a directory	40′ (50′ including instructions)
	1 (Booklet I for 9:00 to 10:11 Booklet II for 11:00 to 15:11)	9:00 to 15:11	Series 2	*Reading maps, graphs, tables and diagrams*: Reading maps; Reading graphs; Reading tables; Diagrams and charts; Reading pictorial material	40′ (50′ including instructions)
(level A)	1 (Booklet P for 11:00 to 12:11 Booklet S for 13:00 to 15:11)	11:00 to 15:11	Series 3	*Reading study skills*: Location skimming (scanning); Outlining and summarising; Getting information from a page; Differentiating fact and opinion; Judging relevancy; Summarizing	40′ (54′including instructions)

Comments: The aim of the test was to measure the skills used by pupils in locating, interpreting and acquiring verbal and graphic information. Additionally, the skills involved in reading for particular purposes were to be tested. The italicised headings show the three major areas in which items were written. The sub-headings indicate the content. There was no assumption that these three aspects of study skills are independent. The evidence presented in the manual shows that they are not, as most teachers would have anticipated. After extensive pilot work, the test was standardised on representative samples of 1 100 pupils at each class level. Raw scores can be converted to percentile rank norms for six monthly age groups. Percentiles for each class level were also obtained. Thus relative attainment on the three tests can be assessed in relation to age peers or to the class level nationally. In order to sensitise users to the unreliability inherent in test scores, it is advocated that percentile *bands* be used indicating the amount of variation likely to occur in scores on retesting. Raw score means and standard deviations grouped by class level and by sex are reported. In Series 1 and 3, girls tend to score higher than boys. In Series 2, at the older ages boys obtain slightly higher scores than girls. Despite these differences, only common norms are provided. Very extensive information is presented supporting the reliabilities and validities of these three measures.

The intercorrelations between the tests are fairly high, indicating that they tap certain common abilities. Factor analyses of the tests together with a battery of fourteen others did not reveal a clear 'study skills' factor. This limits the diagnostic interpretation of the results, a note that is sounded throughout the manual. However, the normative comparisons are of value. The manual also provides a breakdown showing the skill or skills each *item* was written to assess, together with their difficulty levels. Thus it is possible to see where, on any items, a class stands in relation to national norms. This seems a useful way of highlighting relative strengths and weaknesses, but it has an obvious attendant danger – the temptation to teach to the test. This, of course, is *not* advocated. The manual does suggest ways in which schoolteachers might use the information to improve their students' study skills.

TRN	Name of test	Author	Country	Publisher	Year
154	*Proof-Reading Tests of Spelling (PRETOS)*	Croft, C., Gilmore, A., Reid, N. and Jackson, P.	NZ	New Zealand Council for Educational Research	1981

Type	No. of forms	C.A. range	Skills tested	Time
Group, individual, attainment, diagnostic (level A)	1 at each of 5 levels	8:00 to 13:00 (Standards 2 & 3 and Forms I & II)	*Spelling:* Production (misspelt words identified and corrected, error free lines correctly identified) Recognition (Production score plus words identified as errors but not correctly respelt) *Additional Error Analyses:* (ii) Misspelt words identified but not respelt correctly (iii) Misspelt words not identified (iv) Correctly spelt words identified as being misspelt (v) Words incorrect by context rather than by spelling	30′

Comments: After an extensive amount of pilot work, *PRETOS* has been developed primarily as a teaching aid. It comprises five tests of increasing difficulty. Each test consists of either three or four passages of prose preceded by a practice section. Each paragraph contains misspellings generated according to three criteria. In *PRETOS*, 85% of the misspellings (if corrected) are among the most frequently used 3 500 words. The student has to identify and correct misspellings.

A student's responses are scored for Production and for Recognition as defined above. A further four categories of errors are then identified. *PRETOS* was standardised on representative samples of about 1 000 students attending state schools at each of the five age levels covered by the test. Tables of sex × age trends in both Production and Recognition scores are presented. Class norms covering three monthly periods in the school year are provided. Raw scores are converted to percentile ranks for both Production and Recognition. To avoid the false sense of precision such figures can give, it is recommended that test performance be reported as a percentile band using the standard error of measurement of the test to specify the range. The significance of differences between Production and Recognition scores is calculated using standard scores. It would have been of value to have had a table giving the intercorrelation between the error categories. Taken with the information from the additional error categories, the results provide a basis for decisions concerning class strengths and weaknesses, programmes for groups and individuals and a means of evaluating the efficacy of a spelling programme. Test-retest reliabilities, using samples of 100 students at each of the five age levels with a six months gap between testing, range between 0·86 and 0·92. Internal consistency Kuder–Richardson formula 20 coefficients at each age level are all 0·94 and above. The content validity of the test is based on the rationale underpinning its development. Concurrent validity is strongly supported by correlations with twelve other spelling tests using samples of between 31 and 149 pupils. The coefficients ranged between 0·79 and 0·90.

The content of many of the passages has (understandably) an antipodean flavour probably not well-suited to an industrialised urban society such as in Britain. However, it can be argued that the thematic content is less important than the spelling errors therein, bearing in mind the purposes of the test. The strategy developed in this instrument is an interesting one with considerable promise.

TRN	Name of test	Author	Country	Publisher	Year
158	*Reading Evaluation Adult Diagnosis (Revised) (READ)*	R. J. Colvin and J. H. Root	USA	Literacy Volunteers of America	1982

Type	No. of forms	C.A. range		Skills tested			Time
Individual, diagnostic, criterion-referenced	1	Adults with reading difficulties	Part 1	Sight words			Untimed
			Part 2	Word analysis skills			
				A Letter sounds and names	G	Variant vowels	
				B Reversals	H	Suffixes	
				C CVC (Consonant-vowel-consonant)	I	Soft c and g	
				D CV(CC) (4 letters – 3 sounds)	J	Silent letters	
				E Blends (initial and final)	K	Multi-syllabic words	
				F Digraphs (initial and final)			
			Part 3	Reading/listening inventory			
				A Word recognition			
				B Reading comprehension			
(level A)				C Listening comprehension			

Comments: Adult and teenager illiteracy is a serious problem in many countries. It has been estimated that there are 26 million adult Americans who are functionally illiterate. Literacy Volunteers of America is but one of many organisations attempting to help alleviate this problem. The *READ* test will be of interest to workers in other English speaking countries involved in reducing adult illiteracy. LVA train *all* their volunteers to use *READ*. 'This test results from the distillation of the experience of hundreds of Literacy Volunteer tutors who have been instructing adults and teens in basic reading for more than a decade.' If a volunteer is faced with a group of potential clients, he is advised to use a group screening test provided by LVA before carrying out the individual testing required by *READ*. The information provided by the *READ* test is linked to a handbook for tutors. It is claimed that the handbook entitled *Tutor* provides 'a complete programme for teaching the skills identified by *READ*'.

No data on the reliabilities or validities of the test are presented in the manual. Work has been done on the evaluation of the LVA programme and on the validity of the *READ* test, but this work is very limited in scope and detail in the LVA document before the reviewer.

Many teachers of reading will question the model of the reading process underpinning the *READ* test and its associated instructional programme. Three advantages of the instrument are that it can be used to make testing an integral part of teaching, allows behaviourally defined objectives to be set and progress towards them monitored. A cassette tape, text and guide for training tutors to administer and interpret *READ* was produced in 1982.

TRN	Name of test	Author	Country	Publisher	Year
159	*Reading Miscue Inventory (RMI)*	Y. Goodman and C. Burke	USA	Macmillan	1972

Type	No. of forms	C.A. range	Skills tested	Time
Individual, oral, diagnostic (level A)	1	5:06 +	Comprehension Grammatical relationships Sound/graphic relationships Retelling Miscues: Substitution Omission Insertion Reversal Repetition	Untimed (about 15′–20′)

Comments: The 'miscues' made when a person reads aloud from a text are not random. They are determined by what the reader expects to follow on the basis of his understanding, experience and use of meaning (semantics), grammar (syntax) and sound/graphic relationships. One part of the *RMI* requires the subject to retell the material he has read. Such prompts as are needed are provided by the tester. The testing session should be recorded on tape in order that the tester can check on the analysis. The difficulty of the text used has to be such that sufficient miscues are elicited to provide a basis for an analysis, a minimum of 25 is suggested, but should still allow the reader to continue with the task. The pattern of miscues provides insights into the strategies being used by the reader in dealing with the text orally. The extensive handbook gives strategy lessons linked to the findings from such analyses.

A revision is about to be published. It is to be less complex than the original *RMI* in the anticipation that the approach will then be more widely adopted. TRN 102 (p. 142) represents a British development along similar lines.

TRN	Name of test	Author	Country	Publisher		Year
164	*Roswell-Chall Diagnostic Reading Test of Word Analysis Skills*	F. G. Roswell and J. S. Chall	USA	Essay Press	First published	1956
						1959
					Revised and extended	1979

Type	No. of forms	C.A. range	Skills tested	Time
Individual, diagnostic, criterion-referenced (level A)	2 (Forms A & B)	6:00 to 10:00 (or older students with reading difficulties)	Word analysis skills: High frequency words Decoding skills: 1A Consonant sounds 1B Consonant digraphs 1C Consonant blends 2A Short vowel sounds (in CVC* words) 2B Short and long vowel sounds (in isolation) 2C Rule of silent 'e' 3A Vowel digraphs 3B Diphthongs and vowels controlled by 'r' 4 Syllabication (and compound words) Extended evaluation: W Naming capital letters X Naming lower case letters Y Encoding single consonants Z Encoding regular (CVC) words	Untimed (about 10′–15′)

Comments: The test is not intended only for a specific age range but for use with readers of any age whose reading is between the six-year-old and ten-year-old levels. It has been used with children in the early stages of learning to read and also with others who have been referred to reading clinics. The test covers phonic skills considered by many teachers as important underpinnings of fluent reading. Further strengths are that it comes in two parallel forms and takes a relatively short time to administer. Because the tests are graded in approximate order of difficulty, the entire battery need not be used with any one individual client. The test has been warmly reviewed by one well-known British authority (Bookbinder, 1980). A client's score is appraised against quantitative criteria for instructional needs. For each sub-test scores representing *mastery of the skill* (all or nearly all items correct), *need for review* (approximately 50% of items correct) and *systematic instruction indicated* (less than 50% of items correct) are specified.

* CVC = consonant-vowel-consonant words such as 'cat'.

There are extensive data supporting the original test. These include parallel form correlations of 0·98 and sub-test reliabilities ranging from 0·78 to 0·99. With seven- to eight-year-old pupils, concurrent validity coefficients of 0·91 and 0·92 with oral and silent reading respectively were obtained. With a reading clinic population having a more restricted range of skills, the test correlated 0·73 with oral reading, 0·64 with silent reading and 0·57 with spelling. Evidence for the reliabilities and validities of the revised test is included in a separate technical manual. It is based on a group of 203 students aged between six and ten years and a group of 46 with reading difficulties aged between approximately eight and ten years attending the reading clinics at two universities. Parallel form reliabilities ranged from 0·89 to 0·98 for the total test and subtotals. For the sub-tests, coefficients were predominantly in the range 0·84 to 0·94. The internal consistency coefficients of the sub-tests are also high. Test-retest reliabilities for the school and clinic groups were in the range 0·94 to 0·99. Concurrent validity is supported by high and significant correlations with the *Gray Oral Reading Test*, the *Metropolitan Readiness Test* and the *Metropolitan Achievement Tests*, the latter including sub-tests on Word Meaning, Word Analysis, Reading and Spelling. These are not the same for school and clinic goups.

The mean number and percentage correct on each sub-test for Forms A and B are given for each year group. Thus the normative and criterion-referenced aspects of measurement can be seen as complementary. The key issues are the validity of the cut-off criteria for instructional needs and the number of false negative and false positive identifications.

BOOKBINDER, G. (1980) 'Review of the Roswell-Chall Diagnostic Reading Test of Word Analysis Skills.' *Reading*, **14**, 1, 40.

TRN	Name of test	Author	Country	Publisher	Year
165	*St Lucia Graded Word Reading Test*	R. J. Andrews	A	Teaching and Testing Resources	1973
				9th impression	1980

Type	No. of forms	C.A. range	Skills tested	Time
ndividual, ttainment, ormative level A)	1	6:00 to 12:00	Word reading	Untimed (about 10′–15′)

Comments: The test contains 100 words arranged in ascending order of lifficulty. Its major purpose is to provide an accurate estimate of word eading ability for children in grades 2 to 7. The test can be used to assess rogress in this area also. It is suggested that the errors made by children when aking the test provide a 'preliminary diagnosis of pupil reading difficulties by evealing methods of word-attack employed and allowing an analysis of error atterns' (Manual, p. 5). Such a diagnosis would have to be extremely entative. The reviewer questions the utility of the instrument for this latter urpose.

Construction was undertaken in order to avoid some of the inadequacies of existing word reading tests and was based on earlier work into the use of word reading tests carried out by the author. Few details are given in the manual of how items were initially selected and pre-tested. Standardisation was based on a sample of 435 pupils chosen randomly from pupils attending grades 2 to 7 in twelve randomly selected primary schools in Brisbane, Australia. Using a group of 105 pupils in grades 4 and 5, the test-retest reliability was 0·947.

Raw scores are converted to Reading Ages, a system having considerable appeal to teachers. An examination of the words in the test does not show a preponderance of those having dominantly Australasian connotations.

TRN	Name of test	Author	Country	Publisher	Year
166	*St Lucia Reading Comprehension Test*	J. Elkins and R. J. Andrews	A	Teaching and Testing Resources	1974
				2nd impression	1982

Type	No. of forms	C.A. range	Skills tested		Time
Group, attainment, normative (level A)	2 (A & B)	6:00 to 9:00	Reading comprehension	Grade 2	20′
				Grade 3	15′
				Grade 4	12′

Comments: 'Cloze' procedure has been used in the construction of this test of reading comprehension. Forms A and B each consist of six passages and are designed for use with pupils in grades 2 to 4. The passages containing the deletions are arranged in increasing order of difficulty; the overall difficulties of forms A and B for each passage are approximately the same.

The test was standardised using 202, 393 and 250 pupils at each of the grade levels attending twelve Brisbane primary schools that had been selected as a stratified random sample. The internal consistency coefficients of reliability using Cronbach's coefficient alpha are reported for forms A and B at each grade level. The six coefficients range between 0·93 and 0·96. Parallel form reliability using a sample of 86 pupils was 0·86. Test-retest reliabilities using four small groups containing 21 and 30 pupils range between 0·70 and 0·8[illegible] The validity of the test was investigated by correlating the test results wit[illegible] other reading tests and carrying out a series of factor analytic and canonic[illegible] analyses using data from 144 pupils.

For each grade level, raw scores can be converted to standard scores on a 1[illegible] point scale having a mean of 8 and a standard deviation of 3 (a somewha[illegible] unusual scale). Percentiles and age norms can also be obtained. Unless loc[illegible] norms are built up, users of this test must recognise the problems of normativ[illegible] interpretation when an instrument has been constructed and standardised in [illegible] local area.

TRN	Name of test	Author	Country	Publisher	Year
177	*Standard Achievement Recording System (STARS)*	J. M. Smith, D. E. P. Smith and J. R. Brink	USA	Academic Press	1977

Type	No. of forms	C.A. range	Skills tested	Time
Group, individual, criterion-referenced, attainment, diagnostic	1	5:00 to 13:00	See below	Untimed

Skills tested

(A) *Letter skills*:
- L1 Shapes (8)*
- L2 Manuscript form (14)
- L3 Cursive form (11)
- L4 Names (8)
- L5 Letter-sound equivalents (12)
- L6 Functions – alphabet (6)

(B) *Word skills*:
- W1 Shapes (5)
- W2 Phonology (18)
- W3 Word recognition (11)
- W4 Spelling (5)
- W5 Vocabulary (syntactic) (13)
- W6 Vocabulary (range) (20)
- W7 Vocabulary (semantic) (9)
- W8 Vocabulary (classification) (12)
- W9 Vocabulary (fluency) (7)

(C) *Sentence skills*:
- S1 Oral reading (3)
- S2 Spaces between words (1)
- S3 Sentence memory (2)
- S4 Dictation (6)
- S5 Capitalisation (10)
- S6 Punctuation (21)
- S7 Transformations (17)
- S8 Directions (2)
- S9 Questions (6)
- S10 Sentence meaning (3)
- S11 Figurative language (4)

(D) *Paragraph skills*:
- P1 Form convention (2)
- P2 Grammatical patterns (4)
- P3 Phonological patterns (5)
- P4 Universe of discourse (2)
- P5 Topic (4)
- P6 Plot (8)
- P7 Referential links (2)
- P8 Relational links (6)
- P9 Information (9)
- P10 Summarisation (5)
- P11 Induction (6)
- P12 Deduction (3)
- P13 Focus (5)
- P14 Points of view (4)
- P15 Mood (3)
- P16 Oral reading (4)

*The figure in brackets indicates the number of tests at each level

Standard Achievement Recording System continued

Skills tested

(E) *Book skills*:
- B1 Fiction (7)
- B2 Nonfiction (5)
- B3 Textbooks (7)
- B4 Reference works (9)
- B5 Periodicals (3)
- B6 Letters (6)

(level A)

Comments: *STARS* is designed as a complete testing system for pupils aged from 5:00 to 13:00 years. It is based on a hierarchical model of language development formulated by Pike and Pike (1973). *STARS* provides a system of criterion-referenced measures that can be used to monitor the progress of individuals and groups, to identify strengths and weaknesses and to help in the development of instructional material throughout the primary and early secondary school reading programmes. It consists of 48 series of tests. Each series contains between one and twenty-one sub-tests. Overall, in the domains of letters, words, sentences, paragraphs and discourses, some 350 sub-tests are described.

The validity of the tests is assessed against three criteria: task analytic, psychometric and systemic or functional properties (Smith *et al.*, 1977, p. 5). The first of these relates to the degree to which the items represent an acceptable specification of the tasks involved in each sub-test. Thirty-six pages are devoted to this aspect of validity. Psychometric validity includes internal consistency reliability coefficients for the eighteen phonology tests. These range from 0·88 to 0·38 with thirteen exceeding 0·50, based on a sample of 132 students in First Grade. Correlations between *STARS* scores and other attainment tests are reported for very small samples of pupils. The authors present tables showing the proportions of pupils obtaining 100% Mastery Scores for groups of different ages representing the general school population and for certain 'special projects'. The third aspect of validity is related to the practical impact of the introduction of *STARS* into schools and its backwash effect on the teaching and testing of the reading programme. Critics of the task analysis approach embodied in *STARS* will claim that reading is far more than the sum of its parts. They will also question the validity of teaching the tasks operationally defined in the system. Supporters will see a means of being explicit about their instructional objectives and of being demonstrably accountable. The system exemplifies the 'bottom-up' approach to the teaching of reading. As such, it is controversial.

PIKE, K. L. and PIKE, E. (1973) *Grammatical Analysis*. Santa Ana, CA: Summer Institute of Linguistics.

SMITH, J. M., SMITH, D. E. P. and BRINK, J. R. (1977) *Criterion-referenced Tests for Reading and Writing*. New York: Academic Press.

TRN	Name of test	Author	Country	Publisher		Year
179	*Stanford Diagnostic Reading Test (SDRT)*	B. Karlsen, R. Madden and E. F. Gardner	USA	Harcourt Brace Jovanovich	3rd edition	1984

Type	No. of forms	C.A. range		Skills tested	No. of items	Time
Group, individual, diagnostic, criterion-referenced, normative	2 (A & B)	7:06 to 9:06	Red level 1	Decoding:		
				Auditory discrimination	30	15′
				Consonants	15	
				Single consonants	5	
				Consonant clusters	5	
				Consonant digraphs	5	
				Vowels	15	
				Short vowels	5	
				Long vowels	5	
				Other vowels	5	
				Phonetic analysis	40	20′
				Consonants	24	
				Single consonants	8	
				Consonant clusters	8	
				Consonant digraphs	8	
				Vowels	16	
				Short vowels	8	
				Long vowels	8	
			2	Vocabulary:		
				Auditory vocabulary	36	20′
				Reading and literature	14	
				Maths and science	10	
				Social studies and the Arts	12	
			3	Comprehension:		
				Word reading	30	15′
				Reading comprehension	48	35′
				Sentence reading	28	
				Kernel sentences	12	
				Sentence transforms	12	

Stanford Diagnostic Reading Test continued

C.A. range		Skills tested	No. of items	Time
		Riddles	4	
		Paragraph comprehension	20	
9:00 to 11:06	Green Level 1	Decoding:		
		Auditory discrimination	30	20′
		Consonants	15	
		Single consonants	5	
		Consonant clusters	5	
		Consonant digraphs	5	
		Vowels	15	
		Short vowels	5	
		Long vowels	5	
		Other vowels	5	
		Phonetic analysis	30	20′
		Consonants	15	
		Single consonants	5	
		Consonant clusters	5	
		Consonant digraphs	5	
		Vowels	15	
		Short vowels	5	
		Long vowels	5	
		Other vowels	5	
		Structural analysis	48	24′
		Word division	24	
		Compound words	6	
		Affixes	9	
		Syllables	9	
		Blending	24	
		Compound words	6	
		Affixes	9	
		Syllables	9	
	2	Vocabulary:		
		Auditory vocabulary	40	20′
		Reading and Literature	18	

Stanford Diagnostic Reading Test continued

C.A. range		**Skills tested**	**No. of items**	**Time**
		Maths and Science	12	
		Social Studies and the Arts	10	
		3 Comprehension:		
		Reading comprehension	48	30′
		Literal comprehension	24	
		Inferential comprehension	24	
11:00 to 15:06	Brown Level	1 Decoding:		
		Phonetic analysis	30	15′
		Consonants	15	
		Single consonants	5	
		Consonant clusters	5	
		Consonant digraphs	5	
		Vowels	15	
		Short vowels	5	
		Long vowels	5	
		Other vowels	5	
		Structural analysis	78	30′
		Word division	48	
		Compound words	6	
		Affixes	18	
		Syllables	24	
		Blending	30	
		Affixes	10	
		Syllables	20	
		Vocabulary:		
		Auditory vocabulary	40	20′
		Reading and Literature	16	
		Maths and Science	12	
		Social Studies and the Arts	12	
		3 Comprehension:		
		Reading comprehension	60	40′
		Literal	30	
		Inferential	30	

Stanford Diagnostic Reading Test continued

C.A. range		Skills tested	No. of items	Time
		and		
		Textual	20	
		Functional	20	
		Recreational	20	
		4 Rate:		
		Reading rate	33	3′
14:06 to 19:00	Blue Level	1 Decoding:		
		Phonetic analysis	30	12′
		Consonants	15	
		Single consonants	10	
		Consonant digraphs	5	
		Vowels	15	
		Short vowels	5	
		Long vowels	5	
		Other vowels	5	
		Structural analysis	30	12′
		Affixes	15	
		Syllables	15	
		2 Vocabulary:		
		Vocabulary	30	15′
		Reading and Literature	10	
		Maths and Science	10	
		Social Studies and the Arts	10	
		Word parts	30	15′
		Affixes	15	
		Roots	15	
		Vocabulary total	60	30′
		3 Comprehension:		
		Reading comprehension	60	40′
		Literal	30	
		Inferential	30	
		and		
		Textual	20	

Stanford Diagnostic Reading Test continued

(level A)

Skills tested	No. of items	Time
Functional	20	
Recreational	20	
4 Rate:		
Scanning and skimming	32	19′
Scanning	16	
Skimming	16	
Fast Reading	30	3′
Rate total	62	22′

Comments: *SDRT* was devised for use by classroom teachers and the interpretation of the test results is related to classroom reading instruction. The test is also of value in clinical settings. Its purpose is to diagnose pupils' strengths and weaknesses in reading and reading related abilities. In particular, it is focused on pupils experiencing reading difficulties. In most of the sub-tests, the scores that are above average bunch together whereas below average scores are well spread out, thereby increasing the utility of the information obtained when assessing the abilities of children who are low achievers. It follows that pupils with problems in reading will find the *SDRT* less threatening than many other reading tests. The *SDRT* is based on a developmental model of reading involving decoding skills, vocabulary, comprehension and rate. As reading attainments develop, the relative importance of these components changes. These changes are reflected in the content and form of the sub-tests included at each of the four levels of the *SDRT*. Since the publication of the second edition of the test in 1976, theorists have increasingly criticised such hierarchical models. Despite this, it is claimed by the publishers that the *SDRT* is the most popular diagnostic reading test in the USA.

The third edition of the *SDRT* was standardised in both the autumn of 1983 and the spring of 1984. A full range of normative scores is available for each sub-test and also for Total Reading on the battery. The availability of both autumn and spring data is of particular value in measuring reading development over the period concerned. Evidence of reliabilities is generally satisfactory. The intercorrelations and reliabilities of the sub-tests, essential to profile interpretation, are clearly presented. The validity of the battery is based largely on the instructional objectives identified after an extensive analysis of curriculum guides and reading series. It is in schools using such materials that the test will be particularly appropriate. In constructing the battery, care was taken to avoid sex stereotyping in its content.

Raw scores can be converted into both local and national stanines and percentile ranks. Grade equivalents, scaled scores and normal curve equivalents can also be obtained. The students' tests can be scored either manually or by machine. Results can be summarised in a variety of ways including a very helpful Individual Diagnostic Report form. The manual for interpreting and using test results is comprehensive and well-organised. Practical advice is given on the development of educational strategies designed to enhance attainments in particular areas in the handbook of instructional techniques and materials. Additionally, there is a range of software providing drills, practices and exercises for remediating specific reading skills and for testing the efficacy of the instruction.

SDRT provides the teacher with a variety of criterion-referenced information. The Individual Diagnostic Report (IDR) specifies the skills assessed by the test, the number of items correctly responded to by the pupil out of the number possible and a Progress Indicator Cutoff Score (PI) for each of the skills tested. Pupils scoring below specified score levels are deemed not to have sufficient competence and suggestions for developing individual programmes to improve a pupil's performance are provided. The justification of the cut-off points is questionable and it is suggested that users of the *SDRT* treat them with due caution. The IDR also provides the full range of normative information specified in paragraph 3 above.

There is little doubt that the *SDRT* is one of the best constructed diagnostic reading tests currently available, provided that the assumptions concerning the nature of reading abilities and their development on which it is based are valid. Many teachers consider that this is the case.

In the autumn of 1985 a microcomputer software package will be available. It will assist in the analysis of the *SDRT* results. It is thought that this will enable teachers to use the battery more effectively in their reading programme in each classroom.

TRN	Name of test	Author	Country	Publisher	Year
83	*Test of Adolescent Language (TOAL)*	D. D. Hammill, V. L. Brown, S. C. Larsen, and J. L. Wiederholt	USA	Pro-Ed	1980 4th impression 1982

Type	No. of forms	C.A. range	Skills tested	Time
Group,* Individual,† Attainment, Normative, Diagnostic (Level A)	1	11:00 to 18:05	*Sub-tests*:	Untimed
			* 1 Listening/Vocabulary	(about 15′–25′)
			* 2 Listening/Grammar	(about 10′–30′)
			† 3 Speaking/Vocabulary	(about 5′–15′)
			† 4 Speaking/Grammar	(about 5′–20′)
			* 5 Reading/Vocabulary	(about 10′–25′)
			* 6 Reading/Grammar	(about 10′–25′)
			* 7 Writing/Vocabulary	(about 10′–25′)
			* 8 Writing/Grammar	(about 15′–35′)

Composite variables:

(1) Listening (sub-tests 1, 2)
(2) Speaking (sub-tests 3, 4)
(3) Reading (sub-tests 5, 6)
(4) Writing (sub-tests 7, 8)
(5) Spoken Language (sub-tests 1, 2, 3, 4)
(6) Written Language (sub-tests 5, 6, 7, 8)
(7) Vocabulary (sub-tests 1, 3, 5, 7)
(8) Grammar (sub-tests 2, 4, 6, 8)
(9) Receptive Language (sub-tests 1, 2, 5, 6)
(10) Expressive Language (sub-tests 3, 4, 7, 8)

Comments: *TOAL* was designed to identify students falling significantly behind their peers in language development, to appraise the pattern and extent of language strengths and weaknesses of individuals, to monitor progress consequent on instruction and for research into adolescent language development. The test is based on a three dimensional model of language. The dimensions are Form (Spoken; Written), Features (Semantic [Vocabulary]; Syntactic [Grammar]) and System (Expressive; Receptive). Sub-tests were developed from field trials of various formats testing the eight aspects of the model. By combining the results from sub-tests, ten composite variables shown above can be estimated. The sum of all sub-test scores provides an Adolescent Language Quotient (ALQ).

Standardisation was based on a sample of 2 723 students attending schools in seventeen States of the USA and in three Canadian Provinces. From evidence concerning sex distributions and residence characteristics, the obtained norms are assumed to be 'based on a representative collection of American youngsters' (Manual, p. 15). Some readers might require further evidence on this point. Internal consistency reliability coefficients for all eight sub-tests, ALQ and ten composites are presented for each grade level from 6 to 12, together with the standard errors of measurement. 70 % of the sub-test coefficient Alphas exceeded 0·80 and 99 % of the composite scores did so. Inter-scorer reliability is reported because three sub-tests involve subjective judgments. The data reported show median percentage agreements of 95 %, 97 % and 97 %. Test-retest coefficients of reliability based on one sample of 52 students ranged from 0·74 to 0·90 for the sub-tests and from 0·85 to 0·98 for the composite scores. Concurrent validity of the nineteen *TOAL* indices is supported by significant correlations with five criterion tests based on a small sample of 32 students. Age differentiation by the test is presented as evidence of validity. This appears somewhat circular as age differentiation was built in at an early stage.

Raw scores were converted to scaled scores with a mean of 10 and a standard deviation of 3 points for each sub-test for groups of six months of chronological age and the results compared. Only six normative tables were required. These cover chronological ages 11 : 00 to 12 : 11, 13 : 00 to 13 : 11, 14 : 00 to 14 : 05, 14 : 06 to 15 : 05, 15 : 06 to 16 : 05 and 16 : 06 to 18 : 05. The pattern is unusual to say the least. A profile of *TOAL* sub-test scaled scores can be drawn up, as can one of the composite scores. Specific sub-test remediation is *not* advocated (Manual, p. 46). After scores have been recorded for normative evaluation, discussion of these with the student is advocated. Then, if required, follows the 'challenging clinical task' of uncovering 'the factors that are involved in arriving at *whatever* score(s) an individual student makes' (Manual, p. 46). Advice is given on how such exploration could be carried out based on the notion of testing the limits of the student's performance by varying conditions and by probing questions. The limitations of the initial normative test data are stated.

In one sense the test moves from performance to process. Whether *TOAL* is a 'highly reliable, multidimensional, nationally standardized and experimentally validated assessment instrument' (Manual, p. 5) of utility to the teacher is, as yet, still open if evidence of information of improved instructional decision making and a consequent alleviation of language difficulties is required. Further work in this field is necessary as the authors acknowledge.

TRN	Name of test	Author	Country	Publisher		Year
86	*Test of Language Development (TOLD) Primary*	P. L. Newcomer and D. D. Hammill	USA	Empiric Press		1977
					2nd impression	1982

Type	No. of forms	C.A. range	Skills tested		Time
Individual, diagnostic	1	4:00 to 8:11	Picture vocabulary Oral vocabulary Grammatic understanding Sentence imitation Grammatic completion	Principal sub-tests	Untimed (about 40′)
			Word discrimination Word articulation	Supplemental sub-tests	
(Level A)					

Comments: Some people enjoy living dangerously! After their attacks on the *Illinois Test of Psycholinguistic Abilities* (TRN 88) (Newcomer and Hammill, 1976), the authors have devised a test that employs the idea of 'process'. *TOLD* is based on a two-dimensional model of language structure. One (linguistic) includes the constructs of semantics, syntax and phonology; the other, designated a 'Process dimension', incorporates the receptive and expressive aspects of language.

It is claimed that *TOLD* will identify children with significant problems in either understanding or using oral language. It will also enable the specific strengths and weaknesses to be isolated and serve as a basis for criterion-referenced testing and teaching. *TOLD* was standardised on an unselected (for convenience?) sample of 1 014 children in fifteen States of the USA. It is claimed that the sample was characteristic of the national population.

TOLD raw scores can be converted to language ages, scaled scores and a linguistic quotient. The latter is obtained by summing the scaled scores obtained on the five principal sub-tests. Sub-test scaled scores have a mean of 10 and a standard deviation of 3. Separate tables for each six months of chronological age are provided for converting raw scores to standard scores in each sub-test. The *TOLD* sub-tests do *not* provide direct information for remedial instruction, but identify an area of difficulty called by the authors 'primary linguistic deficits'.

A separate booklet gives technical details of the construction and statistical characteristics of *TOLD* (Hammill and Newcomer, 1977) Internal consistency coefficients of the sub-tests are shown to be sufficiently high (0·80 or above) in the vast majority of the 72 presented to warrant use with individual children. Test-retest reliability estimated from a sample of only twenty-one children gives coefficients for all sub-tests exceeding 0·80. Evidence for content, concurrent and construct validity of the test is presented. The substantial intercorrelations between the sub-tests is seen as supporting their theoretical stance concerning the integrated nature of language development. Factor analyses based on the test results of 114 'Normals' are claimed to support the construct validity of *TOLD* though this could be a matter of controversy. *TOLD* discriminated between children with language problems and normal speakers. It is therefore claimed that the administration of *TOLD* to a child with a previously unidentified language handicap would lead to a valid assessment of his disability. Less consistent but linguistically coherent results were obtained using a group of children suffering from articulation problems. However, the small sizes of the groups involved suggest caution. Indeed, the authors claim that the diagnostic validity of *TOLD* is substantiated by these studies but rightly ask that replications with larger groups be carried out before any firm conclusions are drawn.

A version of the test designed for pupils aged 8 : 06 to 12 : 11, *TOL Intermediate*, was published in 1982.

NEWCOMER, P. L. and HAMMILL, D. D. (1976) *Psycholinguistics in the School* Columbus, OH: Charles E. Merrill.

HAMMILL, D. D. and NEWCOMER, P. L. (1977) *Construction and statistic characteristics of the Test of Language Development*. Austin, TX: Empiri Press.

RN	Name of test	Author	Country	Publisher	Year
37	*Test of Reading Comprehension (TORC)*	V. L. Brown, D. D. Hammill and J. L. Wiederholt	USA	Pro-Ed	1978

ype	No. of forms	C.A. range	Skills tested	Time
ndividual, nall group, ttainment	1	6:06 to 17:11	*General comprehension core*:	Untimed
			General vocabulary	(10′ to 20′)
			Syntactic similarities	(10′ to 25′)
			Paragraph reading	(15′ to 30′)
			Sentence sequencing	(15′ to 30′)
			Diagnostic supplements:	
			Mathematics vocabulary	(10′ to 15′)
			Social studies vocabulary	(10′ to 15′)
			Science vocabulary	(10′ to 20′)
evel A)			Reading the Directions for schoolwork instruction	(15′ to 30′)

omments: Viewing reading comprehension as a constructive cognitive rocess, the authors have attempted to devise a battery of tests assessing the upil's ability to establish meanings between words, sentences and notions ontained in more continuous prose. Certain of the sub-tests represent an novative attempt at devising tasks based upon linguistic theory. Opinions ill differ on the extent to which they have been successful. The authors freely ccept that the sub-tests of *TORC* are but a fraction, albeit a representative ne, of the behaviours comprising reading comprehension.

The theoretical basis, sub-test and item generation are described in the anual. The initial version of *TORC* was tried out on 120 pupils from one chool in Austin, Texas. This formed the basis for item analysis and sub-test evision. The test was standardised on an unselected sample of 2 707 pupils esiding in ten different States of the USA. Such standardisation poses roblems in interpreting local norms unless the latter are built up in-ependently. The issue is discussed briefly. Internal consistency coefficients re quite high for the sub-tests. In grades 1 to 12, 62 (79%) of the 78 oefficients presented were equal to or exceeded 0·80. In grades 2 to 12, for whom the test is primarily recommended, 60 (95%) of the 63 coefficients presented round up to 0·90. Test-retest reliability on a small sample (N = 59) ranged between 0·91 and 0·65 on the respective sub-tests. Evidence of the test's criterion-validity, construct validity and age differentiation is presented. Intercorrelations between sub-tests indicate substantial relationships. This is interpreted as supporting the test's construct validity because of the holistic nature of reading comprehension.

From this point it follows that specific sub-test remediation is not generally recommended although guidelines to diagnostic questions and instructional strategies are provided. At times this contains very specific advice such as using a particular instructional programme to increase competence in Reading the Directions for schoolwork instruction. It is suggested that the normative profile of scores on the sub-tests can usefully be related to a test of general conceptual/language ability (intelligence), usually abbreviated to 'intelligence' in the UK. The suggestion is controversial. The relatively small number of items used to cover the wide age range for which the test is intended will be seen as a weakness by some critics.

TRN	Name of test	Author	Country	Publisher	Year
197	*Woodcock Reading Mastery Tests*	R. W. Woodcock	USA	American Guidance Service, Inc. (NFER-Nelson and Educational Evaluation Enterprises act as agents)	1973 1983*

Type	No. of forms	C.A. range	Skills tested	Time
Individual, diagnostic (level A)	2 (A & B)	5:00 to 18:00	1 Letter identification 2 Word identification 3 Word attack 4 Word comprehension 5 Passage comprehension 6 Total reading power (combination of 1-5)	30′–45′

Comments: These five tests provide continuous scales of measurement from kindergarten to the eighteen-year-old level. Thus the tests are geared to a hierarchy of attainments which can be considered as a criterion-referenced scale of reading abilities. The initial interpretation of the results is on the instructional implications for the child, rather than to compare him with his peers. For teachers wishing to consider inter-individual differences, raw scores can also be converted to traditional normative scores. The use of the test as a diagnostic instrument is based on the interpretation of the child's performance profile on the five tests and through the use of a criterion-referenced scale. The interpretation of a pupil's mastery score in any area of the test can readily be related to Informal Reading Inventory standards. This is a consequence of a novel method of item analysis that has been used.

The test has been under development since 1966, and is based on an extensive programme of research. The normative data are based on 3000 subjects specially selected to represent grades K to 12 (five to eighteen-year olds) throughout the USA. The test appears acceptably reliable.

This test is an interesting development, though whether a criterion-referenced test and a normative one, *of value to the reading teacher*, can be based on the same material raises many complex technical issues of test construction and validation. The manual is most impressive, combining clarity and brevity. The British Intelligence Scale Unit under the direction of Dr C. D. Elliott of the University of Manchester has developed a number of ability scales, including one of reading, based on techniques used by Woodcock.

* In 1983 a microcomputer programme for 'instantaneous score conversions, record storage and retrieval of the Woodcock scores' was available for use on the Apple II Plus microcomputer with 48K memory.

4 Attitude to reading scales

(a) British

TRN	Name of test	Author	Country	Publisher	Year
14	*Attitude Scales (Primary Survey)*	T. P. Gorman, J. White, L. Orchard and A. Tate	B	Department of Education and Science Assessment of Performance Unit	1982

Type	No. of forms	C.A. range	Skills tested	Time
Group, attitudes (level A)	1	10:09 to 11:08* *(spread of C.A. of pupils when data collected)	*Attitudes towards aspects of reading*: 1 Pleasure in independent, extended reading (8 items) 2 Preference for reading as a leisure activity (6 items) 3 Preference for factual reading (7 items) 4 Reluctance towards extended reading (10 items) 5 Preference for reading aloud rather than to self (7 items) 6 Dislike of reading aloud (7 items) 7 Reading for self improvement (7 items)	Untimed (about 30′)

Comments: The Assessment of Performance Unit (APU) is involved in the national monitoring of children's skills and attitudes that contribute towards literacy. The above battery of seven scales towards different aspects of reading behaviour was developed by the APU. Building on earlier work in May 1979 with 1 172 eleven year old pupils in 196 schools and in November with a further 1 000 pupils, the responses of a different stratified random sample of 1 124 pupils were obtained to a pool of items designed to reflect the scales as hypothesised. The results were factor analysed and the above scales identified. The pattern of scales revealed was practically the same as on the previous occasion. All of the scales contain relatively few items. Each item is a positive statement to which the pupil responds on a five point scale ranging from 0 to 4. The pupil's scores on the items are summed to give a score for the particular scale. Sex differences were found on scales 1, 2 and 3.

The construct validity of the scales rests largely on the factor analyses carried out. Each scale correlates significantly and in the predicted direction with reading attainment. The internal consistency, as measured by Cronbach's coefficient alpha, of each of the scales is reported as (1) 0·83, (2) 0·73, (3) 0·42, (4) 0·66, 5) 0·79, (6) 0·73 and (7) 0·76 respectively. No evidence of test-retest reliability is given. There are a number of technical points concerning the construction of the scales that are not clear in the source given below. These include the factor analytic method used and the intercorrelations between pupils' scores on the factors. Such considerations do affect interpretation of the results obtained using the scales.

The scales have at least two major weaknesses. The first is their relative shortness with its associated tendency to unreliability. The second concerns the visibility of what is being assessed coupled with the social desirability of responses in given directions. In such scales the tendency to 'fake good' can operate.

DEPARTMENT OF EDUCATION AND SCIENCE ASSESSMENT OF PERFORMANCE UNIT (1982) *Language Performance in Schools: Primary Survey Report No. 2*. London: HMSO.

TRN	Name of test	Author	Country	Publisher	Year
5	*Attitude Scales (Secondary Survey)*	T. P. Gorman, J. White, L. Orchard and A. Tate.	B	Department of Education and Science Assessment of Performance Unit	1983

Type	No. of forms	C.A. range	Skills tested	Time
Group, Attitudes (level A)	1	15:00 to 16:00	*Attitudes towards aspects of reading*: 1 Pleasure in independent, extended reading (14 items) 2 Reluctance towards extended reading (14 items) 3 Reading for self-improvement (8 items) 4 Preference for factual reading (10 items) 5 Attitude towards reading aloud (8 items) 6 Attitude to school activities associated with reading (8 items)	Untimed (about 25′)

Comments: After pilot work using a stratified random sample of 1 062 fifteen-year-old pupils attending 303 schools in November 1979, plus work with a further 1 000 pupils in January 1980, a further stratified random sample of 1 091 fifteen-year-old pupils attending 282 schools completed an attitude questionnaire. Factor analyses of these data were used in identifying the six scales listed above. Each scale consists of positive statements to which students respond using a five point scale. Scores on items can be summed to give a total score on a scale. Sex differences were found in scales 1, 2, 3, 4 and 5.

The construct validity of the scales rests largely on the factor analytic procedures whereby the scales were identified. Correlations between four of the scales and reading attainment were significant ($p < 0{\cdot}05$). Using Cronbach's coefficient alpha as a measure of internal consistency, values for each of the scales are (1) 0·91, (2) 0·87, (3) 0·77, (4) 0·79, (5) 0·83 and (6) 0·84. No evidence of test-retest reliability is presented. Although the scales are described in the publication listed below, many technical points concerning the construction of the scales are not included, for example the factor analytic method used and the intercorrelations between pupils' scores on the factors. These do affect the interpretation of the results obtained when using the scales.

As with the *Primary Survey Scales* (TRN 14), major weaknesses with these scales is the visibility of what is being assessed coupled with the social desirability of responses in certain directions. The tendency for students to 'fake good' can occur.

DEPARTMENT OF EDUCATION AND SCIENCE ASSESSMENT OF PERFORMANCE UNIT (1983) *Language Performance in Schools: Secondary Survey Report No. 2.* London: HMSO.

TRN	Name of test	Author	Country	Publisher	Year
16	*Attitudes to Reading Test 1 (situational) (ATR 1)*	J. M. Ewing and M. Johnstone	B	Dundee College of Education*	1981

Type	No. of forms	C.A. range	Skills tested	Time
Group, attitude, Likert scales (level A)	3 (1 for each of three situations)	8:00 to 16:00	*Attitude to reading* (situational): A Affective (How much do I *like* this kind of reading?) B Instrumental (How *useful* is this reading to me?) C Evaluative (How *important* is this for me at school?)	Untimed (about 8′†) (about 8′†) (about 8′†)

(†Primary pupils take longer)

Comments: With the support of the Scottish Education Department, the development of attitude to reading measures suitable for use with pupils attending both primary and secondary schools was undertaken. After extensive pilot studies, it was decided to use Likert scaling based on five point responses to items. Twenty reading situations were identified. These formed the items. Three forms of the same twenty items were prepared varying in (a) item sequence and (b) aspect of reading to be rated. The three aspects were as defined above. *ATR 1* was tried out on 5911 pupils attending a representative sample of nineteen primary and five secondary schools in the Tayside region. About 16% of the primary sample and 10% of the secondary sample returned incomplete or unclear responses. (This must have been a blow to the researchers!) The split-half reliabilities of the three *ATR 1* scales A, B and C, were 0·74, 0·79 and 0·85 at the primary school level and 0·80, 0·84 and 0·87 at the secondary school level. The validities of the scales were assessed using criterion group comparisons and factor analyses. As a consequence of the latter, the Evaluative scale has been dropped (personal communication). The manual lists in an appendix the ordinal rankings of the twenty items in each o[f] the three situations A, B and C. The lists make fascinating reading[.] Comparisons between and within groups in a school or a class could b[e] illuminating.

This scale was constructed simultaneously with *ATR 2 (global)* (TRN 17)[.] The relationships between pupils' scores on the two measures are discussed[.] Important primary-secondary school differences are noted. The problem[s] involved in trying to produce scales suitable for both primary and secondar[y] school pupils with the crucial differences in maturity and curricular demand[s] involved, is well documented. The account of the research contained in th[e] manual contains important lessons for anyone pursuing this field of study[.]

* EWING, J. M. and JOHNSTONE, M. (1981) *Attitudes to Reading: Measuremen[t] and Classification within a Curricular Structure*. Dundee: Dundee College o[f] Education.

RN	Name of test	Author	Country	Publisher	Year
7	*Attitudes to Reading Test 2 (global) (ATR 2)*	J. M. Ewing and M. Johnstone	B	Dundee College of Education*	1981

ype	No. of forms	C.A. range	Skills tested	Time
iroup, ttitude, ikert scale evel A)	1	8:00 to 16:00	Attitudes to reading (global)	Untimed (about 5′ – 10′†) (†Primary pupils take longer)

omments: The Scottish Education Department funded the research roject that led to the construction of *ATR 2 (global)* and also of *ATR 1 situational)*. After extensive pilot work, *ATR 2* was constructed with ighteen items characterising positive and negative attitudes towards reading. here are nine of each. Pupils respond using a five point scale on each item anging from 'definitely agree' to 'definitely disagree'. Ratings are summated o give scores indicating a range of attitudes towards reading. From a sample f 2 923 pupils at age levels P5, P7, S2 and S4, 2 593 usable replies were eceived. This represented a loss of over 7 % from the primary and 9 % from he secondary sample.

Split-half (internal consistency) reliability coefficients for the primary and econdary age groups were 0·80 and 0·88 respectively. On *ATR 2*, primary upils obtained higher mean scores than secondary school pupils and girls ad, on average, more positive attitudes than boys. The data were then factor nalysed. This failed to produce a global factor. Three different factors were identified. Factor 1 (nine items) is interpreted as characterising the non-involved reader. Factor 2 (five items) taps a 'pleasure or enthusiasm factor' and Factor 3 (three items) a 'utilitarian or learning factor'. This finding underlines the complexity of attitudes to reading, as also did the related work on *ATR 1*. The problems of unidimensionality are not readily overcome. Presumably work will continue with the refined scales, or at least with the nine items comprising Factor 1. The manual containing the description of how the scale was constructed will be of value to other workers in this field. Reading between the lines, it is possible to identify some culs-de-sac that future researchers should avoid. This work was a valuable and important initiative.

* EWING, J. M. and JOHNSTONE, M. (1981) *Attitudes to Reading: Measurement and Classification within a Curricular Structure*. Dundee: Dundee College of Education.

TRN	Name of test	Author	Country	Publisher	Year
56	*Dunham Attitude to Reading Scale*	J. Dunham	B	Unpublished dissertation*	1956

Type	No. of forms	C.A. range	Skills tested	Time
Group, attitude (Thurstone-Chave scale) (level A)	1	Juniors	Attitude to reading	Untimed (15′)

Comments: This is a twenty-item scale covering the entire range of children's attitudes towards reading. The children with whom it is used usually know what is being assessed and therefore might give incorrect responses to please the tester or teacher. The scale is acceptably reliable and valid according to Dunham (re-test reliability 0·77; correlation of scale with teachers' ratings 0·59).

Whether it is legitimate to consider 'attitude to reading' to be unidimensional trait is open to question.

* University of Birmingham, Department of Education, 'Attitude an Achievement in Reading'.

TRN	Name of test	Author	Country	Publisher	Year
74	*Georgiades' Attitude to Reading Scale*	N. Georgiades	B	Article by Georgiades in DOWNING, J. and BROWN, A. L. (1967), *The Second International Reading Symposium*, London: Cassell.	1967

Type	No. of forms	C.A. range	Skills tested	Time
Group, oral administration (Likert-type scale) (level A)	1	Primary school	Attitude to reading	Untimed (25′)

Comments: This attitude scale contains twenty-two items of which only seven are related to reading. Thus the children are unaware of the specific focus of the scale. This scale is enjoyed greatly by children because of the novelty of its presentation. Georgiades gives few details of standardisation o reliabilities. Despite this, the test technique has considerable potential fo development.

RN	Name of test	Author	Country	Publisher	Year
)6	*Williams' Reading Attitude Scale*	G. Williams	B	Unpublished dissertation*	1965

ype	No. of forms	C.A. range	Skills tested	Time
roup or individual, oral dministration Thurstone-Chave model) evel A)	1	8:06 to 9:06	Attitude to reading (25 items)	Untimed) (25′)

omments: This scale comprises twenty-five statements ranging from a ighly unfavourable to a highly favourable attitude towards reading. The ale was constructed on the basis of statements contributed by teachers of ading. It was tested for reliabilities and validities with groups of nine-year-ld children. The use of the scale involves considerable preparation and is best sed with small groups of children. Its major weakness is its 'visibility'—it is irly clear what the tester is getting at and this might cause some children to present the response they feel is required rather than their real attitudes to reading. It seems likely that the test could be used with other ages, but this requires further investigation.

* University of Manchester, Department of Education, dissertation for the Diploma in the Education of Handicapped Children: 'A study of reading attitude among nine-year-old children'.

(b) Others

TRN	Name of test	Author	Country	Publisher	Year
18	*Attitudes toward Teaching Reading in Content Classrooms*	J. L. Vaughan, Jr	USA	International Reading Association*	1977

Type	No. of forms	C.A. range	Skills tested	Time
Group, attitude, Likert scale (level A)	1	Teachers	Attitudes towards teaching reading in content classrooms (subject specialisms)	Untimed (about 10′–15

Comments: Developed at the University of Arizona, this scale measures the attitudes of teachers towards reading in 'content area classrooms'. Content area classrooms appear equivalent to the subject specialisms typically found in British secondary schools. The scale consists of fifteen statements, nine positive and six negative, each of which is responded to using a seven point scale. In the article accompanying the scale, evidence of a satisfactory internal consistency reliability is given. Cronbach's coefficient alpha = 0·87. The median coefficient of stability is quoted as 0·77 with a range of 0·66 to 0·89. The validity of the scale is attested to in that it discriminated effectively in the predicted direction between two groups known to have differing viewpoints both by total score and on each of the fifteen items. The scale also identified change in attitude in members of a graduate education course designed to familiarise specialists with the teaching of reading in content areas. T sample sizes and characteristics on which the scale was developed are n given in the article on which this comment is based. Such details can obtained.

Despite the unfamiliarity of the terminology, the scale is of interest. T teaching of reading in subject specialisms in schools in Britain is an importa professional concern. The attitudes of teachers towards this responsibility of great significance. Even if this scale is not entirely suitable as it stands, provides a basis on which one could be devised for British usage.

* VAUGHAN, J. L., JR (1977) 'A scale to measure attitudes towards teachin reading in content classrooms.' *Journal of Reading*, **20**, 7, 605–9.

TRN	Name of test	Author	Country	Publisher	Year
54	*Dulin-Chester Reading Attitude Scale, Form I*	K. L. Dulin and R. D. Chester	USA	International Reading Association*	1980

Type	No. of forms	C.A. range	Skills tested	Time
Group, forced-choice (level A)	1	Middle and secondary school pupils	Attitude towards reading	Untimed (about 15′)

Comments: This attitude scale contains twenty items. In each item the pupil chooses between either reading a book or some other individual and solitary indoor activity. The situations contained in the items are presented by written statements. The pupil is allowed to show equal preference. He is therefore scoring on a three point scale. Each time he opts for 'read a book' he gets two marks whereas an equal preference scores one mark. Thus theoretically scores can range from 40 to 0.

In a study involving over 800 pupils, correlations of 0·60 and higher are reported with a previously validated test, Estes' *Scale to measure Attitudes towards Reading* (TRN 168). This is seen as evidence of concurrent validity. Significant correlations with both teacher-judgment and self-judgment attitude-rating scales are reported. Internal consistency coefficients are reported as having reached 0·90. As yet, no test-retest reliability coefficients are available.

* MONSON, D. and McCLENATHAN, D. (eds) (1980) *Developing Active Readers: Ideas for Parents, Teachers and Librarians.* Newark: International Reading Association.

TRN	Name of test	Author	Country	Publisher	Year
55	*Dulin-Chester Reading Attitude Scale, Form II*	K. L. Dulin and R. D. Chester	USA	International Reading Association*	1980

Type	No. of forms	C.A. range	Skills tested	Time
Forced-choice rating scale (level A)	1	Middle and Secondary School Pupils	Attitude towards reading	Untimed (about 15′)

Comments: The scale consists of twenty items. Each item specifies two activities, one of which is reading a book. The student has to indicate his preference between these activities on a five point scale with 5 indicating a marked preference to 'read a book' rather than engage in the alternative indoor, solitary activity with which reading a book is paired. The five point, rather than the three point, scale is the significant difference between this scale and the *Dulin-Chester Reading Attitude Scale, Form I* (TRN 54).

It is reported that the scale has gone through a similar validation procedure as Form I. Thus Form II correlates with other validated attitude scales, with teacher-judgment and self-judgment attitude rating scale results. Internal consistency coefficients of over 0·90 have been reported in several studies. The technique looks interesting with possibilities for development despite the high level of 'visibility' in its present form.

* MONSON, D. and MCCLENATHAN, D. (eds) (1980) *Developing Active Readers: Ideas for Parents, Teachers and Librarians.* Newark, DE: International Reading Association.

TRN	Name of test	Author	Country	Publisher	Year
73	*Generalised Attitude Scales*	H. H. Remmers	USA	Best source is SHAW, M. E. and WRIGHT, J. M. (1967) *Scales for the Measurement of Attitudes*, New York: McGraw-Hill	1960

Type	No. of forms	C.A. range	Skills tested	Time
(All group or individual)				Untimed
Thurstone-type scale	2 (A & B)	18:00 +	Attitude towards any practice	(10′)
Thurstone-type scale	2 (A & B)	18:00 +	Attitude towards any occupation	(10′)
Thurstone-type scale	2 (A & B)	15:00 +	Attitude towards any school subject	(10′)
(level A)				

Comments: Generalised attitude scales have been shown to have acceptable reliabilities and validities, but they are still rather crude psychometric instruments. The above group are referred to because each can be adapted to a variety of aspects of reading as a skill, an occupation or a subject. The book by Shaw and Wright discusses the strengths and weaknesses of such scales.

TRN	Name of test	Author	Country	Publisher	Year
105	*Mikulecky Behavioral Reading Attitude Measure (MBRAM)*	L. J. Mikulecky	USA	Indiana University*	1979

Type	No. of forms	C.A. range	Skills tested	Time
Group, attitude (level A)	1	13:00 to Adult	Attitude to reading	Untimed (about 10′)

Comments: The *MBRAM* was developed to assess attitude towards reading of mature readers. An initial pool of forty items, based on a theoretical model of attitudes, was eventually reduced to twenty items. Each item is a statement to which students respond on a five point scale. Using a method for scaling a simplex developed by Kaiser, it was demonstrated that the theoretical framework was empirically supported (Mikulecky, 1976). Concurrent validity of the scale is supported by correlations with other attitude to reading scales ranging from 0·446 to 0·70. Correlations between five informal criteria of reading attitudes (teacher and classmate judgments of attitude to reading, self-reported liking and amount of reading, and the number of books read in six months) and scores on the *MBRAM* were all significant at the 0·001 level, with indices ranging between 0·500 and 0·791. The test-retest reliability of the scale is reported as 0·91.

Data on 1 750 subjects aged from 13:00 to Adult from urban, suburban and rural populations were obtained using *MBRAM*. A stratified random sample representative of the Wisconsin population model was obtained. Norms are reported 'for each grade level . . . and also in terms of urban, suburban and rural populations'. Mean scores of students on *MBRAM* decreased slightly in each successive age group. The most readily available source of normative information and of the *MBRAM* itself is a recent edition of a learned journal (Mikulecky *et al.*, 1979).

MIKULECKY, L. J. (1976) 'The developing, field testing, and initial norming of a secondary/adult level reading attitude measure that is behaviorally oriented and based on Krathwohl's Taxonomy of the Affective Domain.' Unpublished doctoral dissertation, University of Wisconsin-Madison.

* MIKULECKY, L. J., SHANKLIN, N. L. and CAVERLY, D. C. (1979) 'Adult reading habits, attitudes, and motivations: a cross-sectional study.' *Monograph in Language and Reading Studies*, No. 2.

TRN	Name of test	Author	Country	Publisher	Year
149	*Primary Pupil Reading Attitude Inventory (PPRAI)*	E. N. Askov	USA	Kendall Hunt	1973

Type	No. of forms	C.A. range	Skills tested	Time
Group, forced-choice (level A)	2 (one for boys, one for girls)	6:00 to 11:00	Attitude to reading	Untimed (about 15′)

Comments: The *PPRAI* is based on the notion that, given the choice of two activities, a child who prefers one involving books and reading is likely to have a more positive attitude towards reading than a child who opts for the alternative activity. The test consists of 30 pages. Each page displays two activities and the child has to indicate his preference. Twelve sets of picture-pairs are unscored distractors, neither of the activities pictured being visibly related to reading. This is a deliberate strategy to make what is being assessed less apparent to the child. Separate versions for boys and girls are provided. The majority of the activities are the same for both sexes, the exceptions being four non-reading activities. The highest possible score of 18 indicates an extremely positive attitude towards reading.

The reliability of the inventory, tested using a generalised item analysis programme, gives coefficients ranging from 0·77 for first grade girls to 0·87 for third grade boys. Askov has reported a test-retest reliability coefficient, obtained over a gap of one week, of 0·906 using a sample of 78 primary school pupils. The test was validated using the 'known groups' technique. *PPRAI* was administered to 94 second and third grade pupils drawn from three classes. The children's teachers were not present at the administration. Subsequently, each of the three teachers was asked to nominate the five pupils with the highest and the five with the lowest interest in leisure time reading. The former group was shown to have a significantly higher score on the inventory than the latter. It must be mentioned that the validity of the forced-choice technique can be seriously questioned and that the evidence of validity indicated does not rule out the possible differences in reading attainment and/or general mental ability between the contrasted groups. Despite such comments, the technique is an interesting one with considerable potential for further development.

TRN	Name of test	Author	Country	Publisher	Year
156	*Reading Attitude Scales*	W. H. Teale and R. Lewis	A	W. H. Teale, University of Texas at San Antonio	1980

Type	No. of forms	C.A. range	Skills tested	Time
Group, normative, diagnostic, Likert scale (level A)	1	14:00 to 18:00	Attitudes toward reading: I Individual development factor; II Utilitarian factor; III Enjoyment	Untimed (about 10′)

Comments: Extensive empirical studies based on the assumption that secondary school students' attitudes towards reading were multi-dimensional rather than unidimensional led to the construction and refinement of a three scale instrument. Thus the first scale measures the extent to which students value reading as a means of Individual Development, the second measures their valuing of reading as a means of achieving Utilitarian goals whilst the third measures Enjoyment.

There is, as yet, no manual to the scales known to the reviewer. Information concerning them is most readily obtained from articles in journals. The senior author has been particularly helpful in providing information in reply to letters sent to him by the present reviewer. The above scales are combined in one form taken by students. Scoring the separate scales can be easily done using a template.

The construct validity of the distinction between the scales has been supported by factor analyses of the scores from 14:00 and 18:00 year old pupils carried out in 1978 and 1979. The scales used at that time were shown to have an acceptable level of internal consistency. Using sixty-five and forty-three of the younger and older students, test-retest reliabilities over a two to four week period of 0·72 and 0·90 are reported. Validity is also supported in that students nominated by their peers as 'high' or 'low' on the scales differed in the anticipated directions in their respective mean scores (Lewis and Teale, 1980). Both authors are continuing their work in this field and have recently reported on the applicability of the model to primary school pupils (Lewis and Teale, 1982). It is encouraging to find a notion that makes considerable sense from the theoretical viewpoint being empirically substantiated.

LEWIS, R. and TEALE, W. H. (1980) 'Another look at secondary school students' attitudes toward reading.' *Journal of Reading Behavior*, **XII**, 3, 187–201.

LEWIS, R. and TEALE, W. H. (1982) 'Primary school students' attitudes towards reading.' *Journal of Research in Reading*, **5**, 2, 113–22.

TRN	Name of test	Author	Country	Publisher	Year
162	*Rhody Secondary Reading Attitude Assessment*	R. Tullock-Rhody and J. E. Alexander	USA	International Reading Association*	1980

Type	No. of forms	C.A. range	Skills tested	Time
Group, Likert scale (level A)	1	13:00 to 18:00	Attitude to reading	Untimed (about 15′)

Comments: There are twenty-five items in this Likert scale. Some are positive and some negative in relation to the value of reading and books. Agreement with the former and disagreement with the latter are deemed to indicate a favourable attitude towards reading. As each item is scored on a five point scale, scores can range from 125 (highly favourable attitude) to 0. The test appears to be acceptably reliable and valid. A detailed account can be found in the reference given below. Problems of students tending to 'fake good' when the items are very clearly measuring a socially valued attribute can present problems of interpretation. The scale was developed using students attending six urban and two rural schools in one state.

* TULLOCK-RHODY, R. and ALEXANDER, J. E. (1980) 'A scale for assessing attitudes towards reading in secondary schools.' *Journal of Reading*, **23**, 609–14.

TRN	Name of test	Author	Country	Publisher	Year
168	*Scale to measure Attitudes towards Reading*	T. H. Estes	USA	International Reading Association*	1971

Type	No. of forms	C.A. range	Skills tested	Time
Group, attitude, Likert scale (level A)	1	9:00 to 18:00	Attitude to reading	Untimed (about 10′–15′)

Comments: This is a twenty item Likert type attitude scale using a five point response to each item. It contains twelve negative items and eight positive ones. The scale was refined from an original twenty-eight items tested on 283 pupils aged from 9 : 00 to 18 : 00 years. Two classes were used at each age level. The classes were deliberately chosen for their heterogeneous composition in order to get a wide spread of attitudes. In the pilot work, a comparison of younger and older students showed the former to have a significantly higher mean score on the scale, i.e. more positive attitudes towards reading. The internal consistency of the pre-test scale is given as 0·92 for the younger (9 : 00 to 12 : 11) and 0·96 for the older (13 : 00 to 18 : 00) students. No information is given in the article on the reliabilities and validities of the refined twenty item scale. An important weakness is that it is quite clear what is being assessed. The tendency for conforming responses, possibly at variance with the individual's actual attitude, to be produced when acknowledged socially accepted attitudes are known to the respondent and seen to be under scrutiny, can lead to faking. Such problems can be overcome. It would be interesting to establish changes in students' attitudes to reading in both longitudinal and cross-sectional studies.

* ESTES, T. H. (1971) 'A scale to measure attitudes toward reading.' *Journal of Reading*, **15**, 135–8.

Some other sources of scales measuring attitudes towards reading

ALEXANDER, J. E. and FILLER, R. C. (1977) *Attitudes and Reading*. Newark, DE: International Reading Association.

DECK, D. and JACKSON, B. J. (1976) *Measuring attitudes towards Reading in Large Scale Assessment*. Pennsylvania: Pennsylvania State University, Centre for Cooperative Research with Schools.

ESTES, T. H., ROETTGER, D. M., JOHNSTONE, J. P. and RICHARDS, H. C. (1976) *Estes' Attitude Scales: Elementary Form*. Charlottesville, VA: Virginia Research Associates.

HEATHINGTON, B. S. and ALEXANDER, J. E. (1978) 'A child-based observation checklist to assess attitudes towards reading.' *Reading Teacher*, **31**, 769–71.

KENNEDY, L. D. and HALINSKI, R. S. (1975) 'Measuring attitudes: an extra dimension.' *Journal of Reading*, **18**, 7, 518–22.

PENNSYLVANIA STATE DEPARTMENT OF EDUCATION (1976) *Attitudes toward Reading Scale*. ERIC Document ED 117647.

ROETTGER, D., SZYMEZUK, M. and MILLARD, J. (1979) 'Validation of a reading attitude scale for elementary school students and an investigation into the relationship between attitude and attainment.' *Journal of Educational Research*, **72**, 138–42.

ROWELL, G. C. (1972) 'An attitude scale for reading.' *The Reading Teacher*, **25**, 442–7.

The complexity of attitudes to reading

Children's attitudes towards reading may be more complex than some of the preceding scales might suggest. The uses of Osgood's (Osgood *et al.* 1957) semantic differential and Kelly's (1955) repertory grid techniques in attitude measurement have met with some success. Certainly these techniques assume that attitudes are multi- rather than uni-dimensional. Both techniques have been used to measure children's attitudes towards reading in this country.

References

KELLY, G. A. (1955) *Psychology of Personal Constructs*. New York: Norton.

OSGOOD, C. E., SUCI, G. J. and TANNENBAUM, P. H. (1957) *The Measurement of Meaning*. Urbana, IL: University of Illinois Press.

Blank test summary sheets

TRN	Name of test	Author	Country	Publisher	Year

Type	No. of forms	C.A. range	Skills tested	Time

Comments:

TRN	Name of test	Author	Country	Publisher	Year

Type	No. of forms	C.A. range	Skills tested	Time

Comments:

TRN	Name of test	Author	Country	Publisher	Year

Type	No. of forms	C.A. range	Skills tested	Time

Comments:

TRN	Name of test	Author	Country	Publisher	Year

Type	No. of forms	C.A. range	Skills tested	Time

Comments:

TRN	Name of test	Author	Country	Publisher	Year

Type	No. of forms	C.A. range	Skills tested	Time

Comments:

TRN	Name of test	Author	Country	Publisher	Year

Type	No. of forms	C.A. range	Skills tested	Time

Comments:

Appendix 1

Publishers and distributors of reading tests and test information

British

Adult Literacy and Basic Skills Unit, 229-31 High Holborn, London, WC1V 7DA

Arnold-Wheaton, Parkside Lane, Leeds, LS11 5TD

Assessment of Performance Unit, Department of Education and Science, Elizabeth House, York Road, London, SE1 7PH

Allyn and Bacon (London) Ltd, 42 Colebrooke Row, London, N1 8AF

Barking and Dagenham Local Education Authority, Town Hall, Barking, Essex, IG11 7LU

Bell and Hyman Ltd, Denmark House, 37-9 Queen Elizabeth Street, London, SE1 2QB

Basil Blackwell, Publisher, Ltd, 108 Cowley Road, Oxford, OX4 1JF

Cambridge University Press, The Edinburgh Building, Shaftesbury Road, Cambridge, CB2 2RU

Cassell Educational, *see* Holt-Saunders Ltd

Centre for Information on Language Teaching and Research, 20 Carlton House Terrace, London, SW1Y 5AP

Centre for the Teaching of Reading, University of Reading School of Education, 29 Eastern Avenue, Reading, Berkshire, RG1 5RU

Chatto and Windus (Educational) Ltd, *see* William Collins Sons and Co. Ltd, Collins Educational

William Collins Sons and Co. Ltd, Collins Educational, 8 Grafton Street, London, W1X 3LE

Crosby Lockwood Staples Ltd, *see* William Collins Sons and Co. Ltd

Dundee College of Education, Gardyne Road, Broughty Ferry, Dundee, DD5 1NY, Scotland

Education Evaluation Enterprises, Awre, Newnsham, Gloucestershire, GL14 1ET

* Esquire Educational International, 42 Colebrooke Row, London, N1 8AF

Evans Brothers Ltd, *see* Bell and Hyman Ltd

Robert Gibson and Sons, Glasgow, Ltd, 17 Fitzroy Place, Glasgow, G3 7SF, Scotland

Ginn and Co. Ltd, Prebendal House, Parson's Fee, Aylesbury, Buckinghamshire, HP20 2QZ

Gwasg Gomer, Llandysul, Dyfed, SA44 4BQ

Godfrey Thomson Unit for Academic Assessment, University of Edinburgh, 24 Buccleuch Place, Edinburgh, EH8 9JT

* Harcourt Brace Jovanovich Ltd, 24-8, Oval Road, Camden Town, London, NW1 7DX

George G. Harrap and Co. Ltd, *see* NFER-Nelson Publishing Co. Ltd

Hart-Davis Educational Ltd, *see* William Collins Sons and Co. Ltd

Heinemann Educational Books Ltd, 22 Bedford Square, London, WC1B 3HH

Hodder and Stoughton Ltd, Tests Department, PO Box 702, Mill

* English branches of American companies

Road, Dunton Green, Sevenoaks, Kent, TN13 2YD

olt-Saunders Ltd, 1 St Anne's Road, Eastbourne, East Sussex, BN21 3UN

ıner London Education Authority, County Hall, London, SE1 7PB

ıterprint Graphic Services Ltd, Half Moon Street, Bagshot, Surrey

earning Development Aids, Aware House, Duke Street, Wisbech, Cambridge, PE 13 2AE

IcGraw-Hill Book Co. (UK) Ltd, McGraw-Hill House, Shoppenhangers Road, Maidenhead, Berkshire, SL6 2QL

Iacmillan Education Ltd, Houndmills Estate, Basingstoke, Hampshire, RG21 2XS

Ietropolitan Borough of Sandwell, Department of Education, Child Psychology Service, Child Guidance Centre, 12 Grange Road, West Bromwich, West Midlands, B70 8PD

FER-Nelson Publishing Co. Ltd, Darville House, 2 Oxford Road East, Windsor, Berkshire, SL4 1DF

Iational Hospitals College of Speech Science, Test Library, 84a Heath Street, Hampstead, London, NW3 1DN

orthern Ireland Council for Educational Research, The Queen's University of Belfast, 52 Malone Road, Belfast, BT9 5BS, Northern Ireland

liver and Boyd, Robert Stevenson House, 1-3 Baxter's Place, Leith Walk, Edinburgh, EH1 3BB (inspection copies from Longman Group Ltd, Pinnacles, Harlow, Essex, CM19 5AA)

xford University Press, Walton Street, Oxford, OX2 6DP

sychological Test Publications, Scamps Court, Pilton Street, Barnstaple, Devon

.oyal National Institute for the Deaf, 105 Gower Street, London, WC1E 6AH

*Science Research Associates Ltd, Newtown Road, Henley-on-Thames, Oxon, RG9 1EW

Scottish Council for Research in Education, 15 St John Street, Edinburgh, EH8 8JR, Scotland

Sheffield City Polytechnic, Language Development Centre, 37 Clarkehouse Road, Sheffield, S10 2LD

Staples Press, later Crosby Lockwood Staples Ltd, *see* William Collins Sons and Co. Ltd

The Teacher Publishing Co. Ltd, Derbyshire House, Lower Street, Kettering, Northamptonshire, NN16 8BB

Test Agency, Cournswood House, North Dean, High Wycombe, Buckinghamshire, HP14 4NW

*Transatlantic Book Service Ltd, Education Division, 8 High Street, Arundel, Sussex, BN18 9AB

West Sussex Local Education Authority, Education Department, County Hall, West Street, Chichester, West Sussex, PO19 1RF

Further useful sources of information on the assessment of reading (British)

The following organisations produce materials related to the testing and assessment of reading and related abilities as part of a more general concern with the facilitation of children's learning.

1 *United Kingdom Reading Association* (UKRA), Administrative Office, c/o Edge Hill College, St Helens Road, Ormskirk, Lancashire, L39 4QP

The UKRA publishes a journal, *Reading*, three times yearly. Another periodical, the *Journal of Research in Reading*, is published twice yearly. The reports of its annual conferences are published each year. A series of monographs on topics related to reading is also available. Eleven have been published since 1972; in-print titles are listed on p. ii. UKRA also acts as distributor for materials published by the International Reading Association (see p. 304).

2 *National Association for Remedial Education* (NARE), Central Office, 2 Lichfield Road, Stafford, ST17 4JX

This association publishes a journal, *Remedial Education*, four times yearly. It has also moved into the field of publishing in its own right, as the books by Atkinson and Gains (1981) and by Gregson and Thewlis (1983) described in Appendix 2 indicate.

3 *The Centre for the Teaching of Reading*, University of Reading School of Education, 29 Eastern Avenue, Reading, RG1 5RU

The Centre provides a valuable service both locally and nationally. Schools, institutions and individuals anywhere may become members of the Centre. Members receive all new and updated publications by the Centre as they appear. The current publications order form lists 38 available pamphlets covering many measurement topics of value of the teacher of reading. *Diagnosis in the Classroom, Readability* (includes the Spache graph), *The Literacy Schedule* and *How and Why of Cloze* are examples. The Centre also publishes the *Reading Research Review* and the *British Register of Reading Research.*

4 *Centre for Information on Language Teaching and Research* (CILT), 20 Carlton House Terrace, London, SW1Y 5AP

CILT was established in 1966 with the aim of collecting, coordinating and disseminating information about all aspects of modern languages and their teaching. It is maintained as a national resource by grant support from the Department of Education a[nd] Science, the Scottish Education Department and the Departme[nt] of Education for Northern Ireland. In cooperation with the Briti[sh] Council it maintains a Language Teaching Library. In addition [to] its own publications, CILT and the British Council compile a[n] abstracting journal, *Language Teaching*, which appears quarterl[y].

5 *The Remedial Supply Company*, Dixon Street, Wolverhampto[n], Staffordshire, WV2 2BX

The above small company provides an interesting catalogue [of] remedial materials and apparatus with particular emphasis [on] reading.

6 *The National Book League* (NBL), Book House, 45 East Hi[ll], London, SW18 2HZ.

The many travelling exhibitions organised by the NBL re[p]resent but one aspect of the work of this national asset. Th[e] exhibition entitled 'Help in Reading' includes books for teachers [on] the assessment and diagnosis of reading disabilities plus a lar[ge] amount of reading materials suitable for children of all ages wh[o] have difficulties in reading.

7 *The Reading Centre*, Alastair Hendry, Head of the Department [of] Primary Education, Craigie College of Education, Ayr, KA8 OS[N], Scotland.

The above centre was given as an example of the centres being s[et] up as many Colleges of Education throughout Britain when the fir[st] edition of this monograph was published. Since then its resourc[es] and the service it provides have continued to expand. It represen[ts] the type of development that is, unfortunately, not available to a areas. At such centres one is likely to be able to discuss the contribution of the assessment of reading abilities and attitudes to the improvement of standards of literacy. In addition, such centres stimulate the production of innovative materials and methods. An overview of the quite considerable national and local sources of information in the field of reading has been presented elsewhere (Pumfrey, 1977).

Metropolitan Borough of Sandwell Child Psychology Service, Child Guidance Centre, 12 Grange Road, West Bromwich, West Midlands, B70 8DP.

The above psychological service has been deliberately selected as an example of one whose pioneer work in the remedial teaching of reading continues to develop. Remedial Teachers and Educational Psychologists have pooled their expertise, have always emphasised the importance of the contribution made by colleagues involved in the teaching of reading, and have produced booklets that have been found of value by teachers throughout the country. In Appendix 2 readers will find brief reviews of some of the service's latest publications. The work done at Sandwell (formerly West Bromwich) has encouraged many School Psychological Services and Remedial Education Services to develop similar systems but tailored to the particular needs of their own areas. Having been, in turn, a recipient of and contributor to such work, the reviewer has found that it has been one of the most effective means of helping the teaching profession become increasingly aware of the mutually supportive functions of testing and teaching. Publications described in Appendix 2 from Warwickshire (1983) and Stockport LEA (Reason and Boote, 1983) and the assessment/teaching materials developed by the ILEA (TRN 38; TRN 45) at Barking and Dagenham LEA (TRN 22) and at East Kilbride (TRN 155) strongly support the point.

Whilst not a part of Britain, the Republic of Ireland has within its borders an organisation paralleling the UKRA.

The Reading Association of Ireland, Educational Research Centre, St Patrick's College, Dublin 9, Republic of Ireland

American and other English-speaking countries

Addison-Wesley Publishing Co. Inc., South Street, Reading, MA 01867, USA

Allyn and Bacon Inc., 7 Wells Avenue, Newton, MA 02159, USA

American Guidance Service Inc., Publishers' Building, Circle Pines, MN 55014, USA

American Testronics, PO Box 2270, Iowa City, IA 52244, USA

Ann Arbor Publishers, PO Box 91, Esher, Surrey, KT10 ORL.

Australian Council for Educational Research, PO Box 210, Hawthorn, Victoria 3122, Australia

Bobbs-Merrill Co. Inc., 4300 West 62nd Street, Indianapolis, IN 46206, USA

Book Society of Canada Ltd., 4386 Sheppard Avenue East, PO Box 200, Agincourt, ON M1S 3B6, Canada

Wm C. Brown Group, 2460 Kerper Boulevard, Dubuque, IA 52001, USA

Bureau of Educational Measurements, Kansas State Teachers College, 1200 Commercial, Emporia, KS 66802, USA

Bureau of Educational Research and Services, C-20 East Hall,

University of Iowa, Iowa City, IA 52240, USA
Bureau of Publications, Teachers College, Columbia University, 525 West 120 Street, New York, NY 10027, USA
Buros Institute of Mental Measurement, University of Nebraska-Lincoln, 135 Bancroft Hall, Lincoln, NE 68588, USA
Center for Applied Linguistics, 3520 Prospect Street NW, Washington, DC 20007, USA
Center for Applied Research in Education Inc., West Nyack, NY 10995, USA
Chapman, Brook and Kent, 1215 De La Vina, Suite F, Santa Barbara, CA 93101, USA
Committee on Diagnostic Reading Tests Inc., Mountain Home, NC 28758, USA
Consulting Psychologists Press Inc., 577 College Avenue, Palo Alto, CA 94306, USA
Cooperative Tests and Services, Educational Testing Service, Princeton, NJ 08540, USA (refer to Addison-Wesley)
CTB/McGraw-Hill, Del Monte Research Park, 2500 Garden Road, Monterey, CA 93940, USA
CTC/McGraw-Hill Ryerson Ltd, 330 Progress Avenue, Scarborough, ON M1P 2Z5, Canada
Department of Psychological Testing, De Paul University, 25 East Jackson Boulevard, Chicago, IL 60604, USA
Educational and Industrial Testing Service, PO Box 7234, San Diego, CA 97107, USA
Educational Co. of Ireland Ltd, Ballymount Road, Walkinstown, Dublin 12, Republic of Ireland
Educational Performance Associates, Inc., 563 Westview Avenue, Ridgefield, NJ 07657, USA
Educational Research Centre, St Patrick's College, Dublin Republic of Ireland
Educators Publishing Service Inc., 75 Moulton Street, Cambridg MA 02238, USA
ELS Publications, 5761 Buckingham Parkway, Culver City, C 90230, USA
Follett Publishing Co., 1010 West Washington Boulevard, Chicag IL 60607, USA
Garrard Publishing Co., 1607 North Market Street, Champaign, I 61820, USA
Ginn and Company, 191 Spring Street, Lexington, MA 02173, US
Grune and Stratton Inc., 4805 Sand Lake Road, Orlando, FL 3280 USA (UK orders to Academic Press Inc., Books Departmen Foots Cray High Street, Sidcup, Kent, DA14 5HP)
Guidance Centre, University of Toronto, 252 Bloor Street Wes Toronto, ON M5S 2Y3, Canada
Guidance Testing Associates, 1 Camino Santa Maria, San Antoni TX 78284, USA
Harcourt Brace Jovanovich Inc., 757 Third Avenue, New York, N 10017, USA
Harper and Row, Publishers, Inc., 10 East 53rd Street, New Yor NY 10022, USA
Heinemann Educational Australia Pty Ltd., 85 Abinger Street, P Box 133, Richmond, Victoria 3121, Australia
Holt, Rinehart and Winston Inc., CBS Educational and Professiona Publishing, 383 Madison Avenue, New York, NY 10017, USA
Houghton Mifflin Co., One Beacon Street, Boston, MA 02108, US
Human Sciences Research Council, Private Bag 41, Pretori Republic of South Africa

make explicit what has to be achieved, how it will be achieved and the extent to which the programme has been effective. The first section of this book provides the essential background of theory, research findings and practice required by the teacher of reading in eleven units. The second section contains eleven modules, parallelling the units, for competency-based learning. There is an excellent unit on reading tests entitled 'Determining needs and assessing progress'.

2, 1) HARRIS, A. J. and SIPAY, E. R. (1981) *How to increase Reading Ability: A Guide to Developmental and Remedial Methods* (7th edition). New York: Longman.

The latest edition of this well-known text on the identification and alleviation of reading difficulties has been extensively revised and extended. Particular attention is given to early identification and prevention of reading difficulties, and to a diagnostic/prescriptive approach to teaching. In nineteen chapters and 763 pages, a wealth of ideas concerning the nature of the reading process at different stages in its development, the aetiology of reading difficulties and their treatments, is presented. The chapters on 'Differentiated Reading Instruction' and on 'Basic Principles of Remedial Reading' merit the attention of all teachers. Chapters 8 and 9 are specifically devoted to the assessment of reading and likely to be of particular interest to readers of this monograph. Topics covered include an examination of the strengths and weaknesses of normative and criterion-referenced testing. A range of techniques used to test aspects of reading is presented together with descriptions of a number of frequently-used American reading tests.

(1, 2) HARRISON, C. (1980) *Readability in the Classroom*. Cambridge: Cambridge University Press.

The assessment of readability is fraught with dangers. Harrison guides the reader judiciously through these. He describes the concept of readability, considers its educational importance and points out the dangers that can result from an uncritical acceptance of any readability formula. The relationship between readability and reading comprehension, a crucial issue if one hopes to match books to readers, is considered in depth. In Chapter 3, nine readability measures are described and worked examples of each are provided. The validity and reliability of such measures is critically considered. A *Which?* magazine-type table summarises the respective merits of the nine measures. Four uses of cloze procedure as measures of readability are discussed. The classroom uses at successive stages from the infant to the secondary school of readability measures are considered. Harrison's cautionary comments are adroitly made. Consideration is given in Chapter 6 to the dangers of using readability formulae in writing texts. In an appendix, a computer programme for estimating the readability of texts is presented. The reviewer cannot be alone in deciding that it is worth trying out at least some of it on a microcomputer! There is little doubt that this book will achieve a wide popularity among teachers.

HEATON, J. B. (1975) *Writing English Language Tests*. London: Longman (7th impression 1983).

Some teachers become interested in the construction of tests that are intended primarily for use in the classroom. Premissed on the interdependence between the testing and teaching of language skills, this book is for such teachers. In ten chapters Heaton shows the reader how to construct a range of language tests including grammar and usage, vocabulary, listening comprehension, oral production, reading comprehension and writing skills. Although written primarily as a practical guide to teachers of English as a foreign or second language, the book contains a wealth of helpful suggestions and concrete examples that will be of value to anyone interested in the educational uses of language testing. The ability to construct reliable and valid educational tests requires a considerable investment of time and effort, if it is to be mastered. The author provides a well-planned programme that will enable his readers achieve this end. The absence of an index is one blemish in an otherwise highly commendable book.

(2, 1) HENDRY, A. (ed.) (1982) *Teaching Reading: The Key Issues.* London: Heinemann Educational in association with the United Kingdom Reading Association.

Sixteen papers were selected from those read at the eighteenth Annual Conference of the UKRA for presentation in this book. Part I provides developmental, multicultural and social disadvantage perspectives respectively to the teaching of reading. Part II contains nine papers devoted to motivational, organisational and instructional aspects of the reading programme. The final chapter in this section provides a useful overview of classroom diagnosis. Part III consists of four papers looking at some of the challenges of the 1980s for teachers of reading, concluding with a stimulating contribution by Frank Smith. It was clearly a Conference worth attending.

(1) JEFFERY, P. and JOHNSON, B. (eds) (1983) *Australian Council f Educational Research – Annotated Catalogue of Educational Tes and Materials.* Hawthorn, Victoria: Australian Council f Educational Research.

The use of a loose-leaf ring folder storage system facilitat updating this very well-organised catalogue. It includes a helpf glossary of test terminology designed specifically for teacher There is also some sound advice on selecting a test from the ver extensive range described in the catalogue. The section on readin tests describes 25 instruments. A related section on readin materials gives details of seven useful resources. A separate sectio devoted to language tests contains descriptions of twelve tests an is followed by descriptions of seven sets of materials of value i language development.

(2) JEFFREE, D. and SKEFFINGTON, M. (1980) *Let me Read.* Londo Souvenir Press.

Set in a developmental framework that emphasises both th individualisation of learning and the importance of home-scho co-operation, the authors present a wealth of practical ideas o optimising the reading development of young people with seve reading difficulties. The ideas of symbol accentuation and lan guage experience are central. Their practical applications a pertinent to all pupils who experience problems in learning to rea The use of checklists in finding the appropriate level at which t start work with a child, and also as a means of recording progres is explained. The games and exercises described are designed t capitalise on the involvement of the adults in the young person family as well as to provide ideas for the teacher that have been evolved during an extensive period of research and development.

(1) JOHNS, J. L., GARTON, S., SCHOENFELDER, P. and SKRIBA, P. (1977) *Assessing Reading Behavior: Informal Reading Inventories*. Newark, DE: International Reading Association.

For readers interested in the development of Informal Reading Inventories (IRIs), this annotated bibliography provides key references to publications concerning their history, construction, use and development. The dilemmas involved in their uses are also documented. Comparisons of IRIs and standardised tests form an important section for those wishing to know more about research findings in this field up to the middle 1970s. Psycholinguistic insights into the process of reading and its development through miscue analysis is given a section on its own. The final section contains a pot-pourri of factors related to the use of IRIs including examiner competence, motivation and special measurement techniques. The 36-page pamphlet concludes with a list of eight commercially-produced IRIs.

(1, 2) JOHNSON, B. (1979) *Reading Appraisal Guide*. Hawthorn, Victoria: The Australian Council for Educational Research (3rd impression 1982).

This short book (79 pages) is intended for teachers with students of any age who are finding difficulties with reading. It aims to sensitise the teacher to the idiosyncratic and unique needs of individual students. An assessment of a student's attitudes towards reading coupled with a description of the difficulties characterising his reading performances, allows a more rational approach to the planning of an effective educational intervention than would have otherwise been possible. The *Reading Appraisal Guide* (*RAG*) developed in response to teachers' requests for diagnostic materials suited to top junior and early secondary school pupils. The empirical basis for the *RAG* involved only a small number of pupils at top junior and lower secondary school levels (N = 18). A four-stage assessment procedure is advocated. Stage 1 involves the use of one of four reading tests developed in Australia in order to identify those children who are falling behind in their reading. The children identified are then seen individually and an informal but structured appraisal of language background, reading preference, reading at home and reading in school is carried out. This is followed by an analysis of the pupil's oral reading miscues. It is recommended that the child's oral reading be recorded and transcribed. Whilst accepting that the most comprehensive means of assessing oral reading involves using the *Reading Miscue Inventory* (*RMI*) devised by Goodman and Burke in 1972, Johnson presents a far less time-consuming version than the original. Its marking and interpretation is described. Case studies are used to illustrate the approach. The book concludes with a section on the improvement of children's attitudes towards and attainments in reading.

GOODMAN, Y. M. and BURKE, C. L. (1972) *Reading Miscue Inventory: Manual. Procedure for Diagnosis and Evaluation*. New York: Macmillan.

(1) JOHNSTON, P. H. (1983) *Reading Comprehension Assessment: A Cognitive Basis*. Newark, DE: International Reading Association.

A complex of behaviours is involved in reading comprehension. The vast number of formal and informal tests and techniques used in assessing apparently different aspects of reading comprehension underline this point. At present there is no single agreed coherent theoretical framework specifying the nature of reading comprehension. There is no commonly accepted method of generating or selecting test items. As the author says, 'It is difficult to measure something of which we do not have a clear concept' (p. 79). Fortunately, quantification can help to clarify the latter. Johnston addresses issues of critical theoretical and practical importance by reviewing research-based changes in views concerning the nature of reading comprehension by highlighting the 'process' versus 'product' and the 'single-factor' versus 'subskills' approaches to its conceptualisation and assessment. He points towards a partial resolution of such issues that avoids some of the restrictive effects of earlier notions. This is followed by an outline of factors affecting reading comprehension and its assessment which emphasises the structure, content and language of the text and the importance of the reader's background experience and knowledge. A critical consideration of assessment methodology includes strictures on the limitations of standardised tests because of their 'product-type' orientation. The importance of the processes involved, and means of tapping these, are considered. Emphasis on processes and metacomprehension is argued. The need to assess reading comprehension using a variety of different reading tasks and the importance of teaching students to use self-assessment procedures are emphasised. The final chapter explores some new directions in the assessment of reading comprehension. The author is to be congratulated on the succinct presentation of his material. It is recommended reading for all interested in the teaching, learning and assessment of reading comprehension.

(2) JONGSMA, E. A. (1980) *Cloze Instruction Research: A Second Look*. Newark, DE: International Reading Association (in association with the ERIC Clearinghouse on Reading and Communication Skills).

The use of cloze procedure as an instructional technique is developing rapidly. In this slim volume (46 pages), the author provides a succinct overview of the literature in this field during the ten year period 1970 to 1980. In addition he identifies fields for further research. The review is in eight sections. These are: comparative studies; instructional goals; materials; age, grade level and reading ability; teaching procedures; deletion strategies; scoring methods; and the analysis of student attitudes towards cloze instruction. Future directions considered include the uses of different deletion policies and sequencing instruction. Jongsma is to be congratulated on the balanced and informative account he has given. Any teachers wishing to use cloze procedure in their teaching would benefit considerably from reading this book.

(2) KELLY, T. (ed.) (1979) *An Approach to the Acquisition of Basic Skills*. Sandwell: Metropolitan Borough of Sandwell Child Psychology Service.

A team of educational psychologists and remedial and advisory teachers working for the Sandwell Child Guidance Service present a structured and sequential pre-reading programme using mainly commercially available materials. The programme is based on nine years' use in schools. It is intended to fit into the normal school activities and can be used with children entering schools for the first time. It can also be used with individuals or small groups of children shown by an assessment profile chart to be in need of the type of activities included in the programme. A record sheet lists 68 materials/activities. Each activity is seen as involving between one and five (usually related) skills. A simple system for recording the progress of either a class and or individuals is described. No evidence is presented for the efficacy of the programme other than that it has been found of value by teachers in a number of local education authorities.

(2) KELLY, T. and HINSON, H. (eds) (1983) *The Classroom Compendium of Reading and Writing Resources*. Sandwell: Metropolitan Borough of Sandwell Child Psychology Service.

In capitalising on the knowledge and energies of experienced teachers by means of working parties, the Sandwell Child Psychology Service has produced this useful 160-page book. It provides a systematic and extensive review of available materials in five related fields: phonics (26 pages); reading and writing materials (62 pages); handwriting (14 pages); spelling (30 pages) and dictionaries (25 pages). Notes on the classroom uses of the materials described are given. In addition, the materials can be inspected by potential users at the Book Exhibition Room organised by the Child Psychology Service. The above book is complemented by another publication by the Service described in the next entry.

(2) KELLY, T., HINSON, H. and MOON, B. (eds) (1981) *Evaluation of Reading Books: A Teacher's Guide*. Sandwell: Metropolitan Borough of Sandwell Child Psychology Service.

The earliest variant of the current volume appeared in 1953. A teacher's guide, *Reading Schemes for Slow Learners*, first appeared in 1968 and was subsequently updated. The present publication has a completely revised format devised to meet current educational needs. It will help teachers select reading materials suited to the abilities and interests of individual pupils from the infant to secondary school stage. The system has been developed to improve basic reading skills thus most of the books described have reading ages of below ten years. There are 35 pages of information on reading schemes and 81 pages on a wide range of supplementary readers. The interest levels, number of books and the reading age range of all entries are summarised in a valuable quick reference index at the front of the book. A way of using the Guide to help organise a reading resource scheme in both primary and secondary schools is clearly described and illustrated by reference to variations developed within particular schools. Sandwell's teachers are doubly fortunate in that all of the books and materials described can be inspected at the Book Exhibition Room run by the Child Psychology Service. Teachers who take advantage of the expertise made so conveniently available to them are likely to become more efficient in meeting the reading requirements of their pupils.

(1, 2) KIRK, S. A. and KIRK, W. D. (1972) *Psycholinguistic Learning Disabilities: Diagnosis and Remediation* Urbana, IL: University of Illinois Press.

This book contains an exposition of the rationale of the *Illinois Test of Psycholinguistic Abilities*. Relationships between *ITPA* sub-test scores and certain reading disabilities are reported. Patterns of disability in psycholinguistic profiles and their interpretation are discussed. The last two chapters offer guidelines for the remediation of psycholinguistic disabilities in specific functions.

(1) LATHAM, W. and OVERALL, L. (1981) *Assessment Procedures in the Teaching of Reading*. Sheffield: Sheffield City Polytechnic Language Development Centre.

This twelve-page booklet is the third edition of an introductory guide to assessment produced by the Language Development Centre. It is intended for students in initial training as teachers and for qualified teachers taking in-service courses. Commercially published reading tests and teacher-devised assessment procedures including checklists and Informal Reading Inventories are described. There is a short annotated bibliography of texts on the assessment of reading. Advice is given in two appendices on the administration of standardised tests and on the selection of a test. Accepting its brevity, the pamphlet represents a constructive attempt to meet an important educational need. The above edition is nearing the end of its print run. A revision is under consideration (1984).

(2) LUNZER, E. A. and GARDNER, K. (eds) (1979) *The Effective Use of Reading*. London: Heinemann Educational for the Schools Council.

From work done during a major study of the reading of ten- to 15-year-old pupils of average and above-average reading attainment, Lunzer and Gardner have prepared a stimulating and valuable account of various aspects of the research. The contents fall into three main sections. The first begins with a theoretical analysis and an empirical study of reading comprehension. Also included is a study of readability of textual material and its curricular implications. The second section describes the incidence and context of classroom reading carried out in relation to topic work. Of considerable importance is the finding that school reading is characterised by 'short bursts' of from 1″ to 15″ in any one minute in about 50% of all reading across all subjects. Such intermittent reading is incompatible with the reflective thinking that the authors consider the essence of reading comprehension. The final section reports on school-based practices having considerable promise in promoting the more effective use of reading. The efficacy of the SRA *Reading Laboratories* in developing particular aspects of pupils' reading is convincingly displayed. Of far greater importance is the report of pilot work on five different but related approaches to the improvement of reading through group discussion. The promise of these approaches merits the attention of all teachers interested in the nature of reading comprehension and the development of approaches that will enable them, irrespective of their subject specialisms, to help their pupils read more effectively.

Subsequent work suggests that these approaches can be of value to pupils of all abilities.

(1, 2) MALATESHA, R. N. and AARON, P. G. (1982) *Reading Disorders: Varieties and Treatments*. London: Academic Press.

This book is devoted to the controversial topic of specific and/or developmental dyslexia, namely difficulties in learning to read found among children of 'good intelligence' suffering from no emotional problems and having adequate educational opportunities. The twenty-two chapters are divided into three major sections. Part I is devoted to a consideration of neuropsychological, cognitive and biological aspects of developmental dyslexia. Part II concerns acquired alexia and its various forms. The final section consists of seven chapters describing various approaches to the treatment of dyslexia. Approaches deriving from neuropsychology, psychopharmacology, psychology and education are described and their efficacy considered. These approaches include a few that appear, to the reviewer, to be based on highly speculative theorising. The overall impression given by this interesting and important section is that the types and causes of such reading difficulties are so varied that the search for means of alleviation requires a multidisciplinary approach. Professor O. L. Zangwill of the University of Cambridge who wrote the Foreword to this book emphasises the weakness of the scientific rationale underpinning most of the remedial methods and also the need for a more rigorous evaluation of existing approaches to treatment. Despite such comments, this book is one that has many important messages for all members of helping professions whose clients experience the variety and degree of reading difficulties on which this book is focused.

(2, 1) MASON, G. E., BLANCHARD, J. S. and DANIEL, D. B. (1983) *Computer Applications in Reading* (2nd edition). Newark, DE: International Reading Association.

The 'winds of change' in education have often blown to Britain from the USA. Issues raised by the advent of computer technology represent challenges to society, to teachers in general and also to those interested in the learning and teaching of reading. Most schools now have one, or more, microcomputers. At present, a minority of teachers are interested in them. Many pupils have microcomputers at home and these are used by them and their parents for various purposes. The enriching potential of computer technology could be as important as the discovery of the wheel. It is to be hoped that teachers of reading will increasingly become involved in helping to realise that potential.

In this book the authors point (briefly) to the past, and then concentrate on the present and future. Details of computer-based reading programmes at universities, colleges and schools are provided. Computer assessment of text readabilities and of text book analysis are detailed. Information on computer services is given. The recommended uses of computers in both the reading programme and in reading research are discussed. Sources on computers in education are given together with details (over 50 pages) of software and services. The book ends with a consideration of the future of the computer as an aid to reading instruction. Changes during the five years since the publication of the first edition of this book confirm the accelerating importance of this technology. In Britain we have a number of research and development projects in this field. Despite these, the specific focus of this book makes it a key resource. Presumably it will not be long before it comes in disc or tape format! The authors are to be congratulated on producing such a timely, informative and, above all, challenging book.

(1) MILES, T. R. (1983) *Dyslexia: The Pattern of Difficulties*. London: Collins Educational.

In the past, dyslexia has been described as 'the Unidentified Flying Object of Educational Psychology'. Professor Miles, a psychologist who has been involved in the field since 1949, is convinced that such a concept is needed to describe a situation in which 'adequate intelligence in other respects is accompanied by stunted growth of the lexicon'. The medical notion of a syndrome, symptoms which are regularly associated without the assumption that there is a particular cause, is one he views as 'entirely correct' when applied to dyslexia. This book charts his search for the parameters of the syndrome. Among 291 clients he has identified 223 cases of dyslexia, a further seven cases with 'slight dyslexia', and the remaining clients falling into other categories. Thirty-four clients, for example, are grouped as having incomplete records. The dyslexic clients have undergone testing in standard conditions but have not been given a standard assessment. The data he has collected from this work forms the core of the book although related work with 132 control subjects is also presented. Miles uses individual case study material to great effect in describing his assessment procedures and the characteristic intra-individual incongruities in the skills of dyslexics. Separate chapters are devoted to an analysis of the spelling errors made and also to each of the ten indicators included in the test for dyslexia contained in the appendix to the book (*see also* TRN 21). The case studies reveal Miles' clinical sensitivity and the severity and complexity of the problems presented by clients who are mainly of above average general ability. Many questions concerning the empirical basis of his dyslexia test remain unanswered. Miles himself states that it is not intended as a means of definitive diagnosis.

(2) MOON, B. and MOON, C. (1983) *Individualised Reading: Comparative Lists of Selected Books for Young Readers*. Reading: University of Reading Centre for the Teaching of Reading.

Individualised Reading emphasises the importance of the match between the readability level of a text and the reading skills of the pupil. The approach is based on the integration of reading and related language skills within the programme. According to the authors, it can make formal reading schemes unnecessary. There is no need to test children's reading ages in introducing them to an individualised reading programme, but reading tests are accepted as having important screening and diagnostic functions. The books listed are categorised under fourteen progressively complex categories, the simplest being Stage 0. Each level is identified by a colour code. All books included meet up to five criteria deemed important by the Moons. The books are also listed alphabetically.

The readability of the books is not based on the use of readability formulae, in part because such formulae do not have sufficient validity at the earliest stages of reading. The grading of the books is based on '. . . the ability of children to read them', where the children are already involved in an established programme of individualised reading. Practical advice is given on the organisation and extension of such a programme. Many schools use variants of the system in addition to using basal reading schemes.

(2, 1) MOON, C. and RABAN, B. (1981) *A Question of Reading* (revised edition). London: Macmillan Education.

This is an expanded and completely revised version of a book that was first published in 1975. The opening chapters outline current thinking concerning the nature of the reading process and its development. This is followed by a detailed consideration of the books and resources required if individualised reading programmes are to become a reality in schools. The authors provide a structure for organising the primary school reading programme. The final section includes details of techniques for matching books and resources to the needs of the individual reader. It also contains checklists that can be used to assess pupils' progress. The reference section includes a list of books for children, reading games and reading tests. The book will be of value to all teachers who want practical advice and suggestions concerning the improvement of the teaching of reading.

(2, 1) MOSELEY, D. (1975) *Special Provision for Reading: When will they ever learn*? Windsor: NFER-Nelson.

After an extensive review of provision for helping children with reading difficulties, Moseley concludes that the wider implementation of approaches already tried and found effective would greatly reduce the incidence of reading failure in our schools. The book outlines a variety of promising practices whilst, equally valuably, pointing to weaknesses that could be rectified. Whilst claiming that considerable progress has been made in the remedial teaching of reading both within particular schools and by certain LEA remedial education services, much remains to be done. Inner-city schools and secondary schools are two situations where the needs of children with reading difficulties are frequently not met. The book documents many interesting innovations.

(1, 2) MOSSE, H. L. (1982) *The Complete Handbook of Children's Reading Disorders: A Critical Evaluation of their Clinical, Educational and Social Dimensions, Volumes 1 and 2*. New York: Human Sciences Press.

At the end of a long and distinguished career, a British academic might produce a book entitled *An Introduction to* . . . Mosse has no such tendency to meiosis. For teachers in normal schools used to the educational/psychological orientation to the identification and alleviation of reading difficulties, this book will present a relatively unfamiliar viewpoint. Written by an eminent school psychiatrist, it demonstrates how the detailed clinical examination of individual children can identify factors involved in the causation of reading difficulties, provide valid diagnostic categories and hence a sound rationale for both treatment and prevention. The first volume begins with a discussion of the clinical method. It includes sections on the organic, psychogenic and sociogenic bases of reading disorders and their treatment. Volume 2 consists of six chapters devoted to specific disorders and syndromes typically associated with reading disorders. It concludes with a further thirteen chapters on unspecific and general symptoms associated with such difficulties. The account includes reference to thirteen individual clients in Volume 1 and a further eighteen in Volume 2. Inevitably, many professionals will disagree with some of Mosse's analyses and conclusions. It is *not* a *Complete Handbook* as its title claims. It *is* an interesting and important one.

(1, 2) MOYLE, D. and AINSLIE, J. (1981) *Teaching Reading: An Annotated Bibliography* (2nd edition). London: National Book League.

The publications listed in the above booklet are in two major sections. The first lists books suitable for initial teacher education. The second section is more pertinent to readers of this monograph. The section includes information on publications in the following fields: language development and difficulties; reading materials and methods; the testing and diagnosis of reading difficulties; extending reading skills; reading research and, finally, the selection and appraisal of books for children. Although some of the books described are out of print and a few date from the early 1970s, this NBL initiative provides a means of obtaining a rapid overview of what was available up to 1981 in the specified areas.

(2, 1) MOYLE, D. and SYKES, E. (1983) *Games for language and reading development*. London: Holt, Rinehart and Winston.

The authors have brought together details of a wide range of games and activities that, in the main, can be made inexpensively and readily by teachers. The activities are intended for children at the early stages of education and also for those pupils in the primary school who have difficulties in mastering aspects of language and/or reading skills.

The introduction rightly emphasises the many advantages of teacher-made equipment and materials both to the teacher and pupils. Such games can provide motivating and enjoyable experiences that help develop positive attitudes towards literacy. They also facilitate the overlearning that can be helpful to the acquisition of more complex skills. Four chapters give details of the games. The aims behind the games, the materials required to make them and the rules of play are clearly presented.

An appendix contains checklists intended to help the teacher record and monitor the progress of individual pupils. The checklists are linked to suggestions for activities that will consolidate skills that have not been mastered.

This book will appeal to many teachers. Many of the ideas can be adapted, extended and varied to be of value to older pupils. The absence of an empirical validation of the efficacy of such activities must be weighed against the extensive experience in the teaching of reading that the authors bring to their chosen task.

(1, 2) NATIONAL BOOK LEAGUE (1975) *Help in Reading* (6th edition). London: National Book League.

This is the annotated catalogue of a specially selected NBL exhibition. The teaching of reading, diagnosis of disabilities and remediation are represented therein by eminent authorities. Books for children are graded by reading and interest ages.

1) NATIONAL HOSPITALS COLLEGE OF SPEECH SCIENCES (1980) *Test Library Catalogue*. London: National Hospitals College of Speech Sciences.

Established in 1978, the Test Library of the National Hospitals College of Speech Sciences produces the above catalogue. It contains a collection of the most frequently used instruments for assessing aspects of verbal communication and is revised periodically. The above edition contains details of 44 tests and, wherever possible, the price has been given. The address of the college is given in Appendix I of this book.

1) OLLER, J. W. (1979) *Language Tests at School: A Pragmatic Approach*. London: Longman.

This book is an important contribution to the development of language testing. It challenges many traditional assumptions concerning the nature of language and of the testing procedures in common usage and suggests ones that the author considers more adequate. The book is in three sections. The first describes the theoretical and research bases supporting the pragmatic approach to language testing advocated by the author. The second focuses on the currently most popular approach to language test construction, discrete point testing. This avenue is seen as suspect both theoretically and in practice. It is suggested that the diagnostic aims of discrete point testing can be better met by more flexible integrative, pragmatic tests of language competence. The final section provides a wide range of suggestions for this integrative approach to testing in fields such as dictation and other related auditory tasks, productive oral communication, essays and other writing tasks. The section ends with a consideration of the development of new language tests in relation to a coherent language curriculum. The Australian research programme at Mount Gravatt is seen as a good example of the benefits that flow to learner and teacher when the children's natural patterns of language development are identified and built into instructional materials. Oller's approach stems, in part, from his view of the integrated nature of language abilities, an issue on which evidence is adduced in a technical appendix in addition to that contained in earlier sections.

(2, 1) OTTO, W. and SMITH, R. J. (1980) *Corrective and Remedial Teaching* (3rd edition). Boston, MA: Houghton Mifflin.

This book is concerned with corrective and remedial teaching in all the basic subjects but is mainly focused on aspects of literate behaviour. The statement that 'Diagnosis in reading, as in all the basic skill areas, amounts to finding out what children need in order to become better achievers' will strike a chord in many readers of the book. On the same page, it is stated that 'The process of diagnosis is a complex one that must be guided as much by common sense and intuition as by test scores' (p. 129). Most teachers are likely to agree, although such agreement does not imply that the search for explicit public knowledge on which instructional decisions are based is to be abandoned. The authors stress the need for a balanced educational programme for underachieving pupils. Oral and silent reading, listening, spelling, writing, oral expression and arithmetic difficulties are dealt with using a diagnostic-prescriptive approach. In the final chapter, ten guidelines for corrective and remedial teaching admirably and, from a teacher's viewpoint, realistically summarise the authors' constructive approach to the topics they cover.

(1) PIKULSKI, J. J. and SHANAHAN, T. (eds) (1982) *Approaches to the Informal Evaluation of Reading*. Newark, DE: International Reading Association.

In an overview of this field which has been an increasing focus of professional interest over recent years, seven types of informal assessment are described and related to seven applications. The types of evaluation include the 'Inner-ocular Technique' (IOT), Conferences, Informal Reading Inventories, Cloze Procedures, Attitude Inventories, Interest Inventories and the use of Workbooks/Worksheets. The importance of teachers' observations during everyday teaching is underlined as one of the most reliable and valid approaches to the diagnosis of reading behaviours. Promising practices dealt with in more detail include the uses and limitations of miscue analysis and also new informal approaches to the evaluation of word-recognition and reading comprehension (TRNs 94 and 102). Variations on cloze technique are also included. An account of innovative work in the informal evaluation of content reading in relation to the teacher's instructional goals shows how this can be done in relation to text readability and reading skills. The application of informal assessment procedures to children's writing using teacher, self and peer evaluation is outlined. Criteria for evaluation expository and narrative writing are presented. The book concludes with a valuable chapter emphasising the importance of reliability and validity in any assessment procedure, whether informal or formal. The important relationship between these two approaches in the testing and teaching of reading is emphasised. A critical review of research on Informal Reading Inventories is presented. Readers of it will become appropriately judicious concerning the promise and the limitations of this important technique.

(1) POTTON, A. (1983) *Screening*. London: Macmillan Education.

The Bullock Report emphasised the need for early action in the identification of children's actual and potential difficulties in learning to read and in the development of interventions designed to overcome the former and reduce the likelihood of the latter. Subsequently, much time and energy have been spent on developing screening tests intended to help with these tasks.

Using the experience of the medical profession, Potton demonstrates the important differences between a test used for *classificatory screening* (in which a specific and existing disorder is identified) and *speculative screening* (in which the predictors or risk factors associated with the *later* appearance of the disorder, are assessed), i.e. a current versus a future disorder. The analogous situation in education concerning the identification and prediction of reading difficulties is then discussed. The reader is taken systematically though the nature of handicapping disorders, the validity of screening procedures and the ways in which decisions are made about children based on the information provided by screening tests.

Potton then presents an example of screening in practice using the relatively well-known nineteen-item *Croyden Check List* (CCL). Pupils screened at the age of 5:00 were followed up and their reading attainments tested three years later. From studies of the instrument's predictive and concurrent validities, he argues that the use of the CCL does not reduce the incidence of children's reading difficulties. He demonstrates that, for a given sample, only six of the nineteen CCL items were valid discriminators in relation to the criterion of reading difficulty he used. At the age of 7:00 years for pupils, he shows that the seven predictors of low 'ability' (intelligence) form an almost perfect classificatory screening test of reading difficulty. Potton also asks whether the predictors, found at age 5:00 years, of later reading problems 'owe their efficiency to the same reason'. The challenges to the teaching profession implicit in Potton's exposition are considerable.

As teachers can '. . . forecast and influence the reading handicap pattern of a group of 5:00 year old children three years later as well, or as badly, without a checklist as with one' (p. 48), the value of speculative screening is called into question. Subsequent but less extensive work using the *Lindsay Infant Rating Scale* (1981) gives cause for no greater optimism.

Checklists do have a value! According to teachers and head teachers, they help in directing observations and in individual record keeping. The lists can help in enhancing the teacher's vigilance, a point taken up by Joan Dean in an appendix to the book.

Not all readers will accept Potton's verdict. Technical issues concerning criteria, coupled with the predictive validity paradox, are but two reasons. Despite such reservations, Potton's message is extremely important and cannot be ignored.

(1) PUMFREY, P. D. (1977) *Measuring Reading Abilities: Concepts, Sources and Applications* London: Hodder and Stoughton (obtainable from the author at the University of Manchester).

Intended for the non-mathematician, the book considers the role of measurement and assessment in the monitoring and improvement of reading attainments and attitudes.

(1, 2) QUIN, V. and MACAUSLAN, A. (1981) *Reading and Spelling Difficulties: A Medical Approach*. London: Hodder and Stoughton.

The authors of this book are members of the staff of the Learning Difficulties Clinic at St Thomas' Hospital, London. Their concern is not with children who have identified defects such as impaired hearing, cerebral palsy or Down's Syndrome but with children whose failure in class appears incongruous to adults who know them. The assessment unit checks whether there is a learning difficulty, identifies medical and other conditions that may be implicated, and offers advice on the basis of the findings of a multidisciplinary team of professionals. The orientation is an eclectic one of which many teachers in mainstream education are relatively unaware. The topics dealt with include elementary neurology ('It is a mistake to bother about a child's underachievement at school and at the same time ignore his brain': p. 11). Coordination and orientation, speech difficulties, reading, writing and spelling problems are also discussed. Psychiatric illness and giftedness are considered. Be not put off by such a list! Forty case histories are used to illustrate the contributions made by members of the various professions involved. The cases underline both the great variety of presenting problems in reading, writing, spelling and speech dealt with at the clinic and the importance of a multidisciplinary assessment. Selected follow-up data on small samples of clients are presented.

(1) RABAN, B. (1983) *Reading*. London: Macmillan Education.

This 63-page book is one in a series of guides to assessment in various fields of education produced by Macmillan. The author's purpose, admirably achieved, is to introduce teachers and teachers-in-training to the uses and limitations of a variety of tests and assessment procedures. The importance of assessment as an integral aspect of teaching is well made and the various purposes served by reading tests and assessment techniques are specified and discussed. Consideration is given to the measurement concepts underpinning tests of various types at a level that should not prove aversive to readers unfamiliar with these important notions. Inevitably, the fuller expositions that some readers will require must be sought in more advanced texts. Two chapters are devoted to the description of reading tests related to early and later stages respectively in the development of reading abilities. The final chapter focuses on informal assessment procedures including simple miscue analysis, the assessment of pupils' attitudes to reading and some practical advice on record-keeping.

(1) RAGGETT, M. ST J., TUTT, C. and RAGGETT, P. (1979) *Assessment and Testing of Reading*. London: Ward Lock Educational.

There are five major sections in this book. The first deals with the problems of assessment caused by controversies concerning the nature of the reading process and its development and different approaches to assessment. In the second part extended consideration of the uses and limitations of standardised tests, item banking, cloze tests, the informal testing of reading and the importance of ongoing classroom assessment are included. The third section deals with national and regional aspects of the testing of reading, with the use of group tests and with the utility of individual diagnostic testing of reading. Part 4 includes four recent and in some cases still ongoing, developments in the assessment of reading. These are the Barking Reading Project (TRN 22) the development of the ILEA London Reading Test (TRN 100), the Aston Intervention Programme (TRN 13) and a primary school based development of Informal Reading Inventories. The final section underlines the importance of valid assessment in this field and to some of the challenges that this presents to the profession. This is one of the relatively few books in this field in which the contributors are all British.

(2, 1) REASON, R. and BOOTE, R. (1983) *Helping Pupils with Specific Learning Difficulties in Reading, Writing and Spelling: A Course Manual*. Stockport: Stockport LEA.

An educational psychologist employed by an LEA Psychology Service and a reading specialist working at a Reading Centre have combined their respective expertises. They have also co-ordinated the expertise of teachers in the LEA in the development and evaluation of this manual. It focuses on the remediation of children's specific learning difficulties within the mainstreams of education by their teachers and is primarily for children who do not require formal assessment. As such, it is a pragmatic approach to meeting the spirit and requirements of the 1978 Warnock Report and the 1981 Education Act. Motivation, assessment and programme planning are key elements in the strategy. Concrete advice is given on what can be done to identify and capitalise on a pupil's strengths and weaknesses in particular aspects of literate behaviour. The manual's ten chapters are well-organised and written in a commendably jargon-free style. The authors make no claim for originality. They have (wisely) drawn widely from various sources. Nonetheless, the final synthesis *is* theirs (and that of their colleagues). An important facet of the project is the emphasis on mastery learning and parent participation. The authors' initiative is to be welcomed. The materials to be developed in the subsequent two years of this three year project are likely to have more than local interest.

(1, 2) REID, J. F. (ed) (1977) *Reading: Problems and Practices* (2nd edition). London: Ward Lock Educational.

This is a selection of papers covering theoretical aspects, research findings, and practical considerations of the assessment, diagnosis and treatment of reading difficulties.

(1, 2) RUBIN, D. (1982) *Diagnosis and Correction in Reading Instruction*. New York: Holt, Rinehart and Winston.

The five units contained in this book are arranged to help teachers develop skills in diagnostic teaching. Information on a wide range of tests and their applications is provided. The first two units outline the considerations underpinning the setting-up of a diagnostic assessment and correction programme together with an account of the factors affecting children's reading attainments. Unit 3 is concerned with techniques for the assessment of attainments, the diagnosis of difficulties in reading and the alleviation of difficulties identified. The penultimate unit provides description and discussion of a wide range of literacy skills. These include word-recognition skills, reading comprehension skills and vocabulary expansion skills. It emphasises the importance of diagnosis and remediation and of their interaction. The relationship between reading competence and study skills is also discussed. The final unit describes the diagnostic reading and remedial teaching programme in practice. The particular problems presented by children with special educational needs are given due attention. The development of favourable attitudes towards reading by children and the importance of parents or guardians as teachers' partners in the diagnostic reading and remediation programme are both considered and suggestions for achieving these ends are indicated. Although its American orientation is at variance with certain aspects of English educational practices, the common ground between teachers of reading in both countries makes this a well-organised and valuable book for teachers in the United Kingdom who wish to develop their skills in this particular professional field.

(2) RUSSELL, D. H. and KARP, E. (1981) *Reading Aids through the Grades: A Guide to Materials and 501 activities for Individualising Reading Instruction* (4th edition, revised by A. M. MUESER). New York: Bureau of Publications, Teachers College, Columbia University.

The activities listed stress the developmental importance of various reading and reading-related activities. The suggestions presented emphasise the importance of individualising instruction and learning. The book is in five major sections: I Arranging Reading Environments; II Activities for Reading-Readiness; III Basic Reading Skills; IV Advanced Reading Skills; and V Published Reading Material.

(2) RUSSELL, D. H. and RUSSELL, E. R. (1959), with HENNINGS, D. G. (1979) *Listening Aids through the Grades. Two Hundred and Thirty-two Listening Activities* New York: Bureau of Publications, Teachers College, Columbia University (11th printing).

A very popular and useful handbook of 232 suggestions for improving children's listening skills.

(1, 2) RYE, J. (1982) *Cloze Procedure and the Teaching of Reading.* London: Heinemann Educational.

Rye provides an informed and lucid exposition of the wide scope of cloze procedures and their value to both teacher and learner. The procedure's usefulness in assessing pupil's progress, in diagnosing difficulties and in appraising the readability of text, is demonstrated. With respect to the latter, cloze is shown to have advantages over various readability formulae primarily because it involves the child's interaction with prose. The author also outlines the constructive use of cloze to develop the reader's awareness of the cues which can assist in prediction from text. The learning and teaching benefits of group discussion based on cloze materials are also discussed. The book concludes with a chapter stressing the value of the technique to all members of the teaching profession irrespective of subject specialism or age-range taught. The chapter shows how cloze procedures can permeate the whole curriculum to advantage.

(1, 2) SAMPSON, O. C. (1975) *Remedial Education.* London: Routledge and Kegan Paul.

From a pioneer educational psychologist and researcher in the field of the remedial teaching of reading comes a valuable overview of the development and current position of remedial education in Britain. The effects of the remedial teaching of reading are critically examined, as are the skills of the remedial teacher in relation to (i) testing and recording and (ii) selection of methods and materials. The complexity of the remedial teaching of reading is lucidly discussed, some important current conceptual and practical problems are considered and constructive suggestions made for resolving these.

(1) SCHELL, L. M. (ed.) (1981) *Diagnostic and Criterion-referenced Reading Tests: Review and Evaluation.* Newark, DE: International Reading Association.

The aim of this monograph is to help professionals select the best available diagnostic and criterion-referenced reading tests for their particular purposes. The instruments to be reviewed and evaluated were identified by sending a list of 34 tests to 44 acknowledged authorities. Each was asked to identify the tests that they considered sufficiently important to be reviewed in an International Reading Association publication. The twelve most frequently listed tests were chosen for review. The majority of the reviews were written by members of the Association's Evaluation of

Tests Committee. Each review was criticised by another reading specialist. Criteria against which the tests were reviewed and evaluated are listed. These include content, construction, validity, reliability and utility. The test manual receives considerable attention. Of the twelve tests reviewed, nine are individual and three group tests. None of the tests is British.

(1) SCHREINER, R. (ed.) (1979) *Reading Tests and Teachers: A Practical Guide*. Newark, DE: International Reading Association.

This book has been produced by the International Reading Association's Committee on the Evaluation of Tests. It consists of five chapters by different authors. Testing is presented as an important professional activity, about which all teachers need to be informed if they are to be professionally accountable. However, the activity is put into an appropriate perspective by the acknowledgment that it is but *one* aspect of evaluation. The reader is then taken through a consideration of the criteria by which reading tests should be selected and evaluated. This is followed by a description of how valid and reliable reading tests in five major fields can be constructed. The organisation of test results and their uses in planning instruction is discussed and many interesting practical suggestions that will appeal to teachers are put forward. The final chapter is devoted to an explanation of fifteen key measurement concepts. The book will be of value in providing an introduction to this topic for teachers in training and on in-service courses. It is a pity that it has no index.

(1, 2) SCHONELL, F. J. and SCHONELL, F. E. (1962) *Diagnostic and Attainment Testing*. Edinburgh: Oliver and Boyd.

This book starts with a discussion of testing in educational practice. The tests contained in the section concerned with reading are described and commented on in Chapter 4, page 189.

SPACHE, G. D., McILROY, K. and BERG, P. C. (1981) *Case Studies in Reading Disability*. Newton, MA: Allyn and Bacon.

Case studies are presented from two reading clinics associated with American universities and from one in New Zealand having less formal links with a university. The purpose of the collection is to improve the diagnostic and remedial skills of teachers and reading clinicians. The ages of the subjects involved range from the primary school level to the adult illiterate. A wide range of physiological, neurological, temperamental, emotional, intellectual and environmental factors related to reading disabilities are illustrated by means of the studies. Marked methodological contrasts between the approaches exemplified in the two American clinics and in the more informal (and less well funded) New Zealand clinic become apparent. The major author skilfully draws together the many complex issues highlighted by the cases. The individual cases are fascinating. For readers who sometimes think that the individual client all too often disappears in books on reading disabilities, this publication will be like water in the wilderness.

SPOONCER, F. (1983) *Testing for Teaching*. London: Hodder and Stoughton.

Spooncer outlines the contemporary climate of accountability in education and discusses some of the important implications for teachers and schools. The content of the book focuses on the applications and implications of testing in British primary schools. Chapters 6 and 7 deal with 'The assessment of reading' (13 pages) and 'The assessment of written work' (22 pages) respectively and are likely to be of particular interest to readers of this monograph. The final chapter is an eminently practical one on strategies for dealing effectively with the reporting and recording of assessments. Other aspects of testing discussed include mathematics and abilities (intelligence). The book is written clearly. It is informed by the author's widely known work and experience in constructing tests.

(2) STOTT, D. H. (1971) *Programmed Reading Kit* (2nd edition). Edinburgh: Holmes McDougall.

The kit comprises a series of thirty graded, largely self-correcting, card games. These are claimed to enable a complete non-reader to achieve a reading age of nine years on completion of the series. The material has been found of considerable value in both the normal classroom and in the remedial teaching situation.

(2) STOTT, D. H. (1972) *Flying Start—Learning-to-Learn Kit*. Edinburgh: Holmes McDougall.

This kit of materials consists of individual and group games which are mainly self-corrective. The materials are claimed to be a systematic programme at the pre-reading level, of activities in which good learning strategies are reinforced in situations which allow the child opportunities for initiative and choice. It leads into Stott's *Programmed Reading Kit*.

(1, 2) TANSLEY, P. and PANCKHURST, J. (1981) *Children with Specific Learning Difficulties*. Windsor: NFER-Nelson.

This Department of Education and Science sponsored major review of research on children with specific learning difficulties (SLD) is to be welcomed. It focuses on children with severe difficulties in reading, but takes into account evidence that spelling, writing, number and language difficulties must also be considered. The, at times, uneasy relationship between medical and educational/psychological viewpoints is demonstrated and the case for greater professional tolerance is supported by the evidence presented. A similarly uneasy relationship between the public sector of education and a sub-section of the private sector involved in educational provision for such children highlights another area in which tolerance has often been noted by its absence. Fortunately, in the best interests of the children for whom both sectors exist, there is evidence that this antipathy is decreasing. For example, in 1983 at the Annual Conference of the British Psychological Society, representatives of LEA and private sector interests jointly contributed to a symposium on 'Specific Learning Difficulties'. Attitudes change in the light of developing understanding. The terminological complexities involved in the meaning and relationships between such concepts as dyslexia, backwardness in reading, retardation, specific reading retardation and specific learning difficulties are discussed. Teachers need to be informed on these issues if communication with colleagues and clients is not to break down. Aetiological considerations point to constitutional, environmental and attitudinal evidence. The incidence of reading difficulties is shown to be a function of definition and measurement. Studies on incidence both in the UK and other countries are reported. The low incidences reported in both China and Japan are striking. For the teacher of children with severe and prolonged reading difficulties, Chapter 5 on 'Remediation' will be particularly stimulating. The efficacy of remedial treatments together with promising practices in identification, alleviation and assessment are described. The individualisation of instruction, over-learning and structure, and the importance of utilising a pupil's strengths, are advocated. The value of this chapter probably lies more in the possibilities that it opens up rather than the answers it provides, given our present state of knowledge.

It is not until page 259 in the final chapter that a definition of SLD is given. The definition has the clarity of oxtail soup. Its operational specification has unfortunately, but understandably, been avoided probably because there could be no consensus at present. The summaries at the end of the six chapters and the overall summary are helpful in pulling together the many strands in the vast amount of research covered.

1, 2) VINCENT, D. and CRESSWELL, M. (1976) *Reading Tests in the Classroom*. Windsor: NFER-Nelson.

Any teacher who wishes to understand more about the psychometric and psychological bases, including their limitations, of normative reading tests in particular will find the book a helpful introduction. Apart from the 34 pages of information concerning published tests given in the final chapter, the four major chapters of the remaining eleven are devoted to scales and scores, the content of reading tests, backward readers and diagnostic testing. Other chapters, albeit somewhat slighter ones, deal with criterion-referenced testing and with informal test procedures.

VINCENT, D., GREEN, L., FRANCIS, J. and POWNEY, J. (1983) *A Review of Reading Tests*. Windsor: NFER-Nelson.

Vincent and his colleagues describe and review 74 tests of reading and other language skills. The majority of the tests are British. There are separate sections on standardised attainment tests (33), diagnostic and classroom tests (32), checklists (5) and spelling tests (4). Within each of these sections the tests are ordered alphabetically. Thus looking for a test appropriate to a given stage of education requires a rapid scanning of the instruments described in a given section. The description of each test tends to follow a standard format. The heterogeneity of the tests in terms of purpose, form and content accounts for occasional departures from the general format which provides twelve items of information. The book is intended as an initial guide to help teachers in the selection of tests and assist members of the profession to become aware of the strengths and weaknesses of tests currently in use. It is a valuable addition to the professional literature. Its use will help dispel some of the myths concerning the utility of testing reading and other language skills.

(1) WARWICKSHIRE COUNTY READING ADVISORY SERVICE (1983) *Guidelines on the Use of Reading Tests*. Warwick: Warwick County Council Education Department.

This 79-page booklet provides an introductory guide to the availability, uses and limitations of a number of well-known reading tests. It also includes reference to the levels of reading ability typically associated with Informal Reading Inventories (Independent; Instructional; Frustration). Nine examples in sheet form are given of ways of recording reading test scores based on data from a (hypothetical) primary school. Fourteen sheets give examples of reading test score recording based on results from a secondary school. Appendix V presents results obtained from the same group of pupils over a period of four years. The results are related to the UNESCO criterion for functional literacy in western society. The penultimate appendix show how a reading survey of the upper school in a comprehensive school might be summarised and used. One sheet concerns pre-option selection testing carried out in the third year in order to assist option allocation. Reading test scores can also be used to consider the appropriateness of the school's setting system in English. Certain of the documentation at both primary and secondary levels shows alternative ways of recording the same data. The identification of pupils who, without further help, might leave school functionally illiterate can be readily seen using the sheets provided. Thus resource implications can be more readily appraised. More adequate explanation of the use of some of the sheets would be an advantage. Despite this, the document is a good example of an LEA Reading Advisory Service disseminating a better understanding of the ways in which schools can utilise reading tests.

(2) WEBSTER, J. (1982) *Reading Matters: A Practical Philosophy.* Maidenhead: McGraw-Hill.

Aimed at those involved in helping less-able readers at all stages in the educational system, this book is a statement of personal beliefs based on Webster's own synthesis of theory and practice. It invites the reader to '. . . think about reading'. In the twenty-seven relatively brief sections comprising the book, suggestions fo activities, materials and approaches to alleviating reading di ficulties emerge as consequences of the issues that Webste addresses. His Visual-Verbal method is described (as in his earlie book, 1965), together with suggestions for apparatus that th teacher can make and adapt to the needs of children with readin difficulties. The advent of microcomputers, of speech synthesise and other sophisticated electronic devices now (theoretically available make some of Webster's suggestions seem very basic This, in fact, is their strength. There is no need for the teacher t wait for next year's capitation allowance to obtain the material required to make the simple apparatus and use it.

In the field of testing reading Webster's assertions are con troversial. 'Will this test help me to teach this child to read?' i undeniably one important criterion of a test's validity and utility. I your focus is solely on the individual child, it is the correct one However, tests that allow group comparisons with national an local norms can, by quantifying the nature and extent of low attainments in reading, galvanise whole systems. The impressio one gets is that Webster's awareness of the nature of reading test and of the relationship between the teaching and testing of readin had ossified some years ago. Five lines on the analysis of miscues three paragraphs on readability and cloze procedure in thi particular section, reinforce this point. Cloze procedure does com into other sections and is synonymous with 'Informed Contextua Guessing' of which Webster approves. The book concludes with a list of 30 'Facts' linked to actions. Whilst not all readers will agre with either all the 'Facts' or the actions, the suggestions contain th essence of his 'Practical Philosophy'.

Index of Names

Reading tests are indexed separately, by title, on pages 47–51

(1, 2) BROWN, D. A. (1982) *Reading Diagnosis and Remediation.* Englewood Cliffs, NJ: Prentice-Hall.

The fourteen chapters in this book present a well-structured, contemporary and pragmatic approach to the diagnosis and remediation of reading difficulties. A diagnostic model of reading behaviour, based on an analysis of the progression of skills that are progressively elaborated during the development of reading, provides a framework against which the progress of the child with reading difficulties can be appraised. Extrinsic, intrinsic, physiological and sociological causes of reading difficulties are described and the implications for remedial programmes are considered. The bases for diagnosis, diagnostic practices and procedures are described. Constructive suggestions for diagnosis by classroom teachers that are considered in detail include the uses and limitations of criterion-referenced and normative individual diagnostic reading tests. A number of reproducible self-contained diagnostic tests and assessment procedures are included in an appendix. Intensive instructional approaches for extremely disabled readers are described. Chapters are also devoted to remedial and corrective programmes, teaching basic skills, improving higher cognitive reading skills and the organisation and management of a reading programme.

(2, 1) BUSH, C. L. and HUEBNER, M. H. (1979) *Strategies for Reading in the Elementary School.* New York: Macmillan.

'The teacher of the 1980s is expected to prepare for, and to cope with, the needs of *all* children in an educational environment committed to the concept of mainstreaming. The strategic importance of individualization of instruction has been emphasised throughout the book.' These two themes are set in a developmental context. The book is in four major sections. The first provides a theoretical background, the second deals with important reading skills and instructional processes. The third section deals with the planning and organisation of and effective reading programme. The final section is concerned with the evaluation of children's progress in reading and contains some very helpful information and suggestions concerning the range of assessment techniques with which teachers need to be familiar if they are to be professionally accountable in their work.

(2) CHAPMAN, L. J. (ed.) (1981) *The Reader and the Text.* London: Heinemann Educational in association with the United Kingdom Reading Association.

Sixteen papers on insights from linguistics and psychology to the understanding of reading are presented in three related sections. Part I contains six contributions on a range of factors concerning text. In the five papers comprising Part II, textual considerations related to the reader and the reading process are considered. Part III contains five papers focused on various ways in which texts can be made more accessible to the reader. The contributions underline the complexities of the interaction between the reader and textual material. They contain important messages for teachers of reading.

(1, 2) CHEEK, M. C. and CHEEK, E. H., Jr (1980) *Diagnostic-prescriptive Reading Instruction: A Guide for Classroom Teachers.* Dubuque, IA: Wm C. Brown.

The joint authors' experience as classroom teachers, reading specialists and university lecturers represents an impeccable professional pedigree in relation to their chosen topic. Their aim is to present practical diagnostic-prescriptive techniques for use by both classroom teachers and subject specialists. The judicious use of these techniques should enable suitably prescribed reading instruction to be provided for each student. The book begins with three chapters dealing with the nature of the diagnostic-prescriptive approach to the teaching of reading and the respective implications for the class teacher and the subject specialist. The remaining twelve chapters are organised in five steps comprising the diagnostic-prescriptive model. Step 1 describes a range of widely used formal and informal techniques for assessing and observing pupils' strengths and weaknesses. Step 2 is concerned with synthesising the data obtained and Step 3 with ways in which teachers can organise the classroom to ensure that diagnostic-prescriptive reading instruction can be effectively implemented. Chapters 8 to 14 comprise Step 4 and cover ideas related to pre-reading, word-recognition, comprehension, study-skills and personal reading skills. Ways of identifying and helping pupils with special educational needs are also described. Step 5 shows how the various aspects of diagnostic-prescriptive teaching can be integrated. Eleven useful appendices, an excellent bibliography and indices conclude this eminently practical guide. Whilst not all teachers and/or reading specialists will agree with some of the assumptions made by the authors concerning the nature of the reading process and the value of the approaches to diagnostic-prescriptive teaching advocated, the authors' message is likely to appeal to many practitioners.

(1, 2) CORNWALL, K. F., HEDDERLY, R. G. and PUMFREY, P. D. (1984) *Specific Learning Difficulties: The 'Specific Reading Difficulty' versus 'Dyslexia' controversy resolved*? Report of a Working Party of the Division of Educational and Child Psychology. Leicester: The British Psychological Society.

Teachers and educational psychologists are engaged in identifying and alleviating severe and prolonged reading difficulties experienced by children. This Report describes the background to the enquiry and LEA policy and practice in a controversial situation. The views of professional psychologists in both the public and private sectors are presented as are those of involved individuals in universities. A section deals with current practices in assessment. This is followed by a wide-ranging review of the literature on remediation. The policies and practices of examination boards are described in relation to submissions made on behalf of individual examinees having specific learning difficulties. The Report ends with a summary of conclusions and a helpful list of recommendations. Set in the context of the 1981 Education Act, an Act that became operative as from April 1983, the publication is timely. It merits the attention of both professionals and members of the general public interested and/or involved in what can be done to help children with reading difficulties at the levels of national and local policy, the classroom and the clinic.

(1, 2) DANIELS, J. C. and DIACK, H. (1979) *The Standard Reading Tests*. London: Chatto and Windus, 14th impression.

A very useful handbook of tests ranging from pre-reading to the fourteen-year-old level. For details see page 194.

1, 2) DECHANT, E. (1981) *Diagnosis and Remediation of Reading Disabilities*. Englewood Cliffs, NJ: Prentice-Hall.

In thirteen chapters divided into five major sections, Dechant takes the reader systematically through the diagnostic teaching process. The first section is concerned with conceptualising the reading difficulties that are under consideration. This is followed by an account of the detailed diagnosis of reading disability and includes accounts of seven approaches to diagnostic testing. The causes of reading difficulties are considered in the third section and the remediation of these is the focus of the fourth. It is a substantial section containing five lengthy chapters on a variety of remedial approaches to differing reading difficulties. The final section discusses the organisation of effective corrective and remedial teaching of reading. Not all readers will agree with Dechant's initial analysis of the characteristics of various groups of children with reading difficulties, called (ambiguously) 'poor readers', i.e. 'Slow Learner', 'Reluctant Reader', 'Disadvantaged Reader', 'Disabled Reader' and 'Underachiever'. The means of differentiating pupils who are 'genuinely disabled in reading and who need corrective and remedial instruction from those who simply need adapted instruction' (p. 31) is a controversial area as Dechant well knows. Despite such comments, the book contains many practical suggestions and cautions that the teacher committed to the diagnostic teaching of reading will find of value.

1) DEPARTMENT OF EDUCATION AND SCIENCE ASSESSMENT OF PERFORMANCE UNIT (1981) *Language Performance in Schools: Primary Survey Report No. 1*. London: HMSO.

DEPARTMENT OF EDUCATION AND SCIENCE ASSESSMENT OF PERFORMANCE UNIT (1982) *Language Performance in Schools: Primary Survey Report No. 2*. London: HMSO.

DEPARTMENT OF EDUCATION AND SCIENCE ASSESSMENT OF PERFORMANCE UNIT (1984) *Language Performance in Schools: 1982 Primary Survey*. London: Assessment of Performance Unit.

The Assessment of Performance Unit (APU) monitors nationally various aspects of pupils' attainments. The above four reports describe work done on the first four surveys of the language attainments of eleven-year-old children attending schools in England, Wales and Northern Ireland. Their focus is not on the individual pupil, school, LEA or region, but on a national assessment. The baselines established will enable subsequent statements concerning attainments by eleven-year-old pupils to be more precise concerning the nature and extent of changes that have occurred. This may sound deadly boring to many dedicated class-teachers whose dominant concerns include enhancing the language attainments of children in a particular class and school. These books are treasure troves of carefully collected facts, opinions and analyses of considerable educational importance. Attainments in reading, attitudes towards reading, and writing skills have been assessed using a variety of approaches. The implications of the findings for developing a school's language programme are considerable. In addition, the reports contain information on pupils' language performance in relation to important background variables such as sex, whether English is a first language, region, size of age group, size of school, pupil-teacher ratio and percentage of free school meals. APU reports are now 'in-house' publications.

(1) DEPARTMENT OF EDUCATION AND SCIENCE ASSESSMENT OF PERFORMANCE UNIT (1982) *Language Performance in Schools: Secondary Survey Report No. 1.* London: HMSO.

DEPARTMENT OF EDUCATION AND SCIENCE ASSESSMENT OF PERFORMANCE UNIT (1983) *Language Performance in Schools: Secondary Survey Report No. 2.* London: HMSO.

DEPARTMENT OF EDUCATION AND SCIENCE ASSESSMENT OF PERFORMANCE UNIT (1985) *Language Performance in Schools: 1982 Secondary Survey.* London: Assessment of Performance Unit.

Are the language attainments of fifteen-year-old secondary school pupils changing? If so, in which fields and to what extent? The above three reports are part of an initial five-year programme of annual monitoring in England, Wales and Northern Ireland of this age group. The assessment of reading attainments, of attitudes towards reading, and of writing has been carried out. The results help considerably towards answering the two questions posed above. They also reveal the complexity of the task. Pupils' responses to the wide range of tests given are discussed and difficulties they find with particular tasks spelled out by reference to some of these. The table of contents reveals a wealth of professionally important issues: for example, pupils' preferences for content and type of reading materials, the assessment of pupils' writing performances and pupils' attitudes towards reading and writing. The relationships between reading and writing and important background variables are clearly described and discussed. This series is not solely for the administrator interested in the accountability of the educational system. Its contents merit the attention of every teacher. Critical consideration of the issues raised is likely to enhance the efficacy of the language programmes in many school: These APU reports are now published 'in house'.

(1) EPSTEIN, I. (1981) *Measuring Attitudes toward Reading.* Princetor NJ: ERIC Clearinghouse on Tests, Measurement and Evaluatio in cooperation with Educational Testing Service.

Produced under contract to the USA Department of Educatio this book provides a background to attitude scale construction i the context of reading. The importance of the value attributed t reading by individuals and groups is probably of greater signif cance than the ability to read. The nature of attitudes in genera and of attitudes to reading in particular, are reviewed. Concise nor technical but informative accounts of various approaches t attitude measurement are given. Thus Thurstone's method c equal-appearing intervals, Likert's method of summated rating Guttman's cumulative scaling technique, Osgood's semantic di ferential, the method of paired-comparisons, questionnaires, inte views, observational scales and projective techniques are describe Additionally, other sources of data and techniques for attitud assessment are outlined. These include peer appraisal and a rang of 'unobtrusive' (low visibility) measures. References are given tha will enable readers to follow up the detail of any of thes approaches. The technical issues of validity, reliability and employ ability (utility) are discussed. A guide for evaluating an attitude t reading measure is provided. The second part of the book give details of fourteen instruments for measuring attitudes to readin

1, 2) FRANKLIN, A. W. and NAIDOO, S. (1970) *Assessment and Teaching of Dyslexic Children*. London: Invalid Children's Aid Association.

Irrespective of whether one agrees with the value of the concept of dyslexia, this book contains a wealth of practical suggestions for helping children with severe reading difficulties. Fifteen years and more after its first publication, this still holds true.

2, 1) GILLHAM, B. (Ed.) (1983) *Reading Through the Curriculum*. London: Heinemann Educational in association with the United Kingdom Reading Association.

From a wealth of papers read at the nineteenth Annual Conference of UKRA, Gillham has selected nineteen for inclusion in this publication. The first eleven are grouped under the umbrella heading 'Broader aspects of language and reading through the curriculum'. Contributions on the influence of values on the language curriculum, the past, present and future of the language curriculum, the teacher's role in planning and implementing a reading curriculum and the practical implications of the findings from the Schools Council Project 'Extending Beginning Reading' are but five. The hidden curriculum in children's books, first curriculum stories, the problems of vocabulary in the early reading curriculum and the lessons that we can learn from other countries appealed particularly to the reviewer. Part II contains eight papers dealing with rather more specific curriculum considerations than those in Part I. A contribution on cloze procedure is likely to be of interest to readers of this monograph. A paper on reading in school and employment presents an up-to-date account of work on assessing the reading difficulty of texts and points to a mismatch between the reading demands of school and those in the early stages of employment. One is always delighted with the variety of interests represented in the papers read at UKRA Conferences, even if this presents editors with impossible problems of classification.

(1) GIPPS, C., STEADMAN, S., BLACKSTONE, T. and STIERER, B. (1983) *Testing Children: Standardised Testing in Local Education Authorities and Schools*. London: Heinemann Educational.

This book is largely based on the findings of the 'Evaluation of Testing in Schools' Project funded by the Schools Council from 1 February 1980 to 31 December 1982. Whilst the testing of reading was but one part of the study, it was an important one. The testing of mathematics and of intelligence were the other central concerns. The use of standardised tests to monitor attainments in schools, to screen for learning difficulties and to facilitate the transfer of pupils between schools are discussed. The explicit and public nature of standardised test data has important bearings on the accountability of LEAs and schools. The strengths and weaknesses of standardised tests are discussed and advice to LEAs and schools on the best uses of such instruments is offered.

(1, 2) GOOD, M. and HOLMES, J. (1978) *How's It Going? An Alternative to Testing Students in Adult Literacy*. Bagshot: Interprint Services.

Produced by members of the Adult Literacy Unit for tutors involved in the scheme, the handbook is based on experience of working with organisers, tutors and students over several years. The authors accept the importance to all engaged in this venture to reduce illiteracy (more positively, to increase levels of literacy) that progress is seen to be made by the individual student. The particular problems of assessment, recording, teaching, learning and motivation in helping adults who have a history of failure, who know that they are illiterate or semi-literate but who are motivated to become literate, is addressed. The book is in four sections. The first sets out its objectives. These include giving tutors some insights into the relationships between attitudes, skills, knowledge and purpose in the learning process; distinguishing between learning to read and learning to write (though it is advocated that these be learned simultaneously); and to show how checklists can be used to help in the teaching and learning of literacy. In Part 2, the integration of informal testing and teaching is emphasised. Checklists for recording progress in reading and writing are presented. Examples of the records of individual students are discussed. Sections 3 and 4 deal in greater detail with the items in the checklists related to reading and writing respectively. For most qualified teachers this booklet will tell them little they do not already know. The authors' explicit rejection of the use of 'tests' (p. 19) is belied by their subsequent exposition. Presumably they had in mind normative tests on which their students had experienced only failure. Despite this comment, it is salutory to read an account of work with students whom many people would say the system of compulsory education has largely failed.

(2) GREGSON, D. and THEWLIS, S. (1983) *Comprehension and Research Skills: An Index of Classroom Resources*. Stafford: National Association for Remedial Education.

In a seventeen-page Introduction to this three-part book, the authors acknowledge that the term 'sub-skills' is controversial in connection with comprehension. They argue that the value of a sub-skills approach lies, in part, in dividing language development into manageable teaching units. Put simply, because sub-skills correlate quite highly (for example, punctuation and spelling) it does not mean that knowledge of the one indicates that the other need not be taught. Skills do have specific aspects as well as components in common with other skills. The varied research/reference skills towards which the book is directed are important. Their mastery cannot be assumed to take place on the basis of what they have in common. 'The index is comprised of material which is designed to encourage children to think, and/or to give practice at a particular skill' (p. 2). Part Two contains annotated lists of selected books, games and materials for (a) infants and lower juniors, (b) junior, middle and lower secondary school pupils, (c) secondary and adult literacy students and (d) kits for various age groups. The final section provides book and page references for each sub-skill of comprehension and research in the nearly 200 books listed. This is a valuable compendium that will be appreciated by practising teachers.

(2, 1) HARRIS, A. J. and SIPAY, E. R. (1979) *How to Teach Reading: A Competency-based Program*. New York: Longman.

The essence of any competency-based course includes the specification of objectives, assessment of the student's pre-instruction performance, activities to facilitate increased competence and assessment procedures to check that the objectives have been achieved by the learner. It has been described as the epitome of diagnostic teaching. Its strength is that it requires the teacher to